THE

Elvis

FILM ENCYCLOPEDIA

Elvis Presley

THE

Elvis

FILM ENCYCLOPEDIA

ERIC BRAUN

B.T. Batsford Ltd • London

ACKNOWLEDGEMENTS

My grateful thanks are due to many people for their support and active encouragement in the preparation of this book. I list them alphabetically, as it is not possible to judge the order in which their co-operation may by fairly placed: two ladies, to whom word processors are everyday working facts of life, surrounded by none of the mystery and terror with which they are associated in my mind, Jenny Branscombe and Kate Bryson have between them eased my shaky typing into vibrant actuality; Pearl and Tony Cattemull, Branch Leaders of the Middlesex Branch of the Official Elvis Presley Fan Club of Great Britain, have provided unstinting generosity in giving me their time and sharing their considerable knowledge of matters Elvisian; my editor Gerard McLaughlin has imposed order and fluently honed my copy; my friend, film historian and critic David Quinlan has, as always, been unfailingly generous in providing stills, information and the expertise of his book for B.T. Batsford, *The Illustrated Guide to Film Directors*; I am indebted to Paul Robinson of RCA, now BMG Enterprises, for further invaluable information about Elvis's film recordings, while author/biographer Michael Thornton has been ever ready with newspaper files and press cuttings; my agent Carolyn Whitaker has been most supportive in checking my many entries. I would also like to acknowledge Art Wood, brother of Ronnie Wood of the Rolling Stones, for his help and advice. To him and everyone my thanks and appreciation.

Some of the illustrations in this book are stills issued to publicize films made and/or distributed by the following companies: Allied Artists; Metro-Goldwyn-Mayer; Paramount; National General Pictures; Twentieth-Century-Fox; United Artists; Universal Pictures.

Photographs have been made available by the Eric Braun Collection, Pearl and Tony Cattemull, Julie Mundy, The National Film Archive, David Quinlan, the Cliff Richard Organization. Cuttings from local and national newspapers are acknowledged in the text where possible. Credit should also be given to *Photoplay, Variety, Record Mirror*, and *New Musical Express*.

The information in this book has been compiled from many sources, often acknowledged within the text, though much derives from personal observation and conversation with other enthusiasts. Although every effort has been made to trace present copyright owners, the publishers apologize in advance for any unintentional omission or neglect and will by happy to insert appropriate acknowledgement to companies or individuals in subsequent editions of this book.

First published in Great Britain 1997

© Eric Braun 1997

A CIP record for this book is available from the British Library.

ISBN 0 7134 8128 5

Printed in Hong Kong

For the Publishers

B.T. Batsford Ltd
583 Fulham Road
London SW6 5BY

INTRODUCTION

There is a popular belief that people who had reached the age of reason when President Kennedy was assassinated can remember when and where they were at the time they first heard the news of his killing. Similarly, the betting is that many will be able to pinpoint the circumstances in which they first heard of Elvis Presley's death. Having been a keen fan since I first heard 'Blue Suede Shoes' and later saw his first film *Love Me Tender*, I had watched with dismay his physical deterioration from 1968 when he stopped making his Hollywood musicals and set out on his vastly successful concert tours. However, inspite of this later deterioraton it seemed inconceivable that he would not regain his earlier physique and energy.

While putting the finishing touches to my biography of Deborah Kerr, I was working as a part-time caretaker at an infants' school off Sloane Square. It was my wont to stay the night, sharing the floor beneath a large glass skylight with my Alsation, Sabre. The night of August 16th, 1977, Sabre and I retired about 10 p.m. after supper, awaking to an almighty thunderstorm – with rain beating on the glass skylight with the force of hailstones. Sabre was terrified and crawled under the desk for protection; I switched on my cycle radio to gauge the time and heard the announcement 'Elvis Presley died at his Graceland home this afternoon'. The storm seemed entirely appropriate. I kept the radio on for most of the night to hear the tributes that flowed in almost ceaselessly, only interrupted by a steady diet of Presley records.

As I had closely followed Elvis's work in the movies besides collecting almost all of his records, I had long cherished the ambition to tackle him as a biographical subject, but with the vast amount of Presley material that has appeared since his death – the first biography, unbelievably, within a month of the announcement – a suitable format proved elusive. That is, until Glenn Mitchell's brilliantly innovative *Laurel and Hardy Encyclopedia* came my way: it seemed that Presley's kaleidoscopic life and film career might be ideally suited to the Encyclopedic treatment, although it should be noted that I have only discussed in detail those songs which are featured in Elvis's films. These have been classified, as have the films, by my own personal rating system. A further inducement was that, going through my Elvis material, including half-a-dozen closely knit scrap books covering his film career, I re-discovered a mine of fascinating material.

Since his death, 'El' himself has been canonized, if not positively deified. Hopefully this survey, without being irreverent, will become even more revealing than the 1964 Bible for the fans, *The Elvis Presley Pocket Handbook*. That and the authorized version of the Bible went everywhere with me on my world-wide travels by bicycle. And I'm not at all eccentric!

ERIC BRAUN
LONDON 1997

AARON

Elvis's middle name, spelt wrongly by his mother, Gladys (*qv*). Either deliberately, or inadvertently through ignorance, she used one 'a' as in Elvis Aron, instead of the correct way as in the Old Testament. Aaron features prominently in the Book of Exodus as the brother of Moses, whom the Lord, being angry at Moses's self -confessed lack of eloquence, appointed to be his spokesman in spreading His Word: 'Aaron the Levite is thy brother. I know that he is eloquent: behold, he cometh forth to meet thee... speak to him and put my words into his mouth: and I will be in thy mouth, and in his mouth, and will show you what you must do.' His powers were such that it meant the death penalty for those who should refuse to submit to his priestly authority. The name Elvis is from an ancient Norse word, meaning 'all wise'.

Elvis, not especially noted for his eloquence as a speaker, nevertheless more than matched up to Aaron as a disseminator of the word as a song stylist, whose lyrics moved the masses. Dr. William Robert Hunt, the physician who delivered Elvis and his stillborn twin brother, Jessie Garon, spelt the surviving boy's name on the birth certificate correctly as 'Aaron' but wrote 'Evis' for Elvis, which was evidently the way it was pronounced.

His parents, especially Gladys, were great fantasists: from her way of slanting the truth to make it fit with her preconceptions, a Presley mythology emanated that was often at variance with the facts.
(See also: Presley, Gladys Love Smith; Presley, Vernon Elvis)

ANIMALS

In the video tour of Graceland (*qv*) we meet Elvis's Aunt Delta, who was at that time supervising the staff. Cradled in her arms is Edmund, a small, brown fox terrier, who had 'adopted' her after his master died. One of the reasons Elvis loved being at Graceland was that it fulfilled his childhood dreams of being surrounded by all kinds of animals. Priscilla explains that often when Elvis went out in the car he would return accompanied by some fuzzy, furry or feathery thing – 'It was the most natural thing in the world to him!' Priscilla enumerates some of the creatures which he delighted in adopting. 'There was a regular zoo here: there was a turkey called Bowtie; there were peacocks, mynah birds, ducks, guinea pigs, hens, monkeys' – and here we get a close up of his beloved chimp, Scatter, with a little eulogy about his life style and the house Elvis built for him. If any of his animals died while he was on tour his companions would try to keep it from him for as long as possible; the news could send him into a decline. One thing he had in common with his wife was a love of horses and here the video

takes us on a tour of the stables and we meet some of his favourites who were then still alive. Elvis personally oversaw the feeding and care of the horses. When he bought a farm in Mississippi he insisted all of his friends should have a horse so he bought seventeen, each with a custom-built saddle. Further, so everyone had access to his horse, he bought them all a pick-up truck. Slightly redundantly, Priscilla explains, 'Elvis never did anything by halves.'

Of the five surviving horses in 1985, Elvis's top favourite was a golden Palomino called Rising Sun, bought in 1967, who had his own stable known as the House of the Rising Sun. Elvis regularly used to ride him down to the front wall to show him to the fans who were always gathered there. There was also a black horse called Mayor Ingram, named after the Mayor of Memphis at the time, and a champion walking horse named Ebony who, after eight years of being out to pasture, was retrained over a period of forty days and performed an exhibition to a medley of Elvis's songs at the Tennessee Walking Horse Celebration to a wildly enthusiastic crowd. Finally we meet another black beauty, Memphis, the last survivor of the original seventeen horses bought by Elvis.

Lisa Marie's pony, Maria, shared the stables with the others. Priscilla tells a story of Elvis trying to shock his grandmother, Minnie Mae, by taking

Elvis and co-star Ann-Margret enjoy a private picnic between scenes of *Viva Las Vegas* (*Love In Las Vegas* in Britain), fuelling speculation that they were lovers off screen as well as on. Though they both married others they remained friends until the end of Elvis's life. (1964)

Maria right into the den, whereupon the pony did what comes naturally to ponies. Grandmother was not amused and Elvis received the dressing down of his life.

For all his love of animals, the nadir of his singing career on film must have been his serenade to a bull, 'Dominick', which was never released on record – to date. *Stay Away Joe* enshrines the aberration.

(See also: Dogs; Graceland; Presley, Lisa Marie; Presley, Priscilla Beaulieu; Scatter; *Stay Away Joe*)

ANN-MARGRET

(b. 1941)

Presley's leading lady in *Viva Las Vegas* is arguably the only real star in his film career who could match him for charisma, professionalism and photogenic quality. The one exception would be Barbara Stanwyck (*qv*), had they been of the same generation, but by the time they made *Roustabout* (*qv*) together her days of top stardom were over: she was making few films, and frankly confessed in an interview about her penultimate movie that she took the part for the 'exposure'.

At the time of *Viva Las Vegas* (*qv*), Ann-Margret had come a long way from the insipid ingénue she portrayed as Bette Davis's daughter in *Pocket Full Of Miracles* – to the extent that she was being called 'the female Elvis Presley'. At the start of the filming relations between the stars were strained since Elvis thought that director George Sidney was favouring Ann-Margret with the best camera angles and the greatest number of close-ups – something unheard of in a Presley film of the time (1963). He complained to his *éminence grise*, Colonel Tom Parker (*qv*), who tried to put pressure on the film's producer, Jack Cummings, but found himself up against a customer as tough as he and even more powerful, being the son-in-law of the formidable Louis B. Mayer,

boss of Metro-Goldwyn-Mayer (*qv*), who were making the film in Las Vegas. The matter resolved itself by the end of the production; not only did Elvis recognize her ability and a talent that enabled her to hold her own consistently without help from the director she was dating, but the star himself had fallen in love with her.

They began a brief but passionate affair, which was apparently broken off suddenly by Presley himself without explanation. None was really needed, as her main dedication was to her career, which did not suit Elvis at all. Besides, he was already committed to marry Priscilla Ann Beaulieu (*qv*) when she came of age: she was only fourteen when they met.

Ann-Margret went on to become an international star. After her sensitive performance in Mike Nichols' *Carnal Knowledge* earned her a nomination for an Oscar, she starred in a number of highly successful TV specials and top Las Vegas nightclubs. She recovered from a near-fatal accident in 1972 when she was thrown 22 feet from a platform during a performance at Lake Tahoe, but she was back at work within a year, and went on to even greater successes, including a highly acclaimed dramatic performance in a British TV drama opposite Claudette Colbert, *The Two Mrs Grevilles*, in 1987.

(See also: Girls! Girls! Girls! (Not the movie); Parker, Colonel Tom; Presley, Priscilla Beaulieu); Stanwyck, Barbara: *Viva Las Vegas*)

AUDLEY, MAXINE

(1923-1992)

The TV movie *Prime Suspect* starring Helen Mirren as Inspector Jane Tennison contains a strange echo of Elvis Presley that demonstrates forcibly how ubiquitous has been his influence in the world's culture, which his death only served to enhance. There's a moving little scene in an Old People's Home in which

the Prime Suspect, George Marlow, played by John Bowe, visits his mother, a great beauty in her day, fittingly played by the late Maxine Audley. He puts his hands over her eyes and starts singing 'I Could Spend My Whole Life Through, Loving You' and she finishes the song for him. This must have been one of her last appearances before her sudden death at 69 in 1992, and a touching valedictory to a distinguished career on stage, screen and TV, including the late Eighties revival of *42nd Street* at Drury Lane theatre, starring Frankie Vaughan, and *Light Up The Sky* with Kate O'Mara.

(See also *Loving You*, film and disc.)

BANKHEAD ON PRESLEY

Tallulah Bankhead, best described as the Madonna of the Twenties through the Forties – actress, ambivalent bon viveuse, whose life-style revolved around how many people she could shock, was a hell-raiser who was expelled from England after allegedly over-stepping the mark at her tea parties for the boys of Eton. Among some of her pet phrases were 'I didn't recognize you with your clothes on' and 'Dahling – how could you say such a thing: you know some of my *best* friends are women!' She also cut discs – unlike Madonna she was a spectacularly awful singer: 'Don't Tell Him What Happened To Me' is a classic of unbelievable hideousness.

Were she a contemporary of Elvis's she would have been banned from his parties – if there ever was an upstager it was she. If things were a little quiet a ploy of hers was to wander naked among the guests saying 'Don't worry, Dahlings – I'm going to wash that man right out of my hair!'

Stars of her era were agog to hear what she thought of Elvis. Her reply was 'I've only seen Elvis on TV when he was on Frankie's show, and his pompadour, my dear, was up to here, which I thought was ridiculous. I liked him, aside from that and I wouldn't be at all surprised if he turned out to be a good actor. They make such fun of him I have to be on his side a little. And I do think,

if he had just a little less fat in his face, he'd be a very good looking boy.

'I'm sure that, if the time and the place were right, he could turn out to be quite a Dahling.' History does not record whether he took the hint.

BENNETT, BRUCE

(b. 1909)

Born Tacoma, Washington, he was educated at Washington University, one of the unusual facets of a career which did not seem to point to Hollywood. His initial distinction was as a champion shot-putter and he represented the USA in the 1932 Olympic Games in Los Angeles. His athletic prowess and good looks attracted the attention of Hollywood and he became the screen's eighth Tarzan in 1935 in two independent studio productions in serial and feature versions of *The New Adventures of Tarzan*, under his real name of Herman Brix.

Brix changed his name to Bruce Bennett in 1940 and did well in such action movies as *Atlantic Convoy* and *Sabotage Squad* in 1942, graduating to major productions in *The More The Merrier* with Jean Arthur. His macho personality made him much in demand by such Warner stars as Joan Crawford, Bette Davies, Ida Lupino and Ann Sheridan although he was seldom the male lead; usually the dour husband or, paradoxically, the athletic stud. His finest moment came as the desperate

prospector in John Huston's classic *Treasure of the Sierra Madre* in 1948. Joan Crawford, on whom he had made a big impression in her Academy Award winning *Mildred Pierce*, sent for him again in the 1952 *Sudden Fear*.

After *Love Me Tender* (*qv*) in 1956 he said, 'The writing was on the wall. At 54, if you can't even get a part in an Elvis Presley film and Tarzan is out of the question, real estate seems the only alternative.' His last movie to date is *The Outsider* in 1962.

(See also: *Love Me Tender*)

BIRTH

Elvis was born on January 8th, 1935, in East Tupelo, Mississippi, in a thirty feet long, two-room wooden cabin, comprising two square rooms: a kitchen at the rear and a bedroom at the front. There was also a small porch. The whole building was elevated on bricks to avoid the flotsam liable to float up from the several creeks adjacent to the area. His father, Vernon Presley (*qv*), built the house with help from his father and brother and money borrowed from a local dairy farmer, Orville S. Bean, for whom Vernon drove a truck and delivered milk in the neighbourhood. Both Elvis's parents came from share-cropping families, originally settled in the Carolinas in the 1740's. The Presleys have been traced back to an English or Irish immigrant called David – the surname being initially spelt with two s's.

His mother, Gladys Love Smith (*qv*), was born in 1912 in Saltillo, four years previous to Vernon's birth in 1916 in Fulton, Mississippi. Both families subsequently moved to East Tupelo: Vernon's after the First World War, when the farm on which his parents worked was sold; Gladys's at the start of the Depression. The Smiths had a house in Berry Street, not far from Vernon's on Old Saltillo Road, where he lived with his three sisters and brother Vesper. Gladys was the second born of five sisters and two brothers and had found work as a sewing machinist. Although the hours were long and the work monotonous she made a better living than she could have done working on a farm.

After their first meeting, the courtship was brief and they were married on June 17th, 1933, in Pontotoc Church twenty miles west of Tupelo. Initially the newly weds moved in with Vernon's parents, but when Gladys found herself pregnant a year later the couple made plans to build their own home. Gladys had been obliged to stop working and it was hardly an ideal situation: heating was provided by a brick chimney stack affording a fire in the front room and a stove at the back; there was no bathroom, the toilet was outside and running water had to be obtained from a tap shared with neighbours.

Gladys had divined, rightly, that she would bear boy twins and chose their names in advance. The first, Jesse Garon (*qv*), was stillborn: Elvis Aron, as she mis-spelt it, arrived thirty minutes later at 4.35am. The births were attended by a local doctor, William Robert Hunt, who waived his usual fifteen-dollar fee, which the Presleys were simply unable to afford. The body of Jesse Garon was kept overnight in a cardboard box in the front room and buried the following day in an unmarked grave under a tree in Princeville Cemetery, north-east of Tupelo. Gladys, naturally distraught, suffered additional trauma when told she would not be able to bear any more children which almost cerainly accounts for her fierce over-protectiveness of her surviving son.

(See also: Presley, Gladys Love Smith; Presley, Vernon Elvis)

BLACK MARK

To a press tired of writing about Elvis's escalating success as teenage idol and potential world movie star, with glowing accounts from his co-workers about his gallantry and exemplary behaviour – other than pelvic thrusts that smacked of obscenity to the Purity League – the punch-up at Hopper's petrol station in Memphis was a godsend. A small incident was blown up into world news: Elvis had pulled up at Hopper's to refill his brand new Lincoln Continental and a crowd began to gather, asking for autographs, with which he was always happy to oblige. Hopper asked him to leave. When Elvis continued to sit in his car signing autographs Ed Hopper hit him on the back of his head, shouting 'I said move on!' He received a punch in the eye for his pains, blood flowed and the police were called. Happily they arrived just as Hopper was pulling a knife from his pocket and both men were arrested. Hopper was later fined twenty-five dollars for 'taking the law into his own hand' and Elvis was cleared. The incident made international headlines in the October of 1956 and a month later a nineteen year-old was fined for trying to assault Elvis in Toledo, after finding that his wife carried a photo of Elvis in her wallet. To add fuel to the growing press attention *Love Me Tender* (*qv*) opened that same November and did such phenomenal business at the box office that the film's costs were recouped within three days. Elvis was learning that fame could have it's drawbacks. It was now obvious that he could no longer travel without a companion.

(See also: *Love Me Tender*)

BLUE HAWAII * * *

Released by: Paramount Pictures (Panavision, Technicolor); **Producer:** Hal B. Wallis; **Director:** Norman Taurog; **Screenplay:** Hal Kentner; **Art Directors:** Hal Pereira, Walter B. Tyler; **Director of Photography:** Charles Lang Jr; **Technical Advisor:** Colonel Tom Parker; **Music:** Joseph J. Lilley, vocal background by The Jordanaires; **Running Time:** 101 mins; **Opened:** November 22, 1961.

Cast: Elvis, Joan Blackman, Angela Lansbury, Nancy Walters, Roland Winters, John Archer, Howard McNear, Steve Brodie, Iris Adrian, Jenny Maxwell, Flora Hayes, Edward Atienza, Hilo Hattie, Pamela Kirk, Marlene Renkin, Kristin Kay, Red West.
Chad Gate (Elvis), discharged from army service, flies into Honolulu airport from Europe, met by his girlfriend, Maile (Joan Blackman). He is driven to his beach home, where he joins four of his native beachboy buddies for a song fest, with guitar. He takes Maile to meet his parents, Sarah Lee and Fred Gates (Angela Lansbury and Roland Winters) at the welcome home party they have arranged for him. Mother is an inveterate snob and the party very starchy: she does not appreciate his attempts to liven things up with his beach boy friends, hired as musicians for the occasion, by singing a really beaty song, 'Rock Hula Baby', nor does she appreciate his choice of girlfriend. His parents have a cushy job all lined up for him in his father's pineapple cannery business, while mother has her own ideas about a suitable girl for him to marry. He and Maile make excuses to get away from the party so they can go on to her grandmother's birthday celebrations. Grandmother Nihila (Flora Hayes) is delighted to see them and with the musical box Chad gives her for an anniversary gift. He sings to her and the party is a happy contrast to the one at his home.

Elvis as Chad Gates, son of a pineapple
merchant millionaire, enjoys a reunion
with his beach friends in Honolulu after
his discharge from the army.
Blue Hawaii (1961)

Maile tells Chad about a job vacancy at the travel agency where she works as a tour guide; he is happy to accept as he is keen to make a life for himself away from his family's influence. His first assignment is to show a group of teenage girls and their attractive teacher Abigail (Nancy Walters), over the island. Before long he finds that one of the girls, Ellie (Jenny Maxwell) is a neurotic troublemaker, whose flirting causes a brawl in the club where Chad is singing. Chad knocks out a drunken rough, Tucker Garvy (Steve Brodie), whose wife (Iris Adrian) has him and his band arrested for assualt. They are put in jail and his father bails them out, but Chad loses his job; his mother blames the whole thing on Maile's bad influence.

Abigail, impressed by Chad's demeanour decides to keep him on to escort her and the girls around the island. Ellie, up to her old tricks after a tough day of sightseeing, forces her way into Chad's room, making it clear what she is after. He is saved by the bell – the telephone bell – in the nick of time: Maile is downstairs with their friend Jack (John Archer), Fred Gate's partner. They ask him to meet them in the lobby, but he is stopped by an influx of teenagers, Ellie's friends, looking for her. Another knock at the door turns out to be Abigail: Chad hurriedly hides the teenagers and lets her in to hear her good news. She tells him excitedly she's in love, Ellie overhears, and gets the wrong end of the stick and runs screaming into the night. Meanwhile Maile, tired of waiting in the lobby, comes up to Chad's room, sees him with Abigail and fears the worst. More tears and another furious exit: before he can follow to explain, Ellie's friends rush in and say that she had puloined a jeep and driven off. The hag-ridden Chad goes looking for her and finds her by the roadside, having driven the jeep into a tree. As he calls her, Ellie runs into the sea and tries to drown herself. He follows and drags her out, telling her that until she learns to

like herself no one will like her. She tells him that even her parents have always shunted her off to school or on holiday far away from them – they have not even cared enough to give her the spanking she deserves. Chad solves that problem by putting her over his knee and giving her a good hiding.

The next morning is tough for Chad, Maile refuses to speak to him although he explains that it is Jack that Abigail is in love with. When she sees Abigail and Jack together with her own eyes she gladly accepts the truth. The one person who appears not to be confused over the breakfast table is Ellie, who is polite and no longer a crosspatch. When Abigail asks her if she has a headache, Ellie smiles for the first time and says 'No – just the opposite!' (Amazing what a spanking from Elvis can achieve!)

Jack is determined to get Chad and his father together and arranges a meeting. Over a drink they come to a compromise, Chad will work with his father's pineapple business if he and Maile can run their own tourist agency to run the firm's 317 sales representatives to Hawaii for holidays, so they will go home refreshed and work harder than ever. Fred salutes his son's business acumen, a happy agreement is reached and he calls Sara Lee to tell her of an impending wedding. She faints dead away, but recovers in time to travel to Kauai for the nuptuals, happy at last, when she learns that Maile is of royal descent.

This, the first of Elvis's South Seas trilogy and his second under the direction of Norman Taurog (*qv*) was the start of Presley's love affair with the islands and grossed $14 million, three times more than *G.I. Blues* (*qv*). Elvis, often in skintight swimming gear, is in peak form and handles the Crosby-esque songs with grace and ease, along with the nebulous plot, a trend that escalated as film followed film. Charles Lang's sumptuous technicolor photography is a considerable

asset, given the slight storyline by Hal Kantnor, which includes a few telling lines – 'tourists aren't people' says Angela Lansbury's hairbrained socialte wife, 'they're just .... tourists'. Her deep Southern Belle is a splendid piece of character acting, in the days when she was always playing several years older than her age. Now, some thirty-five years later, she had kind of caught up with herself. As Fred Gates, Roland Winters neatly counterbalances his wife's dizziness with his wry humour. Joan Blackman's French Hawaiian Maile – part Juliet Prowse (*qv*) walked out of due to 'artistic differences' – turns Chad out of her room after a lover's quarrel, saying 'Men – you can have them'. He answers 'I don't want them – I want you!' She makes a charming heroine.

Another of the roster of Thirties showgirl blondes in their maturity to brighten his cast, raucous Iris Adrian runs true to form by taking a swipe at him when he floors her husband. Presley films usually boasted the cream of Hollywood supporting players, even if the script writers were not always top class.

BLUE HAWAII
(RCA LPM – 2426) October 1961
(Original Soundtrack Album)

BLUE HAWAII * * *
Written by Leo Robin, Ralph Rainger
(1937)
Elvis sings over the credits, Charles Lang's camera roving over shots of enticing seashores etc., – a typically Bing song written by his favourite firm of Robin and Rainger suits Elvis a treat, without advancing his recording career in any way: his low-key delivery is pure romanticism, complemented by Hawaiian guitars and The Jordanaires singing happily along.
LPs: 'The Alternative Aloha'; 'Elvis – A Legendary Performer – Vol. 2); 'Elvis in Hollywood'; 'Mahalo from Elvis'.

ALMOST ALWAYS TRUE * *

Written by Fred Weis, Ben Weisman.
Chad Gates gives a tuneful account of what was going on in his life away in the forces: Maile obviously doesn't take him too seriously, having found him in a deep embrace with an air hostess as the plane door swung open. Jolly, inconsequential travelling ditty, ideal for beating time in the car while the girl drives – guitar, saxes, drums in the background, while Joan Blackman echoes a few bars here and there.

ALOHA OE
(Farewell To Thee) * * *

Written by Queen Liluokalani of Hawaii (1878).
Chad sings with his Hawaiian beachboy friends as they paddle their canoe to shore: male chorus and Hawaiian guitars accompany another happy and very Bing effort: shades of Crosby in *Waikiki Wedding* waft round the shores.

NO MORE * *

Written by Don Robertson, Hal Blair.
(Based on La Paloma).
Chad sings to his friends, seated on the side of the canoe, twanging his guitar, back by Hawaiian guitars, as before. Instead of Bing, this conjures up, for me, the vision of Bette Davis, going mad as the Empress Carlotta in *Maximillian and Carlotta* – to the strains of 'La Paloma'.
LPs: 'Burning Love'; 'Hits From His Movies – Vol. 2'; 'Elvis Aaron Presley – Forever'; 'Mahalo From Elvis'

CAN'T HELP FALLING
IN LOVE * *

Written by George Weiss, Hugo Peretti, Luigi Creatore.
Chad and Maile visit her grandmother Nihila for her 78th birthday party: he gives her a musical box for a present, which plays the above tune and Chad sings it to her, tenderly with a background of guitars and female chorus.
Single B/W: Rock-A-Hula Baby
LPs: 'Aloha From Hawaii via Satellite';

'The Alternate Aloha'; 'Elvis, Elvis – A Legendary Performer'; 'Elvis Aaron Presley'; 'Elvis As Recorded at Madison Square Garden'; 'Elvis in Concert'; 'Elvis in Person'; 'Elvis Recorded Live on Stage in Memphis'; 'Elvis TV Special'; 'Elvis 50 Golden Award Hits – Vol. 1'; 'From Memphis to Vegas/From Vegas to Memphis'; 'The Top Ten Hits'; 'A Valentine Gift For You'

ROCK-A-HULA BABY * * *

Written by Fred Wise, Ben Weisman, Florence Kaye.
To liven up the Gates' wecome home party for their son Chad, his beachboy friends, hired to provide music for the occasion, decide to liven up proceedings with a wild rocker, to Hawaiian guitars, bong drums and their own male chorus, with The Jordanaires. Chad sings about the Hula Baby he wants to hold in his arms all night, but she is more interested in dancing. His mother Sarah Lee is shocked to the core: her husband Fred tells her she has been experiencing the sound of youth, in answer to her query 'What was that?'
Single B/W: 'Can't Help Falling In Love'
LPs: 'Elvis in Hawaii'; 'Elvis: Worldwide Gold Award Hits – Vol. 1'

MOONLIGHT SWIM * *

Written by Sylvia Dee, Ben Weisman.
Acting as a guide to four teenage girls and their attractive teacher, Abigail, Chad drives them to a moonlight swim, while he and the girls sing along to guitars and drums.

K-U-U-I-P-O
(Sweetheart) *

Written by George Weiss, Hugo Peretti, Luigi Creatores.
At a torchlight party Chad, accompanied by his friends and the girls, sings of how he loves them today but will do so even more tomorrow. Guitars and drums play along, prior to the whole party hauling in the fish catch for a barbeque. Youthful high spirits predominate while guitars,

drums and The Jordanaires play and zing along.

ITO EATS * *

Written by Sid Tepper, Roy C. Bennet.
After the barbeque Chad and his friends serenade one of the beachboys Ito O'Hara, who's finishing off the leavings – being a big fat man, he eats all night and all day. Elvis sings in his best Hawaiian accent, stepping to a bongo rhythm with the boys and girls, all singing along. These beach capers are symptomatic of the festive mood of the whole movie.

SLICING SAND * * *

Written by Sid Tepper, Roy C. Bennet.
Elvis and company continue their beach party – a charming dance and song scene, to a rocking guitar beat: they kick up the sand and generally have a ball: Charles O'Curran's choreography is sharp and spot-on, as in all his arrangements for the film.

HAWAIIAN SUNSET * *

Written by Sid Tepper, Roy C. Bennet.
Elvis sings of the beauties of the sunset, on stage, accompanied by his ubiquitous beach friends, while two hula girls, both wearing leis dance to the Hawaiian guitar rhythm and the beating of bongo drums. The lull before the storm: the neurotic member of the teenagers, Ellie causes a riot in the club, involving Chad in a punch-up. Next scene he is behind bars, singing.

BEACH BOY BLUES * * *

Written by Sid Tepper, Roy C. Bennet.
Chad sings a lament to a slow blues beat in his prison cell, as laid-back in tempo as 'Jailhouse Rock' was frenetic. His friends are in the nick with him – handy for accompanying the song with their guitars and bongos, while in the next cell, a prisoner tearfully plays a mouth organ. The songs explains that he got into this position through drinking his daddy's liquor – a romantic twisting of the facts, until a punch-up starts in the

next cell over Chad's singing – again by Steve Brodie's Tucker Garvey.

ISLAND OF LOVE (Kauai) * *

Written by Sid Tepper, Roy C. Bennet. More of the same Hawaiian romantic island serenade – Elvis in smoochy, romantic mood, sings along to Hawaiian guitars and the Jordanaire's vocal accompaniment.

The above songs are among the most effective Tepper and Bennet wrote for Elvis. It is noteworthy that they penned some very successful songs, including 'The Young Ones' and 'Travelling Light' for Cliff Richard (qv) at that time emulating Presley's successful musical films.

HAWAIIAN WEDDING SONG (Ke Kali Nei Au) * * *

Written by Charles B. King (1926); English lyrics by Al Hoffman and Dick Manning (1958).
Chad and Maile celebrate their wedding on the island, suitably garlanded and being paddled along in flower-decked boats. Both sing in Hawaiian and English, accompanied by guitars and the rest of the South Seas panoply – the heavenly chorus swelling to a spectacular finale.
LPs: 'Elvis Aaron Presley – Forever'; 'Elvis in Concert'; 'Mahalo From Elvis'

BOONE VERSUS PRESLEY

The fight that never was. Hollywood and the pop world decided there is nothing like a feud to drum up sales. And, if the contest is denied, as it almost always is, that's even better. In the Thirties there were Garbo and Dietrich, top foreign glamour girls of MGM and Paramount respectively – supposedly at each other's throats. One announced, 'We have never met.' The other replied, 'And never will.' There was Gloria Swanson, a top star of the Twenties, still in there battling in the

thirties and Constance Bennett. Swanson was publicized as 'The Highest Paid Star in the World', married to playboy the Marquis de la Falais. In the Thirties along came Bennett, to annexe both title of Highest Paid… and Gloria's titled husband. Very ladylike, both. Said one, 'I wish her all the luck in the world – she may need it.' Said the other Marquise, 'Miss Swanson and I simply do not mix in the same circles.' More down to earth were mature sex symbol Mae West (qv), queen of the *double entendre*, and Gracie Fields (qv), queen of knock-about comedy and top notes in British movies, signed up for Hollywood by Darryl F. Zanuck at a sum said to exceed that of the 'Come up and see me sometime' girl. Said Mae, 'I could treble her takings if I cared to make more movies!' Gracie's reply: 'I have to work for my wages.'

The late Fifties saw Elvis and Pat Boone both selling records by the million and both making movie debuts. While *Love Me Tender* (qv) in 1956 was fairly heavy drama, with Paramount's new contractee on loan to Twentieth-Century-Fox, Pat Boone's films in the following years for the same company, to which he was under contract, were both musicals, *Bernadine* and *April Love*. Then Paramount rushed Presley into *King Creole* (qv), having secured a deferment from his army call-up, while Twentieth-Century-Fox put Boone into *Mardi Gras*. Both films were set in New Orleans, both announced as musical dramas, with both studios saying their singing idols were getting their biggest acting challenge to date. *King Creole* is about a high school kid tempted into crime; *Mardi Gras* concerns military school students chasing thrills.

Said Presley, 'I rate Pat Boone the best around today.' Said Boone, 'I sometimes envy him – he can afford to be eccentric. I've become the stereotyped image of a guy who never makes a mistake.' Discland entered into the fray

with RCA putting out 'Elvis Golden Records', a collection of 14 Presleys that had sold over a million copies. Boone's London label countered with three LP's recently issued and the singles 'Sugar Moon' and 'Cherie, I Love You'. During his army service Private Presley's progress was punctured by recording sessions arranged by RCA during his leaves. Nothing was left to chance. At that time Colonel Parker's (qv) orchestration was masterly; hardly an edition of the press went by without the latest Presley special, mostly on the lines of (a) his romances with countless German fraulein and (b) will he be remembered? You bet your sweet life he was – the Colonel had made darn sure of that. By the time the new, post-military Presley was ready to go before the Technicolor/Metrocolor cameras in the 1960 *G.I. Blues* (qv) – he was never again to make a film in black and white – the Second Coming of the King of Rock was geared to swing into action. Europe's most swinging young Princesses – Margaretha, now Queen of Denmark; Astrid of Norway and Margaretha of Sweden – were in attendance on his set, though By Appointment Only, as ordinary visitors were not allowed, to counter Elvis's nerves and slight difficulty with his lines after so long away. There was also an audience on the set with the King and Queen of Thailand. Mad passionate love was rumoured to be on the cards with his new leading lady, South African dancer Juliet Prowse, in whose affections Elvis had reputedly supplanted Frank Sinatra. Additionally, Presley was tipped to inherit the role of a jazz pianist, intended for Sinatra, in *Solo*. This was not to be, but his next role in *Flaming Star* (qv) in the same year as the son of a white man and an Indian woman, played by Mexican born Dolores Del Rio (qv), glamour girl from the Twenties through the Forties, was already announced as a strongly dramatic role in

One of the first photos of the new phenomen, 'Elvis The Pelvis', driving teenage audiences wild at a concert in Miami. His act had been called 'dirty and obscene' by many civic and religious leaders. (1956)

contrast to the light-hearted *G.I. Blues*. His other new LP, 'Elvis is Back' produced hits galore and mostly enthusiastic reviews.

Though his records continued to by extremely popular, how could Pat Boone possibly compete film-wise against all this? *Journey to the Centre of the Earth* in 1959 was a straight and hardly sensational role; the Fox remake of the charming musical *State Fair* was mainly notable for teaming Boone with Ann-Margret (*qv*) and for the brief come-back of Fox's top musical star of the Thirties and Forties, Alice Faye. After that, the names of Presley and Boone were peripherally linked again when the Boone British-made *Never Put It In Writing* (*qv*) went on release as the lower half of a bill with *Kissin' Cousins*. Thereafter both stars went their separate ways, Boone appearing fairly regularly in movies and continuing to cut recordings and to please family audiences: he also did very well with the books he wrote, supplying a religious approach to teenage problems.

(**See also: Ann-Margret; Crooners for Swooners; Del Rio, Dolores; Fields, Gracie;** *Flaming Star*; *G.I. Blues*; *King Creole*; *Kissin' Cousins*; *Love Me Tender*; **Parker, Colonel Tom; West, Mae)**

BOXING AND ELVIS

Dedication and discipline are qualities Elvis possessed in abundance in the days when his film work still presented a challenge. Faced with the role of a boxer in *Kid Galahad* (*qv*), he took his role very seriously and went into training like a real boxer. He did road work, went on a strict protein diet (not with conspicuous success), shadow-boxed and walloped the punch-bag and boxed several hours with several good young professionals. He was coached by Mushy Callaghan, former junior welterweight champion of the world, who also acted as technical advisor on all the fight scenes without Coloner Parker relinquishing his customary billing.

Mushy is full of praise for Presley's boxing aptitude. 'He's my best pupil yet' he claims 'and he could have made a really good boxer.'

This is praise indeed for a professional who has also trained Burt Lancaster, Montgomery Clift and Kirk Douglas for their boxing movies.
(**See also:** *Kid Galahad*; **Parker, Colonel Tom)**

CAPRICORN

Elvis's birth under the sign of Capricorn, falling under the rulership of the planet Saturn, accounts for one of his most dominant characteristics – ambition. His salad days of time-filling occupations included being a cinema usher, where the main attraction was being able to watch his acting heroes, such as Marlon Brando, Rod Steiger and Tony Curtis, who were the guiding lights in his unformulated dream of one day becoming an actor. At the opposite end of the scale, while working as a truck driver, he took time out to cut his first disc as a present for his mother, Gladys (*qv*). Thereafter it was always Elvis himself who would take his demos round and force DJ's to listen to them. Immense power of concentration and meticulous attention to detail are other prominent characteristics of those born under this sign and he was to become famous in recording studios for knowing exactly the result he wanted and would work at it until it was achieved to his complete satisfaction.

It is notable that people born at this particular period work at their best in co-operation with another person, so the scene could be said to be set for Colonel Tom Parker (*qv*) to take over the guidance of the Presley career. The unparalleled heights to which their partnership led has tempted some to say that without the Colonel Elvis would not have got as far as he did, but who can

tell? While the Colonel's promotional abilities were phenomenal, they were also one-track and blinkered: within them lay the seeds of disillusion and ultimate destruction. With his unique talents Elvis would have surely found a mentor and his place in the sun – arguably someone who would have encouraged him to develop all his powers to the full. One way or another, Elvis's driving force of industriousness and sheer dogged persistence would have taken him to the top. The year he turned 30 it was still possible for people to write of his 'stable personality and good sense of proportion', his thrift and the disciplined lines on which his life was run and how he never allowed his 'slight inborn moodiness' to show outwardly and interfere with his natural good manners.

There speaks the authorized version of the Presley bible, based on his natural good qualities and assiduously honed to an image of near sainthood by Colonel Tom Parker. It was even possible to explain the inordinate profusion of movies that followed each other with such monotonous regularity by saying that people born under the sign of Capricorn tend to concentrate on one aspect of their talents at a time and perfect that before trying anything new. The snag was that as time went by the movies themselves were less and less to do with the quest for perfection. Elvis had soon gone as far as he could in expressing as much as his scripts would

allow. Only by getting away from them could he return to grass roots and do what he did best: bring his music to live audiences for their delectation. But the discipline had gone with the wind of self-indulgence and limitless affluence. (See also: **Parker, Colonel Tom; Presley, Gladys Love Smith**)

CHANGE OF HABIT * * * *

Released by: Universal Pictures and NBC (Technicolor); **Producer:** Joe Connelly; **Director:** William Graham; **Screenplay:** James Lee, William Schweitzer, Eric Bercovoci from a story by John Joseph and Richard Mor; **Art Director:** Alexander Colitzon; **Director of Photography:** Russell Metty; **Music:** William Goldenberg; **Running Time:** 93 mins; **Opened:** November 10, 1969.

Cast: Elvis, Mary Tyler Moore, Barbara McNair, Jane Elliot, Leora Dana, Edward Asner, Robert Enhardt, Regis Toomey, Richard Carl, Doro Mirandi, Ruth McDevitt, Nefti Millet, Lorena Kirk, Laura Figuera, Virginia Vincent, David Renard, Ji-Tu Kumbaka, Bill Elliott, Rodolfa Hayes.

Dr. John Carpenter (Elvis) is a young physician in an urban slum who accepts, with some reluctance, three young ladies who offer their services as assistants in his free clinic in the grandly named Washington Street, Michelle (Mary Tyler

Elvis as Dr. John Carpenter, a physician working in an urban ghetto, with Sister Michelle Gallagher (Mary Tyler Moore), one of three nuns sent to assist in his work. He only discovers their true vocation when the sisters are instructed to return to the convent by the Mother Superior. *Change of Habit* (1969)

Moore), Irene (Barbara McNair) and Barbara (Jane Elliott). He takes them to be Park Avenue debutantes whereas in fact, they are all qualified in various ways

to help the desperately overworked doctor. One of his enterprises is the concerts he gives with the youth of the area.

Knowing the young ladies were sent by the Catholic Action Group he does not fancy their chances of getting through to disadvantaged and chronically poor people. What he does not know is that the girls are nuns, sent into the world by their Mother Superior (Leora Dana) to gain practical experience

before taking their final vows. The old fashioned parish priest Fr. Gibbons (Regis Toomey) makes it clear he does not welcome them or their unconventional approach, but has to accept them on the bishop's orders. Two tight-lipped spinsters (Ruth McDevitt and Dora Mirano) are always hanging out of the window and reporting on their activities to Fr. Gibbons. Seeing Irene in a mini-skirt, enticing some local toughs to help her in with some heavy furniture, and hearing music and laugher late at night while the nuns are painting their squalid apartment, the old ladies assume they are prostitutes. When their love and persistence, helped by Dr. Carpenter, turn Amanda, a young autistic into a girl who can talk and take her part in life, John finds himself attracted to Michelle and cannot understand her reticence at sharing any physical contact with him, but he admits the girls are doing a wonderful job in the clinic. When Fr. Gibbons appeals to the Bishop (Richard Carlson) to remove the sisters from the clinic, Michelle defends their attitude vigorously and they are allowed to go ahead with their plans for a carnival on the local saint's day, but the Mother Superior insists they resume their nuns' habits for several reasons, among them being their own personal safety. John feels hurt and betrayed.

Mother Joseph attends the carnival which seems to be going well until Barbara, the black nun of the trio, confronts the virtual godfather of the community, a ruthless hawker from whom she has raised a loan, by declaring a moratorium in the name of the patron saint on all his hawk loans to the local community. The banker assaults her, Dr. John punches him and a fracas breaks out. Peace is only restored by the black contingent who had threatened Barbara if she does not do something to help their race. Two victories are won – the change of attitude of the coloured people and the exposure of the banker – but Mother Joseph insists the nuns return to the convent the next day. Michelle is heartbroken, but worse is to come: Julio, a psychotic teenager, is apprehended and sent to prison when Fr. Gibbons catches him trying to return one of the Stations of the Cross he had stolen from the church. Michelle had made him her special charge, but he breaks into her bedroom and tries to rape her when out on bail.

Dr. John arrives in the nick of time to save her. Julio is recaptured but avoids prison by being sent to a psychiatric unit on the recommendation of Fr. Gibbons.

Irene, who had her own

confrontation with a supermarket extortioner with varying results, declines to rejoin the Order of St. Mary and goes her own way as a crusader. Michelle is torn between her love for John and her vocation. Mother Joseph says she must make up her own mind and brings John to see her. He begs her to follow him but she insists she still needs time to think. When she goes to hear him at the folk mass, at which he is singing and playing she raises her eyes to the crucifix and we never know her decision.

This is an astonishing film for several reasons. To begin with it is the

only movie I can remember since *The Nun's Story*, Fred Zinneman's masterpiece, to have presented a sympathetic and, as far as it went, truthful story of nuns and their vocation. William Graham's best known work as a director has been for television. *Change of Habit* is a case in point, having been virtually ignored by serious critics as the bottom of the pit for Elvis Presley's career as a cinema actor, while in Britain its premiere was limited to BBC TV on August 24, 1971, two years after it was made and probably released due to the then current success of the documentary *Elvis – That's The Way It Is*. In the States it was accorded some kind of recognition as *Variety's* no. 17 in the list of top-grossing films. The performance of the idealistic young medic was one of Elvis's best ever – top marks to the screenplay by James Lee, S.S. Schweitzer and Eric Borcovici and the direction of William Graham, who miraculously coaxed out of Presley arguably the most sensitive performance of his career at a time when it was no secret how disenchanted he was with the business of making movies. Similarly, Mary Tyler Moore, two years Elvis's junior, makes her sincerity towards her vocation and the agony of her indecision over whether to settle for God or Elvis worthy to rank alongside that of Audrey Hepburn's title role in *The Nun's Story* or Deborah Kerr's in Powell and Pressburger's 1947 *The Black Narcissus*. If it is a fact David Stanley quotes in his sympathetic summary of his step-brothers life and career, *The Elvis Encyclopedia* that Tyler Moore was one of his least favourite co-stars, it certainly does not show here: their work together is exemplary and touched with understanding.

There are other fine performances in the movie, not least that of six-year old Lorena Kirk as the autistic child cured by the doctor and the nun – her screams of agony are quite shattering. Richard Carlson, handsome hero of the Forties, is sympathetic as the Bishop and

Dr. Carpenter (Elvis) finds himself attracted to Michelle and is confused by her seeming lack of interest in him. When they originally meet all three nuns are in civilian clothes. This embrace is for publicity purposes only (she apparently was one of his least favourite co-stars). *Change of Habit* (1969)

Elvis chats with one of his favourite directors, William Graham, between scenes of what proved to be his final fictional movie. His role as a doctor not only turned out to be a change of habit for the actor, but a real switch in dramatic emphasis. Had he and Graham worked together before disillusionment with the film industry set in, the course of Elvis' career might have taken a different turn. (1969)

Nefti Millet is splendid as Julio. McNair and Elliott are totally convincing as nuns over the wall and there are nice cameos by Doro Mirandi and Ruth McDevitt bring light relief as the two gossips. Regis Toomey, leading man of the thirties, brings conviction to the role of Father Gibbons.

CHANGE OF HABIT * * *

(Single Release)

Written by Ben Weisman, Buddy Kaye. Elvis, as Dr. John Carpenter, sings the title song over the credits, after the three nuns, Michelle, Irene and Barbara have been sent into the world in civilian clothing to gain practical experience. Their vocation is a secret to everyone but the church officials. Cute lyrics with a *double entendre*, and a list of the changes of attitude and heart they need for their new lives. Guitars, drums, piano most prominent.

LP: 'Lets Be Friends'

RUBBERNECKIN' * * *

Written by Davy Jones, Bunny Warren. The sisters introduction to the surgery is unconventional in that the strains of Dr. Carpenter's concert with the local teenagers filter out and they are surprised when one of the girls comes downstairs to find out why the music session is interrupted. The doctor plays his guitar for this rocker and a couple of young people have guitars also, while the rest of them clap to the rhythm. The philosophy is to stop, look and listen.

Single B/W: 'Dont' Cry Daddy'

LPs: 'Almost in Love'; 'Double Dynamite'; 'The Memphis Record'

DON'T CRY DADDY
(not included in movie)
Written by Mac Davis.
Single B/W: 'Rubberneckin'
LPs: 'Always On My Mind'; 'Worldwide
50 Gold Award Hits – Vol. 1'; 'The
Memphis Record'; 'The Top Ten Hits'

HAVE A HAPPY * * *
Written by Ben Weisman, Buddy Kaye,
Dolores Fuller.
A song of jubilation, on the swings and
roundabouts, after John and Michelle
between them have discovered that
Amanda is not really autistic but
suffering from a traumatic childhood –
love and persistance have brought about
the change, but on the roundabout she
looks fretful, so John sings to her,
twisting around the horses, on the theme
that she must have a happy face. At last
he gets her to smile and they go off with
their ice creams, still happy. The music is
cute, to a hurdy-gurdy beat.**LPs:** 'Elvis
Sings for Children and Grown-ups Too';
'Lets Be Friends'

LET US PRAY * * * *
Written by Ben Weisman, Buddy Kaye.
The final song in the church by Dr.
John, with a backing of guitars and
drums, at a folk mass attended by sisters
Michelle and Irene, is a hymn with a
rocking rhythm and quite delightful.
One day it will be discovered for the
current Ocumenical church movement.
Sister Michelle's sad dilemma; God or
marriage to the doctor is more easily
resolved in current terms of attitudes to
Jesus and Elvis – the film was clearly
ahead of its time!
LP: 'You'll Never Walk Alone'

CHARRO! * * *
Released by: National General Pictures
(Technicolor); **Executive Producer:**
Harry Caplan; **Producer:** Charles
Marquis Warren; **Director:** Charles
Marquis Warren; **Screenplay:** Charles
Marquis Warren from a story by Frederic
Lewis Fox; **Art Director:** James Sullivan;

Director of Photography: Ellsworth
Fredericks; **Music:** composed and
directed by Hugo Montenegro, **Running
Time:** 98 mins; **Opened:**
March 13, 1968.
Cast: Elvis, Ina Balin, Victor French,
Lynn Kellog, Barbara Werle, Solomon
Sturges, Paul Brinegar, James Sikking,
Harry Landers, Tony Young, James
Almanzar, Charles H. Gray, Rodd
Redwing, Gary Walberg, Duane Grey, J.
Edward McKinley, John Pickard, Robert
Luster, Crista Land, Roberts Karns.
On his way to visit a friend, Jess Wade
(Elvis) runs into his old gang leader,
Vince Hackett (Victor French), from the
days when Jess rode with the ruthless
desperado. Hackett and his crazy

brother, Billy Roy (Solomon Sturges),
take Jess prisoner and ride on to their
mountain hideout, where they have
hidden the priceless treasure of their
maraudings: the cannon that fired the
final shot against the Emperor
Maximillian and set Mexico free from
Spain. They intend to sell it to the
highest bidder and when Jess tells them
they will be hunted down by the forces
of both sides of the border Vince tells
him, 'Not us – you.' His brother and the
rest of the gang tie Jess down and brand
him in the neck with a red hot iron in
accordance with a fake 'Wanted' poster
which reads 'Jess Wade – Dead or Alive'
and tells how he had stolen the cannon
and received a brutal wound in the neck

**Jess Wade (Elvis) persuades his old love,
Tracy Winters (Ina Balin) that he is
innocent of charges trumped up against
him. *Charro!* (1968)**

while escaping from the forces of the law. Jess, badly beaten and in agony, is left on the ground, but manages to stagger up and lasso a wild mustang, on which he is able to ride across the border to the US village of Rio Seco, where Sheriff Ramsay (James Almanzar) has faith in his innocence, although even he had warned him not to throw in his lot with the Vince Hackett gang. Billy Roy arrives in the village and seriously wounds the Sheriff in a gunfight. Jess captures Billy Roy and hustles him into gaol. The wounded Sheriff makes Jess Deputy Sheriff, much against his will, and his first act is to arm the townsfolk, knowing that Vince Hackett will ride into town in a bid to save his brother. Also in town is a saloon girl, Tracy Winters (Ina Balin), who aroused Vince's hatred by falling for Jess when Vince had considered her his girl. Jess lets himself into her apartment, knowing where the key is hidden, to look for the gun she had promised to look after for him. She emerges from her bath and slips on a robe to confront Jess, whom she half believes guilty of the charges trumped up against him. She, however, cannot bring herself to turn him over to the law and becomes convinced of his innocence when she witnesses the Sheriff make him his deputy.

Vince returns and threatens that unless Jess frees Billy Roy he, Vince, will destroy the cannon along with the township of Rio Seco. Tracy confronts him in the bar and tells him that before he was arrested his brother had tried to make it with her; she also reveals that Ben Ramsay was shot in cold blood, not in self-defence, as Vince would like to believe. As Vince leaves the Deputy's office he notices the townspeople lined up outside their homes with guns aimed at him. From his sick bed Ben Ramsay orders Jess not to free Billy Roy. Even Ben's wife, Sara's (Barbara Werle) impassioned pleas cannot persuade Jess to go against the Sheriff's orders. When the Mexican federals cross the border to

accuse Jess of having stolen the cannon, he warns Vince that unless he heads them off it will be the worse for Billy Roy. Hackett persuades the Mexicans to return home and on their return across the river he orders his men to train the cannon on them – all are destroyed. Vince then orders his men to manoeuvre the cannon down the hill so that it can be trained on Rio Seco in case his brother is not released by sundown. While he and Jess are parleying, forty minutes before sundown, shots destroy the church and then the Sheriff's house with him in it. Sara frantically beats at Jess, telling the appalled townsfolk that he has killed her husband as surely as if he had shot him himself. She also produces the fake 'Wanted' poster and everyone in town insists Jess free Billy Roy before they and the town are all destroyed. Tracy comes over to add her pleas that Billy Roy be freed. When the residents, headed by Sara, march on the gaol to free Billy Roy he has already gone, led out by Jess who tells Vince to surrender. If they fire, he'll kill Billy Roy, who is tied up in a tree. In the resultant gunfire most of the gang are shot: the cannon breaks loose and crushes Billy Roy. At last Vince Hackett is broken and defeated; Jess drives him into town as his prisoner. He hands the Sheriff's badge back to the widowed Sara and tells Tracy to wait – he'll be back for her, as he drives his prisoner away into the sunset, with the cannon in tow.

Charro!, Elvis's third from last movie, is a one-off – though something of a flashback to *Flaming Star* being a cowboys and horses film. Elvis is bearded, the only time in his career, tortured, by being branded, the only time ever, and sings only one song – over the titles. The reviews were mostly dismal – even *Variety* was uncharacteristically tepid! 'Presley strolls through a tedious role that would have driven many another actor up the wall.' In fact, the film came at a stage in his career when whatever he did would have only produced yawns and/or moans from the critics – not given a credit for

doing something different. The storyline, as Westerns go, is intriguing, the famous cannon being, along with Ina Balin as a saloon lady, one of the bones of contention between Elvis's ex-bad boy turned deputy sheriff and the leader of the gang to which he once belonged. With tauter direction this could have been a winner, but producer-director-scriptwriter Charles Marquis Warren was no Don Siegel (*qv*) and the gratuitous torture scene could well have been truncated with advantage. Presley's rivalry with Victor French's Vince Hackett is played with conviction by both actors, while the debut of cult comedy director Preston Sturge's son Solomon is the most effective portrayal of gigglingly insane villainy since Richard Widmark's in the 1947 *Kiss of Death*. We know that he went on to a successful career, but what happened to Solomon Sturges? Ina Balin, too, made a promising impact opposite Paul Newman in her second film *From the Terrace* without fulfilling her early Most Promising Actress of the Year accolade. The best female performance in *Charro!* is from Barbara Werle as Sara, the wife of the Sheriff, also a nice performance by James Almanzar.

This interesting departure came too little and too late to provide a shot in the arm for Presley's film career.
(See also: *Flaming Star*; Siegel, Don)

CHARRO * * *

Written by Billy Strange, Mac Davis.
Recorded for the film *Charro!*
Unique in that it is the only Presley film with just one song, sung over the credit titles and coming to a climax as Elvis rides into a Mexican border town. The theme describes a man who not only walked out on his commitment to gang leader Vince Hackett but also took his girl away with him. He knows that Hackett will never let him get away but Charro has only one thought in his mind: to meet the woman, Tracey Winters, he has stolen. He knows his time is running out. A message from the

lady in question has brought him into town – a ruse by his adversary to lure him into a confrontation. The ballad is strongly evocative of so many cowboy movie songs of the Fifties and Sixties, usually sung by Frankie Laine. The lyrics say it all, are trenchantly written, and sung by Presley at full throttle – guitars and drumbeats predominating.
Single B/W: 'Memories'
LPs: 'Almost in Love', 'Elvis in Hollywood'

MEMORIES
(not included in movie)
Written by Mac Davies, Billy Strange.
Single B/W: 'Charro'
LPs: 'Elvis – TV Special', 'This is Elvis'

CLAMBAKE * *
Released by: United Artists (Technicolor, Techniscope); **Producers:** Arnold Lavan, Arthur Gardner, Jules Levy; **Director:** Arthur H. Nadel; **Screenplay:** Arthur Browne Jr; **Art Director:** Lloyd Papez; **Director of Photography:** William Marguilws; **Technical Advisor:** Colonel Tom Parker; **Music:** Jeff Alexander, vocal background by The Jordanaires; **Running Time:** 97 mins; **Opened:** November 22, 1967.

Cast: Elvis, Shelley Fabares, Will Hutchins, Bill Bixby, James Gregory, Gary Merrill, Red West, Suzie Kaye, Hal Peary, Marj Dusay, Jack Good, Angelique Pettyjohn, Olga Kaye.

Rich and bored, Scott Hayward (Elvis) heads off to see the world and also to do something that doesn't require the family fortune. At a filling station/roadside bar, he receives an irate call from his father, Duster (James Gregory), who is outraged when Scott tells him there is more to living than money and declines to return to become vice-president of his father's company, which owns more oil wells than he can even remember. He insists he wants to be able to do something on his own and hangs up. Tom Wilson

hears him say whose son he is and invites him to call by the Shores Hotel in Buimi Beach, where he's going to be a water-ski instructor. When Scott says he's got problems, Tom says 'what problems?' With all that money he could happily change places and experience some of those problems. Tom takes Scott's opulent car, Scott follows him on Tom's motorbike and whilst duetting the theme song of the movie, 'Who Needs Money?' with his new friend Scott finds time to make up his mind about his proposition to change places.

By the time they pull up at the Shores Hotel the metamorphosis has taken place: Tom tells the hostile doorman that he is, in fact, Scott Hayward, son of the famous Duster Hayward. The doorman's attitude changes like magic as he haughtily tells Scott (Elvis) he can't park outside the hotel. The manager, alerted by the doorman, is aghast at Tom's clumsy antics in the hotel foyer until he realizes that it is the millionaire's son who is looking for a room without reservations. He is then, of course, offered the presidential suite. Scott, checking in with Tom's skis, gets a haughty brush-off from the manager until he explains that he is the new ski instructor. A young woman called Diane Carter (Shelley Fabares) insists that Scott gives her a course in ski-instruction at once. In fact, she is a fortune-hunter looking for a rich husband and has set her cap at the super-rich James Jamison (Bill Bixby), in town for the season and the races. She is not in need of instruction on water-skis and, in fact, is able to do some fancy stunts to impress Jamieson, who is always surrounded by nubile nymphs.

Diane, mistaking him for one of her own kind, confesses her intentions and he, attracted and impressed by her honesty, agrees to help her in her husband-hunting so he can see more of her. He has decided to continue to play the humble ski-instructor, rather than to win her the easy way by revealing how

rich he is. Meanwhile, he meets a man called Sam Burton (Gary Merrill) who has invented a power boat with blazing speed – a sure winner, if he can find a way to prevent it from tearing itself apart at high speed. They go into business together, and Scott remembers a hardening agent he once developed for his father's laboratory when he was fooling around. It was flawed, but he has confidence that he can make it work to strengthen Burton's boat in time for the race. When he contacts his family and asks for the chemical to be sent to him, his father finds out where he is and travels to Florida to find out what is going on. Scott sets to work with the 'help' of some dancing bimbos provided by his friend Tom: to music and between kisses, they apply the magic formula 'gump' that hopefully will ensure the boat holds together under pressure. Sam Burton also lends a hand. When Hayward Senior arrives looking for his son, Sam, who has learned the truth about the switch of identities, seeks him out to tell him what a great job Scott has been doing. Tom, in his borrowed Prince Charming plumage, surrounded by hotel lovelies and renowned for buying drinks for all-comers to the bar, tries the same procedure on Duster Hayward, swapping cigar for cigar and nearly swallowing one when he realizes he is hoist with his own petard. But the awe-inspiring tycoon, after treating his son to a fearsome dressing down, reveals that his heart is as big as his bank balance and tells Scott he'll be backing him to the hilt when he enters the race, even though the formula has arrived too late to test its efficacy under race conditions.

Favourite to win is the super-stud, super-playboy James J. Jamison, for whom Diane is apparently making a big play as the husband of her dreams. When 'ski instructor' Scott interrupts the big seduction scene with Diane, who is wise to Jamison's every move having been primed by Scott who arrives at the crucial moment. James, on having

**Rich and bored, Scott Hayward (Elvis)
sets out to make his own way in the
world, ending up in Miami Beach.**
Clambake (1967)

proposed marriage, is following up the proposal by getting physical; the unrequited Lothario challenges him to a karate duel. When Scott, with a contemptuous 'Shut up!', fells him with a single blow, Diane thanks him for his timely intervention and tells him she will be leaving for home right after the big race. Inevitably Jamison takes the lead, but Scott overtakes him and after nail-biting suspense when his boat splutters ominously under the strain of the great speed imposed upon it, 'gump' saves the day and Scott wins, hands down. Diane tells Jamison she can't marry him, as she loves another; and makes to leave. Who should pick her up in his convertible but Scott, having bribed the doorman to get rid of the taxi she had ordered. Scott produces a proposal of marriage and a fabulous ring which she, thinking him still to be ski-instructor Tom Wilson, insists he cannot afford. When Scott finally convinces her of his real identity, she conveniently faints dead away onto his shoulder. Scott has not only won the respect of his father but gained the love of a good woman.

The reception accorded to *Clambake*, Elvis's 25th film, was extremely mixed. British TV producer/entrepreneur Jack Good, credited with 'virtually inventing' rock 'n' roll, and who had produced the *Shindig* television show among others as well as having a small part in the *Clambake* film, says the film was 'one of the really, really awful ones.' Bill Bixby, years away from rising to the position of the Incredible Hulk, is a charmingly convincing playboy as Jamieson, despite sporting the strangest shade of marmalade-coloured hair. He acted with Elvis more than once and said of him, 'He is a performer, he is an actor. He is worth considerably more than people have given him credit for. Frank Sinatra once said, "The best singers are the best actors," and I think he's absolutely right. He's a good example. When Frank decides to act, man, stand aside. Elvis

Presley has the same kind of presence. That's the only word I can think of. They both have it and I am not making a comparison. When they take stage, they take stage. They are it.'

American Variety practically glowed: 'Elvis at his best in a well-motivated yarn... one of the singer's top offerings to date, backed by a legitimately premised story line, melodic songs, acceptable acting and winding with a spectacular water race. The film has all the making of being one of Presley's heaviest grossers.' (Unfortunately, it wasn't.) Shelley Fabares provides pretty distaff interest... technical credits are all first rate, including Lloyd Papez' lush art direction, Tom Rolf's fast editing and Jess Alexander's appropriate music score.'

Who could ask for anything more – except the British Film Institute's *Monthly Film Bulletin*, who wrote, 'Elvis Presley floats amiably through a flimsy story enlivened only by an occasional touch of humour and an engaging performance from James Gregory as a drawling Texas oil millionaire. The script is sometimes embarrassingly naïve, but in general this is painless Presley fare, and the only really jarring note is the very unpersonable heroine.'

Poor Shelley Fabares, one of Elvis's favourite leading ladies, made three films with him, although she does not figure in any of the reference books to which I have had access. She does, in fact, have that Priscilla Presley look and hair and the film was made within months of Elvis's wedding. Fabares purveys a touching innocence and naïveté, which belies her gold-digger role.

The story line by Arthur Browne Jr., resembles *Cinderella*: Prince Charming, herein Elvis, changes places with his major-domo, interpreted by Will Hutchins as an amiable girl-chasing slob. Happy endings for all, except discomforted snake-in-the-grass Bill Bixby. Shelley Fabares is an acceptable Cinderella substitute – the poor girl who ends up with a prince, who has won the big boat regatta against almost

insuperable odds. In the circumstances the actors acquit themselves well, though it must have been embarrassing for that serious actor, Gary Merrill, not far from the time when he made an unsuccessful bid for the Republican nomination for Maine's legislature, to be involved in the ridiculous scene where Will Hutchins' capering floozies help to reinforce his racing boat with magic formula 'gump', while Elvis sings 'Hey, Hey, Hey' to them as part of their engineering tuition. No wonder Elvis was unhappy about the songs, although the ever-reliable Jordanaires give him stalwart backing in the best of them, notably the angst-ridden ballad 'The Girl I Never Loved'.
(See also: Presley, Priscilla Beaulieu)

CLAMBAKE
(RCA LPM 3893) November 19, 1967

GUITAR MAN
(not included in movie)
Written by Jerry Reed (1967)
Single B/W: 'High Heeled Sneakers'
EP: 'Stay Away'
LPs: 'Clambake'; 'Elvis in Nashville'; 'Elvis Sings Hits From His Movies – Vol. 1'; 'Elvis – TV Special'; 'Guitar Man'
This bonus number is certainly one of the best on the record. Elvis gives it all he's got. A veritable guitar fest, harking back to the Elvis of the Sun days.
The guitar man can't interest anyone, sleeps rough, until he makes it with his own combo.

CLAMBAKE * *
Written by Sid Wayne, Ben Weisman.
Fast introductory number as rich boy Scott Hayward heads off in his convertible to try and do something to prove himself without the backing of his oil tycoon father, Duster. It's the usual, jolly 'shake the dust off my heels' number, with promises of picnics and lots of pretty girls, reprised at suitable moments in the movie. Backed by guitar, drums, saxophone, double bass, piano dominant.
EP: 'Clambake'

WHO NEEDS MONEY * * *

Written by Randy Starr.

Duet between rich boy Elvis and poor boy Will Hutchins, who have switched roles and vehicles, Elvis driving the bike, Will the convertible. This is a fun number, with swingy orchestral backing, reminiscent of the Sinatra–Celeste Holm duet from the 1956 musical *High Society*, 'Who Wants To Be A Millionaire?' Elvis is smoothly in tune, Will sometimes deliberately flat.

A HOUSE THAT HAS EVERYTHING * *

Written by Sid Tepper, Roy C. Bennet. Elvis after swapping places with his poorer friend, watches the girl he loves chasing millionaire James Jamison and sings about how lonely she'll be in her mansion, without love. Drums, harmonica and guitar predominate.

CONFIDENCE * * *

Written by Sid Tepper, Roy C. Bennet. This is one of those songs with children Elvis does so well. It's no good complaining he should be doing rock 'n' roll – in this case; as *Variety* observed in their surprisingly eulogistic review, each of the seven song numbers is logically inserted in the story sequence. This is a delightful scene, with a flock of youngsters on swings.

LPs: 'Elvis Sings Hits From His Movies – Vol. 1

HEY, HEY, HEY *

Written by Joy Byers.

Joy Byer's undeniably catchy number, written solely to help the plot along, is just too silly for words, especially as it is supposed to illustrate how, fighting against time, Elvis's invention, 'gump', makes the boat he is to drive in the regatta resistant to the conditions. Skimpily-clad girls jig about with their paint brushes, wiggling their bottoms and distributing kisses – at that rate it's a safe bet the job would never have been completed.

YOU DON'T KNOW ME * *

Written by Eddy Arnold, Cindy Walker. In sentimental mood, Elvis expresses his unrequited love for heroine Shelley Fabares. Piano and strings prominent. Vocal accompaniment by The Jordanaires – once again neatly placed in the story-line. This prompted Tony Blackburn writing in the *Daily Sketch* to ask, 'Frankly Elvis, is it time to quit?' He says, 'The zest and the punch have gone.' Ballads hardly call for zest and punch. At the time of writing, Tony Blackburn himself has not quit.

Single B/W: 'Big Boss Man'
EP: 'Clambake'
LP: 'Elvis Sings Hits From His Movies – Vol. 1'

THE GIRL I NEVER LOVED * * * *

Written by Randy Starr.

This switches from the jaunty mood of 'Who Needs Money' to one of those 'longing' ballads Elvis sings so well. Under a handy tree – one of a kind that proliferate in so many Presley films of this period, Elvis once again expresses his love for Shelley Fabares, the girl he thinks is out of reach as long as she thinks he's an impecunious ski instructor. She creeps up beside him for the last few bars, with a look that should tell him 'it won't be long now'. Most noticeable in the background is the piano, and those ever-soothing Jordanaires.

HOW CAN YOU LOSE WHAT YOU NEVER HAD?

(Bonus) (not included in movie)
Written by Sid Wayne, Ben Weisman. The Wayne–Weisman team, who wrote the gutsy title song, produce more in the same vein; main distinguishing feature being the prominence of the harmonica.

BIG BOSS MAN

(bonus) (not included in movie)
Written by Al Smith, Luther Dixon. Along with 'Guitar Man', 'Big Boss Man' is the other number with its honky-tonk piano effect and harmonica. Tony

Blackburn presumably did not choose to review the A side, or he could not have accused the singer of having lost his zest and punch, nor could he, in all conscience, have said 'Are the skids under Elvis Presley as a pop force?'

Single B/W: 'You Don't Know Me'
EP: 'Stay Away'
LPs: 'Double Dynamite'; 'Elvis Sings Hits From His Movies – Vol. 1'; 'Elvis – TV Special'
SINGING TREE (Bonus) (not included in movie)
Written by A. Owens, A. Solberg.

JUST CALL ME LONESOME

(bonus) (not included in movie)
Written by Rex Griffin.

It could be relevant that the bonus songs of the LP were recorded after Elvis's marriage to Priscilla on May 1, 1967, shortly after Brenda Lee, once friendly with Elvis said, 'It's impossible for his friends to reach Elvis since his marriage. No one sees him anymore, unless he's making a movie. He's pretty well secluded up there in his Hollywood mansion, but a few of us keep trying to see him. It's a very, very sad situation.'

CROONERS FOR SWOONERS

With the possible exception of Al Jolson, who introduced talking pictures with *The Jazz Singer* in 1927 and remained a major star until his death at the age of 64 in 1950, Rudy Vallee was the first popular singer to be called a 'crooner' and induce mass swooning in audiences, young and old. In a book devoted to Presley it may seem lèse majesté to record the fact that Vallee was the original most popular recording artist and is still considered by some to be the greatest entertaining talent of all time. Vallee's first feature film was *The Vagabond Lover*, named after his most famous song and despite his decidedly unromantic looks with batwing ears and eyes which his detractors considered crossed, he starred in several Thirties musicals until he found his true métier as a character actor caricaturing eccentric millionaires.

As a film star he was supplanted in the recording and movie stakes by the far more photogenic Bing Crosby, whose protruding ears were less prominent than Vallee's and who had an engagingly laid back warmth as an actor. After he recorded 'Where the Blue of the Night', the title of his own radio show, his records began selling in millions. Among his most popular films were the series of *Road* movies with Bob Hope and Dorothy Lamour made between 1941 and 1962, although in the final film Dorothy Lamour was relegated to 'Guest Star', while the much younger Joan Collins became leading lady. Crosby won an Academy Award for his portrayal of a Catholic priest in *Going My Way* in 1944, the year after Frank Sinatra, the new claimant to the throne of idol to swooning, screaming bobby-soxers, played his first acting part in *Higher and Higher*. Bobby-soxers were a breed that had grown up since Rudy and Bing wowed their mums and dads. No one was more influential in giving teenagers their place in the sun than Sinatra, who soon acquired an acting talent to match his unique way with a song. In 1953 he, too, won an Oscar for *From Here to Eternity* and in 1956 he co-starred with Crosby and Grace Kelly in the musical remake of *The Philadelphia Story*, *High Society*, with roles played respectively by James Stewart, Katherine Hepburn and Cary Grant.

By this time both Crosby and Sinatra, while retaining immense popularity as film stars and recording artists, had moved over to make way for the latest in teenage raves, the icon of the early Fifties 'Crying Crooner' Johnnie Ray. He had a gimmick – and an unusual one: the tears flowed as he sang and the cash flowed equally prodigiously with his million selling 'Cry'. His blond good looks were those

of an up-dated matinée idol, but an all-American boy version, likely to appeal to the more mature as well as the bobby-soxers, although his uninhibited body language was met with pursed lips and head-wagging by many of the older generation. At his London Palladium debut it was standing-room only. I stood at the back with excited fans of both sexes, mostly youngsters but with a sprinkling of appreciative older theatregoers. Among the latter was perennial musical comedy star, American-born Dorothy Dickson, who had delighted audiences on both sides of the Atlantic since World War One, when she was a star of *The Ziegfeld Follies*. She was preparing for a play satirizing the Johnnie Ray cult – about a crying crooner who creates havoc when he takes refuge from his hysterical fans in the home of an actress and her staid business man husband. The crooner was played by the musical idol of London, Paris and New York from the Twenties, Jack Buchanen. His laid-back style was the antithesis of Johnnie Ray's, so like other members of the cast he went along to the Palladium to gain a few pointers. The play *As Long as They're Happy*, ends with him and the whole family bawling 'Cry!' into a microphone; Dorothy had come along to see what all the fuss was about. Greatly impressed though she was by the audience reaction, she was not sure whether Ray or Al Jolson was the better entertainer.

Johnnie's film debut, *There's No Business Like Show Business*, with a scintillating all-star cast including Ethel Merman, Marilyn Monroe, Mitzi Gaynor and Donald O'Connor, was a box office smash, but it was also his movie swansong. Cast as an unlikely priest, a member of a show business family with Ethel Merman as the redoubtable Mama, he did not film particularly well, possibly because of his inherent deafness which he was able to surmount on stage but which gave him

an unfair disadvantage with spoken dialogue. He continued to record and give live performances with great success, though by June 1956 Presley, having topped the pops with 'Heartbreak Hotel' had created major ripples – waves really – in the established order of things in the chart world and Johnnie's excellent 'Ain't Misbehavin' failed to climb as high as it would automatically have done before. Among other top recording stars to feel the breeze were Doris Day, Frankie Laine, Eddie Fisher and Rosemary Clooney. In Britain Ruby Murray (the only girl singer then to have had six discs in the Top Twenty concurrently), Dickie Valentine, Joan Regan and Frankie Vaughan were no longer automatic best sellers, though most of them were getting on with successful stage shows and the occasional film. British comedian Dave King pushed Dean Martin's version of 'Memories Are Made of This' from the top spot with his first disc.

Johnnie Ray, back at the Palladium, in 1957, showed no ill-will. He said 'I don't like Rock 'n' Roll, but I admire Elvis Presley. He's going to be around for some time, I reckon. Because he's got the experience now. He's becoming stable.'

Like Bing Crosby, who died of a heart attack in 1977 aged 73 – and some reference books say more – while playing golf, his favourite pastime, Johnnie Ray stayed around in show business till almost the end, though some unfavourable publicity in later years put something of a blight on his career. He was in great form and little changed when I reviewed him at the Back Theatre, Hayes, Middlesex, in 1990. Sadly he died soon after the same year.

DANCING IN THE STREET

In June, 1996, BBC TV put out the first of a ten part history of rock 'n' roll. The term, coined by white D.J. Alan Freed for rhythm and blues, was, in fact, the black slang term for sex. Hence, the Fifties hostility to the new music was rooted in racism. One snarling mid-westerner in the film called a meeting to counter the new 'threat', saying that rock 'n' roll was obviously a means by which the white man can be driven to the 'level of the nigger.'

The programme traced a fascinating pattern of how black and white rhythms and, eventually, singers came together to form a new mode of musical expression that appealed equally to all races. The way was being prepared for Elvis Presley, from the banks of the Mississippi through Chicago, New Orleans, right up to Memphis and beyond, in two small recording studios. The Little Mississippi in Chicago, run by the Chess Brothers, Phil and Leonard, was where Bo Diddley introduced his innovative percussive electric guitar sound. In New Orleans the great Fats Domino, pianist extraordinary, with his 'Ain't That A Shame?' had been the first to break away from the exclusively black labels to which Negro artists were confined and switch over to a mainstream company and sell in millions. Probably the greatest catalyst in the movement was

actually Sam Phillips, who started his recording studios in Memphis in 1950, later to be the home of Sun Records. He would take great pride in recording black and white entertainers without discrimination and his is the most impressive interview among several fascinating ones in the BBC's first programme. He describes how they were all 'just beginners' and how fierce the opposition was; they were accused of causing white people to love niggers and of mutilating and trying to destroy all that was good in music.

Phillips was having hits with numbers like 'Rocket 88' by black pianist Ike Turner, recommended to him by grateful guitarist B.B. King, who had cut his first record at the studio. Phillips was convinced that if he could get the black musicians into his studio without any preconceptions that they were playing for white men sitting behind that glass panel and just be themselves, the result would be rewarding. 'Rocket 88' broadened the base from which young white males and females began to get interested in rhythm and blues; the radio was the most potent disseminator of this levelling out, when young people heard the records in their cars at night. Little Richard, young, black, totally uninhibited, with his make-up and outrageous pompadour hair styles started to have hits for Sam Phillips – 'I guess he thought he was Queen of the May' said a contemporary – and

regarded himself as the architect and innovator of rock 'n' roll.

Thus the scene was set for the 18 year-old trucker from Memphis to take the world by storm as the white Southern boy who could sing with the black sound that Sam Phillips had always prayed for. The one blemish in his otherwise exemplary account of the way things were is his claim that the moment Elvis Presley walked in the door he recognized that his prayers had been answered. In fact Sam wasn't even there and. It was his studio manager, Marion Keisker, who recognized Elvis's potential, turned on the tape recorder, caught much of his first session and took the trouble to make a note of the telephone number at which a message could reach him. However, it is a simplification of the truth for which the man who did so much to set him on his way can be forgiven.

From Elvis's original backing team Scotty Moore and D.J. Fontana contribute positively to the film and the flashbacks to them at work are riveting. Director David Espar's comprehensive survey is a must for any serious study of Presley's work and is fully complemented by the narration of Sean Barrett.
(**See also: Boone versus Presley**)

DEATH THREAT – HAWAIIAN STYLE

On 10th July, 1966, the *Sunday Express* in London printed the following review:

'Paradise, Hawaiian Style (Plaza) is the latest Elvis Presley vehicle, and not a whit different from any of his others. That means it will be Paradise for Presley fans, and Purgatory for anyone else who gets trapped in the cinema.'

The author was Michael Thornton, London's youngest national critic in 1964, at the age of 23. The review provoked an outraged female fan of the star to threaten to hurl acid in his face. The lady in question wrote to him at the *Sunday Express*.

No acid thrower materialized and at the time of writing some thirty years later, Thornton's attitude to Presley has mellowed. He says, 'I remember I had given some dismissive reviews to several earlier Presley vehicles. I think I did give some attention to *Roustabout* (*qv*), largely because of Barbara Stanwyck's (*qv*) presence, but otherwise I have to admit that I found Mr. Presley infinitely resistible. In this I was completely out of tune with my own generation. My cousin, Dudley Gillham, who was three years my senior, was a Presley aficionado, but I just didn't dig Elvis. I found his singing unexciting, his acting atrocious and his screen presence wooden. I much preferred his younger British counterpart, Cliff Richard, even though I recognized at the time that Cliff was 'merely' (sic) an ersatz Elvis and had based his entire career at that point on the most blatant imitation of Presley – the same singing style, and even accent, the slicked back hair, the shirt torn open to the navel and even the gyrating hips. But Cliff had far more charm and vulnerability than Elvis. Charm was what Presley lacked, for me at any rate, though I have to confess that now I find him much better that I did then. Some of the films still stink, though, and I agree with Doug Tomlinson, in *The International Dictionary of Films and Filmmakers* when he says that "No major star suffered through more bad movies than Elvis

Presley. Of the 31(sic) movies he made as a movie star, arguably Don Siegel's (*qv*) *Flaming Star* (*qv*) – a non-singing role for Presley – has any redeeming value beyond the star's appearance."'

Tomlinson's assessment smacks of intellectual snobbery and is in any case inaccurate: Elvis does, indeed, sing in *Flaming Star*, including the title song, although the LP 'Elvis Sings Flaming Star' (*qv*) is, in effect, something of a cheat. After reviewing all his movies I have compiled a list of other productions of quality, pointing out what, in my estimation, makes them special. Heading the comedy list has to be Gordon Douglas's (*qv*) *Follow That Dream* (*qv*). *Paradise Hawaiian Style* (*qv*), coming at a period in the Presley career when Elvis was growing disillusioned with the way his movies were being ground out from Colonel Parker's (*qv*) 'Technical Advisor' sausage machine suffered from being virtually a regurgitation of the 1961 highly successful and far superior *Blue Hawaii* (*qv*). In a way, Michael Thornton's assessment of the later film as being 'not a whit different from any of his others' is justified. It was, indeed, more of the same of which even the staunchest fans were beginning to tire. (See also: *Blue Hawaii*; Douglas, Gordon; *Flaming Star*; *Follow That Dream*; *Paradise Hawaiian Style*; Parker, Colonel Tom; *Roustabout*; Siegel, Don, Stanwyck, Barbara)

DEL RIO, DOLORES
(b. 1905)

In *Flaming Star* (*qv*), Elvis Presley's second movie in 1960 after his discharge from the army, he was blessed with three assets; a worthwhile and serious script that had been intended for Marlon Brando, a great director in Don Siegel (*qv*) and one of the world's most glamorous and prestigious stars, Dolores Del Rio, as his mother, Neddy Burton, a Kiowa Indian. Del Rio's presence in the plot creates the tension that ends in tragedy, both for Neddy and her son

Pacer (Elvis), caught up in the animosity between the Kiowas and the white settlers. Both of them ultimately head off into the hills to die, in search of what Neddy calls their 'Flaming Star'. The film was the beginning of the end of Presley's quest for meaningful roles in serious films: for all its qualities the movie was rather less successful than his previous ones – perhaps partly because of the minimal singing – there was only the title song and one other, neither particularly distinguished, although 'Flaming Star' did reach No. 3 in Elvis's Top Forty. What weighed against its appeal to the fans were his death at the end, although unseen, and the thought of him playing a half-caste.

Del Rio herself showed great fondness for Elvis and, as with other distinguished actors who appeared with him, was loud in her praises for him and his attractive qualities. She referred to him as her 'lithe Black Panther', and at the London press showing when mother and son shared a kiss, one of the critics was heard to murmur to his neighbour, 'She's playing his *mother*?' For all this, the following year when Paramount offered her the chance to play his mother again, she graciously declined. The part went to Angela Lansbury, who at 36 was only ten years older than Elvis. Dolores, at 56, would have seemed a more suitable choice , for all her youthful beauty. The part with Presley in the Siegel film was obviously a challenge that aroused her curiosity and, like Barbara Stanwyck (*qv*), she realized the film would receive world-wide coverage; moreover the role, though not a long one, was sympathetic and called for some of her considerable dramatic powers, while the *Blue Hawaii* (*qv*) mother, that of a slightly scatty society dame, would have been the kind of part that Billie Burke could have been ideal for in her younger days.

Dolores Del Rio was born in Durango, Mexico, in 1905 and first married at 16 to writer James Del Rio, a name she adhered to through her two subsequent marriages, the second to MGM's top art director, Cedric Gibbons. In 1925 director Edwin Carewe was struck by her exotic beauty at a Mexico City tea party and invited her to Hollywood to appear in his film *Joanna*. She went on to star in many silent films and made the transition to sound successfully, although her Latin accent made type-casting inevitable. She sang the title song 'Ramona' not only on screen but in prolonged tours nationwide for promotional purposes; the idea of a singing screen heroine was a novelty that proved successful. During a liaison with Orson Welles she made *Journey Into Fear* for him in 1942: when they parted gossip maliciously suggested that Dolores' nightly routine of covering herself with preserving oils had made their relationship a slippery one from the start. In fact her role in the Welles film was ill-defined and unrewarding; even her adagio act with a muscular partner was so clumsily cut little remained to remind filmgoers that she was one of the most graceful of dancers on screen. The following year, dissatisfied with her Hollywood career, she returned to Mexico to sign a lucrative film contract that gave her a percentage of the profits and, as Mexico's top star, had the pick of the roles, including the title in *Maria Candelaria*, released in Britain as *Portrait of Maria*. Her Mary Magdalene-like part as a pure peasant girl hounded to her death by malicious gossip prompted some critics to compare her incandescence and spirituality with that of Garbo, who had just turned her back on her spectacular career; at 36 she was the same age as Del Rio.

Dolores, on the other hand, was embarking on the most productive stage of her acting life: she married producer Lewis Riley, they opened their own theatre and she received the affectionate title of 'Uncrowned Queen of Mexico'. During one of her occasional visits to the US to look for plays, she contracted to play her role in *Flaming Star*, released

about the same time in 1961 as her Mexican movie *La Cucuracha* about the Pancho Villa revolution, in which, as a glamorous society widow, she not only got her man, a General played by Emilio Fernandez, but made sure the public knew she did not have to play mothers – even Elvis's! This may have weighed with her when she turned down the role in *Blue Hawaii*.

As late as 1971 she made one of her biggest stage successes in *Camille*, aged 66, playing the famous courtesan role in which Garbo gave her memorable performance in 1937 aged 32. Actress Dorothy Dickson, wrote in *Films and Filming*:

'Helen Hayes, at whose home in Mexico City I was staying, asked me along when she went to unveil a plaque to Dolores Del Rio at her theatre in Mexico City, where she was playing Camille. I was not looking forward to sitting through Dumas' play yet again at this stage in history. However, before the evening was through I was completely won over by the quality of the production, the staging and, above all, the artistry and absolutely contemporary beauty of Dolores Del Rio, whose death scene was an exquisite achievement, worthy of ranking with the greatest.'
(See also: *Blue Hawaii; Flaming Star;* Stanwyck, Barbara)

DOGS

Two of the most famous Presley songs are associated with dogs, a species for which he had a lifetime of affection. Dogs featured in several of his films and he had a series of his own canines. The first notable 'dog' song was 'Old Shep', a tear jerking ballad recalling a beloved pooch, written in 1933 by Red Foley and Willis Arthur and first recorded by Foley himself. The song was first sung by Elvis at the tender age of ten in his initial public appearance at the 1945 Mississippi–Alabama Dairy Show. Inevitably, there was not a dry eye in the

place, including young Elvis. He had to stand on a chair to reach the microphone and sing unaccompanied in the talent contest. He won the second prize of five dollars and free rides at the fair.

Being a profound dog lover myself, I simply can't listen to the song in public for fear of breaking down – the words are so terribly sad. I was interested to note in *Elvis – The Movie* (*qv*) that Ronnie McDowell as the voice of Elvis omitted the unbearably tear-provoking line about taking the old dog to be put down and finding himself unable to pull the trigger.

On a far lighter note is, of course, 'Hound Dog', which created a furore when Elvis, wearing a tuxedo, sang it to a solemn-looking bloodhound with a top-hat on its head on the *Steve Allen Show* – demeaning for both dog and Elvis, but hysterically popular with the viewers. 'Hound Dog', by Jerry Lieber and Mike Stoller was written in 1952 and recorded by Willie Mae (Big Mama) Thornton in 1953 and by Freddie Bell and the Bellboys in 1955. Elvis's version was recorded on July 2nd 1956 for RCA, New York City. The flip side was 'Don't be Cruel'. Elvis and his dog friend are featured on the record sleeve – presumably from the *Steve Allen Show*. On the British charts the disc reached No. 2; on the US Charts it was No. 1. Sales in 1956 reached 6 million – 9 million overall. It would be fascinating to learn what the eponymous bloodhound received as his share. Repeats, reissues, LP and CD releases would fill a page on their own.

Dogs also featured in Presley movies. In *Kissin' Cousins* (*qv*) a bloodhound, billed as Hezekiah, raises piteous howls whilst being sung to by Glenda Farrell (*qv*). This is presumably no reflection on her singing. In the plot she has lost her husband somewhere and Hezekiah is pining for his missing master. Every time the word 'Pappy' comes up both she and Elvis have to spell it out, 'P A P P Y'.

The dog featured in *Live a Little,*

Elvis and furry friend. (1962) (It's not a poodle!)

Love a Little (qv) is a Great Dane called Karl, who helps heroine Bernice (Michele Carey) in a bizarre plot to involve photographer Greg Nolan (Elvis) in her life. Bernice has spotted Greg sitting on the beach, singing to himself: she lets Karl chase him into the sea and keep him there until the sun sets on the Pacific. By the time the dog lets him crawl ashore Greg is too weak to say no when Bernice takes him home and tucks him into bed. This was 1968 and Elvis was reaching the end of his tether with such films, with only another three to go before his commitment to Hollywood ran out. *Stay Away, Joe* (qv) featured five endearing hairy dogs with whom Elvis shares a blanket while he sings 'All I Needed Was The Rain' to them.

There's a much quicker
Back to 1957 and his third movie *Jailhouse Rock* (qv), when Elvis was still enchanted with the idea of being an actor. The two King Charles spaniels, although unnamed and referred to as 'the dogs', provide incidental plot motivation as the catalysts in the worsening relations between Vince Everett (Elvis), new TV star, and his ex-cellmate, Hunk Houghton (Mickey Shaughnessy), whom he has put on his payroll, but treats with some contempt, having discovered that Hunk had double crossed him in prison by bribing a warden to withhold fan mail after Vince's sensational TV debut in a Spectacular from the prison. One of the chores the resentful Hunk considers demeaning is having to walk Vince's dogs: he trails them eight miles round every bar in town and they return exhausted. Hunk picks a fight in a drunken rage with his employer, who refuses to retaliate and is in danger of losing his voice after a severe punch in the throat. The dogs then disappear from the plot.

There's a much quicker disappearance in *Spinout* (1966) when Mike McCoy (Elvis) is enjoying an al fresco meal with his band when a handsome wolfhound joins him at the table, snatches some food and is never seen again. More doggy disruption occurs in *Paradise, Hawaiian Style* when pilot Rick Richards (Elvis) is ferrying a group of pedigree dogs to an important dog show in his helicopter. They're happy when he sings to them 'It's A Dog's Life', natch, but when he mentions the word 'steak' they go beserk, scrambling all over him until he loses control of his aircraft and finally delivers his charges to their outraged owner much the worse for wear.

Much earlier in Elvis's career, in *Wild in the Country* (1961), the heroine, Irene Sperry's (Hope Lange) Red Setter, Rosie, plays a dramatic role in the movie when she raises the alarm on finding her mistress has shut herself in the garage and is intent on committing suicide. Rosie saves the day and Irene's life.

Among the many dogs who played a large part in Elvis's affections throughout his life, one of his favourites was a Chow Chow called Getlo, who used to sleep on the end of his bed. Getlo died after an operation in 1975 and Elvis took the loss very badly. Some of his other favourites were Duke (after John Wayne (qv)), Boy, Foxhugh and Sweetpea.

(See also: Animals; *Elvis – The Movie; Jailhouse Rock; Kissin' Cousins; Live a Little, Love a Little; Paradise, Hawaiian Style; Scatter; Stay Away, Joe; Wild in the Country*)

DOUBLE TROUBLE * *

Released by: Metro-Goldwyn-Mayer, a B.C.W. Production (Panavision, Metrocolor); **Producers:** Judd Bernard, Irwin Winkler; **Director:** Norman Taurog; **Screenplay:** Jo Heims, based on a story by Marc Brandel; **Art Directors:** George W. Davis, Merrill Pye; **Director of photography:** Daniel L. Fabb; **Technical Advisor:** Colonel Tom Parker; **Music:** Jeff Alexander; **Running Time:** 92 mins; **Opened:** April 5, 1967.

Cast: Elvis, Annette Day, John Williams, Yvonne Romain, Chips Rafferty, Norman Rossington, The Weire Brothers, Monty Landis, Michael Murphy, Leon Askin, John Alderson, Stanley Adams, Maurice Marsac, Walter Burke, Helene Winston, The G. Men.

Society entertainer Guy Lambert (Elvis), singing in London, is pursued by two attractive women: Jill Conway (Annette Day), a seventeen year-old student, English and outgoingly naïve, and the sophisticated, glamorous Claire Dunham (Yvonne Romain), something of an enigma. Guy does not know that Jill is heiress to a fortune until her uncle, Gerald Waverly (John Williams), introduces himself on the phone and enlightens him. He also says that Jill imagines herself in love with Guy and he thinks it's time they met. Gerald summonses him to what appears to be his stately home – until the camera pulls back to reveal that the stately mansion is a painting by Constable. He asks if Guy's intentions are honourable to ensure he has marriage in mind. Guy makes a quick exit. Gerald, having observed Jill's enraptured greeting when she meets him, decides to get her out of harms way by sending her to school in Belgium, unaware that Guy's next singing engagement is in that country.

While crossing the Channel Jill moves from deck to deck looking for Guy, eventually finding him. On the trip Guy and Jill have narrow escapes from a number of bizarre accidents: a gangway gate springs open, almost precipitating him into the sea; a heavy trunk narrowly misses them, as he pushes Jill out of the way. Two bumbling smugglers watch their every movement: Arthur Babcock (Norman Rossington) and Archie Brown (Chips Rafferty), who are using Guy's luggage to smuggles diamonds. Guy is certain the incidents on the boat were pre-planned, but hopes that things will get easier in Brussels. Far from it. The pace hots up: Guy is surprised, but not displeased to find Claire smiling at him in the club where he is singing 'The City By Night'. She is less than delighted when Jill also turns up, 'bag and

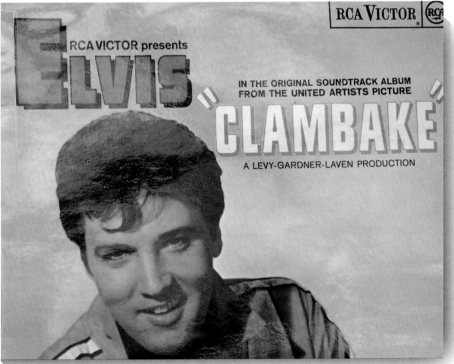

Blue Hawaii, complete with Hawaiian shirt, Roland Winters and Angela Lansbury.

Clambake – the soundtrack album

IN' COUSINS!

El doubles with himself in his latest for M.G.M. Here's a R.M. special on the film

A dramatic scene from the film—with the two Elvis's fighting.

...have never... ...ever, had ...In "Kissin' ...shown to ...in London ...re are two ...e song-star. ...ith his first ...as a young ...officer—and ...ountain boy, ...of one of ...'est clans in

...include ...one of the ...d him but ...t Happened ..."; Cynthia ...ustin; Glenda ...a fabulous ...med "Heze-

...TIVE

...ase of girls, ...e way; along ...gs, songs, ...new ones, ...parody with ...on "Won't ...ome, Bill

...newies is a ...on the title ...ew beat for ...ey Mountain ...march tempo ...fective. Then ...troubles of ...ith two girls ...Ballad, "One ...Girls."

...n the Moun- ...the setting ...he film—it's ...y section of ...e Mountains. ...Past" is a ...number in ...ined by the ...cluding the ...Kittyhawks," ...who prowl ...e.

...RY

...t Ballad," ..." number. ...of tempo

in the same movie, if you get the gist.

Says Elvis: "I'm nowhere near those greats. But I guess I have some right in playing this sort of role seeing as how I am in real life the survivor of identical twins.

COUNTRY GARB

"The bit about 'Kissin' Cousins' that I enjoyed most was when I fight myself. As Josh, the lieutenant, I tackle Jody, the hillbilly, in a free-swinging, hard-hitting, no-holds-barred sort of scrap—and I throw myself over my shoulder, hurl myself in the air, then flatten myself on my back! That was a gas!"

Of course, El had to have

pulling power at the cinema should ponder on this: he was named by the Motion Picture Herald poll as one of the ten stars who brought in most money at the box office in the States last year ... and was also named as one of the ten most popular stars in Britain.

Incidentally, "Kissin' Cousins" introduces an interesting mother-and-son partnership. Glenda Farrell, for long one of the most glamorous stars and now a character-player, works with her young son, Tommy Farrell.

And Tommy told Elvis: "Funny thing is that when I began in this business, my mother did everything in her power to discourage me. It wasn't that she was against

same time. He wears a blond wig for one of the characters — and his own jet-black styling for the other.

Revealed Elvis: "We had a wedding during the shooting of 'Kissin' Cousins. Pam Austin, who is a wonderful girl, got married to Charles Britt, a Los Angeles Rams' football star, while we were working on the early stages. She actually isn't the girl I get in the film—I go for Yvonne Craig eventually. Pam ends up with Tommy Farrell ... though I guess I shouldn't give too much of the plot away."

DANCER

Film also features a lot of dance sequences, with Elvis showing how he's developed

Elvis sings in *Girls! Girls! Girls!* (left)

***Kissin' Cousins*. Elvis hugs Pam Austin and Yvonne Craig (above)**

A dramatic moment from *Kid Galahad*, with Lola Albright and Gig Young (below)

Frankie and Johnny – the soundtrack album
Elvis shows his strength in *Follow That Dream*

**Elvis as Society Entertainer Guy
Lambert, trying to protect a young
heiress whom unknown forces are trying
to murder, gets into the right spirit when
he runs into carnival time in Antwerp.**
Double Trouble (1967)

baggage'. Guy invites her to his hotel to talk; he has realized she is running away from school and her uncle. As they arrive at the hotel a car narrowly misses Guy. As they go upstairs Babcock and Brown are still tailing them and a sinister character called the Iceman (John Alderson), who was lurking on the boat, is also hanging around. In Guy's room Jill slips into a negligee and makes big play for him: when she lets slip that she is not yet eighteen he forces her to put her clothes back on, but she persuades him to let her stay with him until they get to Sweden, where she says she has an aunt. As they sneak out of the back entrance a gun is fired at them, hitting the door. Deciding that discretion is the better part of valour, they jump on a passing chicken cart and hitch a ride to Antwerp, the venue of Guy's next engagement.

It is carnival time and the two bumbling jewel thieves, dressed up in Humpty Dumpty costumes, are hovering about in an attempt to snatch Guy's suitcase. He sings along with the festival folk in their costumes and then finds Claire has turned up again. She invites him back to the sculptor's studio where she is staying. A furious Jill in a child's mask trips Guy up. Claire gives him her phone number and Jill wanders off, still wearing her mask. The Iceman appears about to attack her when some revellers intercept and the man disappears. She runs into a charming young man she met on the boat; he lures her into a deserted barn to look at an ancient well, then reveals himself in his true colours. He has been working for her uncle, who has been dipping into her inheritance and has sent him to kill her. Guy has traced her by the carnival mask she dropped. Hearing her screams he tackles the assailant with expert karate chops and he falls into the ancient well to his death. They fight their way through the revellers to try to get a lift on a tramp steamer whose eccentric captain has planted a bomb in the hold. Fortunately he turns them off the ship and they check in at a

sleazy seaport hotel, where Guy leaves Jill while he slips out to phone Claire, asking her to look after Jill. Outside the phone box Guy is arrested by three eccentric detectives (the Weire Brothers) and taken to police headquarters on a charge of kidnapping. Uncle Gerald arrives to substantiate the charge but Guy is unable to convince the Inspector (Leon Askin) that Jill is in danger of being killed before she turns eighteen at midnight.

Guy tricks his way out of the police station, steals the inspector's car and hurries to Claire's apartment, unaware that she is an accomplice of Uncle Gerald and has first drugged Jill, then turned the gas on to asphyxiate her. Just as the sinister man who has been trailing Jill lifts her off the bed, Guy bursts in and knocks him out, along with Claire, then smashes the window to let the gas out. Gerald and Claire are finally arrested; Guy and Jill, who has extracted a confession of love from him, set sail for England – on the boat with the bomb in the hold. The ship blows up and the lovers are left on a raft in the English Channel, with a suitcase full of valuable jewels while Babcock and Brown flounder in the water, bereft of the ill-gotted booty.

The English setting, opening with Elvis singing in a London nighterie, is just one of the unusual aspects of this MGM musical, one of a cluster which came just before his marriage. Another is the bona fide cast of authentic British character actors in support. Annette Day, who received much publicity by being discovered in London's Portobello Road, makes a pretty, beleaguered heroine, both innocent and apparently eager to bed Elvis at the earliest opportunity. The sames goes for Yvonne Romaine, except that she's far from innocent and turns out to be the mistress of the villain, who is none other than our own John Williams, playing the heroine's wicked uncle – an unusual role for Williams, more often cast as the chief inspector. Then there are

English comedians Norman Rossington, as the silliest jewel thief ever, with Australian Chips Rafferty as his extemely tall and bumbling partner. Even stranger are the variety comedy trio the Weire Brothers, as inept Belgian police officers.

Director Norman Taurog (*qv*) keeps his hands on the directorial reins in his usual efficient way, but it is the comedy approach that lets the film down. Elvis looks beautiful, with some stylishly different hair fringes by Mary Keats and elegant suits by Don Field: alas, he looks slightly bored, with a conspicous lack of his customary enthusiasm. Britain's *Monthly Film Bulletin*, official organ of the British Film Institute, summed it up neatly: 'All is brisk, painless and rather dull.'
(See also: Taurog, Norman)

DOUBLE TROUBLE

(RCA LPM – 3787) June 1967 *
Written by Doc Pomus, Mort Shuman. Guy Lambert (Elvis) singing at a London night-spot laments, with hep gestures and much clicking of fingers, that he's in love with two girls, which gives him twice as much trouble as anybody else. During the song the girls in question turn up – sophisticated Claire Dunham and innocent 17 year-old Jill Conway. He's accompanied by his cockney friend and travelling companion, Georgie, another guitarist, a drummer and a pianist, all with slightly Beatle-orientated haircuts, which does nothing to disguise the banality of the lyrics, interchangeable with almost any opening number of a Presley movie of the period. As he finishes the song two harmonizing cigarette girls ask if it's true he's leaving for Belgium the next day. When he says 'yes' they go 'Boo Hoo' in unison and he says, 'That's a good title for a song': giving anxiety that he may be about to launch into just such a number – but we are spared that experience.
LP: 'Elvis in Hollywood'

BABY, IF YOU'LL GIVE ME ALL OF YOUR LOVE *

Written by Joy Byers.

The second song comes soon after the first, after some repartee between the two girls and Elvis – he does not get away with pleading innocence to either of them. This is something of a rocker, in which he threatens to embrace the girl until she begs for mercy. He beats out his own rhythm on a tambourine, having plucked at a bass bassoon with a girl's blonde, bewigged head on top to which he addresses his declarations of love – until a real blonde pops up out of the jiving, hand-clapping audience on the dance floor. Close-ups of Jill and Claire giving him adoring looks are interpolated with the action shots, until he ends with one of his modified bump and grind movements. There's the same accompaniment by the G. Men as in the first song, who join in the chorus from time to time. More insipid lyrics, given a certain punch by Elvis's delivery.
LP: 'Mahalo from Elvis'.

COULD I FALL IN LOVE *

Written by Randy Star.

Jill has virtually lured Guy to take her to his flat on the premise that if they are ever going to get together, this will be the last opportunity. When she gets there she fusses around, with various ploys to keep him at arm's length – making tea etc., chattering on about her family background. She asks him to put something on the record player and reminds him that this is the songs he had said was 'our' song. She asks him to sing it to her, after he has stolen his first quick kiss. The orchestral backing features piano and vocals, presumably by the G. Men. With his arms around her he answers his own question that he could fall in love, for the very first time, as long as she is the girl in question. A very short song, at the end of which Jill is fast asleep on his shoulder. No wonder; such a dreary dirge is enough to send anyone to sleep. They smooch a

little until he sits on the tea service; while he changes she slips away, writing down his phone number as she goes. A peal at the doorbell sends Guy to open it, rubbing his hands in anticipation: it is not Jill, but a perfect stranger who knocks him out with a single blow then observes he mistook the number on the door. This incident can only be explained as a desperate ruse by director Norman Taurog to inject a punch into the somnolent scene we have just endured. Not featured on any other LP.

LONG LEGGED GIRL (WITH THE SHORT DRESS ON) *

Written by J. Leslie McFarland, Winfield Scott.

Guy sings this to the enthralled passengers on the boatdeck, his backing band behind him, while he moves around among the jigging travellers, singing of his world-wide search for the girl of the title, searching high and low, until at the end of the song Jill appears on cue to prove she's who he's been looking for all along. She explains that she's on the ship en route for Brussels, where her uncle is sending her to finishing school, apparently unaware that Guy is on his way to sing in Bruges. This has to be one of the low spots on a not particularly distinguished LP.
Single B/W: 'That's Someone You Never Forget'
LPs: 'Almost in Love', 'Elvis Sings From His Movies – Vol. 1'

CITY BY NIGHT * * * * *

Written by Bill Giant, Bernie Baum, Florence Kaye.

Guy sings this one at his Bruges gig in his most effective outfit: red open-necked shirt, white jacket, dark trousers. Naturally, at the end of the song there's the lovely Claire, ready with a few pointed ripostes ('You must like travelling an awful lot to come here for a one night stand'. 'I hope you're referring to the itinerary.') Equally obviously, there is also Jill. The song opens on an

ingenious jump-cut from Norman Rossington's despairing scream on the steamer at the ineptitude of his partner in crime, Chips Rafferty, to a close up of Georgie's trombone. Various instruments combine to make a marvellously atmospheric start to lyrics describing a mysterious night-life in crowded clubs and cafes, teeming with dancing sillhouettes – a city that never sleeps and is full of surprise, enchanting to the unwary visitor. There are exciting tempo changes, piano interludes and much use of muted trumpets. This is a personal favourite, beautifully interpreted by Elvis in his moody blues vein. Seemingly too stylized for repetition.

OLD MACDONALD *

Traditional Children's Song

Down to earth with a bump from the rarefied atmosphere of the 'City By Night', as Guy and Jill hitch a lift on the back of a farm truck, with chickens clucking behind them in cages. Elvis sings with every semblance of enjoyment, with Annette Day making the appropriate gestures beside him, as the remorseless chorus song grinds its way to a close via a gaggle of animal noises, while hero and heroine ride off on their way to Antwerp and his next song date. It must have been this that prompted Dave Marsh to write in his book *Elvis*, 'Who could sing such drool and make it stick? Who could put across such drivel and keep the customers lined up for more? Only Elvis.'

I LOVE ONLY ONE GIRL * *

Written by Sid Tepper, Roy C. Bennett. Established in Antwerp, Guy joins the carnival folk, jumps on the roundabouts and sings to the gaily disguised crowds in their masks. Behind one of them is the jealous Jill, keeping an eye on him as he makes a provisional date with the inevitable Claire. And what does he sing? Messrs Tepper and Bennet have set new lyrics to the traditional French ditty 'Aupre de ma Blonde' to give him a girl

in every capital. With fairground-type backing, it is a jolly accompaniment to a pretty, colourful scene.
LPs: 'Elvis Sings for Children and Grownups Too!' 'Elvis sings From His Movies –Vol. 1'.

THERE IS SO MUCH WORLD TO SEE *

Written by Sid Tepper, Ben Weisman. Guy and Jill have to share a room in a seedy Antwerp hotel. They lie down on the bed together and she does her best to trap him into marriage, but his song explains his attitude that he does not want to get tied up yet because he has not finished exploring the world. He prefers them to remain friends, not lovers, as he doesn't want to break her heart. Drums, strings and clarinets help along the orchestral backing to this inevitable pot-boiler, keeping the lovers apart until the final close-up clinch.
The remainder of the songs on the 'Double Trouble' LP are bonuses:

THAT'S SOMEONE YOU NEVER FORGET

Written by Red West.
Single B/W: 'Long Legged Girl (with the Short Dress On)

IT WON'T BE LONG

Written by Sid Wayne, Ben Weisman. Recorded for the film *Double Trouble*, but not used.

NEVER ENDING

Written by Buddy Kaye, Phil Springer.
Single B/W: 'Such a Night'

SUCH A NIGHT

Written by Lincoln Chase.
Single B/W: 'Never Ending'
LPs: 'Elvis Aaron Presley'; 'Elvis is Back'

BLUE RIVER

Written by Paul Evans, Fred Tobias.
Single B/W: 'Tell Me Why'

TELL ME WHY

Written by Titus Turner.
Single B/W: 'Blue River'
LPs: 'Elvis: The Other Sides – Worldwide Gold Award Hits – Vol. 2'; 'Essential Elvis Vol. 2'; 'A Valentine Gift For You'

WHAT NOW, WHAT NEXT, WHERE TO

Written by Don Robertson, Hal Blair.
LP: 'Separate Ways'

DOUGLAS, GORDON
(1909–1993)

This generally under-rated director made only one movie with Elvis Presley, *Follow That Dream* (*qv*) – regrettably so, as they obviously had a rapport which brought out the best in Elvis as a comedy actor. It was perhaps his early experience as a child stage actor that gave Douglas an insight into how an actor's mind work. He went to Hollywood in the late Twenties and after some time at both MGM and Paramount, joined the Hal Roach studios as actor, casting director and occasional gagman. He appeared in *The Boy Friends* comedy series and in 1936 began directing 'Our Gang' comedy shorts, as well as the 'Our Gang' feature special *General Spanky*.

He directed Oliver Hardy in *Zenobia* (1939), in which the main character is a circus elephant – the title in Great Britain was *Elephants Never Forget* – and Stan Laurel and Oliver Hardy in *Saps at Sea* the following year: the two films were far from being the finest hour for either the comedians or the director, but it appears that he was working under difficulties in both cases, due to circumstances beyond everyone's control. Douglas's most successful association with a comedy team, after years of directing a diversity of movies, including *The Falcon in Hollywood* in 1944, was with Eddie Cantor and Joan Davis in 1948's *If You Knew Susie*, which Cantor also produced. Albeit a B

musical, cast and director infused a good deal of warm humour into the time-honoured story of a show business family's ups and downs. Personally, I always found Eddie Cantor highly resistible, but Joan Davis, one time wife of Bert Lahr, the Cowardly Lion of *The Wizard of Oz*, was one of the funniest of the gangling slapstick comediennes of the ilk of Cass Daley, Martha Raye and Charlotte Greenwood. Subtlety was never their stock-in-trade and they were either loved or hated by the public.

Gordon Douglas had a tricky time directing Doris Day and Frank Sinatra in *Young at Heart*, the musical version of the early Warner Brothers Fannie Hearst drama, *Four Daughters*, starring John Garfield. Though Doris was top-billed and her husband, Marty Melcher, was as usual technical advisor – there goes that term again – on his wife's films, Sinatra had considerable power around the set and created a situation by taking such an instant dislike to Melcher that he insisted Douglas keep him off the lot. Doris handled the awkwardness with her usual tact and has said nothing but gracious things about her co-star in public, but the tensions were inevitable. Melcher stood in the same Svengali–Trilby role to Doris Day as Tom Parker did to Elvis Presley. At his death Doris found he had run her into debts of millions of dollars – something the Colonel (*qv*) was far too shrewd an operator to have done with his protégé. There is nothing to suggest that relations between Gordon Douglas and Colonel Tom Parker were ever anything but cordial, and *Follow That Dream* (*qv*) benefited as a result.

Douglas was to work with Sinatra again in 1974 in *Robin and the Seven Hoods* and twice in 1978 in *The Detective* and *Lady in Cement*, both hard-hitting gangster movies which showed how adeptly he could handle themes dealing with the seamy side of life. It also indicated that he had cleverly negotiated the shoals of the

Day–Melcher–Sinatra situation.
Probably one of the director's most
popular films was *They Call Me Mr.*
Tibbs in 1977.

The devoted Albert Hand, who
originally ran the Elvis Presley Fan Club
of Great Britain, accorded Gordon
Douglas a real accolade for directing
Elvis in 'one of the funniest movies ever
seen' and castigates the power-that-were
for failing even to nominate him for an
Oscar. He could, of course, be accused of
being biased – his adoration of the King
and his work was unremitting during the
years he looked after the club – but there
was more than a glimmer of justification
for what he said in the first section of his
El-Cyclopedia in 1968. In this Albert
Hand was ahead of his time with the
ingenious idea of producing an A–Z of
Presley information in a red mock-
leather folder, securely stapled, to be
added to every so often with a further
eight or nine pages.
(See also: Fan Clubs; *Follow That*
Dream; **Parker, Colonel Tom)**

EASY COME, EASY GO * * * *

Released by: Paramount Pictures;
(Technicolor); **Producer:** Hal B. Wallis;
Director: John Rich; **Screenplay:** Alan
Weiss, Anthony Lawrence; **Art
Directors:** Hal Perreira, Walter Tyler,
Robert Benton; **Director of
Photography:** William Margules, ASC;
Technical Advisor: Colonel Tom Parker;
Music: Joseph J. Lelley, vocal
background by The Jordanaires;
Running Time: 95 mins; **Opened:**
March 22, 1967.

Cast: Elvis, Dodie Marshall, Pat Priest,
Pat Harrington, Skip Ward, Sandy
Kenyon, Frank McHugh, Elsa
Lanchester, Ed Griffith, Read Morgan,
Mickey Elley, Elaine Bennett, Shari
Nims, Diki Lerner, Robert Isenberg.

Navy frogman Ted Jackson (Elvis), on
duty in the Pacific, finds a treasure chest
in the hull of an old ship. While he is
diving, Dina Bishop (Pat Priest) and her
boyfriend Gil Carey (Skip Ward) take
photos. Ted refuses her offer to join
them for a cocktail on the grounds that
he is on duty. At the local marina Ted
meets the eccentric Captain Jack (Frank
McHugh) who tells him that a
descendant of the original owner of the
Port of Call, Joe Symington, will be able
to give him the history of the vessel.
Arriving at the Symington house, Ted
finds himself inducted into a yoga class,

conducted by Madame Nehrina (Elsa
Lanchester), where hippies of both sexes
are practising transcendental meditation.
Removing his officer's uniform, Ted, clad
in more suitable all black gear, finds
himself next to the descendant of the
ancient sea captain. This is Jo, a girl
whose form he has already admired when
he saw her diving. Having failed to live
up to Madame Nehrina's expectations of
him as a yoga expert, Ted persuades Jo to
talk in a more secluded place. Her
mission in life is to take care of the
town's artistic types. After Ted has
convinced her he is only interested in the
Port of Call as research for a manual he is
writing on sunken vessels Jo confirms
that the ship went down with a cargo of
coffee and a chest of gold coins.

Discharged from the navy, Ted
seeks out his old partner, Judd (Pat
Harrington), and persuades him to help
in the quest for the treasure using
equipment hired from Captain Jack. Jo is
outraged when she finds Ted's motives
are the same as the other mercenary
creeps who are after the gold, but when
Captain Jack gets seasick at the mere
sight of the sea, she agrees to take over as
skipper on condition that the money
goes towards an art centre for her
friends. Captain Jack admits he's a
phoney – his only claim to the title
Captain is that he used to run a
children's programme on television, *The
Good Ship Lollipop*, in which the water
was not salt and the only fish were

plastic ones suspended from the ceiling.
With Jo in charge, Ted and Judd head
out to sea. When they get to the diving
site they find Dina and her yacht are
already there, with Gil on board: the
rich, pleasure seeking blonde has already
made a play for Ted and only quick
action by Jo prevented Gil from
throwing a punch at him. Taking a closer
look at the photos he took, Gil spots the
treasure chest. He and Dina are
determined to get there first and he takes
a dead battery cable, invoking the rule of
the sea that Ted must tow them to shore.
Gil goes to see Captain Jack and
recognizes him from the TV programme,
of which he was an avid watcher and
finds it easy to turn the Captain against
Ted. Wrathfully Captain Jack goes to
Ted's boat to reclaim his diving
equipment – over the arguments of both
Ted and Gil. This time he really does
provoke a fight as he refuses it to both of
them. Ted persuades Jo to do her best to
change Captain Jack's mind.

Dina and Gil then kidnap Jack and
he finds that they have stolen his diving
equipment. They head for the treasure
site and by the time Ted and Judd get
there they find their rivals have already
gone diving. Ted, with his navy expertise,
is able to head them off under water and
retrieve the chest. Captain Jack is
jubilant that through his enforced trip he
has conquered his fear of the sea and
sides with Jo and her crew. Watching
them through binoculars Dina sees them

Elvis, as frogman Ted Jackson, searches for a descendent of the original owner of the vessel *Port of Call* – a quest which leads him into a yoga class of Madame Neherina (Elsa Lanchester). Trying to follow her movements, Ted gets himself tied up in a knot and Madame singles him out to join her in an expository song/dance 'Yoga Is As Yoga Does'.
Easy Come, Easy Go (1967)

counting the 'bullion', which turns out to be copper. They have it evaluated and accept $4,000 for the coins, which both agree would be a nice down payment for her art centre. Dina, landed with the surly Gil, raises the inevitable glass of champagne and goes on her merry way.

This is one of the better Presley vehicles of this period, though the ingredients mix a bit of everything – the search for treasure, the rich nymphomaniac with a yacht, the ex-serviceman trying to prove himself by his own efforts. The cocktail is full of basic Elvisian themes, but the script by Allen Weiss and Anthony Lawrence, who were actually nominated for more awards by the Screenwriter's Guild for *Roustabout*, *Paradise Hawaiian Style* and *Spinout* – though not, strangely enough, for this one, does contain a couple of tasty garnishes. They include the ample shapes of Frank McHugh as a dotty sea captain who's allergic to the sea and Elsa Lanchester (*qv*) as the no less dotty Madame Nehrina, who runs the yoga class. Both shine through rich characterizations, with McHugh's famous mad laugh to the fore, even if the so-called hippies in the yoga classes are so freshly scrubbed and perfectly made-up that they do not ring entirely true. However, the scene affords Elvis with an unusual opportunity to tie himself in knots – a new departure for him I would wager. Another quite delightful cameo comes in the camp form of Diki Lerner as an artist who is a motor nut, with a penchant for turning automobiles into mobiles. When Elvis finds his car missing this character beckons them into a garage and says proudly 'I've just made my first automobile mobile' – and there is Presley's car suspended from the ceiling. When Jo reproves him gently, 'You shouldn't do that without permission, Zoltan', the artist tosses his head petulantly. His own car is a nice op-art creation. To start it you press a button marked 'go-go' and the speedo registers 'rare, medium and well-done'.

The underwater scenes tend to go on too long – it is difficult to generate tension submerged (without a giant octopus lurking in the deeps), but the stars look happy enough, even during the songs, which may have been a feat of acting as they are not particularly distinguished. Elvis is as convincing as a diver as he is a pilot, racing driver, boxer, motor mechanic, swimmer or trapeze artist, while leading lady Dodie Marshall has a freshness that makes her believable as the girl who really does care about hippies and artistic types. Pat Priest's blonde sexpot has a nice line in repartee, 'I don't give rain checks' and there's a sexy toy boy in Skip Ward; perhaps he did Red West out of a job, dodging the punches.

Murf's verdict in *Variety* deserves a quote: 'Somewhat slimmer here than in recent pics, Elvis looks great and ageless, although his maturity shows in the acting department'.

(See also: Lanchester, Elsa; Memphis Mafia; Paradise Hawaiian Style; Roustabout; Spinout)

EASY COME, EASY GO

(EP) (Released 1967) * *
Written by Sid Wayne, Ben Weisman.
Elvis sings his first song in a speed boat after climbing down from a suspension ladder from his ship , as he speeds with his buddies towards shore. The credit titles roll during the song, which is the norm Presley starter: up-tempo and suggesting fast travel, no more or less distinguished than the usual. It was hardly headed for the charts with its inevitable references to kissing girls all over – all clever stuff. Trumpets, saxes, drums etc. abound and The Jordanaires are all working overtime, leading to Dodie Marshall as Jo jigging in front of a combo, which seems to belong to Judd Whitman, Ted's ex-partner before his naval stint.

LPs: 'C'mon Everybody'; 'Double Dynamite'

THE LOVE MACHINE * * *
Written by Gerald Nelson, Fred Murch, Chick Taylor.
Ted, in uniform, spins a giant wheel with girls' faces etc on as he sings about the wheel perhaps being about to turn up his lucky number – be it June, Wendy or whomsoever. Catchy and for jigging to – but not one to set the charts ticking over. Combo plays away in the background – saxes, guitars, zylophone and those hard-working Jordanaires.
LP: 'I Got Lucky'

YOGA IS AS YOGA DOES * * * * *
Written by Gerald Nelson, Fred Burch.
A Duet with Elsa Lanchester. Ted finds himself an unwelcome member of Madame Nehrina's (Elsa Lanchester) yoga class, which he interrupts with his noisy questions. Madame reprimands him, 'Either shut up, or ship out!'. She spreads her arms like a giant red-headed moth and, pointing at Ted, launches into her song, while he gets all twisted up in the lotus position. He joins her in the song and movement, the while manoeuvering Jo towards and out of the door. One of the wackiest numbers Elvis has ever duetted to and with the unlikeliest partner. A scene straight out of intimate revue, with bouncy backing by the dancing and rolling hippies, having been interrupted by Ted's 'ripples across Madame's area of contentment'. hurdy-gurdy music with zylophone and tambourine, giving a barrel-organ sound to an uproarious scene.
LP: 'I Got Lucky'

YOU GOTTA STOP * * *
Written by Bill Giant, Bernie Baum, Florence Kaye.
Ted fronts a rocker, with his ex-partner, Judd, to see if he can still please the punters. It's a case of 'everybody dance' to the rocking saxes, guitars – especially Elvis's – clarinets etc. At the end of this number, Dina still on the make for Ted, walks down the stairs, uses the old

Tallulah Bankhead (*qv*) line of 'I didn't recognize you with your clothes on' and orders him a drink. The jealous Gil appears and again makes threatening noises.

LP: 'I Got Lucky'

SING YOU CHILDREN * * * *

Written by Gerald Nelson, Fred Burch. Started by a blast on Judd's trumpet, Ted quietens a restive crowd of hippies by singing about Jonah in the belly of the whale. He beats a tambourine and the jolly jingle, boosted by saxophones etc., hurries to its conclusion while Jo, Ted and Judd are able to make a quick exit. The Nelson–Burch team certainly gives a lift to the scene.

LP: 'You'll Never Walk Alone'

I'LL TAKE LOVE * * * *

Written by Dolores Fuller, Mark Barkan. The last number sung by Ted after the treasure has been raised and turned out to be just copper – worth 30 cents a piece. All put together their share add up to a down payment on the arts centre. Ted raises the rhythm at the bash at which he and Judd's combo play, and Jo shakes her marracas to a latin beat – more good beaty fun.

LP: 'C'mom Everybody'

ELLIS, BETTY

Although Elvis Presley did as many of his own stunts as his contract would allow, obviously it was not practicable for him to do them all. In *Roustabout* Elvis spends a good deal of time riding around the dusty hillsides of Thousand Oaks, where the film was shot, and ends up, after his bike is wrecked, working for Barbara Stanwyck (*qv*) in her travelling carnival show. One of the attractions is the Wall of Death where Elvis is involved in a bad accident. The extremely clever direction left no reason to doubt that Elvis was doing all the riding himself, let alone that his double was a woman.

Betty Ellis was born in Croatia of an circus family and grew up perfoming all over Europe. Interned with other travellers and gypsies in Dachau in 1939, friends bribed the guards to free her and she was able to continue performing her act across Germany. After the war she travelled to England and met her future husband, Arthur, also a famous Wall of Death rider. They married in 1955 and performed their stunts in Germany, Russia, Italy, Spain and the USA, where they went into movies.

(See also: *Roustabout*; Stanwyck, Barbara)

ELVIS AND THE BEATLES

Colonel Parker's strategy to try and stem the tide of Beatlemania in America had been to promote a series of awards and medal for Elvis, playing up his image as a great American patriot. Albert Hand, President of the Elvis Presley Fan Club of Great Britain, went to Los Angeles for an official meeting with the King on April 9, while Beatles records were selling like hotcakes. By the end of 1964 Elvis Presley was named 'Best Male Singer' for the eighth year in succession, indicating that he had triumphed over the Beatles: the British invasion was quelled, at least for the time being. In June, 1965 Elvis's single 'Crying in the Chapel' topped the Beatles in England and reached No. 3 in the States; by the end of the year it had sold almost two million copies.

After three long years of speculation, the summit meeting between Elvis Presley and the Beatles finally took place at Elvis's Beverley Hills home – a palatial edifice in early-Hollywood film star style, which Elvis rented for £10,000 a week – on August 27th, 1965. After three days of planning, amid massive secrecy and the highest possible security checks to avoid any possibility of the convergence of joint hordes of Beatles and Presley fans, the Beatles arrived between 9 and 10 p.m., with a couple of bodyguards, the group's manager, Brian Epstein, and the New Musical Express's reporter Chris

Hutchins, who claimed to have organized the whole event. John Lennon, George Harrison, Paul McCartney and Ringo Starr were greeted by a seemingly relaxed Elvis, dressed in his most becoming smart casual style – red shirt, black windcheater and skin-tight grey trousers. Elvis rose while formal introductions were effected flanked by ten of his Guys and his current girlfriend. Soon after Colonel Parker (*qv*) and his assistant, Tom Diskin, joined the group – it seems Brian Epstein was as keen to meet the Colonel as the Beatles were to meet Elvis. At first the Beatles and Elvis just sat and stared at each other, while the jukebox blared their hits alternately and others by up and coming artists until Elvis broke the ice by saying he would go to bed if they just sat and stared at him like that. He suggested they sit and talk and 'maybe play a little – jam a little'. 'We'd love to play with you!' they all cried. One of his men distributed guitars. 'Here's how I play the bass' Elvis told Paul, '- not too good, but I'm learning.' One of the discs was Cilla Black's 'You're My World' to which Paul played piano while Elvis busked bass guitar.

Later there was general talk: Elvis led the way by mentioning the strange experiences encountered while touring and the Beatles entered in with some enthusiasm. Parker and Epstein talked shop before withdrawing to play roulette. Fans and cars were other topics they had in common – nothing at all controversial – while Elvis's companions kept the drinks flowing, none of which he himself touched – nor did he accept any of the cigarettes passed around by those who probably did not accept publicity stories which always stressed he was not a smoker.

The meeting broke up at 2 a.m. It had notched up a victory in diplomacy for Colonel Tom, who had been plotting to bring the two together since the Beatles first became a threat and who had stage managed a constant flow of cordial messages and compliments from his protégé to the Liverpool group, of whom Elvis's original reaction has reputedly been along the lines of 'Hell, I don't want to meet them sons of bitches!' For their part, the Beatles had been genuinely keen to meet Elvis. The next evening, when some of the Memphis Mafia (*qv*) had accepted the Beatles' invitation to visit them in the house on Mulholland Drive they had taken for their week in Los Angeles, John Lennon told them, 'There's only one person in the USA that we have ever wanted to meet – not that he wanted to meet us! And we met him last night. We can't tell you how we felt. We just idolized him so much. When we first came to town, these guys like Dean Martin and Frank Sinatra and all these people wanted to come over and hang around with us at night, simply because we had all the women, all the chicks. We don't want to meet those people. They don't really like us. We don't really like or admire them. We can't tell you what a thrill it was last night.'

John Lennon's most memorable quote to the press was, 'He was just like us... quite normal.' Later Elvis was to meet and become genuinely friendly with the only one of the British contingent to take America by storm whom he really liked and admired – Tom Jones. He went to see Jones's performance in cabaret in Las Vegas and studied his way with an audience. They discussed details after the show and when Elvis had made his sensational comeback he adopted the Welshman's trick of handing out scarves to the women in the front rows.
(See also: *Paradise, Hawaiian Style*; Parker, Colonel Tom; The Memphis Mafia)

ELVIS AND THE COLONEL – THE UNTOLD STORY

Directed for TV by William A. G raham, 1993
This is something of an oddity, starring

and strangely casting Lloyd Bridges as Colonel Parker. It starts interestingly with the judge ruling that Parker shall no longer be able to get his hands on the Presley estate, from which he had been carving great chunks to pay for his gambling debts since the King's death. Vernon, the legal guardian of the estate, has been powerless to put a stop to Parker's depredations.

A grizzled Colonel listens to the verdict fuming, and we then go into flashback about his beginnings as a fairground barker whom the elephants, at least, seem to love. For this metamorphosis, Bridges exchanges one old bald wig for another younger one with jet black fronds draped across the front. It is difficult to decide which looks more weird; in both cases his head appears lopsided and distinctly unpleasant.

We then follow the well-worn story of Parker taking control of Presley's career, obviously with considerable misgivings from Elvis's mother Gladys. Lloyd Bridges is here at his best in shedding light on the Colonel's obvious duplicity as he tries to ingratiate himself with pious platitudes. Elvis is played with considerable vocal skill by Rob Youngblood, who unfortunately bears little physical resemblance to the subject, although he does his best to age convincingly with considerable midriff padding in the Vegas scenes, where the conflict between the two men is played with convincing bitterness.

The most interesting point about the movie is that it was directed by William A. Graham, who handled Elvis with sufficient subtlety in *Change of Habit* to suggest he had both sympathy and insight into the actor, to whom he must have been close enough to witness the stress under which he was living at that time. To that extent the film may be looked upon as a labour of love.

ELVIS AND 'DANNY BOY'

In the television documentary *Danny Boy: In Sunshine Or In Shadow*, (a Strictly The Business Production, made for Granada Television and screened in 1996), 'Danny Boy' (an old Irish Air, with words by an English lyricist, Fred Weatherley) was described by the music writer Julian Lloyd as 'one of Elvis's and his father Vernon's (*qv*) favourite tunes'. It was performed at Elvis's funeral. It was the first piece of music in the funeral service'.

The Presley rendering was very slow, highly emotional and charged with great depth of feeling. The sole backing is a poignant piano accompaniment. In the television documentary Presley is heard singing the song over newsreel shots of his funeral: endless banks of flowers from fans, including one wreath in the shape of a guitar with the word ELVIS picked out in blue flowers on a white background; women being helped and carried away in tears; policemen wiping tears from their faces, and a long and seemingly endless funeral procession of white cars. Over these scenes, the voice of Elvis is heard singing.
(See also: Fields, Gracie Dame)

ELVIS AND THE FACE OF JESUS

As with so many facts about the death of the King of rock 'n' roll, there seems to be controversy as to exactly which book Elvis was reading in the toilet the day he died: some authorities quote *The Scientific Search for the Face of Jesus* on the Shroud of Turin, others *Sex and Psychic Energy*: certainly both books were in the vicinity of his body. The first was provided by Larry Geller (*qv*), Elvis's ex-personal hairdresser, who had been something in the nature of a spiritual advisor to Elvis since 1964. He was feared and disliked by some of the Memphis Mafia (*qv*), as he initiated Elvis into a melange of books on mystical and theoretical systems, including *The*

Impersonal Life which was interesting Elvis when he was filming *Tickle Me* (*qv*), in 1965. He used to take it with him to the studio and try to persuade members of the cast and crew to study it. He was undoubtedly genuinely anxious to explore the reason why he, a humble truck driver of lowly origins, should have been singled out for the pinnacle of fame equivalent to that of Jesus Christ and other prophets and world leaders. He, like his mother Gladys (*qv*) before him, was certain he had a mission on earth. Gladys, herself something of a mystic, had been aware from before his birth that the child – or children as it turned out – she was carrying was destined for something very special, although the King of rock 'n' roll was probably the last thing she envisaged. His mother and his born-dead twin, Jesse Garon, were undoubtedly the guiding influences in his life.

Larry Geller was positively hated by Colonel Parker (*qv*), probably fearing that he might influence his protégé in financial as well as metaphysical matters. It was one aspect where the Colonel nd Priscilla (*qv*) saw eye to eye , probably for different reasons. The situation became so difficult that Geller resigned and when he departed Elvis and Priscilla made a bonfire of all his mystical books. However, he insists that Elvis summoned him to Graceland shortly before his death and he gave him the book on he Shroud he was probably reading when he died.

Which leads to the fact that as the years have passed, Elvis has developed from being someone the fans worshipped, many equating him with Jesus Christ – the pilgrims on Elvis's Death Day on August 16 in Graceland (*qv*) not only carry candles in procession, but also bless themselves and genuflect by his tomb – to the man who was not just a pop legend, but had the most profound effect on social change this century. The King of the enduring cult of rock 'n' roll has

become the new icon of the intellectual elite. The First Annual Intellectual Conference on Elvis Presley met in 1995 in Oxford, Mississippi, to explore the deeper, richer purpose to Presley's music and life. Some would like to believe that he was right in there with them, heavily disguised, on the same mission as they themselves. Mighty claims were made: Peter Nazareth, lecturer in Elvis Presley studies at the University of Iowa, asserted that 'If it weren't for Elvis, millions and millions would still be enslaved in the thinking patterns of the oppressed and culturally colonized'. One writer quoted John Lennon, saying 'Before Elvis there was nothing'. Cliff Richard extended this to include himself in an interview with Julie Mundy, head of the Official Elvis Presley Fan Club and editor of the magazine in the summer issue, 1996, saying that 'without Elvis Presley there would have been no Cliff Richard'. Professor Vernon Chadwick, senior lecturer in English at the University of Mississippi, who had organized the conference to examine 'Elvis as a serious man with a serious message', concluded: 'We should be exploring bi-racial and cross-cultural dimensions of Elvis's life with the aim of evaluating his role in the evolution of the civil rights movement'.

The same Professor Chadwick in his review of Peter Goralnick's biography of the early Elvis, *Last Train to Memphis*, a brilliantly analytical study, agrees with the author that illiterate Fifties critics mistook Elvis's notorious leg wiggles for an obscenely suggestive striptease 'when his moves stemmed in fact from the provincial sub-worlds of Southern gospel, country and blues that combined spiritual exaltation with bodily release'. Try telling that to the marines or to the shrieking teenagers who responded so basically to Elvis's bumps and grinds. Chadwick goes so far in his identification of Elvis's sexuality refined into saintliness as to equate his 'Don't Be Cruel' with the Sermon on the Mount, while the Rev. Howard Finster

elaborated that 'the leg wiggle was a Mission for God: Elvis was sent by God to revive sex, to simulate sex and nature'.

Pilgrims come to Graceland from all over the world, some in wheelchairs, others on crutches, many seeking healing as at Lourdes – mainly spiritual, sometimes physical also. For them Elvis is almost a reincarnation of Jesus; many believe that by immersing themselves in Elvis's pain, encapsulated in a song he wrote a year before his death called 'Hurt', repeating again and again 'I'm hurt' in his most heart-rending vibrato, expressing his own naked, unbearable pain. Another view is taken by Mark Gottdiener, chairman of the department of sociology at the State University of New York, in Buffalo, who sees Elvis as 'the other Jesus' – the permissive saviour, indulgent and carnal, who has one thing in common with the first Jesus in that he gives his celebrants permission, even encouragement, to express love. Here the distinction between love and sex becomes distinctly blurred: absolving the woman taken in adultery, Christ says, 'She has loved much'. The less devout Elvis followers in universities are content to equate him with Abraham Lincoln and the evolution of the contemporary novel and leave it at that.

(See also: **Graceland; Knight, King and Movies; Memphis Mafia; Parker, Colonel Tom; Presley, Gladys Love Smith; Presley, Jesse Garon; Presley, Priscilla Beaulieu;** *Tickle Me*)

ELVIS ON TOUR * * *

Released by: Metro-Goldwyn-Mayer, a Cinema Associates Production (Panavision, Metrocolor); **Producers:** Pierre Adidge, Robert Abel; **Directors:** Pierre Adidge, Robert Abel; **Director of Photography:** Robert Thomas; **Montage Supervisor:** Martin Scorsese; **Technical Advisor:** Colonel Tom Parker; **Running Time:** 93 mins; **Opened:** November 1, 1972.

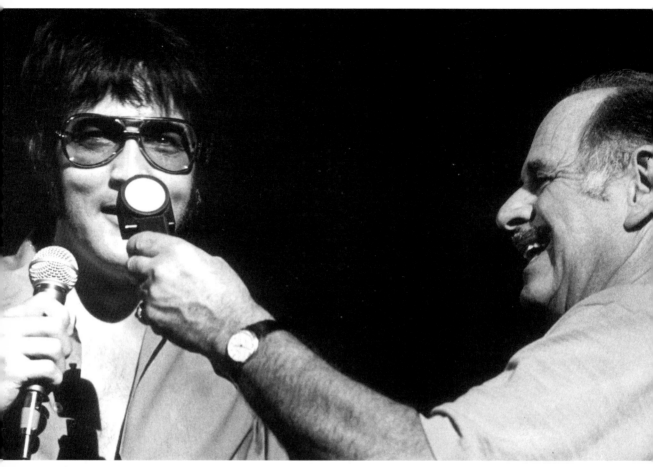

Director of Photography lines up a camera angle of Elvis for Pierre Adidge and Robert Abel's documentary. *Elvis On Tour* (1972)

Cast: Musicians with Elvis, James Burton, Charlie Hodge, Ronnie Tutt, Glen Hardin, Jerry Schell, John Williamson. Orchestra conducted by Joe Guercio. Background vocalists Cathy Westmoreland, The Sweet Inspirations, J.D. Sumner and the Stamps Quartet. Onstage Comedian Jackie Kahane.

An important coda to Elvis's film career, this film, which came 13th on *Variety's* list of top-grossing films, gives a vivid picture of what being on tour with Elvis entailed. Looked at dispassionately, sheer hell on earth – the demands imposed by a concert tour are inconceivable, magnified a hundredfold if the star is

Elvis Presley. At the end of every performance he has to rush off stage and race out of the theatre to leap into the waiting car, avoiding the mob at the stage door who pursue like shrieking harpies. If ever they caught him it seems likely that he would be torn limb from limb like Tennessee William's Sebastian in *Suddenly Last Summer* pursued by the starving beachboys whom he has used for his own gratification. Only these are not rampaging beachboys, but presumably educated and 'civilized' human beings – mostly, but by no means all, young. This brings into focus Presley's Mafia (*qv*), who come into their own as bodyguards of the world's foremost entertainment phenomenon. Devoted to protecting their master, even unto death, they hustle him from concert to concert, city to city, hotel to hotel and state to state, along

roads that must be closed to allow him to travel in some degree of safety. He has to listen to endless boring speeches from a succession of pompous dignitaries and respond with fitting politeness. His previous film *Elvis – That's The Way It Is* has detailed the strain of endless rehearsals which must go on until the perfectionist in Presley is satisfied.

On the other hand, there are the rewards: endless adulation – the stuff that fuels every star to go on and up – contact with the audiences which, towards the end, were the only thing that kept him going. Then there is the power of Superman, reflected in Tom Belew's rhinestone studded costumes, with enormous upstanding collars reminiscent of Elizabeth Tudor at her most regal, jewel-studded belts, which grew wider and more concealing as time passed, magnificent

**Backstage in Las Vegas, Elvis with Sammy
Davis Jr and other friends. (April, 1971).**

cloaks, just made for giving the illusion, with arms outstretched, that the King was about to be assumed into heaven.

The split-screen technique is valuable – if occasionally irritating – for giving prominence to the degree with which the star is dependent on the musical and promotional talents which surround him and which are usually consigned to background atmosphere. Here we get the impression of a ferociously hard-working team supporting the star player. Names which come up again and again in any survey of Presley's work come into sharp, if brief focus. They include D.J. Fontana, leader of the Stamps Quartet, who was in there backing Elvis almost from the beginning, now a little grizzled by time but delivering rounded bass notes with the best, hand cupped to the ear in the time-honoured style of Johnnie Ray and Dorothy Squires herself. Other outstanding talents featured are the brilliant lead-guitarist, James Burton, close-harmonist Charlie Hodge and bass-player Jerry Scheff: on the distaff side the eye-catching girls, The Sweet Inspirations, who not only provide a background chorus but often flank Elvis like heavenly harmonizers. These and others become familiar, lending authenticity in the off-stage scenes, giving the impression that Presley is, indeed, relaxing with friends.

For these insights, at least, the film is to be cherished, although the general effect is one of blandness. For all Elvis's powerful delivery of every kind of music from rock 'n' roll, through emotional balladeering, to gospel, there is little variation from full orchestral backing from every second verse, which is probably acceptable if one is there in the audience, being mesmerized by the Presence, but on the flat screen everything tends to come out sounding much the same. Heresy this may be but, going from the often sublime to the sometimes ridiculous, it gives one pause to recall how effective is Elvis's reflective

soliloquy 'I Need Somebody to Lean On' with a gentle, mainly piano and sax backing in the bar scene in *Love in Las Vegas* (*qv*).

It would seem that the 'technical advisor' wanted to ensure that *Elvis on Tour* would illustrate without analysis and offer family entertainment whilst pleasing all the fans. If the box office takings are anything to go by, the Colonel was successful.

(See also: *Elvis: That's the Way It Is*; **Esposito, Joe**; *Love in Las Vegas*; **Memphis Mafia**; **Parker, Colonel Tom**; **Presley, Vernon Elvis**)

ELVIS ON TOUR

(Song selection)

Of the 26 or so numbers on this final film in the Presley collection, there are inevitable duplications from the previous documentary, *Elvis, That's The Way It Is*. This is a purely personal selection.

JOHNNY B. GOODE * * * * *

Written by Chuck Berry.
Sung over the credits of the movie, this quintessential rocker, slightly pre-dating Elvis but revived by him in concert between 1969 and 1977, is a must. Today it is often included by survivors of the great rock 'n' roll era and Jess Conrad usually begins his concerts with this one.

SEPARATE WAYS * * * *

Written by Red West, Richard Mainegra. Probably the most popular of the songs written for Elvis by his friend Red West (*qv*). Sales exceeded one million and it formed the cover picture for the LP of the same name, showing Elvis strumming his guitar in a Bill Belew outfit, his legs straddling a two lane highway. A great signpost for the latter phase of the Presley career.

BURNING LOVE * * * * *

Written by Dennis Linde.
Another million-seller from Elvis's later period, combining the best of the early

rocker with the passionate manifestation of his maturity.

UNTIL IT'S TIME FOR YOU TO GO
* * * *

Written by Buffy Sainte-Marie.
Revival of the tender, romantic best-seller of the old days.

AN AMERICAN TRILOGY * * * * *

Written by: Dixie (Dan Emmett, 1859), Battle Hymn of the Republic (Julia Warde Howe, 1961), All My Trials (Unknown).
Medley arranged by Mickey Newbury, 1971.
The definitive signature arrangement for the mature Elvis: passionate, sincere and a real workout for Presley's vocal range.

A BIG HUNK O' LOVE * * * *

Written by Arthur Schroeder, Sid Wyche.
Another perennial rocker. Referred to by Gracie Fields (*qv*) as 'Elvis's Stuttering Song'.

ELVIS: THAT'S THE WAY IT IS * * * *

Released by: Metro-Goldwyn-Mayer (Metrocolor, Panavision); **Producer:** Herbert F. Soklow; **Director:** Denis Sanders. **Director of Photography:** Lucien Ballard. **Technical Advisor:** Colonel Tom Parker; **Elvis's Wardrobe Designer:** Bill Belew; **Running Time:** 97 mins; **Opened:** November 11, 1970.

Cast: Musicians with Elvis: James Burton, Glen Hardin, Charlie Hodge, Jerry Scheff, Ronnie Tutt, John Wilkinson Millie Kirkham. Conductor: Joe Guercio. Background Vocalists: The Sweet Inspirations, The Imperials.

This documentary by double Academy Award-winning director Denis Sanders came twenty-second on Variety's weekly list of top-grossing films and was the first of two movies depicting Presley going through the routine of putting his

**A scene from Denis Sanders'
documentary on the life of
Elvis as musician and man.**
Elvis: That's The Way

than the latter-day comparisons with Jesus Christ and Mohammed.

A critic at the time wrote, perhaps unkindly, but with some degree of accuracy, that this film is actually 'Elvis, That's The Way It Isn't'. Little real insight goes into the presentation of the facts but the film is photographed with the accuracy one would expect from Lucien Ballard, though Metrocolor is one of the least subtle colour processes. The highlight is the opening at the Phoenix Hotel, Arizona, on September 9, 1970, of the star's first concert tours in thirteen years. Here we get the master musician-entertainer rousing his adoring audience to various degrees of frenzied rapture, only matched by the intensity with which he hurls himself through an incredible variety of songs. It is a remarkable exhibition of mass communication, with the singer wringing the utmost degree of adulation from his public, orchestrating every mood change in response to the subject of the song. No wonder he uses great swathes of towelling to staunch his freely-flowing sweat like a prize boxer. In view of the frequent karate kicks with which Elvis interlarded his performance, one wonders whether Tom Jones was being brutally ironic in his good luck telegram when he said, 'Hope you have a good opening and break both legs!' The multiplicity of coloured handkerchiefs handed out by the King after he had dashed them across his fevered brow were certainly an effective contribution to the Presley armoury of tricks by the Welsh singing star.

Elvis's devotion to his fans was genuine and on-going: the total effect was that of a mutual adoration society. One interviewee marvels at his tolerance and forbearance in not ordering the fans outside his house to stop cluttering up his driveway. If only he had – just once – done that, the reaction would have added a bit of spice to this always politically correct survey of the Presley phenomenon in action.

stage show together. Here we see rehearsals at MGM Studios followed by his performance in Las Vegas at the Showroom International of the International Hilton Hotel. The director claims to have explored the emotions Elvis inspires in others as well as his own feelings, but it is very much a picture of what is expected of the star, both in his public behaviour and private persona. The interviews at managerial level and with the fans are wholly predictable, from the awed acknowledgement of his total professionalism to the gob-smacked man who declares 'He is an original'. He goes on to say Elvis should be ranked with Marconi and Bell, which is at least putting him on a human level rather

**Elvis leaves the set to take a break during
the making of Denis Sanders' documentary.**
Elvis: That's The Way It Is (1970)

This selective casting, along with the well written script, which by stopping at the King's comeback triumph, avoids what could only have been a distressing and necessarily highly sanitized portrait of his declining years.

Some of the documentaries, like the excellent *Elvis '56*, may have been more detailed and factual, but John Carpenter's lovingly reconstructed picture of an icon is one for the fans to treasure. As Colonel Parker's veto prevented the use of the real Presley voice on the soundtrack, the recording was taken over by Ronnie McDowell who helped to produce a very authentic sound, overseen by Felton Jarvis who had looked after the quality of several of Elvis's later recordings for RCA at Nashville in 1966. McDowell, a relatively little known country singer before Elvis's death, had sprung to fame overnight when his tribute single, 'The King is Gone' sold a million copies within a week. The songs he interprets so faithfully in the film include 'Mystery Train', 'Old Shep', 'Blue Moon of Kentucky', 'Are You Lonesome Tonight?', 'Blue Suede Shoes', 'The Wonder of You' and 'The Battle Hymn of the Republic'.

(See also: **Parker, Colonel Tom, Presley, Gladys Love Smith, Presley, Vernon Elvis**)

ELVIS, THE MUSICAL

November 28, 1977, the first British stage musical tribute to Elvis was staged by Jack Good at the Astoria Theatre, Charing Cross Road, with three actors/singers playing Elvis: the young one of Sun Records days being played by Timothy Whitnall, Welsh Rocker Shakin' Stevens, (already known in the record world but a solid hit maker for several years after the musical), as the mid-period Elvis, and P.J. Proby, who had actually sung on demo discs for Elvis during the early sixties, as the Presley of Las Vegas days. *Elvis* was a tremendous success and ran for several years in London. Critics were, in the main, favourable, which is more that can be said for the current revival, which opened

at the Prince of Wales Theatre on April 19, 1996, when some of the notices were so derisive and patronizing as to suggest personal antipathy to Jack Good, the original presenter of the show with Ray Cooney. Such terms as 'necrophilia', 'the grand-daddy of them all showing its age' are fortunately not going to be taken seriously by Presley fans in this country who are likely to welcome another musical rock down memory lane if it is respectful to their hero. And it is.

Tim Whitnall now plays the middle-aged Elvis with aplomb while the young star is impersonated by Alexander Barr convincingly. He is tipped as a good bet for the future Billy Fury story, but P.J. Proby, back as the sad, overweight Elvis of the last years, has cornered the most outstanding notices, even if one critic can't resist the jibe that he discovers more vowel sounds in one note than even Dorothy Squires thought possible. Maureen Paton in the *Daily Express* heads her piece 'P.J. is the King in this Elvis tribute.' She praises his handling of the ballads to which 'that dark-brown voice does more than justice', saying he 'even makes 'My Way' sound fresh and almost sincere', and that 'the sumptuous voice is in great nick'. She adds that he is 'an astonishing lookalike for the mature Elvis in his rhinestone period as the Las Vegas troubadour'. As good a reason as any for visiting the show.

ESPOSITO, JOE

Although not the longest standing member of the Memphis Mafia – they only met while Elvis was stationed in Germany – he rose to one of the highest positions in the group and his loyalty was second to none. He was with Elvis to the end, having worked for him for 16 years. After Elvis's death he even went so far as to state in a newspaper interview that Elvis took 'no drugs whatsoever'. Greater loyalty had no man and it is safe to say that he would do anything Elvis asked him to, including introducing him to female 'fans'. He has preserved a record

of their friendship in a film called *Joe Esposito's Elvis Home Movies* and a very jolly thing it is, showing the star always with a smile on his face, often entwined with Priscilla (*qv*) and Lisa Marie (*qv*). Joe dedicates the movie to 'My friend Elvis A. Presley'. Elvis is shown driving his magnificent bus across country, idealistically fulfilling his early ambition to be a truck driver. Karate work-outs seem to be a favourite sport, with the boys beating each other up – not for real, but nevertheless revealing some very angy-looking bruises on their arms. Pure boy's games, all along, and sometimes Priscilla, immaculate in white, is seen trying to keep her balance at the edge of some rough terrain where the bus has stopped: ironically, really, for it seems that much of her life with Elvis she was busy trying to keep her balance. This film was made with the blessing of Colonel Tom Parker and it represents an idealized version of everyone's favourite 'teenager', as one waspish critic commented in his review of one of Presley's least distinguised movies, when he was well into his thirties.

This is one film the fans love, the King at play, 'always happy', which is how Esposito likes to remember him. Today he is a businessman in Los Angeles, where his life can hardly be as eventful as it was when he was Elvis's right hand man.

(See also: Memphis Mafia; Parker, Colonel Tom; Presley, Priscilla Beaulieu)

FARRELL, GLENDA
(1904–1971)

The gun-toting, raucous-voiced Ma Tatum in *Kissin' Cousins* (*qv*) was an older version of the character with which Glenda Farrell became identified in her early days in Hollywood. She was a strikingly beautiful blonde in constant demand as gangster's molls – notably opposite Edward G. Robinson in her second movie *Little Caesar* in 1931 –

wise cracking newspaper reporters and man-chasing often as the best friend of Joan Blondell, another tough comedienne who was to be cast opposite Elvis Presley. Born in Oklahoma in 1904, she started in stock in her teens and reached Broadway in 1928. She was one of the *Gold Diggers* of 1935 and 1957, played crime busting newspaper reporter Torchy Blane in several well-liked comedies: by the time she was cast

Glenda Farrell in the 1930's – her wisecracking 'Gold Diggers' era. Thirty years later she was unrecognizable as grizzled Ma Tatum, Mother of one of Elvis' *Kissin' Cousins.*

in *Kissin' Cousins* she had been absent from films for five years in favour of returning to the stage and appearing on television, for which she gained an Emmy Award for her perfomance as best supporting actress in a *Ben Casey* segment in1963.

She was given a song of her own in the role of Ma Tatum – and a very amusing job she makes of it, moving around the kitchen with her cooking pot and stirring one of her remarkable mountain concoctions while she laments the absence of her adored Pappy (Arthur O'Connell) (*qv*) with a take off parody of 'Won't You Come Home, Bill Bailey?' called 'Pappy, Won't You Please Come Home'. She ends up cuddling her bloodhound, Hezekiah, who has returned on his own, howling piteously whenever Pappy's name is mentioned. Also in the film is Glenda's son, Tommy Farrell, as Master Sergeant William George Bailey. He had told Elvis, 'Funny thing is that when I began in this business, my mother did everything in her power to discourage me. It wasn't that she was against me, it's just that she didn't think this was my kind of work.' Elvis replied 'There were times when people tried to talk me out of show business as a career. You've just got to stick to your own belief in yourself.'

Glenda Farrell made only two more movies; terminal cancer forced her to leave the Broadway cast of *40 Carats* in 1969, two years before her death.

The film was a painful one for Glenda: on location for a week at Big Bear, a ski resort a couple of hours from Los Angeles, she broke a bone in her neck during the scene where she has to flip Elvis from the porch of a house. He flipped himself in the stunt and the first time it worked perfectly, but on the second take she didn't let go and fell, hitting her neck on a step. For the rest of the film she wore a brace until it was time to go in front of the camera.

(See also: Dogs; Kissin' Cousins)

FIELDS, DAME GRACIE

(1878–1979)

'I think he's a great entertainer,' Gracie Fields told her agent, Lillian Aza, after catching Elvis Presley in one of his early sensationally successful concerts. 'I just had to go along to see what all the fuss was about. I'm glad I did – the boy is unique. I can't judge his singing – it's just not my style – but the personality is electrifying. There's just one thing, though – I can't help thinking he must stuff a bottle of beer down the front of his pants!' This was in the days when his gyrations shocked TV presenter Ed Sullivan so deeply he swore he would never have Presley on his show. When he had to eat his words and welcome the star who had become the most talked about and marketable entertainment phenomenon in the world, Sullivan issued the famous edict that Elvis must be photographed only from the waist up, so perhaps Gracie had a point. We in England were never privileged to be able to witness in the flesh, as it were, the factor that had prompted the ever plain-speaking Lancashire Lass to make her observation. By the time the sanitized version of Presley's pelvic activity reached the screen, there was no sign of whatever

had provoked her remark. Entertainers who followed went so much further in on-stage outrage that Presley had become an emblem of propriety – girl-chasing in a cheeky, though never overtly sexual way, calculated to win over millions of family audiences world-wide. The plan worked, with great financial success for most of his 13 year film career, until it went slightly sour in the last few movies and he stopped the rot by his gigantically successful return to being a live entertainer.

In her own way, the pre-Second World War Gracie was, for Britain, the icon of anti-depression entertainment. Like Elvis, her background was strictly grass-roots; while the Presleys worked in the cotton fields, the Stansfields worked in the cotton mills, which is where the future Dame of the British Empire began her career. One of her great comedy songs 'Clogs and Shawl' says it all. Their careers followed the same pattern – deep poverty to unprecedented wealth, fame, and vilification, to which idols are always open. Both became superstars of the cinema from having started in concert halls and the record industry, their films, in the main scorned by the critics, but delighting the public; in different times and different genres each became the most highly-paid entertainer of a generation. Adulation was the order of their day; in England, Parliament was once adjourned early so that members could go home to listen to one of her radio broadcasts. When she was near to death following an operation for cancer at the age of 41, regular bulletins were put out by the media as to her condition and prayers were offered up in churches for her recovery. Within a year she was defying medical advice to undertake gruelling tours abroad, entertaining the Armed Forces at war. Like Elvis, she made a great come-back in the theatre – hers was at the London Palladium – where she made her last appearance in Britain in a Royal Command Show shortly before her death at the age of 81 in 1979.

Ironically, having stated that Rock 'n' Roll was not her kind of music, Gracie Fields chose to sing 'Rip it Up' in one of her shows at the Palladium in 1956 – a song recorded by Elvis in September of that year. It had previously been a hit for Little Richard and was an unwise choice for Gracie at that late date in her career. The notices were not kind and she flew back to her home in Capri visibly distressed. EMI, for whom she had also recorded for years, happily talked her out of choosing it for her new disc session: Elvis's version reached the UK Charts in March 1957 and went no higher than 27th, a poor showing for a Presley disc at that time. In the States it didn't show up at all, yet three months later his recording of 'All Shook Up' made No. 1 on both sides of the Atlantic.

FILMS THAT GOT AWAY – AND SOME THAT DIDN'T

The films announced for Elvis Presley that never got made, or underwent a title change – usually into something to do with girls – are legion. The ones on which the Colonel (*qv*) put the mockers, apart from *A Star Is Born* towards the end of Presley's career, include some that would have given him a chance to grow artistically.

The Colonel's veto was understandable over what was first announced to be his first movie *The Rainmaker*. Elvis did a scene from the movie for his first film test, which Hal Wallis, who had signed Elvis to his first screen contract, was about to produce. It was not a leading role, leaving aside whether he would have had an opportunity to sing in it.

Veto number 2 was far more serious: one of Hollywood's greatest directors, Stanley Kramer wanted Elvis to co-star with Sidney Poitier in his 1958 production *The Defiant Ones*, as the white convict and racialist who escapes from prison handcuffed to a black prisoner. Like much of Kramer's work it had a profoundly significant theme – that of racial prejudice and tension. The Colonel objected that there were no songs in it (well, there wouldn't be, would there?) – although his motives may have been deeper than that. The part went to Tony Curtis, one of Presley's favourite actors and mentors (remember the quiff). Curtis was nominated for an Oscar.

The same year, Tennessee Williams, to whom the trucker Presley appealed, mentioned that he could be an asset to his filmed play *Cat on a Hot Tin Roof*. The Colonel was affronted – apart from the song question and the character's sexual ambivalence, his Boy was certainly not going to take second billing to Elizabeth Taylor. Paul Newman played the part and was Oscar nominated.

In 1961 Elvis was sought to play opposite his old friend, Natalie Wood in the award winning musical *West Side Story* which was a massive hit even without Elvis. The Colonel could hardly object to there being no songs – his objection was that his Boy was not going to play second fiddle to Natalie. There would hardly have been problems over the billing. George Chakiris played the part, which called for serious dramatic acting, singing and dancing. And he received an Oscar nomination.

The following year the shadow of Tennessee Williams loomed again. This time the part was that of a young man of womanizing tendencies, kept by a rich older woman. Certainly not an idea to please the Colonel and Paul Newman played eventually the part. This time, by way of a change, he was not nominated for an Oscar. The film was *Sweet Bird of Youth* and co-starred Geraldine Page. Lauren Bacall took the part on stage.

It is impossible to guess what advantages Elvis missed by the following list of titles, which are by no means exhaustive: In 1957 Hal B. Wallis scheduled Elvis for *Lonesome Cowboy*. The title was changed to *Running Wild*, then to *Something for the Girls*. It surfaced as *Loving You* (qv): so they

didn't all get away but Shirley MacLaine, prospective co-star did. And all the time on Sunset Boulevard Elvis Presley badges were selling for 10 cents: these were the 'I Love Elvis' badges. For an 'I Hate Elvis' badge you had to spend 25 cents: one of each, at a cut down price of 15 cents. They all sold out.

A film called *Cowboy*, co-starring Jerry Lewis, after his break up with Dean Martin, came to nothing. Or was it the first idea for *Lonesome Cowboy*?

Sing, You Sinners, first starring Bing Crosby in 1938 did not show as a vehicle for Elvis. Neither did *The Queen of Rock 'n' Roll* with Mamie Van Doren after her hit in *Untamed Youth*. Presumably they would have switched titles.

Another explosive teaming that didn't' quite make it: Elvis was announced as Jayne Mansfield's co-star in the rock 'n' roll spoof *The Girl Can't Help It*. Two numbers were allegedly written into the film for him, but the deal fell through. I wonder why? Miss Mansfield also announced there were rumours of herself and Elvis starring in a rock 'n' roll version of *Romeo and Juliet*! They remained rumours.

A detective story called *Solo*, scheduled for Frank Sinatra, was turned over to Presley: in the event neither made it.

Rodeo, announced as Elvis's come-back film after the army service, from an original story by Erna Lazarus, was replaced in the schedule by *Cafe Europa* which, as that was the name of the cafe where Juliet Prowse danced, became *G.I Blues*.

The 1962 Paramount *Ya Ya Gumbo* – Creole for Everybody Talks At Once – for Hal Wallis, became *Girls! Girls! Girls!* The 'Gay romantic musical' – announced by MGM as the first of four Presley's with a San Diego setting, to be produced by Jack Cummings, surfaced two years later with a Las Vegas locale as *Viva Las Vegas* (qv), having originally been titled *Mister, Will You Marry Me?* This one was preceeded by *It Happened*

at the World's Fair originally called *Take Me to the Fair* and released in 1963, with the background of Seattle State Fair and enlarged to embrace the World Fair (and the Colonel)

The cheapo *Kissin' Cousins* (qv) for Sam Katzman (qv) was rushed into release before the already completed *Viva Las Vegas*.

The production after that, as originally announced by MGM was 'probably' to be based on the life of the Colonel, entitled *Right This Way, Folks*. Elvis as the Colonel? Perhaps even the star – the producers balked at that, and we were spared the spectacle. So the next for the MGM studio was *Girl Happy* in 1965.

Plans for 1966, according to Metro, included *Jim Dandy*, of which nothing more was heard and *You're Killing Me* produced by Judd Bernard and Irwin Winkler, with screenplay by Jo Heims, from an original story by Marc Brandell, eventually released in 1967 as *Double Trouble*. This is not to overlook the second quickie for Sam Katzman in 1966, *Harum Scarum*. Colonel Parker commented, 'It didn't do as well as the first.' No grosses were listed for *Harum Scarum*. Poor Colonel.

In 1975 Barbra Streisand rang to Elvis trying asking him to be her leading man in the re-make of *A Star Is Born* which she was planning with the help of her then constant companion, ex-hairdresser Jon Peters. Elvis was thrilled at the idea of returning to the screen in a classy production with one of the world's great stars. Once again the Colonel put a spoke in the wheel: negotiations broke down over the exorbitant financial demands he made for the services of his protégé. This was to be the last time Elvis would get such an interesting offer, although he would have had to get into strict training to play the role, eventually taken by Kris Kristofferson. Elvis's looks had deteriorated seriously in the interim since their first meeting: the enormous intake of junk food he was assimilating during his tours, combined with an ever-increasing ingestion of drugs had taken their toll and his weight ballooned dramatically, although his stage costumes did their best to disguise the fact. In a film he would never have been able to get away with it. It is debatable whether rigid dieting would have put further strain on his already unstable health. On the other hand, a major film success, if it could have been followed up, might have saved his life.

(See also: Double Trouble, G.I. Blues; Girls! Girls! Girls!: Girls, Girls, Girls (not the movie); Girl Happy; Harum Scarum; It Happened at the Worl'ds Fair; Katzman, Sam; Kissin' Cousins; Parker, Colonel Tom; Viva Las Vegas)

FLAMING STAR * * * * *

Released by: Twentieth-Century-Fox (Deluxe Colour, Cinemascope); **Producer:** David Weisbart; **Director:** Don Siegel; **Screenplay:** Clair Huffaker, Nunally Johnson, based on a novel by Clair Huffaker; **Art Directors:** Duncan Kramer, Walter Simonds; **Director of Photography:** Charles G. Clarke; **Technical Advisor:** Colonel Tom Parker; **Music:** Cyril J. Mockridge, vocal background by The Jordanaires; **Running Time:** 101 mins reduced to 91 mins; **Opened:** December 20, 1960.

Cast: Elvis, Steve Forrest, Dolores Del Rio, Barbara Eden, John McIntire, Rudolph Acosta, Karl Swenson, Ford Rainey, Richard Jaeckel, Anne Benton, Perry Lopez, I.Q. Jones, Douglas Dick.

Pacer Burton (Elvis) a half breed Kiowa, and his white half brother, Clint (Steve Forrest), arrive at the family ranch to discover that their parents, Neddy, a full-blooded Kiowa (Dolores Del Rio), and Sam (John McIntire) have arranged a surprise birthday party for Clint. Among the guests are Clint's fiancée Roz (Barbara Eden), her brother Angus (Richard Jaeckel) and the Howards, Dorothy (Anne Benton) and her brothers, Tom (I.Q. Jones) and Will (Douglas Dick). It's

Elvis as Pacer Burton with his Indian mother Neddy (Dolores Del Rio); the clash between their cultures ends in tragedy for the whole family. *Flaming Star* (1960)

a fun party and Pacer sings 'A Cane and a High Starched Collar' accompanying himself on his guitar. They break up early, as the Howards have a long ride home and the Pierces an even longer ride into town. Back at their ranch the Howards are ambushed by the new leader of the Kiowas, Buffalo Horn (Rudolph Acosta), with a full war party and in the ensuing massacre everyone apparently is killed and the ranch burned to the ground. News reaches the Burtons about the Howard tragedy, just as Dred Pierce

storms into the yard with a band of men, demanding a guarantee that Burton, his wife and sons side with them: to back up their argument they shoot some of the Burton cattle and scatter the rest of the herd. Sam and Clint ride out in the morning to collect their cattle, leaving Pacer to look after Neddy. Buffalo Horn rides up with a brave called Two Moons and demands that Pacer come out to talk to him. Pacer refuses, saying he can talk just as well from the inside: he also refuses to side with the Kiowas in the coming fight with the white man. Neddy insists she will go along to her people's camp in an attempt to prevent the bloodshed. Buffalo Horn rides away, observing that Pacer's mother is a wise woman.

Neddy and Pacer set out for Buffalo Horn's camp, where she hopes to influence her sister to find peaceful ways to resolve the dispute. The Kiowas remain implacable and treat her with contempt for having married a white man. The gentle Neddy tells her sister she goes in friendship and she is allowed to return home with Pacer. His friend Two Moons (Perry Lopez) rides with them. On the way they are assailed by a demented Will Howard, who has somehow survived the massacre. He kills Two Moons and Neddy is badly wounded by an arrow.

Grief-stricken and desperate, Pacer rides to the Crossing, the little mid-West township, where the only doctor in town, Doc Phillips (Ford Rainey), is prevented by the townsfolk from going to Neddy's aid: 'The Doc ain't fixing up any Injun woman!' is the cry. Pacer, driven crazy by anger and fear for his mother's life, reluctantly kidnaps the doctor's little girl, who is out playing with one of the animals. To soothe her he tells her they're playing a game, as he blackmails Doc Phillips into agreeing to come and attend Neddy. 'It's not a game I like very much,' says the child fearfully, as the hostile townsfolk give in and let the Doc go: he tells Pacer he always wanted to anyway. By the time they get to the ranch Neddy, left momentarily in the bed to which Sam and Pacer carried her, has wandered off into the hills to run, then stumble, then crawl to die under the stars. As Tom and Pacer get to her she breathes her last, saying that she has been called out to meet the Flaming Star of Death.

Pacer turns on the doctor, saying 'You know who done it, don't you? You! Wasting all that time arguing at the Crossing. It was just five minutes before we got to her she died!' The doctor protests 'I couldn't have saved the woman if I'd got to her ten minutes after she was hurt!' 'The woman! Ain't she got a name like white folk?' Pacer moves towards the doctor, a knife in his hand. 'A white man shot her and white men let her die!' Clint lunges towards his brother, to wrest the knife away. They fight until Pacer lets the knife fall. He says 'You ought to have let me kill him! Them people that stopped us at the Crossing – I want to see every one of them dead! All Ma and me ever had from whites was insults and mean looks!' Clint's fiancée, Roz, a distressed bystander says, 'That's not true!'

Pacer turns the force of his fury on Roz and says, 'You were the worst. When I was little I liked you a lot – a whole lot. But ever since you were old enough to know, you never looked at me without saying somewhere in your heart – he's a Kiowa. Clint's all right, but keep your eyes out for Pacer!' Clint says unhappily that he never realized, and Pacer tells him 'Nobody knew but Ma and me.' Clint tries to prevent him leaving to join up with Buffalo Horn, but Pacer pulls a gun on him. Clint tells him 'If you can pull a gun on me, your own brother – get out and to hell with you!' Pacer goes to say goodbye to his father, who's digging his mother's grave. Sam tells him he must do what he has to do – he will understand.

That's the last time he sees him alive; Sam Burton dies, riddled with Kiowa arrows. Pacer sets out to join Buffalo Horn, but finds him dead from a marksman's bullet – as the executioner charges his horse at Pacer's he realizes the attacker is Clint and that he's badly wounded, a spear in his shoulder. Clint faints and Pacer picks him up bodily and slings him across his own mount, then grabs the reins of both their horses and guides them home. It is then Clint tells him of Pa's death. Pacer lashes his brother

to Roz's horse and sends him off to the Crossing, then stays to face the Indian attack alone, firing desperately and with deadly accuracy at dark faces daubed with paint. But he is one against too many and receives a mortal wound. He decides he has to get back to the Crossing to see that Clint's all right. Tended by Roz, Clint can just limp down the stairs and try to follow Pacer who, close to death, urges his horse high into the hills to face his own Star of Death – the Indian way. 'Just like Ma...' he thinks. Clint gives up the futile chase, realizing that Pacer must face the end alone.

Evidently much thought went into Elvis's return to the screen after his well-publicized and well-conducted army service. After the light-hearted *G.I. Blues*, a serious vehicle was scheduled to follow. This was in the days when he was being allowed to talk freely about his ambitions as an actor. He said, 'I know I have a long way to go, but a man has to have a goal, and acting's mine. The part I have in *Flaming Star* is the least like myself, but I would like to move on to new dramatic frontiers. I'm hoping in time to be able to handle *only* straight roles.' These sentiments, one suspects, were more the brain child of the film's producer David Weisbart, with his James Dean experience, and director Don Siegel, who later confessed he had hoped to have Marlon Brando in the part of the half-Indian Pacer. At the time Colonel Parker appeared to be echoing their feelings, but sincerity was not one of his more notable characteristics.

Clair Huffaker's original novel was initially announced as about to be brought to the screen as *Brothers of Flaming Lance*, with Nunally Johnson as the other screenplay writer. That was in early July. By the end of the month the title had changed to *Flaming Lance*. The film went before the cameras on August 8th, 1960. By September it was *Black Star*, finally emerging on December 20th,

1960 in the U.S. as *Flaming Star* which it remained when shown at London's Rialto in February, 1961.

The screenwriters have fashioned a story from a not very new or exciting premise that lends itself beautifully to the film medium. From the opening sequence a central theme is established: the fight and ultimate failure of a half-breed son (Elvis) to establish himself either on the side of the whites or the Indians in a war where the neutral party is an enemy to both sides. He cannot throw in his lot with the whites, because of the prejudices towards himself and his Kiowa mother (Dolores Del Rio) (*qv*), equally he cannot condone the violent activities of savage marauders determined to clear the land they believe is theirs by heritage. Tragedy can be the only outcome of such a situation. The pivotal characters are John McIntire as the white farmer Sam Burton, Dolores Del Rio as his Kiowa Indian wife and Elvis as their son, Pacer. Slightly off-centre is Steve Forrest as the white Clint Burton and even less clearly defined is the character of Roslyn Pierce, played by Barbara Eden, the fiancée of Clint. Almost as an after-thought, it is left to Pacer to imply that he loved her himself, until her racist attitude to the colour of his skin, as they grew up, caused him to leave the field open for Clint, who murmurs 'I never knew.' This is an echo of the Debra Paget–Richard Egan–Presley triangle in *Love Me Tender*, but Barbara Eden's performance expresses little interest either way. Nor does Steve Forrest make as clear an impression as did Richard Egan in the same circumstances – although race did not enter into the equation in the earlier film. Director Don Siegel, at his best when dealing with young outcasts, handles Presley with sensitivity and coaxes from him a touching performance, particularly in the scenes with his mother Neddy, a beautifully executed characterization by the incandescent Dolores Del Rio. Their rapport is so evident that one senses

Elvis is drawing on aspects of his closeness to his own mother, Gladys. The change of title subtly underlines the creed they shared in both going to meet the Flaming Star of Death. Del Rio's death scene is protracted and, like much of the violence in this film, painful to watch, notably when John McIntire's body becomes a pincushion for Kiowa arrows. This is, however, unavoidable in bringing home the futility of the conflict and the need for tolerance. Charles Clarke's photography is impressive, but slightly marred by the sometimes muddy quality of the DeLuxe colour.

(See also: Del Rio, Dolores; Love Me Tender; Siegel, Don)

ELVIS SINGS FLAMING STAR (RCA Camden 2304) April 1969

FLAMING STAR * * *
Written by Sid Wayne, Sherman Edwards.
Elvis sings this over the film's titles: director Don Siegel was against him singing at all in the movie, but Twentieth-Century-Fox, mindful of the enormous booster the title song 'Love Me Tender' gave to that film and with the technical advisor strongly on their side, won the day. Producer David Weisbart had, of course, worked on *Love Me Tender*, so Siegel, cult director or no cult director, had no option but to give way, even though he had been accepted in that genre since 1954 in *Riot in Cell Block H* and confirmed in the status in 1957 with *The Invasion of the Body Snatchers*. The song, in fact, is well in the tradition of the Western title-over songs, fast and galloping, and relevant to the theme of the movie, in that both Pacer and his mother Neddie go to meet their Flaming Star of Death. Siegel did not like the title anyway.
Single B/W: 'Love Me'
EP: 'Elvis by Request'
LPs: 'Double Dynamite'; 'Elvis in Hollywood'; 'Singer Presents Elvis Sings

Flaming Star and Others'
A CANE AND A HIGH STARCHED COLLAR *
Written by Sid Tepper, Roy C. Bennett.
A jolly family song early on, when the tensions between the Burton family, with their white father and Indian mother, and the outside world have not surfaced. It is, in the *Love Me Tender*, tradition, a family get together, with Elvis on guitar. Strangely it is not featured on the LP.

The LP (see title) is a flagrant cheat, compiled in 1969 and made up of songs from other movies at a time when Elvis had cut no new pressings for years. The rest of the songs are as follows:

WONDERFUL WORLD
(From *Live a Little, Love A Little*)

NIGHT LIFE
(Recorded for film *Viva Las Vegas* – 1968)

ALL I NEEDED WAS THE RAIN
(From *Stay Away, Joe*)

TOO MUCH MONKEY BUSINESS

THE YELLOW ROSE OF TEXAS/THE EYES OF TEXAS
Written by J.K. 1953 ('Yellow Rose'). John L. Sinclair, 1907 ('Eyes of Texas')

SHE'S A MACHINE
Written by Joy Byers.
LP: 'Singer Presents Elvis Sings Flaming Star and Others'

DO THE VEGA
Written by Bill Giant, Bernie Baum, Florence Kaye.
LP: 'Singer Presents Elvis Sings Flaming Star and Others'

TIGER MAN
Written by Joe Hill Louis, Sam Burns.
LPs: 'Elvis Aron Presley'; 'Elvis in Person'; 'From Memphis to Vegas – From Vegas to Memphis'; 'A Golden

**Elvis as Toby Kwimper with his father
(Arthur O'Connell) and adopted sister
Holly (Anne Helm). The Kwimper's,
an itinerant family, finally win out against
intolerance and bigotry.** *Follow That
Dream* **(1962)**

Celebration'; 'Singer Presents Elvis Sings
Flaming Star and Others'

FOLLOW THAT DREAM * * * * *

Released by: United Artists for the
Mirisch Company, (Deluxe colour,
Panavision); **Producer:** David Weisbart.
Director: Gordon Douglas; **Screenplay:**
Charles Lederer, based on the novel
'*Pioneer Go Home*.' by Richard Powell;
Art Director: Mal Bart; **Director of
Photography:** Leo Tover ASC; **Music:**
Hans J. Salter; **Running Time:** 105 mins;
Opened: May 23, 1962.
Cast: Elvis, Arthur O'Connell, Anne

Helm, Joanna Moore, Jack Cruschen,
Simon Oakland, Herbert Rudley, Alan
Hewitt, Howard McNear, Gavin, Robert
Koon, Harry Holcombe, Roland Winters.
Pop Kwimper (Arthur O'Connel) takes
his son Toby (Elvis) and family on the
road in search of pastures new. Other
members of the family, orphans
unofficially adopted by Pop, are Ariadne
Pennington (Pam Ogles), three years old;
Eddie (Gavin Koon) and Teddy
Bascombe (Robin Koon), eight year-old
identical twins, and Holly Jones (Anne
Helm), nineteen, who takes care of
the youngsters.

Travelling on a new, unopened
stretch of road in Florida, the Kwimpers
run out of petrol and are forced to camp
for the night on a strip of beach alongside
the road. The next morning, H. Arthur
King (Alan Hewitt), State Supervisor of
Highways, is aghast to find them there.

He is further appalled to learn that the
Kwimpers are virtual wards of the
Government, existing on Pop's relief
cheques, Toby's Army disability pension
and the children's state allowance.

At that moment the Governor
(Harry Holcombe) arrives to dedicate the
highway. Pop refuses to leave and informs
the Governor that he is homesteading the
strip of beach from the end of the road to
the water's edge. After a hurried
consultation the Governor and King
depart, the latter vowing to return.

A few hours later, Toby is fishing
from a wooden bridge nearby, when a
passer-by Endicott (Herbert Rudley)
stops and watches in amazement as Toby
struggles to land a giant tarpon. Endicott
offers Toby twenty dollars to let him take
over. He loses the fish, insists Toby takes
the money anyway; Toby declines but
Holly takes it forthwith. The incident

gives her an idea; hurrying to nearby Gulf City, she purchases some fishing equipment and spreads the word that the bridge area is filled with tarpon. In a matter of hours the place is over-run with fishermen, and Holly, Toby and the twins bring in over 90 dollars selling tackle, bait and food.

Spurred on by this initial success, the Kwimpers decide to go into business, with their own pier and fleet of row-boats. They borrow money from the bank through their friend, Endicott, who turns out to be the Managing Director, after an embarrassing incident when Toby is suspected of trying to arrange a heist. The homestead takes on a new look and it is not long before trailers and homesteaders move into the area beside them. The biggest trailer is owned by gambler Nick Poulos (Simon Oakland) with his floating crap game. Discovering the homesite is outside municipal and County jurisdiction, Nick and his chief henchman Carmine (Jack Kruschen) offer Pop $5,000 for his claim. He turns them down.

Meanwhile King, searching for a way to evict the Kwimpers, enlists the support of State Welfare Superintendent, Alicia Claypole (Joanna Moore), who lures Toby into the woods for a word association test, abruptly ended when Holly angrily shoves Alicia into a stream.

Customers flock into Nick's gambling casino and the noise becomes unbearable. The homesteaders elect Toby as sheriff and his first official act is to notify Nick that he is invoking an eleven o'clock curfew. Enraged, Nick orders his hoods to take care of the naïve and unarmed Toby, who effortlessly despatches them with his expertise at karate and judo, learned in the army. In desperation, Nick phones Chicago for reinforcements.

The hired guns arrive the next night and corner Toby in the woods. Mistaking them for playful drunks he disarms them and sends them packing. Later, one of the hoods plants an explosive near the

Kwimpers' doorstep. Holly finds it and, trying to be helpful, returns it to Nick's trailer. Moments later there is a loud explosion as the floating dice parlour is blown to bits. That's enough for Nick and Carmine, who drive away for good.

The following morning the state seizes the children and Pop is ordered to attend a hearing to show why the youngsters should not be turned over to the Department of Public Welfare. Alicia and King lead the fight against the Kwimpers, who spurn legal counsel and plead their own case, with Toby as spokesman. The word association test and Holly's attack on Alicia are the key factors for the prosecution and the judge (Roland Winters) orders Alicia to set a repeat test. She denounces the answers as those of a feckless, drunken layabout and loses the case: the judge, at Toby's prompting, had supplied the answers. Exit fuming, Alicia and King.

That night Holly snuggles up to Toby and asks him to show her what he and State Welfare Superintendent Alicia were doing in the woods. He begins reciting multiplication tables but gradually returns her embrace and draws her closer.

On its release this film was hailed as breaking new ground for Elvis and the notices were, for a Presley movie, almost respectful, ranging from the facetious (in the *Daily Sketch*) 'Why isn't Elvis wiggling any more .... he comes on the screen minus his wiggle – the one that has served him so well all these years, and his loss is our gain ... the boy's not bad ... not bad at all' to the earnest (in *What's On In London*) 'Elvis Presley now has a try at comedy and his gamble comes off handsomely ... it's a fine, funny film and gives Mr. Presley the opportunity to add the epithet "versatile" to those he has already collected in his movie career.' The *Sunday Telegraph* said 'It's a relief to come up against the blamelessly innocent character played by Elvis Presley ... never has his sulky charm been so much in

evidence.' *Picturegoer's* Sarah Stoddart wrote 'Now Hollywood rightly feels he can stand on his own as a comedy actor. This he does here, turning in a likeable, convincing performance as the amiable country boy who manages to outwit his opponents with the sweet innocence of a babe.' *Films and Filming* recorded 'A charming vehicle as well as a nice story based on the American theory that good simple folk will always triumph over city slickers ... the script is witty, the direction clever and Elvis's part brilliantly conceived.' Them's my sentiments and after four viewings I saw no reason to change my opinion, yet when I asked the then Editor of *Films and Filming*, the late and sorely missed Robin Bean, to let me do an in-depth appraisal of Presley's film work, he suggested I turn my attention to Elvis's then biggest British rival, Cliff Richard, whose immensely successful musical, *The Young Ones*, was released the year before *Follow That Dream*. Admirable as he was then and is perhaps even more so today, Cliff was a totally different proposition: the only things they had in common were youth – Cliff was five years younger (an immense appeal to teenagers) – and the fact they they both acheived fame by singing Rock 'n' Roll.

This kind of snobbish attitude has prevailed to the present day, as far as Presley's films are concerned. *Radio Times'* assessment in August 1995, on the re-showing of the film dismissed it with one star (for 'awful') and commented that Elvis's singing of 'On Top of Old Smokey' – a few bars, leading into a fast rocker, 'I'm not the Marrying Kind' – showed how far he had declined in his eleventh film (actually his ninth) but this decline was nothing in comparison with that of screenwriter, Charles Lederer, who penned 'this rubbish'.

In fact, *Dream* had heart, the kind of innocence we don't come across in many films any more, wonderful support from Arthur O'Connell as Elvis's Pa, a sweet leading lady in Anne Helm, a group of not oversentimentalized children, crooks in Jack Kruschen and Simon Oakland, as bumblingly effective as Laurel and Hardy, and the best comedy direction ever achieved by Gordon Douglas (*qv*), whose technical efficiency and visual polish were a by-word in the movies.

As for the 'fallen' Charles Lederer, the scene where Toby and Holly go to try and borrow money from the local bank is one of the funniest I can remember – full credit to all the actors involved and some superbly witty writing and direction. Toby follows the loans manager George (Alan Hewitt) into his self-locking office and stands over his desk. The man looks up fearfully at the jean-clad apparition and asks 'what do you want?' Toby mutters 'Money!' and advances towards him. The nervous George faints and Toby picks him up and carries him to the door. The scene is being watched by alarmed security men with guns, and a gathering crowd of customers, who cry 'He's got a hostage!' The vice president of the bank is summoned and turns out to be the Kwimpers' fishing friend Endicott (Herbert Rudley) who greets Toby warmly, revives poor George and instructs him to advance Toby and Holly the loan they seek, the latter having impressed him with her quick-thinking business acumen.

Presley's portrayel of guileless innocence has never been bettered, even by Stan Laurel! The final scene, where he wins over the judge (Roland Winters – best known as the last actor to interpret the role of Charlie Chan in the late forties) is like the bank heist, comedy acting at its best. Elvis was never again to have the benefit of such ideal fusion between characterization, script writing and direction. This film is a much under-valued gem in the Presley crown. *(See also: Douglas, Gordon)*

FOLLOW THAT DREAM
(RCA EPA 4368) 1962

WHAT A WONDERFUL LIFE * * * *
Written by Sid Wayne and Jimmy Livingstone.
Toby Kwimper sings this song, which was the original title for the movie. Breezy and cheerful, it establishes the mood for the best comedy Elvis ever made, partly due to Charles Lederer's witty and original screenplay and Gordon Douglas' taut direction. The Kwimper family are on the road, driving along the Florida coast in Pop's old jalopy. Toby sings of how wonderful it is with no boss to worry him. He has friends and life is good to him: guitars, drums and The Jordanaires vocalizing make the journey a jolly one.
LP: 'Got Lucky'

I'M NOT THE MARRYING KIND * * * *
Written by Nick David, Sherman Edwards.
Toby, reclining on the beach accompanies himself on his guitar while his adoptive sister Holly listens to his outlook on girls and marriage. He reckons marriage is all they ever think about, whereas he wants to keep his freedom, so tells her to keep her distance. The Jordanaires, more guitars, drums and piano accompany lyrics that are pointed and amusing – the tempo speeds up as the song draws to an end with Elvis relaxed and in great voice.
LP: 'C'mon Everybody

SOUND ADVICE * * *
Written by Bill Giant, Bernie Baum, Florence Kaye.
Toby sings to the Kwimpers the kind of song that had been cropping up in most Elvis films since *G.I. Blues*. Catchy and simplistic philosophy for the young ones, eased along by guitars, piano and vocals by The Jordanaires.
LP: 'Elvis for Everyone'

FOLLOW THAT DREAM * * * *
Written by Fred Wise, Ben Weisman.
Toby sings this in answer to a request from the local welfare officer Alicia Claypole (Joanna Moore) who is there giving him a word test on behalf of the government. First he sings a few bars of the traditional 'On Top of Old Smokey', unaccompanied, then goes into the title song of the movie which happens to be playing on his portable radio, with full orchestral accompaniment – guitars, piano, drums, saxophone and The Jordanaires. He sings of following his dream wherever it takes him. Alicia is much impressed and starts to make a big play for him, until interrupted by the indignant Holly.

WHEN MY BLUE MOON TURNS TO GOLD AGAIN
(not included in movie)
Written by Wiley Walker, Gene Sullivan.
Single B/W: 'Follow That Dream'
EPs: 'Elvis – Vol. 1'; 'Elvis /Jaye P. Morgan
LPs: 'Elvis, Elvis'; 'The Other Sides – Worldwide Gold Award Hits – Vol. 2'; 'A Golden Celebration'

ANGEL * * * *
Written by Sid Tepper, Roy C. Bennet.
Toby, reclining on the balcony of the Kwimper home in a chaise longue with his guitar, sings a dreamy reflective ballad which indicates to Holly that he has begun to appreciate her as something much more than the sister he had envisaged before. At last he views her as a woman and wonders why he hadn't appreciated her before. Holly comes into the room while he is singing, full of admiration for the way he had brought about a happy conclusion to the court hearing that the vengeful Alicia brought claiming that the children need to be taken into care. His guitar solo is backed by piano, drums and clarinet. The last song in the movie is charming and like the other four major songs in *Follow That Dream*, written as an integral part

of the action in true musical comedy tradition.

LPs: 'C'mon Everybody'; 'Elvis Sings for Children and Grown-ups Too'

FRANKIE AND JOHNNY
* * * * *

Released by: United Artists (Technicolor); **Producer:** Edward Small; **Director:** Frederick de Cordova; **Screenplay:** Alex Gottlieb from a story by Nat Perrin; **Art Director:** Walter Simonds; **Director of Photography:** Jacques Marquette; **Music:** Fred Karger; **Running Time:** 87 mins; **Opened:** March 31, 1966.

Cast: Elvis, Donna Douglas, Harry Morgan, Sue Ann Langdon, Nancy Kovak, Audrey Christie, Robert Strauss, Anthony Eisley, Joyce Jameson, Jerome Cowan.

Frankie (Donna Douglas) and Johnny (Elvis) may be lovers and partners on the river boat owned by Clint Braden (Anthony Eisley), for whom they work as a singing act, but she won't agree to marry Johnny until he gives up card playing and gambling, not to mention a roving eye for the ladies. A gypsy fortune-teller (Joyce Jameson) reads Johnny's cards and foretells that he'll be on a winning streak when a certain redhead comes along. She turns out to be Nelly Bly (Nancy Kovak), introduced onto the boat by owner Clint Braden, with whom she used to be 'an item'. Frankie gets the wrong idea when Johnny shows an interest in Nelly, though she doesn't realize that he regards the redhead merely as a good-luck charm. Nor does it behove her to know as Johnny has promised, not for the first time, to give up gambling. Nor is Braden pleased about what appears to be a mutual attraction. In the meantime

In the plot within the real story of the song, Frankie (Donna Douglas) shoots Johnny (Elvis) for doing her wrong with that gal named Nellie Bly; somebody substitutes a live bullet and she believes she really has killed him. *Frankie and Johnny* **(1966)**

Johnny's friend, Cully (Henry Morgan), surveys the scene and is inspired to write a song called 'Frankie and Johnny', which becomes an immediate hit and bids fair to be the number which will send Frankie and Johnny into the big time, as the story is re-enacted in the riverboat scene.

The fortune-teller was right: with Nelly Bly at his side – a position to which she is not at all averse – Johnny is on an apparently unbreakable winning streak. Both Frankie and Braden are becoming more and more incensed over the situation when Braden's bodyguard, Blackie (Robert Strauss), tries to please his master by getting Johnny out of Nelly's life for ever by slipping a real bullet into the gun that Frankie uses to 'kill' her lover in the song's climax when she finds him 'doing her wrong' with Nelly Bly. The gun goes off and hits its target – in this version Johnny's heart – and he goes down like a ninepin. Miraculously, the good luck charm that Frankie gave Johnny to wear close to his heart deflects the bullet and Johnny survives, not only to sing again, but finally to win Frankie's heart when she realizes that she loves him, come what may. Nelly Bly goes back to where she belongs in the arms of Clint Braden. The lovers are immortalized in the annals of riverboats and doubtless go on to take Broadway by storm, fulfilling Cully's dream which he crystallized in his song 'Look Out Broadway'.

This is the only classic musical from olden times that Presley was ever given to re-enact, albeit a 1904 music hall song rather that a full-bodied stage musical like *Showboat*, in which he could have been a charismatic Gaylord Ravenal. Edward Small and his astute director Frederick de Cordova have made do with the next best thing – a gutsy song the world knows as well as the characters involved. They employed a first class script writer in Alex Gottlieb to provide crisp dialogue, notably between Henry

Morgan as Cully and Audrey Christie as his long-suffering wife Peg, and to make suitable adjustments to the original finale which would have broken the fans' hearts and in any case would not be fitting in a musical. My memories of the only other film version of the story are still vivid – strangely enough – the black and white Republic movie directed by Chester Erskine and shown in Britain in some cinemas as second feature to Kay Francis' Florence Nightingale biography, *The White Angel* in 1936. It was filmed in 1934 with a cracking cast including Helen Morgan and Chester Morris in the title roles and Lilyan Tashman as Nelly Bly and Lew Cody as Clint Braden. Both these actors died in 1934, so the movie, played with all stops out for melodrama, was a sombre experience, though a cherishable musical piece.

The individual performances bear comparison: Helen Morgan's Frankie, like the lady herself, the original 'torch singer', is a tragic figure who loves her man with fatal intensity: Helen Morgan herself died of alcoholism at 42. Donna Douglas, cute and bubbly star of the TV series *The Beverley Hillbillies*, of necessity plays Frankie on a lighter note but still manages to make her love for Johnny ring touchingly true. Chester Morris, the square-jawed hero of several *Boston Blackie* movies and an adept at playing gangsters, was just the right Johnny for Morgan's Frankie – intensely male and none too scrupulous. Elvis's Johnny is a sharp dresser, almost feminine in his smooth-talking charm, a guy who's desperately handsome and knows it. In the original version it is not his heart that Frankie aims at, so no lucky charm could have saved him, unless it were very unconventionally suspended. The way Mae West (*qv*) tells it 'Why did you shoot so <u>low</u>?' Lilyan Tashman's Nelly Bly was the traditional blonde vamp par excellence, a part in which Tashman, ex-Ziegfeld Follies girl in *The Follies* starring Dorothy Dickson was the leading exponent of her day. Not for

nothing was she known as the best-dressed woman in Hollywood, with the most valuable collection of diamonds – most of which her Nelly Bly appeared to be wearing. Nancy Kovak in 1966 was a more laid-back Nelly, a sophisticated redhead; beautiful, relaxed but nonetheless lethal.

The characters in Alex Gottlieb's screenplay – one of his best was *Susan Slept Here* – are sharply etched and very well acted. Henry Morgan and Audrey Christie are a credible showbiz couple – endlessly bitching, but devoted – while Sue Ann Langdon brings considerable personality to the role of the love-starved Mitzi. There's a genuine feel of old music hall fun, with attractively bright Technicolor, zippy musical routines and attractive players: in all one of the most entertaining of Elvis's musicals. (*See also: West, Mae*)

FRANKIE AND JOHNNY
(RCA LPM 3553) April 1966 (Original Soundtrack Album)

FRANKIE AND JOHNNY
* * * * *
Written by Hughie Cannon (1904).
Single B/W: 'Please Don't Stop Loving Me'
Johnny (Elvis) sings the song that tell the story of the film. This appears during the reprise of the drama, at the climax of the film and occasions real tension over the outcome – for those familiar with the tragic ending of the song. Piano accompaniment opens the song gently, then builds to the climax as other instruments join in, including the saxophones, brass and drums.
LPs: 'Double Dynamite'; 'Elvis in Hollywood'; 'Elvis Sings Hits From His Movies'

COME ALONG * * *
Written by David Hess, recorded as above.
Typical riverboat song, telling everyone they're going to hit St. Louis tonight

under a full moon. Johnny repeats this sentiment, accompanied by trumpets, cymbals, drums – jolly, in one ear and out the other.

PETUNIA, THE GARDENER'S DAUGHTER * * * * *

Written by Sid Tepper, Roy C. Bennett. Concert party piece for entertaining the passengers, sung by Frankie and Johnny in flowery costumes, while the company caper happily, similarly attired. A delightfully quixotic number, with cutely tricksey lyrics: e.g. 'Make Petunia's tulips' is reprised as 'two lips'. A great one for London's Players Theatre, in the style of Victorian music hall, with piano, drums, tympany, saxes etc bouncing along with the singers.

CHESAY * * *

Written by Fred Karger, Sid Wayne, Ben Weisman.

A paen to strong gypsy wine – the kind to exorcize the devil away, sung by Johnny in czardas vein – very Hungarian, with fiddles, tambourines and male chorus. We might almost be in Ivor Novello-land. With Elvis in Ruritanian costume this is another fun song.

WHAT EVERY WOMAN LIVES FOR * * * *

Written by Doc Pomus, Mort Shuman. This is an 'I wish' song – plaintive melody and lyrics from the adroit Pomus-Shuman team. Johnny yearns for his Frankie to want only to take good care of him though he knows he's unworthy. Elvis in slow romantic tremolo is deeply appealing. Full of chauvinist sentiments, it's a pretty song with a prominent male chorus and the piano to the fore. There's a wistful coda, in which Elvis hopes he's the man she longs to take care of.

LOOK OUT BROADWAY * * * * *

Written by Fred Wise, Randy Starr. A throw back to the Alice Faye–Betty Grable–Don Ameche musicals of the war years, when all the troupes join in together to sing about how they will take Broadway by storm. A terrifically fast and zingy tempo, in which Elvis is joined by Donna Douglas, Sue Ann Langdon, Audrey Christie and Henry Morgan with his amusing basso profundo. Mostly piano and drums lead to a rousing 'pre-interval' climax.

BEGINNERS LUCK * * * *

Written by Sid Tepper, Roy C. Bennett. Gambler Johnny reflects on his luck with cards and in love – slow, melodious, gentle and charming with clever lyrics from which Elvis milks every nuance in his low key register. The choral background is male and restrained, accompanied mainly by piano and drums.

DOWN BY THE RIVERSIDE/WHEN THE SAINTS GO MARCHING IN * * * *

Traditional – adapted by Bill Giant, Bernie Baum, Florence Kaye. The antithesis of the reflective previous song: Elvis in martial vein, uniformed and marching to the beat of cornet, trumpet, tambourines, cymbals, drums etc. Noisy, cheerful and great fun. LP: 'Elvis Sings Hits From His Movies – Vol. 1'

SHOUT IT OUT * * *

Written by Bill Giant, Bernie Baum, Florence Kaye. More extroversion by Elvis's riverboat star: fast and riotous with a male chorus and a backing which includes guitars, drums and cymbals.

HARD LUCK * * * *

Written by Sid Wayne, Ben Weisman. The most bluesy song by Elvis; very down-beat about a black cat blighting his luck and sung with depth of feeling,

accompanied by muted trombones, piano and bass: very dirgy and very effective.

PLEASE DON'T STOP LOVING ME * * * *

Written by Joey Byers. **Single B/W:** 'Frankie and Johnny'. Johnny's saddest song, fearing that Frankie will not forgive his gambling and philandering he pleads that she is his whole world: piano, drums, all very low-key and touching – a contrast to Joe Byer's more customary cheerful style.

EVERYBODY COME ABOARD * * * *

Written by Bill Giant, Bernie Baum, Florence Kaye. Johnny heads the final rousing encouragement for everyone to come aboard and enjoy themselves on the riverboat up and down the Mississippi. There's a strong chorus backing with trombones, trumpets, drums and piano, put over with such gusto that the call is irresistible.

FUN IN ACAPULCO * * * *

Released by: Paramount Pictures (Technicolor); **Producer:** Hal B. Wallis; **Director:** Richard Thorpe; **Screenplay:** Allan Weiss; **Art Directors:** Walter Tyler, Hal Pereira; **Director of Photography:** Daniel L. Fapp; **Technical Advisor:** Colonel Tom Parker; **Music:** Joseph J. Lilley, vocal background by The Jordanaires and the Four Gringos; **Running Time:** 100 mins; **Opened:** November 27, 1963.

Cast: Elvis, Ursula Andress, Elsa Cardenas, Paul Lukas, Larry Domasin, Alejandro Rey, Robert Carricart, Teri Hope, Charles Evans, Alberto Morin, Francisco Gringa, Robert de Anda, Linda Rivera, Tom Hernandez, Linda Melia, Mary Treen, Red West, Musicians – Eddie Cano, Carlos Melia, Leon Cardenas, Fred Aguirre.

Elvis as Mike Windgren, ex-trapeze artist, with his manager, shoe-shine boy Raoul Almeida (Larry Domasin) who has found him a job singing at a resort hotel where social director Marguerita (Ursula Andress) takes a personal interest in him. *Fun In Acapulco* (1963)

Mike Windgren (Elvis), working on a yacht, is fired by the father of a malicious young blonde, Janine Harkins (Teri Hope), whose advances he spurns by telling her to get back to her dolls. When her father (Charles Evans), owner of the yacht, finds his daughter in a low drinking haunt she claims it was Mike who took her there. Out of work and penniless, Mike goes along with an ambitious shoeshine boy with connections, Raoul Almedo (Larry Domasin), who has heard him sing and offers to work as his manager. Mike's disbelief turn to admiration when Raoul persuades the manager of a resort hotel (Alberto Morin), who just happens to be his cousin, to engage him as a singer at his hotel. After his performance Mike is attracted by Dolores Gomez (Elsa Cardenas), a lady bullfighter celebrating her afternoon's triumph in the bullring. The attraction is mutual; she invites him to her table and teaches him to appreciate a potent Mexican drink called Margarita. With Raoul's help he persuades his manager–cousin to hire him as a part-time lifeguard in the hotel swimming pool while Moreno (Alejandro Rey), the conceited high diving champion, takes his siestas. He also happens to be interested in Marguerita, the hotel's social director (Ursula Andress), and is displeased when she, as well as Dolores Gomez, obviously takes a shine to Mike. Seeking to discredit him, Moreno unearths a newspaper report about how Mike, as a member of the trapeze team, the Windgrens, dropped his brother during the act whereupon he fell to his death. It is this that Mike is trying to come to terms with in his life and he takes the lifeguard job in the hope that it will give him an opportunity to overcome his phobia about heights. Moreno challenges him to tackle the high dive and when Mike refuses he calls him a coward; Dolores, overhearing the argument and being a worshipper at the shrine of physical bravery, turns her attentions

towards Moreno. She decides to throw a party and orders Marguerita, as social director, to arrange it.

Moreno picks a fight with Mike, who knocks him out: he tells him he fights pretty well for a coward and pretends to be too injured to perform his nightly high dive at La Quebrada. Moreno hopes to prove to Marguerita that Mike is indeed a coward and that she will come back to him. Mike hears the champion being ordered by loud speaker to perform his daring feat from the cliff top and feels obligated to take his place. Anxiously watched by his young manager, who has in the meanwhile – by sleight of phone that was perhaps inspired by technical advisor Tom Parker himself – secured a much better financial deal, Mike scales the rock face and, after a brief prayer at the local shrine, makes a perfect dive into the sea 136 feet below. He is chaired off to the spectators' stands by the cheering Acapulco fishermen for a happy ending for everyone: congratulations from his no-longer jealous rival, Moreno: kisses from the lady bullfighter and from the hotel's social director, who enquires 'Can anyone get in on the act?'; and a permanent partnership with the jubilant Raoul. Fun in Acapulco indeed.

Tautly directed by the always proficient Richard Thorpe, who had more than 100 films to his credit when he retired, Allen Weiss's screenplay gives Elvis a stronger storyline that most, although never less than predictable and deviating only minimally from the usual plot which sees Elvis proving himself a hero at the end. A lady bullfighter is certainly a variation from the normal romantic interest and Elsa Cardenas is as convincing as possible, considering we are not allowed to see her prowess in the bullring – thank the lord. More conventional is the top-billed Ursula Andress, as blonde as Cardenas is dark, and the ladies snipe prettily at each other in competition for Elvis. The statuesque

Andress seemingly did not think a great deal of her role. Or of the opportunities for her to be sexy. When she arrived in Hollywood she was called the new Dietrich and told to watch all Marlene's old movies. She did and was none too impressed: 'I do not believe in sex being flaunted. Equally I do not believe in being dishonest about it. When they put me in Elvis Presley's film *Fun in Acapulco*, for instance, it was a nightmare. I cried in the producer's office every day. They wouldn't let me wear lipstick or mascara and they put ribbon round my hair, just to please innocent little girls who make up Elvis's audiences. They wouldn't even let me wear a proper bikini. "You can't show your navel in a Presley picture," they said in horror. Oh, it made me so MAD.' Poor Ursula, especially as Elsa Cardenas wore a good deal of lipstick and mascara. But then she was playing a lady whose morals seemed pretty free. The only time in the movie when the great dress designer, Edith Head, who was responsible for several Presley musicals, allowed Andress a slight edge over Cardenas was when she wears a brightly coloured orange and yellow dress in the final scenes, presumably to make it seem likely Elvis would have been able to pick her out from the top of the high cliff off which he was steeling himself to dive. Seeing her was, of course, what finally helped him to conquer his phobia about heights and launch himself into the sea over 100 feet below.

Paul Lukas, a romantic star in early Hollywood and continental movies opposite such stars as Kay Francis and Constance Bennett, gives an amusing character study as Andress's father, an ex-Duke turned chef, which got him away from the villainous roles in which he tended to be cast later in his career. He died in 1971, two films after *Acapulco*. At the other end of the age scale, young Larry Domasin as the bootblack-turned pop star manager, a veritable embryo Tom Parker who demands 50 per cent of his protégé's earnings, is the obligatory bright waif of several Presley films of the period and far more fun and less irritating than Vicky Tiu in his previous oeuvre *It Happened at the World's Fair*. A Hollywood character comedienne, Mary Treen, who had brightened many films for Hal B. Wallis and others as a plain-looking working girl pops up here, uncredited, as a plain middle-aged matron, who, with her husband, 'Just adores bullfights' and can't get over meeting a lady of that ilk.

Elvis gives the role of Mike Windgren all he has got and more than it deserves, looks radiantly fit and trim and extracts every ounce of rhythm from the Mexican-flavoured score. This musical comedy deserved to be a winner, even though he, in the words of an unusually discriminating American *Variety*, deserved better after all his years on the Hollywood treadmill. This was Elvis's 13th movie and his sixth for Hal Wallis.

(See also: It Happened at the World's Fair; Parker, Colonel Tom)

FUN IN ACAPULCO

(RCA LPM – 2576) December 1963

FUN IN ACAPULCO * * *

Written by Sid Wayne, Ben Weisman. Elvis's opening song celebrates the Bay of Acapulco awakening to a new day; he tells us it's time to get up and be ready for fun in Acapulco – time to tell the musicians and last remaining stars to dissappear, while our roving sailor goes out to meet the senoritas with a plan to kiss every one. (Where have we heard that theme before?) Lots of piano, guitars, castanets etc., ending with a rumba beat; all covered by very fetching shots from Daniel Fapp's camera team showing the contrasting views of what appears to be an ideal place for a holiday. The song is in perfect harmony with the locality.

LP: 'Elvis in Hollywood'

VINO, DINERO Y AMOR

* * * *

Written by Sid Tepper, Roy C. Bennet. Torito's waterfront bar, full of smoke, gringos in straw hats, music and noise where Mike Windgren arranged to meet the fishermen who had disturbed the peace of the yacht where he was working as the film opened. The Four Gringos are waiting for him at the bar and say they're going to sing him a song for tequila lovers. As they launch into the opening bars, Mike picks up the refrain and joins in, blanket over shoulder, poncho-style, first in Mexican, then in English, getting down to the usual theme of girls, wine and money, punching it over with enormous zest while the Mexicans shake their maraccas in time to the backing of guitars, mandolins, trombones and the rest. It all adds up to a genuinely Mexican flavour and Elvis again demonstrates his powerful vocal range in this zippy choral effort.

MEXICO * * * *

Written by Sid Tepper, Roy C. Bennet. This catchy number is sung by Mike and his self-appointed manager, Raoul Almeido. Elvis achieves the tricky feat of riding through Acapulco with Larry on the cross bar of his bike – making it look the easiest thing in the world – no trouble at all from traffic lights or anything like that. Drums, piano, maraccas, guitars, trombones and zylophone are among the backing; while samba and rumba beat accompany Elvis's cheerful bass notes. Larry's unrestrained falsetto achieves some outrageous top notes as they sing of what a wonderful place Mexico is.

EL TORO * * * *

Written by Bill Giant, Bernie Baum, Florence Kaye.
Mike's first song at the hotel is sung in a stylish blue matador outfit with white shirt and scarlet cummerbund. The dramatic effect is matched by his

immense dignity and the power of his delivery of the salutory story of the matador who knew defeat and shame because he could not defeat the bull. He goes into the field one night filled with bitterness to even up the score with El Toro, but in the end it is the matador who lays dying. Serves him right, too. Heavy drumbeats, guitars, clarinet and tambourine provide great atmospheric effects, enthusiastically applauded by Margeurita who is not too happy that Mike refuses to let Raoul take publicity pictures. Larry laughs it off by saying he's the man most wanted by the F.B.I.

MARGUERITA * * * *

Written by Don Robertson.
This number is dedicated to the beautiful social director, who gives every indication of appreciating the compliment as Mike sings of how he was once free as a gypsy but is now captivated by her charms. Seven or eight guitars and clarinet are neatly offset by a small girl playing castanets and the inevitable tambourine adds variety to this genuinely sweet love serenade, with Elvis in highly romantic vein and Ursula in a pink bikini, a bowl strategically covering her navel after we have been allowed a brief glimpse. The Jordanaires add enthusiastic support.

THE BULLFIGHTER WAS A LADY

* * * *

Written by Sid Tepper, Roy C. Bennet. Mike, in matador outfit again, with different design and blue shirt this time dedicates a song to the glamorous bullfighter Dolores Gomez in the presence of the manager of the rival Ambassadors Club, invited along by the resourceful Raoul. Elvis manipulates his yellow and pink cape with style and does some fancy stepping with the Mexican backing group. Charles O'Currans choreography is brief but effective.

This bullfighter tale counterbalances the sad fate of the matador in 'El Toro' as the bull is smitten by the beauty of his adversary and refuses to fight: he only wants to kiss. This time it is El Toro's tale that is the sad one – it's above her door. Mandolins, persistent castanets, guitars and tambourine follow the opening trumpet solo as the backers sombreros lift to reveal their beaming faces as they step out in unison. Dolores is clearly delighted and rewards Mike with a kiss, causing Marguerita to storm out with her escort, high diver Moreno. This is another fun number, impeccably performed.

THERE'S NO ROOM TO RUMBA IN A SPORTS CAR
* * *

Written by Fred Wise, Dick Manning. Mike serenades Dolores on the way back from a tryst that narrowly avoided ending in disaster as the car almost goes over the edge of a cliff while they are kissing. A beaty rumba with humour and full orchestral backing. Short but sweet.

I THINK I'M GOING TO LIKE IT HERE * * *

Written by Don Robertson, Hal Blair. The second song Mike sings in Theito's bar, with his friends the Four Gringos, who join in the harmonizing, partly in Spanish, with the same backing music as the Tepper-Bennett song, while Elvis shakes his tambourine. Another paen of praise for the country – peppy and humorous Latin tempo.

BOSSA NOVA BABY * * * * *

Written by Jerry Lieber, Mike Stoller (1962).

Mike auditions at the rival establishment, the Tropican Club, with Marguerita in the audience as well as his ever-attentive manager Raoul. While he is singing Dolores arrives at the club, unaccompanied. The ladies glower at each other while Mike/Elvis performs the swingiest and most energetic song and dance in the film, and his most effective for several years. The eight musicians

with tambourines, maraccas, guitars, drums and organ, which Mike plays briefly while dancing, all join in the movements and chorus. Charles O'Curran has done a great job in choreographing the whole package, which understandably landed Elvis back in the Top Ten after 'One Broken Heart For Sale' from *It Happened at the World's Fair* only reached 11.

Single B/W: 'Witchcraft'
LPs: 'Elvis in Hollywood'; 'Elvis Worldwide 50 Golden Award Hits – Vol. 1'; 'The Top Ten Hits'

WITCHCRAFT

(not included in movie)
Written by Dave Bartholomew, Pearl King.
Single B/W: 'Bossa Nova Baby'
LPs: 'Elvis Golden Records – Vol. 4'; 'Elvis – The Other Sides – Worldwide Gold Award Hits Vol. 2'; 'Return of the Rocker'

YOU CAN'T SAY NO IN ACAPULCO * * *

Written by Sid Fuller, Dorothy Fuller, Lee Morris.

Mike with his peripatetic sombreroed backing group at the edge of the swimming pool, where white capped nymphets swim in rhythm without giving Esther Williams any competition, but lending a splash of originality to the conventionally romantic ballad which is put over by Elvis with genuine feeling, strolling around with accompanying violins, guitars and maraccas, The Jordanaires in soothing tempo, bathing belles swaying in rhythm at the poolside.

GUADALAJARA * * * *

Written by Pepe Guizar.
Mike rounds off the film triumphantly, after having performed his spectacular death-defying dive. Fittingly the song is as Mexican-orientated as Xavier Cugat and his orchestra, who introduced it in the 1944 Esther Williams film *Bathing Beauty*. Perhaps this inspired the pool

belles for extra embellishment in the 'Can't Say No In Acapulco' number. Plenty of violins and guitars. The doughty sombreroed musicians all fling their headgear in the air while Elvis, after singing in fast and fluent Spanish that 'even a Costa Bravan could understand' as one music critic wrote, takes centre stage with a rousing top note as the titles come up. Flamenco steps, tambourines and maraccas all add to the Mexican flavour of a song which Elvis sings with total *joie de vivre*, joined by the Gringos and The Jordanaires in resilient style.
LPs: 'Burning Love and Hits From His Movies – Vol. 2'; 'Elvis – A Legendary Performer – Vol. 3'

LOVE ME TONIGHT

(bonus) (not included in movie)
Written by Don Robertson.
This smoochy ballad, sung with characteristic tenderness by Elvis, is in no way to be confused with the song with which Jeanette MacDonald romanced Maurice Chevalier at full throttle in the 1932 movie of the same title.

SLOWLY BUT SURELY

Written by Sid Wayne, Ben Weisman.
Recorded for Film *Tickle Me* (1965)
EP: 'Tickle Me'
(See also: *Tickle Me*)

G.I. BLUES * * *

Released by: Paramount Pictures
(Technicolor, Cimemascope); **Producer:**
Hal B. Wallis; **Director:** Norman
Taurog; **Screenplay:** Edmund Beloin,
Henry Carson; **Director of
Photography:** Loyal Griggs; **Technical
Advisor:** Colonel Tom Parker; **Music:**
Joseph G. Lilley, vocal accompaniment
by The Jordanaires; **Running Time:** 104
mins; **Opened:** November 15, 1960.

Cast: Elvis, Juliet Prowse, Robert Ivers,
Letitia Roman, James Douglas, Sigrid
Maier, Arch Johnson, John Hutton.

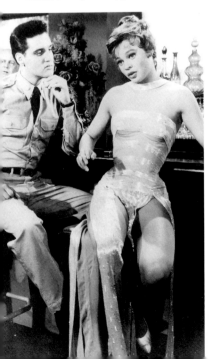

**Elvis as GI Tulsa McLean sizes up his
chances of defrosting dancer–singer Lili
(Juliet Prowse), renowned for keeping
GI's at bay, in his first movie after demob.
GI Blues (1960)**

Three army buddies, Tulsa McLean
(Elvis), Cooky (Robert Ivers) and Rick
(James Douglas), assemble a rock 'n' roll
band to pass the time during their term
of duty in West Germany. They call
themselves the Three Blazes and play
whatever gigs they can get to save up
money to open their own club when
they return to the USA. They get their
big break when they're asked to take
part in an Armed Forces show that is
being arranged.

The Three Blazes' popularity is
largely due to the sex appeal of Tulsa,
plus his wonderful way with a song: he
seems a natural to take over when the
platoon's resident lothario is suddenly
transferred to duty in Alaska before he
can take up a $300 bet for himself and
his buddies that he could win over Lili
(Juliet Prowse), a local cabaret star who
is noted for her allergy to GI's, and
persuade her to spend the night with
him. Tulsa is no shrinking violet and Lili
is a looker, so he does not need much
persuasion to deputise for the absent
Romeo. There is also the added
inducement of making extra money for

his proposed night-club. Overcoming
Lili's initial coolness and resistance, Tulsa
succeeds in making a date and she agrees
to show him the town. As the evening
proceeds he begins genuinely to fall for
her and is in danger of overlooking the
original purpose of the exercise, while
she, for all her former reticence, begins
to feel affectionately towards him in
return. She is, of course, totally oblivious
to the fact that Tulsa's mates are tailing
them to make sure that he keeps the bet
in view.

Tulsa has agreed to baby-sit for one
of his army friends and his fiancée, so
they can slip away and get married so as
to give the child a name. Tulsa turns out
to be a disaster as a baby-sitter and in
despair calls Lili for assistance. She tells
him to come over and bring the baby
with him. Predictably, she proves adept
at soothing fractious babies and, equally
predictably, he spends the night, in the
purest possible way, baby-sitting. In the
street below his scheming buddies swap
ideas about how they will spend their
wager money.

Rehearsals begin the next day for
the Armed Forces show, at which Lili is
scheduled to sing, along with Tulsa and
the Three Blazes, but things go seriously
wrong when she hears Tulsa's sergeant
(Arch Johnson) laughing about Tulsa and
the bet he won. When the commanding

Elvis happily signs autographs for fans during his term of National Service, 1960.

officer gets to know about the bet he is shocked and angry and makes arrangements to transfer Tulsa to another base before the evening of the show. Further, the Colonel himself apologizes to Lili in these memorable words, 'Sorry there was a mercenary motive Ma'am. No offence taken, I hope?' She reassures him that no offence was taken – 'How could there be?'

Probably of more positive influence in soothing Lili's ruffled sensibilities was her meeting with the parents of the baby she and Tulsa looked after during their absence. When the newlyweds return from their honeymoon to collect their child, now a fan of Tulsa's since he won him over by singing 'Daddy Big Boots', they enthuse to Lili about Tulsa's fine qualities and how his looking after the baby has altered their lives by giving them a new start together as a family unit. Lili is persuaded that the whole matter of the bet was a complete misunderstanding and admits her love

for Tulsa is unchanged.

Wedding bells are in the air for Tulsa and Lili, he is retained at base as a necessity for the success of the Armed Forces show and Lili gets to do her scheduled number with the Three Blazes.

Given that the storyline is in the worst possible taste, the post-Army Elvis, sleek, immaculately groomed and glowing with fitness, is able to take the whole thing in his stride in a way that justifies one of the few enthusiastic notices in the British national press: Dick Richards in *The Daily Mirror*, November 11th, 1960, said days before the US release, 'I'm happy to welcome him back and report that his military stint seems to have done Elvis a power of good. He's a changed man and a better actor: his acting is more mature and relaxed'. Most of the others slate the movie and his singing. *The Daily Herald's* Paul Dehn says 'Like

Elvis proudly shows his sergeants stripes at his station in Bad Neuheim, Germany, January 21, 1960.

a gramophone with engine trouble' but cautiously admits to an improvement in his acting. The US press were, in the main, more cordial with *Variety* praising production qualities, Norman Taurog's (*qv*) direction and Elvis's smartened up appearance. *Hollywood Reporter* noted 'A subdued and changed Elvis Presley.'

Jack Good, later to appear with Presley in a film, spearheads the attack in his column in the musical paper *Disc* with 'Why did Presley allow this?' (Possibly because he had no say in the matter.) Good goes on, 'The apparently infallible Colonel Parker (*qv*) seems at last to have made a major mistake.' He quotes derogative notices in the British nationals, asks 'Are his fans morons?' and obliges us morons with a definition of the word: 'MORON: Adult whose mental development is arrested at the stage normal in a child of 9-12 years.' *Oxford Dictionary.*

The film reached No. 2 in *Variety's* weekly list and grossed over four million dollars, quite a successful 'major mistake' on the Colonel's part and one that was to chart the course for the remainder of the Presley film career. There came a stage in the early 'sixties when a hitherto devoted fan wrote to the English *Elvis Monthly*, which normally printed only

Elvis greeted by fans at his arrival in Memphis after his demob from the US army, March 1960.

eulogistic opinions of their star, describing the films of the time as 'Puppet show for not over-bright children.'

Apart from Elvis's bright and charming performance – all his charm was needed make the Tulsa McLean character likeable – a definite asset to the film was Juliet Prowse, with her talents as a singer and dancer, which had already singled her out in *Can Can*, and a gamine quality with a touch of the Lesley Carons. Robert Ivers and James Douglas are acceptable buddies for Tulsa and two bright and attractive young talents, Letitia Roman and Sigrid Maier, were singled out as future stars, although without any noticeable progress in later movies.

After all the speculation about whether Presley could regain his crown and reports about his closed set and his nerves during the filming, he came out a winner. Producer Hal Wallis had no such qualms and predicted, 'Will he be as big

now as he was before the Army? Man, he'll be bigger. He's an even greater entertainer now. No one will take the crown away from him. His National Service didn't do him any harm, as some people think – it did him a power of good. He's won thousands of new admirers as a result of it.' After forty years' experience of Hollywood and stars, Hal B. Wallis knew a thing or two but, like Colonel Parker, his vision was limited as far as Elvis was concerned. Wallis went on to be associated with such prestigious movies as *Becket* (1964) and *True Grit* (1969), but never worked with Presley again.

(See also: Girls! Girls! Girls! (Not The Movie); Parker, Colonel Tom; Taurog, Norman)

G.I. BLUES
(RCA LPM 2556 October 1960)
TONIGHT IS SO RIGHT FOR LOVE * * * *
Based on: 'Barcarolle' by Jaques Offenbach.
Adapted by: Sid Wayne, Abner Silver.
Tulsa McClean on his first date with dancer Lili from the Europa Cabaret is

serenaded in a German bierkeller by the German band. He tells the guitarist who comes to their table playing 'Barcarolle' that they do it differently in the US – 'We just let the rhythm ooze out'. 'Was ist ooze?' asks the musician. Lili suggests Tulsa shows what is 'ooze'. Tulsa is happy to demonstrate; the musician hands him his guitar and Tulsa goes into the Wayne-Silver lyrics to a rock 'n' roll beat, elaborating on the theme of the title, while the band accompanies him joining in the vocal background with accordeons and a girl guitarist in traditional costume. A charming scene, with a happily updated beat to Offenbach – great top note by Elvis at the climax.
LP: 'Burning Love and Hits From His Movies – Vol. 2'

WHAT'S SHE REALLY LIKE * *
Written by Sid Wayne, Abner Silver. Tulsa sings a few bars of this, his first song, in the shower, without vocal accompaniment, although his buddies are then also showering. The same number is played by the band in the Europa when Tulsa and Lili have their first meeting.
EP: 'The EP Collection – Vol. 2'

DOIN' THE BEST I CAN * * *
Written by Doc Pomus, Mort Schuman. Tulsa, with guitar heads the combo of G.I.'s, including his buddies Cooky and Ricky, with whom he is trying to raise the cash to open their own nightclub after demob. He sings the Pomus – Schuman lyrics to slow, dreamy music, to which couples in the German club dance cheek to cheek, accompanied by bass guitar, piano and drums. They are rudely interrupted by one of the G.I.'s putting 'Blue Suede Shoes' on the jukebox, saying he wants to hear the 'original' – an 'in' joke which delighted audiences and leads to the inevitable punch-up. Tulsa gives the owner of the wrecked club (Ludwig Stossel) money to pay for the damage before they run out.

FRANKFURT SPECIAL * * *

Written by Sid Wayne, Sherman Edwards.

Tulsa and his G.I. friends crowd into a train compartment for the ride to Frankfurt. They discuss how they will continue with their bet that one of them will be able to spend the night with the allegedly icy Lili – Tulsa finds himself landed. He and another play guitars and make train noises while the wheel spin along the track in time to the music. The sort of tuneful journey few of us who remember the last war can recall – how it would have enlivened those all night journeys from Cardiff to Edinburgh. Jigging girls outside the doors in low-cut dresses would have been a welcome novelty too.

LP: 'Elvis – A Legendary Performer – Vol. 3'

WOODEN HEART * * * * *

Based on 'Muss Ich Denn Zum Stadtele Hinaus'.

Written by Bert Kempfert, Kay Twomey, Fred Wise, Ben Weisman.

Tulsa and Lili visit a children's puppet show, featuring boy and girl puppets temporarily separated by a wrathful father. The puppet master's recording apparatus breaks down and Tulsa volunteers to sing the boy's song, courting the girl puppet, while the puppeteer accompanies on his accordeon which seems to have built in orchestral effects. Based on an old German folk song, of which Elvis sings a verse in impeccable vernacular, this is a really sweet song, as effective in its own way as Gene Kelly's dance with a cartoon mouse. This may not have pleased the rock 'n' roll fans, but the well over one million sales when released as a single speak for themselves.

Single B/W: 'Blue Christmas'

LPs: 'Elvis – A Legendary Performer – Vol. 4'; 'Elvis sings for Children and Grown-ups Too!'; 'Elvis: Worldwide 50 Gold Award Hits – Vol. 1'

BLUE CHRISTMAS

(not included in movie)

Written by Billy Hayes, Jay Johnson.

Single B/W: 'Wooden Heart'

EP: 'Elvis sings Christmas Songs'

LPs: 'Elvis – A Legendary Performer – Vol. 2'LP's; 'Elvis Aaron Presley'LP's; 'Elvis's Christmas Album'; 'Elvis – TV Special – A Golden Celebration'; 'Memories of Christmas'

G.I. BLUES * * * *

Written by Sid Tepper, Roy C. Bennet.

Elvis's first song with orchestral backing in the movie takes place in the German nightclub where he and his combo, Cookie and Ricky, are playing in the hopes of making enough money to buy their own nightclub after demob. The number is played orchestrally over the credit titles and is a smart military-type marching beat, with snappy lyrics recounting the woes of being a G.I. – all they do is march, never mind the beautiful view of the Rhine, and the frauleins are pretty but out of bounds. The owner of the club, Papa, is impressed enough to reward them with their first pay packet. Bass, guitar, piano, drums are in evidence.

EP: 'The EP Collection'

LPs: 'Elvis in Hollywood'; 'This is Elvis'

POCKETFUL OF RAINBOWS * * *

Written by Fred Wise, Ben Weisman.

Tulsa and Lili ride on one of those romantic suspension cars over the Frankfurt countryside and he sings the kind of song appropriate in the circumstance – apart from the rainbows in his pocket (rather unwieldy, one would think), his heart is overflowing with love. The invitation to kiss him is taken up and they go into their first clinch. Lili's contribution to the song is to chant 'Rainbows' at the start of every verse. They are such a handsome couple that one tends to forgive the banality of the words, accompanied by plenty of strings, heavenly choir, pianos and drums.

EP: 'The EP Collection – Vol. 2'

SHOPPIN' AROUND * * *

Written by Sid Tepper, Roy C. Bennet, Aaron Schroeder.

Tulsa, with guitar, sings 'by special request' at the Europa Club, watched by their star dancer, Lili, at first sceptically, given the big build up his pal Cookie has given him. She has warmed to him by the end of the song, which tells how he has found the dolly he's been shopping around for and tears up his little red book. A fun rocker, delightfully put over by Elvis. First time around, I was under the impression he was singing 'Gonna stop *shoving* around!' which was something of a puzzlement. Apart from beating time, leg wiggles are conspicuous by their absence in a number in which they would have been de rigeur in the pre-war service Elvis. The Europa band features saxophones, piano and much finger clicking.

BIG BOOTS * * * *

Written by Sid Wayne, Sherman Edwards.

Tulsa, baby-sitting for his friend Rick's little boy, sings him a lullaby about his 'daddy big boots', who once wore little boots like him. Of course it's sentimental, but who's scoffing? Elvis has a magic way with babies of all ages.

DIDJA EVER * * *

Written by Sid Wayne, Sherman Edward.

Final song from Tulsa, the finale of the Big Band concert at the end of which he marches down through the audience of G.I.'s to wild applause as they fling their programmes into the air. The complications between the lovers are all sorted out to the accompaniment of the Armed Forces Big Band – trombones, drums, clarinets, bass trombone. The lyrics are about the woes G.I.s are subject to, when everything goes wrong and it isn't worth getting up – all to a martial beat. As Tulsa and Lili go into their final clinch he repeats to the camera, with a wink, 'Didja ever?'.

BLUE SUEDE SHOES * * * * *

Written by Cark Perkins.

Elvis's version of the Carl Perkins hit is played on the juke box by one of his army buddies as an interruption to 'Doin' the Best I Can' which Tulsa and his combo are performing in a German nightclub. The incident ends in a brawl, drowning both songs.

Single B/W: 'Tutti Frutti'

EPs: 'Elvis Presley' (RCA EPA 747); 'Elvis Presley' (RCA EPB 1254); 'Elvis Presley' (RCA SPD 22); 'Elvis Presley – The Most Talked About Personality in the Last Ten Years of Recorded Music

LPs: 'Aloha From Hawaii via Satellite'; 'The Alternative Aloha'; 'Elvis – A Legendary Performer – Vol. 2'; 'Elvis Aaron Presley'; 'Elvis in Person'; 'Elvis Presley'; 'From Memphis to Vegas/From Vegas to Memphis'; 'A Golden Celebration'; 'This is Elvis'

TONIGHT'S ALL RIGHT FOR LOVE * * * * *

Based on 'Tales from the Vienna Woods' by Johann Strauss

Written by Sid Wayne, Abner Silver, Joe Lilley.

Enchanting Elvis version of famous Strauss melody, sung with emotion and considerable depth.

LPs: 'Elvis – A Legendary Performer – Vol. 1'; 'Elvis Aaron Presley'

I NEED YOU SO

(not included in movie)

Written by Ivory Joe Hunter.

EP: 'Just For You'

GIRL HAPPY * *

Released by: Metro-Goldwyn-Mayer, a Eutorpe Production (Panavision, Metrocolor); **Producer:** Joe Pasternak; **Director:** Boris Sagal; **Screenplay:** Harvey Bullock, R. S. Allen; **Art Directors:** George W. Davis, Addison Hehr; **Director of Photography:** Philip H. Lathrop; **Technical Advisor:** Colonel Tom Parker; **Music:** George Stoll, uncredited vocal background; **Running**

Time: 96 mins; **Opened:** April 14, 1965.

Cast: Elvis, Shelley Fabares, Harold J. Stone, Gary Crosby, Joby Baker, Nita Talbot, Mary Ann Mobley, Fabrizio Minni, Jimmy Hawkins, Jackie Coogan, Peter Brooks, John Fielder, Chris Noel, Lyn Edgington, Gale Gilmore, Pamela Curran, Rusty Allen, Dan Hagerty, Red West.

Rusty Wells (Elvis) and his band are preparing to leave Windy City where they have had a record breaking engagement; their aim is to head for Fort Lauderdale and take a well-earned spring break. However, they have made so much money for their employer, the formidable Mr. Big Frank, that he decides to hold the band over for a while to reap the rewards of the new popularity Rusty's band has brought to his night-spot. Big Frank is not easy to refuse, but Rusty's determined to get to Florida and its beaches and when he finds out the Frank's daughter Valerie (Shelley Fabares) is spending the Easter holiday in Fort Lauderdale, he decides on a positive plan of action. Frank is devoted to Valerie, almost to the point of paranoia, and Rusty suggests that he send the band there to look after her welfare. The idea is welcomed with enthusiasm and Rusty and his boys are despatched forthwith to Florida, all expenses paid, where they check into the same hotel as Valerie. She turns out to be an inveterate bookworm, with reading seemingly her only interest, so Rusty decides she is not in imminent need of minding and makes his own plans for relaxation. He meets a beauty called Deena (Mary Ann Mobley) and invites her to the club where he is playing.

While they are on stage Rusty and his combo (Gary Crosby, Joby Baker and Jimmy Hawkins) spot Valerie in the audience: she has obviously left her book behind for the evening for a date with a rich and obnoxious young man called Brentwood Von Durgenfield (Peter Brooks). Rusty leaves Deena at her table

while he sorts out Valerie's escort, but finds out that looking after her is not the simple matter he first thought: she has a proclivity for getting into troublesome situations. Furthermore, he also discovers that he himself is falling in love with her.

Valerie's growing affection for Rusty takes a severe tumble when she finds out he's been sent to the hotel as her minder: she gets furiously drunk in a bar and starts a striptease of her own. Rusty intervenes and a fight breaks out. When things calm down Rusty finds that Valerie has been arrested and is languishing in Fort Lauderdale jail. Never one to do things by halves, he contrives to burrow beneath the cell where she is incarcerated in order to rescue her. All that energy has been in vain; the bird has flown. Her father, Frank, has bailed her out.

Fearful of the consequences, Rusty appeals to Big Frank, whose fury at first knows no bounds, but eventually he realizes that a man who'll risk digging his way into jail to save his daughter has to be admired. He adopts a pragmatic attitude and ends by giving the couple his blessing.

This was watershed time for Elvis, who had just celebrated his thirtieth birthday and, like the Colonel (qv), was all too well aware that the Beatles (qv) had taken over as the world's top record sellers and were making no secret of the disdain they felt for the kind of discs the King was making at the time. At the same time their admiration for him was immense and led to the world famous summit meeting later in the year. Although the plot of *Girl Happy* was more or less the same mixture as before, the inclusion of rock 'n' roll numbers on an LP which included some of the most ridiculous songs Elvis ever recorded, paid some kind of lip service to the Beatles' preferred style of recording. All the same, the film grossed $3.1 million – $100,000 more than the previous film, *Roustabout*. Leading lady Shelley Fabares, whose first film out of three with Elvis this was, herself was making records and joins him in a couple of song and dance routines. In an interview she said all the usual things about how 'nice' and courteous Elvis was and what a good dancer, but added that their only real conversations were to do with the filming and, when that was over, he withdrew 'with his own friends'. According to David Stanley, she later became one of his favourite leading ladies along with Ann-Margret (*qv*), Nancy Sinatra, Mary Ann Mobley and Juliet Prowse. *Variety* says she does well in an 'undemanding' part and glows about the movie in general, including Elvis's 'growing naturalness', which was also commented on by British pop star, Mike Sarne, writing in *Films and Filming* who thought he had developed into a 'first class comedy actor'. Against this we have *British Record Mirror*, who called the film 'the sexiest, smoochiest, craziest romp' he'd ever made but found the scene in which Elvis has to dress as a girl 'sickening'.

One of the most intelligent Elvis biographies of recent years, John Tobler and Richard Wootton's '*The Legend and The Music*' voted *Girl Happy* 'quite awful' and the film did raise the question as to the course his career would take now that he had reached thirty. Later in the year his 'Crying in the Chapel', which he had recorded in 1960, restored him to No. 1 in the Top Twenty in Britain and reached No. 3 in the USA. 'Return To Sender' from *Girls! Girls! Girls!* (1962) was the previous time he had reached that eminence.

Performances to note in this financially successful excursion to Fort Lauderdale by the King of Rock at the time when British pretenders to the throne were beginning to proliferate, include Harold J. Stone as Shelley Fabares' formidable night-club owner father, Bing Crosby's son Gary as one of Elvis's combo, Mary Ann Mobley – another favourite co-star – as the girl

who loses him and Jackie Coogan, amusing as an army sergeant more than forty years after he was the world's biggest child star opposite Charles Chaplin in *The Kid* in 1924.
(See also: Ann-Margret; Elvis and the Beatles; Girls, Girls, Girls (not the movie); Roustabout; Parker, Colonel Tom)

GIRL HAPPY * *

(Original Soundtrack Album)
Written by Doc Pomus, Norman Meade.
Band leader Rusty Wells with his combo sing of a life full of beautiful women who go back to the cradle: the first nurse who rocked him was his first love and now he's always in the mood for loving – mothers are advised to keep their daughters out of the way. The theme of this (and most other Elvis films at the time) is explained over the credits in
Doc Pomus' rocker: drums, guitars, cymbals play along with a persistant vocal background.
LP: 'Elvis in Hollywood'

SPRING FEVER * *

Written by Bill Giant, Bernie Baum, Florence Kaye.
Rusty waxes lyrical, with vocal assistance from Valerie, about nature coming to life signalling that spring is in the air and its time to get outdoors and make love: vocal chorus, piano, drums and guitars accompany beaty lyrics.

FORT LAUDERDALE CHAMBER OF COMMERCE *

Written by Sid Tepper, Roy C. Bennet.
Perhaps the silliest lyrics yet, telling how if you're in Fort Lauderdale Chamber of Commerce and you're not stalking a pretty girl, you'll get arrested – just why is not made clear: the usual piano, drums and guitars plus vocal accompaniment.

7STARTIN' TONIGHT *

Written by Leonore Rosenblatt, Victor Milrose.
More insistence from Elvis about making love: spread a blanket on the shore – call a cop – for reasons not made clear. More nonsense to a rocking beat with vocal chorus, piano, drums and guitars.

WOLF CALL *

Written by Bill Giant, Bernie Baum, Florence Kaye.
Elvis sees a pretty girl standing against the wall and gives her a wolf call which he is sure she won't resist – she's just waiting for him to kiss her. Accompanied by basso profundo male echoes, along with the guitars, drums, piano and of course, wolf whistles.

DO NOT DISTURB * *

Written by Bill Giant, Bernie Baum, Florence Kaye.
Rusty sings to his girl that it's time to put down her book – reference to Valerie's reputation in the film as a bookworm. He is in husky, wooing voice and suggests they hang out the 'Do Not Disturb' sign, turn down the lights and make love. Tango rhythm, to drums, guitars and insistent pianoforte.

CROSS MY HEART AND HOPE TO DIE * *

Written by Sid Wayne, Ben Weisman.
Elvis laments that his girl got things all wrong when she say him with another – he was only doing a favour for a friend and all he wants to do is be forgiven and fly back to her arms. He thought about her all night long. Slow rocker with repetitive vocal chorus, drum, guitars, and piano.

THE MEANEST GIRL IN TOWN *

Written by Joy Byers.
Fast rocker for Elvis as Valerie reveals herself in her true colours: she asks you out for a date, and then stands you up. She'll lead you on, then laugh at you

when you go to kiss her. Guitars, piano, drums.

DO THE CLAM * *

Written by Sid Wayne, Ben Weisman, Dolores Fuller.

Beach party rocker. The vocal chorus on the LP is again much in evidence as Elvis sings this number for dancing – twisting, turning and squeezing to bongos, guitars and drums.

Single B/W: 'You'll Be Gone'

PUPPET ON A STRING * *

Written by Sid Tepper, Roy C. Bennet.
Elvis recorded July 1964 – Radio Recorders.

Elvis in masochistic mood: the girl can do almost anything she wants with him as long as she loves him and is kind to him. It is sung to a slow beat with vocal accompaniment and guitar predominant. No relation to Sandie Shaw's sixties Eurovision Song Contest hit.

Single B/W: 'Wooden Heart'

I'VE GOT TO FIND MY BABY * *

Written by Joy Byers.
Elvis sings a fast rocker, lamenting the loss of the girl he loves, accompanied by vocals, guitar, saxophone and piano.

YOU'LL BE GONE

(Bonus) (not included in movie)
Written by Elvis Presley, Red West, Charlie Hodge.

Single B/W: 'Do The Clam'

GIRLS! GIRLS! GIRLS! * * * *

Released by: Paramount Release;
Producer: Hal B. Wallis (Technicolor);
Director: Norman Taurog; **Screenplay:**
Edward Anhalt, Allan Weiss, from a story by Allan Weiss; **Art Directors:** Hal Peirera, Walter Tyler; **Director of Photography:** Loyal Griggs ASC;
Technical Advisor: Colonel Tom Parker;
Music: Joseph J. Lilley, vocal background by The Jordanaires; **Running Time:** 106 mins; **Opened:** November 21, 1962.

Cast: Elvis, Stella Stevens, Jeremy Slate, Laurel Goodwin, Robert Strauss, Guy Lee, Frank Puglia, Lili Valenty, Benson Fong, Ginny Tiu, Elisabeth Tiu, Beulah Quo, Alexander Tiu, Mary Treen, Red West.

Ross Carpenter (Elvis) built a sailboat called 'West Wind' with his father, who died soon after the boat was completed. Ross, for financial reasons, was forced to sell the boat to Papa Stavros (Frank Puglia), the Greek owner of the charter fishing boat of which Ross is the Captain. Stavros is a straight-dealing, kindly man and allows Ross to continue to live on the boat until he has saved enough money to buy it. One day Stavros and his wife come to see Ross with the sad news that because of Mama's failing health, they have to move to Arizona which means that he is forced to sell everything to raise money, including Ross's beloved 'West Wind'. Ross, depressed by the prospect of losing the boat, goes to his girlfriend, Robin Gatner's (Stella Stevens) club, where she is a singer. He has been less than attentive of late and she accuses him of only going to see her when he wants a shoulder to cry on or to sing a little. A drunk at the club insists someone sing and Ross volunteers. The troublemaker becomes truculent and tells Ross he stinks as a singer; whilst escorting him out of the club, Ross meets the girl who came with the drunk, Laurel Dodge (Laurel Goodwin), and she tells him she admires him and his singing. He escorts her to her hotel and invites her to lunch the next day. Turning up late he sees her in conversation with a man and storms off in a fury, only to be embarrassed when he discovers the man was her father. The next day they go sailing together and he confides his dream of somehow raising the money to buy back the 'West Wind'. They are falling in love, but Ross does not want to be tied down and Laurel has been hurt so many times she does not want to take the risk of making another mistake.

Ross is dismayed to find that Papa Stavros has sold the boat to a broker, Wesley Johnson (Jeremy Slate), who is about to offer it to the highest bidder. Faced with the necessity of making a living as he no longer has a boat to work on, Ross approaches Sam (Robert Strauss), owner of the Pirate's Den, to ask if he can take up his offer of singing there. Sam agrees readily, but Robin, suspecting Ross is trying to take her job away, is furious as Ross's popularity means she is no longer the star attraction. Wesley Johnson is asking $10,000 for the 'West Wind' for which he only gave Stavros $6,000. Ross asks Wesley whether he can go to work for him, fishing for tuna on a percentage rather than a wage, and thus pay him gradually to get the boat back. After much wrangling – Johnson is a sharp dealer – they agree on 5%, but the first trip is a disaster: their catch is small and the net is ripped. Second time out there is a large catch but on a sliding scale differential Johnson only pays Ross seventy-one dollars instead of the hundred and three he had counted on. Ross hits him and a big fight ensues, until Ross notices the 'for sale' sign has gone from the 'West Wind'.

Johnson refuses to tell him who has bought it. In fact, Laurel had got the money from her rich father and had paid with a cheque swearing the broker to secrecy. When she admits to Ross that she had bought the boat for him he walks out on her, outraged that she had tried to 'buy' him. Laurel swallows her pride by going to the Captain's Cabin where Robin is singing and finally elicits the information that when Ross gets mad he goes to stay with his Chinese friends, the Yungs, at Paradise cove, now that the Strauss's have moved away. Robin says she's being far too polite to Laurel, which must mean she's over the guy. With this new understanding the girls bury the hatchet – and not in each other.

Laurel goes to Johnson and

persuades him to take her in the 'West Wind' to Paradise Cove – she just has to see Ross. As she has, indeed, bought the boat and, anyway, he finds her attractive, Johnson agrees to take her to the Cove, but on the trip starts to get fresh. Ross's friend, Chen (Guy Lee), Number One Son of the Yungs (Benson Fong and Beulah Quo), watches through his binoculars and is concerned for Laurel: he phones Ross, who alerts Kin Yung. Together they race along the pier, leap on a speed boat and catch up with the 'West Wind' in the nick of time. Ross jumps on board, knocks Johnson over and gets Laurel into the boat with Kin. He then overpowers Johnson and tells him he's going to buy the boat back from Laurel. Johnson has no alternative but to agree and on the way to a huge celebratory party at Paradise Cove, Ross admits to Laurel that once he thought the only thing that mattered to him was the 'West Wind'. Now he realizes that Laurel is nore important than anything else and proposes that they should build a new boat – together. She asks 'Is that a proposal or a proposition?' His answer is 'either you marry me or live with me in sin.'

Two little Chinese twins, far too knowledgeable for their age, Mai Ling and Tai Ling (Ginny and Elisabeth Tiu), who have been eavesdropping under the balcony as usual, cackle knowingly and drag Ross onto the dance floor, handing him a guitar.

The title, once again, says it all. From this film on right up to the last three fictional movies this was to be the pattern. So long as there could be a plethora of lovelies of as many colours and varieties, Elvis had to be surrounded by them, with a sprinkling of four-legged dogs and other animals to sing to, by way of a change. This time a boat is officially his first love, for which he will sacrifice the affections of even such glamorous cabaret leading ladies as Stella Stevens or such wholesome young

heiresses as Laurel Goodwin. In the end, does the boat get the man? You bet it doesn't. The astonishing factor in this set-up is the fact the actors do, in the most cases, emerge as human beings, rather than just girl-ballast. Thanks to Norman Taurog (*qv*), so adroit at handling Presley, Ross is a character in whom the audience can believe enough to care what becomes of him, no matter with what absurdities he is involved. Leaving aside sex appeal for a moment, there is enough human magnetism in Elvis to have carried him through so many nonsense films that would have swamped a lesser personality. To have had to stop in mid-plot so often to embark on so many frankly piffling ditties and come up smiling for more, proves how much of an instinctive actor he, in fact, was. Writers Anhalt and Weiss have come up with some individual scenes that are funny enough or original enough to help gloss over the cracks in the storyline.

In one scene Laurel Goodwin is working in a hat shop, coping with the usual grotesque and unattractive middle-aged women who proliferate in Hollywood films of that period. One of them is Mary Treen, who contributes so many vignettes in Elvis's movies that one must conclude she was a favourite character lady of Norman Taurog's. There's a hideous bucket-shaped hat that Mary Treen snatches from another customer and when she puts it on there's just her chin showing. 'I'll take this one' she says 'it has so much more élan than the others'. Then there's the scene where Elvis, painting a boat, predicts rain to his host, Kin Yung (Benson Fong). 'We find out' he says and calls 'Kapu! Kapu!' His cream-coloured cat comes running up to the boat. 'He tells weather' says Kin. 'White spots in eyes if rain. No spots, no rain.' Elvis is a disbeliever: 'Better stow away this gear if you don't want it to get wet,' he says. Kapu arches his back and spits at Elvis. 'Very dangerous animal when contradicted,' says Kin.

This, then, is a fun film. No. 6 on Variety's list of top-grossers. Total Gross: 2.7 million. So the Colonel (*qv*) continued on his merry, money-making way.

(See also: Animals; Parker, Colonel Tom; Taurog, Norman)

GIRLS! GIRLS! GIRLS!
(RCA LPM 2621) November 1962 (Original Soundtrack Recording – apart from 'Dainty Little Moonbeams')

GIRLS! GIRLS! GIRLS! *
Written by Jerry Lieber, Mike Stoller. Fisherman Ross Carpenter, seated on the prow of a motorboat, sings while the title credits roll; girls of all kinds, in bikinis, tight sweaters etc., are what he – a real man – can't get off his mind. The Jordanaires seem to be of the same mind judging from their spirited vocal background encouragement on this Lieber/Stoller number – unfortunately the only one on the album and crafted as a lively starter with saxes, guitar, drums and piano at full throttle.
LP: 'Elvis in Hollywood'

The next song in the movie but not on the LP, is Stella Steven's moody 'Never Let Me Go' in the Pirate's Den nightclub where she, as Robin Gatner, Ross's girlfriend, sings. He goes there for consolation on learning that Pappa Stavros has to sell the charter boat of which Ross is Captain, along with all his other boats. (Not on the disc).

I DON'T WANT TO BE TIED * *
Written by Bill Giant, Bernie Baum, Florence Kaye. In the Pirate's Den Ross, at the request of the management, steps in for Robin to sing an expressive rocker, whose words are directed at her; he wants to be satisfied – but fancy free. He's seen couples wed, but their love doesn't last. Elvis twists as he sings in front of the club's combo comprising piano, bass guitar, drums and clarinet.

WHERE DO YOU COME FROM \
(not included in movie)
Written by Ruth Batchelor, Bob Roberts.
Single B/W: 'Return to Sender'
LPs: 'Elvis: Worldwide Gold Award Hits – Vol. 1'

I DON'T WANT TO
2(not included in movie)
Written by Janice Torre, Fred Spielman.

WE'LL BE TOGETHER * * *
Written by Charles O'Curran, Dudley Brooks.
Ross sings this sentimental love song to Mama Stavros as she celebrates her Golden Wedding anniversary to Papa Stavros – since the death of his father they have been family to him. The film's brilliant choreographer, Charles O'Curran, penned this, which celebrates love that lasts for ever. The family and party guests join in, some with guitars, while someone plays piano. Vocals by the Amigos.
LPs: 'Burning Love'; 'Hits From His Movies – Vol. 2'

A BOY LIKE ME, A GIRL LIKE YOU * *
Written by Sid Tepper, Roy C. Bennett.
Ross takes Laurel Dodge sailing and declares his love for her, with The Jordanaires helping out in the vocals while guitar, drums, piano etc., waft up from the ocean. Pretty, but predictable.

EARTH BOY * *
Written by Sid Tepper, Roy C. Bennett.
Ross's second date with Laurel takes place in Paradise Cove as dinner guests of the Kung family. The inquisitive little twins from next door laugh at Ross singing Chinese lyrics to a lute and join in to show him how it should be done. They duet in Chinese and English: very ping-ping, with kettle drum, guitars and lutes.

The next song in the movie is Stella Steven's 'The Nearness of You'
(not on disc)

RETURN TO SENDER * * * * *
Written by Chris Blackwell, Winfield Scott.
Ross sings and swings in the Pirate's Den club, again with their combo, with witty lyrics about what happened when he mailed his letter – which came back the very next day with the title-legend and Address Unknown. The excellent quality of the accompaniment – the usual crew of Scotty Moore (also known as Winfield Scott, one of the writers of the song), D.J. Fontana, Boots Randolph and The Jordanaires were augmented by Los Angeles session stars, including guitarist Barney Kessel and drummer Hal Blaine – and Elvis's energetic twisting to the rhythm, returned Elvis to the No. 1 position in the British charts and 2 in the USA for the first time in years.
Single B/W: 'Where Do You Come From'
LPs: 'Elvis, Elvis, Worldwide Gold Award Hits – Vol. 1'; 'Return of the Rocker'; 'The Top Ten Hits'

BECAUSE OF LOVE * * * *
Written by Ruth Batchelor, Bob Roberts.
Elvis sings of the extra strength being in love gives him and how he'll never let it get away. Elvis in good voice in a romantic mood with backing by The Jordanaires.

THANKS TO THE ROLLING SEA * * *
Written by Ruth Batchelor, Bob Roberts.
Ross and the other fishermen celebrate in song a great catch of tuna. Taken in context a fine sea shanty played to the engine beat of the boat, with one guitarist apparently on deck and a very basso profundo vocal.

SONG OF THE SHRIMP *
Written Sid Tepper, Roy C. Bennett.
Ross serenades his shrimp catch, with lyrics about the shrimp's happy song as it goes into the net. Muted guitars, as befits the most ludicrous number on an LP mainly distinguished by 'Return To Sender'.

THE WALLS HAVE EARS * * *
Written by Sid Tepper, Roy C. Bennett.
Laurel invites Ross to dinner and the roast is burnt to a frazzel in an exploding oven so he does the cooking. A row starts next door among the neighbours: Ross bangs on the wall and soon a rumpus breaks out – pots and pans being hurled and even the floor begins to vibrate violently. He comments that the walls have arms and legs as well as ears and goes into a tango cum flamenco with Laurel. Funny lyrics are descriptive of the occasion: every time you throw things about you cannot hide the noise so it's best to settle for a kiss. The full orchestral score is punctuated by bangs and crashes leading to a crescendo when the ceiling falls down. Elvis took the flamenco beat so enthusiastically that he took extra lessons from choreographer Charles O'Curran.

WE'RE COMING IN LOADED * * * *
Written by Otis Blackwell, Winfield Scott.
Another sea shanty from the surprising team of Scotty Moore and Otis Blackwell – such a contrast to their other contribution to the LP. Elvis with macho chorus again, drumbeats, guitars, this time to a rocking beat.

Stella Stevens sings her final song in the movie 'Love Me' after some sharp remarks to Laurel Goodwin, she comes to terms with the fact that she'll never get Ross and tells Laurel where he's to be found.

Elvis's song to the girl twins Ginny and Elizabeth Tiu, 'Dainty Little Moonbeams' – not recorded – leads into a reprise of the title song spectacularly choreographed by Charles O'Curran where Elvis accompanies, with appropriate movements, the scantily dressed girls from Tahiti, Samoa, Brazil, Manila and the US, all dancing up a storm.

Elvis as Rusty Wells, touring with his band, is subjected to a surprise party.
Girl Happy (1965)

GIRLS, GIRLS, GIRLS

Not the movie

A breakdown, in running order, of some of Elvis's favourite girlfriends:

DIXIE LOCKE

By his own admission, Elvis's first steady date was local girl Dixie Locke at highschool and beyond. After meeting at a roller rink in 1953, they went steady for two years. Their relationship and its breakdown are covered in *Elvis: The Movie* (qv), from her qualified enthusiasm over his early success, through her complaints that she was seeing so little of him because he was spending so much time on the road with his band, to Elvis's mother breaking the news that Dixie was engaged to marry someone else. After their initial closeness when they went to football games together and he attended her prom in 1954, they remained friends and she was active in his first fan club. In an interview towards the end of his army days, he still speaks nostalgically of her as 'The girl I can't forget' while he puts on a record of 'Smoke Gets In Your Eyes' and describes her as having long dark hair to her shoulders and the biggest smile he'd ever seen. For a while he and Dixie were in the same class; he gave her his school ring and saved up his money to buy a beat up old Lincoln so he could drive her home. They played tennis, rode and swam together. After his first hit with 'Good Rockin' Tonight' success set in and soon after Dixie offered him back his school ring. She sounds physically remarkably like Priscilla Beaulieu (qv), whom he was to meet in November of that year, 1959, when she was fourteen: he was immediately smitten and so, it seems, was she. From then on she was his main female preoccupation.

DEBRA PAGET

Although Elvis tried all of his charm on his *Love Me Tender* (qv) co-star, she remained coolly dispassionate, although always friendly and polite. He was apt at that time, when interviewed about romantic attachments to sigh and mention Debra with affection: in fact, he could not quite understand her reluctance to fall into his arms. Years later, she explained and did not pull her punches. 'I didn't date him at all, to be truthful. He wasn't really my cup of tea. Too much backwoods, if you know what I mean. Besides, at that time I wasn't dating anyone: mother was chaperoning me wherever I went.' That included parties, at which Elvis was present, but they were thrown by the studio, for reasons not entirely unconnected with publicity.

NATALIE WOOD

Natalie Wood, later to marry, divorce and remarry Robert Wagner, and to whom she was still married at the time of her tragic death, emphasized that, while she and Elvis had great times together, they were with her mother's permission, after she had talked to Gladys Presley (qv) and been assured that she would look after Natalie. When the press made a big thing of their dating, Natalie hurried back from Memphis to Hollywood.

ANITA WOOD

Anita Wood, talented, blonde and beautiful Memphis DJ and host of the TV show *Top Ten Dance Party*, was introduced to Elvis by Cliff Gleaves and, soon after their first date, he took her home to Graceland to meet his parents. Their attachment was so strong that it was widely thought by family and friends that they would get married. The idea was firmly knocked on the head by Colonel Parker (qv), Elvis met Priscilla and Anita went back to concentrate on her career, later cutting several discs. She eventually married former Cleveland Browns star, Johnny Brewer. She won substantial damages in the late Seventies against a newspaper that stated she had continued to see Elvis after her marriage.

MARGRIT BUERGIN

The press had a field day linking him to 17 year-old Margrit Buergin, from Frankfurt who seems to have been the favourite of his German girlfriends. Elvis spoke of her as 'cute, warm and friendly!' He compared her as 'in some way like Judy Tyler', of whom he was fond, while they were making *Jailhouse Rock* (qv), but who died tragically young, soon after completing the film. But by the time he left Bad Neuheim he had parted from Margrit, seemingly with mutual affection and, unlike some of his ex-Hollywood female associates, she was not known to badmouth him when he was not in a position to hit back.

JULIET PROWSE

Elvis's co-star in *G.I. Blues* (qv), Juliet Prowse, lithe and leggy and something of a cross between Leslie Caron and Cyd Charisse was 23, when they met. She was born in Bombay in 1936, raised in South Africa and started her career as a dancer in London, where she found stardom in *Can Can*. She was such a success she was called to Hollywood and repeated her role in the film opposite Frank Sinatra, who said she was 'the sexiest dancer' he had ever seen. They became engaged, but when she appeared in *G.I. Blues* she and Elvis became part of a starry triangle with Sinatra – a source of endless interest for the world's press gossip writers with constant speculation as to whom she favoured at any one time. The publicity department were not averse to fuelling the flames of conjecture, especially when she broke off her engagement to Sinatra, of whom she said, 'he was a lovely, sweet man, but after a few drinks he could be very difficult'. Rumours of an engagement to Elvis proved unfounded and they went their separate ways. She alternated between films and stage when the days of the big Hollywood musicals ended. She was married and divorced twice, carried on dancing until she became ill with a pancreatic tumour in 1994. She had appeared to be besting the illness, but had a relapse and died in Los Angeles on September 14, 1996.

NANCY SINATRA

Elvis and Nancy Sinatra duetted together in *Speedway* (*qv*), in which she played a tax inspector (!), and in 1968 shared a liaison which again was one of the rare cases in which a genuine, long-lasting friendship developed. When Nancy was in Las Vegas visiting her father she would also go to see Elvis backstage and was one of the few people with whom he was always able to gossip freely.

LINDA THOMPSON

After Priscilla told Elvis she was leaving him to live with Mike Stone, her karate instructor, with whom she had been having an affair for three and a half years, Elvis went into a baffled decline. It was he who had suggested she attend karate classes to alleviate the boredom and loneliness she suffered when deprived of his company while he was constantly on the road. He would not allow her to stay with him or travel with him. She announced her intention of leaving late in 1971 and he met Linda Thompson, former beauty queen, in July 1972 at a midnight movie marathon in the Memphian Theatre, which Elvis had taken over for entertaining his friends as he often did. They were introduced by mutual friend George Klein and Linda's beauty bowled Elvis over. It was, perhaps, inevitable that she would be the one to fill his lonely life and she moved into Graceland, where she was to stay with him for almost five years. She was everything to him, and even, unlike any of his other girlfriends or even Priscilla herself, toured with him and stayed in Las Vegas. He saw to her financial need lavishly, showering her with clothes and jewels, but even she could do nothing to affect his massive dependence on drugs, which were making him impossible to live with. She could stand it no longer

and moved out in 1976. She was accused of taking advantage of him and even of robbing him, but David Stanley (*qv*) has come out firmly in her support: he believes they shared a mutual love.

GINGER ALDEN

She, like Linda, had been a local beauty queen and was the last to stay in Graceland with Elvis, at a time when Lisa Marie was enjoying her longest visit since she moved out with her mother in 1972. Lisa Marie was 9 and had been paying visits to her father on a fairly frequent basis. Ginger stated that Elvis had proposed marriage to her early in 1977 and he certainly presented her with cars and jewellery, in his usual generous way. She was with Elvis on the night he died and was the last person to see him alive.

BARBRA STREISAND

After Elvis's death young ladies were not slow in coming forward with claims of affairs of varying intensity and duration: starlets in particular proliferated with stories of nights of passion which could never be substantiated. One lady who had no need to cash in on a claim of intimacy with the King was Barbra Streisand, almost as much a legend in her own time as Presley. It was never denied that they had met when she was playing the International Hotel while he was preparing to make his Las Vegas comeback in the summer of 1969. David Stanley says Elvis took him to see her show when he was fourteen and not at all keen, being a committed Led Zeppelin fan. As it turned out David was deeply impressed and refers to her as 'wonderful' on her closing night at the International, when he was one of a party of Elvis family and friends.

Another biographer, James Spada, goes much further in *Streisand: Her Life*, saying that they became lovers after Elvis visited her dressing-room backstage one night. Spada's informant was Barbra's ex-lover Jon Peters, who describes a bizarre

scene: apparently Elvis went in, said 'Hi' and broke an awkward silence by crossing to her dressing-table, picking up a bottle of red nail polish and dropping to one knee beside her. He then began to apply the polish to her nails: when the job was completed she appeared stunned and murmured 'Thank you.'

A Presley associate told the author that Elvis had told him he spent the night with Streisand in her suite, but not how long the involvement lasted. He guessed it was a brief fling.
(See also: Presley, Priscilla Beaulieu; Elvis: The Movie; G.I. Blues; The King is Dead – Vivat Rex; Love Me Tender; Parker, Colonel Tom; Presley, Gladys Love Smith; Speedway)

GRACELAND

In 1985 Steve Pinder directed a film with the title of *Elvis's Home*, after it had been opened to the public as a museum-cum-shrine, largely due to the industry and determination of Priscilla Presley (*qv*), who had surprised some and angered others by demonstrating that she was far from being 'just a pretty face'. She was and is that, of course, her hair transferred to titian from the jet black of Elvis's day, with a remarkable resemblance to one of Clark Gable's best-loved girlfriends, MGM contractee Virginia Grey – never a star, but always in demand when a glamorous supporting player was needed.

Naturally, Priscilla Beaulieu Presley is the hostess for this fascinating tour round Graceland and she conducts it with natural grace and charm, taking us all around the rooms that have been restored as far as possible to their original condition. Thanks to the camerawork of Lazlo Kovals ASC, the house comes across as positively palatial and glowing with vibrant colour – not to everyone's taste, obviously, but certainly to that of the King of rock 'n' roll. Nor, in reality, is it as large as it appears without all the

Studio still for *Flaming Star*

With Yvonne Craig
in *Kissin' Cousins*

'Little Egypt'
sequence from
Roustabout. Wylda
Taylor is seated in
front of Elvis (below)

Soldier Boy – *GI Blues*
(left)

With Shelley Fabares in *Girl Happy* **(above)**   **'Do The Clam' from** *Girl Happy* **(below)**

RECORD MIRROR, Week ending April 10, 1965

EL'S 'DO THE CLAM' GIRL

by LANGLEY JOHNSON

ON the grounds that we're obviously in for seeing and hearing a lot of Shelley Fabares in the next month or so, it seemed a good idea to link up with her breathless Californian tones via the trans-Atlantic telephone. before reporting those conversational gambits, let's fill in the facts on Shelley.

She is, of course, the girl you see on television every time we're shown an excerpt of Elvis Presley's "Girl Happy" movie. You see her rolling in a sand-dune, with bongo drum accompaniment, as El sings "Do The Clam."

Shelley started in the business at 5, appeared with **Frank Sinatra**, has starred with **Rock Hudson** . . . but regards "Girl Happy" as being extra-important to her. And she clearly liked working with Elvis.

NERVOUS

Said Shelley: "I was a little nervous when I first saw him. But then I'm the sort of person who gets frightened if I go to a party and see a star! Anyway, when you actually SEE Elvis in the flesh . . . there's just something unreal about him. How can I say it — he just LOOKS like Elvis Presley. There's nobody else in the world looks like this guy.

additions and outhouses which were added as time went by. As Priscilla proceeds with her tour, following the opening shots of the Presley family memorial stones and the mourners at the annual candlelit ceremony that is a yearly event on the anniversary of his death on August 16, 1977, she recounts some of the details of his life, aided by interviews with key figures, notably Marion Keisker, the first ever to detect unusual potential in the young singer and her boss, Sun Studios manager Sam Phillips, an imposing figure if there ever was one. Which is more than can be said about Colonel Tom Parker (*qv*), glimpsed, cigar in mouth, but not interviewed. Priscilla refers to him as 'Colonel', much as a convent girl, which of course she was, would refer to her mother superior as 'Mother', with a certain amount of natural awe.

Made with the blessing of the Presley estate, and of the Colonel himself – this is an Elvis Presley Enterprise Production – of which Priscilla is effectively the controller. It is inevitably a hagiography, but nonetheless one for the fans to treasure and revere. No shadow of darkness ever crosses the narration or the lovely face of the hostess. She speaks affectionately of 'parties' and his friends – 'often ten would sit down to dinner', with no hint of the blight those very parties and friends cast on her life with the man she undoubtedly loved. Some of his ways of 'letting off steam' are enumerated: the private planes, every conceivable form of motorized vehicle; the Memphis Movie Theatre which he used to hire for his friends overnight. Here Priscilla lets drop that he adored any film with Peter Sellers in it.

The film is a touching tribute and ends with a candlelight procession and a young girl crossing herself and genuflecting by the tombstone. The sobbing quality of the song tribute 'Old Friend' by Bill Medley which opens and closes the film will not be to everyone's taste but there can be no doubting its

sincerity. Priscilla Presley and the staff of the Graceland management have certainly done a great job of perpetuating the heroic legend of 'The World's Greatest Entertainer'.
(See also: Parker, Colonel Tom; Presley, Priscilla Beaulieu)

GREAT LOVERS

Ironically, although the Colonel (*qv*) made damn certain that there was never a Presley film in which he didn't sing, he was the originator of many rumours that 'Elvis is going to throw away his guitar'. This statement, made hand on heart in October 1958, generated interest, indignation and scepticism in roughly equal measures. *King Creole* (*qv*), Elvis's last film before his induction into the army, had been well received by the critics and there was an important gap to fill while he was away from the screen. So Colonel Parker evidently judged the time was right to help fill it.

After the pronouncement about the guitar, the Colonel went on, 'Since his film *King Creole* came out – and the British Press raved about his performance in that – we have had to realize that Elvis is really a straight actor. Indeed, I can see him after his return taking his place with the great lovers of stage and screen.... John Barrymore, Rudolph Valentino, John Gilbert, Ramon Novarro.' He paused and became somewhat misty eyed before he added 'I shall wait for him'.

As well he might: by that time Elvis had sold something like 25 million records alone, from which Tom Parker got his share. There were also a couple of years of Presley records 'waxed' to ensure that during his absence in Germany his teenage fans would not go wanting. Never had an army call-up been so brilliantly orchestrated: no facet of the event and its aftermath went unrecorded by the world's press and Elvis played his part with exemplary tact and good taste. With the eyes of the media upon him night and day, he never put a foot wrong. By the time he returned to

civilian life the canonization process was well under way.

Teddy Johnson who, with his wife Pearl Carr, was one of Britain's best-loved recording stars (at the time of writing they are still working and a couple of years back did a nation-wide tour with their own stage show) and had his own column in the music paper *Disc*, echoed the Great Lover thesis and, like the generous man he is, seemed ready to welcome Presley as a straight actor. He also put forward the suggestion that Elvis would be valuable as a disc jockey – those were the days when the possibility of a Presley visit to England could not be far away – with a tremendous pull with teenagers of all nationalities in helping to put across 'the American way of life'. In both cases, it was not to be. Teddy summed up accurately: 'One thing is certain – we are not going to be allowed to forget that Elvis exists.'

Predictably, the loyal admirers of the stars of the past were incensed at the comparisons. Valentino still had an active Fan Club who were outraged that the star, whose early death in 1926 at the age of 31 had brought on a wave of mass hysteria among female fans, should in any way be compared with Elvis. Indeed his image was far removed from that of the clean living all-American boy from Memphis. Nonetheless Elvis's National Service record won over millions of the older generation who had been upset by his music and gyrations, toned down though they were for the screen.

Valentino had, in fact, after a period as a 'taxi dancer' – a euphemism for 'gigolo' – in New York, achieved some success as the partner of Bonnie Glass, a popular dancer of the period, whom he 'inherited' from Clifton Webb (later to become famous in movies as the acerbic 'Mr Belvedere'). Rudy was later sent to a detention centre on charges of petty theft and blackmail, but was released through the influence of exotic film star Nazimova, who was later to star with him in her production of *Camille*, by which time he had become the hottest property on the screen after *The Four Horsemen of the Apocalypse* in 1921. Women fainted in the aisles over his allure: men were not so keen, finding his acting ludicrous, his manner foppish and his screen persona effeminate. He was blasted in *The Chicago Tribune* in an editorial headlined 'Pink Powder Puff' and called 'That Painted Pansy'. This did not prevent Elvis in his 1965 musical *Harum Scarum* (*qv*) giving a stab at playing a Valentino type sheikh in a film within the film. He was very funny, but in no way 'A Pink Powder Puff'.

As for John Barrymore, whose profile Presley's was said to resemble along with that darling of the gods, Adonis, this was stretching the imagination more than somewhat, as the great actor had a perfect, though aquiline, profile while Elvis's, albeit handsome, was more fleshy. There were similarities, though, mainly towards the end of the careers of both actors. Barrymore, youngest member of the family dubbed 'The Royal Family of Broadway' – Grande Dame Ethel and curmudgeonly character actor Lionel were the other two – was born in 1882 and died in 1942. In his long career he had been acclaimed as one of the greats of the theatre, mainly through his inspired interpretation of Shakespeare's *Richard III* in 1920 and *Hamlet* two years later. He entered films in 1913 and became known as the Great Lover even in silent films, through his imposing presence and 'that Profile'. Perhaps his greatest movie success was in the 1920 version of *Dr Jeckyll and Mr Hyde* in which he achieved the metamorphosis from saintly Jeckyll to evil Hyde without the sensational make-up employed by later interpreters of the role, notably Fredric March in the early Thirties.

His early talkies presented him at full throttle as an actor, with his magnificent speaking voice, while he was still able to fulfil his reputation as a Great Lover – a role he relished in real life through turbulent marriages and countless well-publicized love affairs. But then the heavy drinking habit he had accquired in his teens began to ravage his once beautiful features. After being leading man to Garbo in *Grand Hotel* and Katharine Hepburn in *A Bill of Divorcement,* both 1932, by the time he was cast as Mercutio in 1934 with Norma Shearer and Leslie Howard he could no longer remember his lines, nor even, at times, read the cue cards strategically placed all over the set. He went on acting until 1941, but was a parody of himself in the great days – which was something Elvis was spared in his fourteen year film career. In his last romantic movie, *Change of Habit* (1969) (*qv*), Elvis was at thirty-four as handsome and photogenic as ever – nor was any appreciable weight problem apparent. He remained a picture of health and as professional as ever despite the deterioration in the quality of his films – the Colonel had adopted a 'quantity before quality' policy which had long depressed Presley, when he looked back on all those early ambitions to prove himself as an actor. He had indeed done just that, by continuing to appear as fresh and keen as ever, but he was too intelligent not to notice the decline in box office takings as one bland musical followed another. When the time came to return to the stage with concert and night club work his popularity peaked again and the progress was charted in two well-received documentaries, *Elvis – That's the Way It Is* (1970) and *Elvis on Tour* two years later. Elvis was only too happy to turn his back on a Hollywood that had helped make and then almost break him, at least as far as his spirit was concerned. *(See also: Change of Habit; Elvis – That's the Way It Is; Elvis on Tour; Harum Scarum)*

HARUM SCARUM (HAREM HOLIDAY in Britain) * *

Released by: Metro-Goldwyn-Mayer, a Four Leaf Production (Metrocolour); **Producer:** Sam Katzman; **Director:** Gene Nelson; **Screenplay:** Gerald Drayson Adams; **Art Directors:** George W. Davis and H. McClure Capps; **Director of Photography:** Fred H. Jackson; **Technical Advisor:** Colonel Tom Parker; **Music:** supervised and conducted by Fred Karger, vocal background by The Jordanaires; **Running Time:** 84 mins; **Opened:** November 24, 1965.

Cast: Elvis, Mary Ann Mobley, Fran Jeffries, Michael Ansara, Jay Novello, Philip Reed, Theo Marcuse, Billy Barty, Dirk Harvey, Jack Constanzo, Larry Chance, Barbara Werle, Brenda Benet, Gail Gilmore, Wilda Taylor, Red West, Vicki Malkin, Rick Rydon, Richard Reeves, Joey Russo.

While on a goodwill tour of the Middle East with his film *Sands of the Desert*, film star Johnny Tyrone (Elvis) in his sheikh outfit impresses the first night audience with his skills as a swordsman and, even more, as a karate expert, who

Film star Johnny Tyrone (Elvis) tackles a tiger with his bare hands in his film *Sands Of The Desert*, premiering during a goodwill tour of the Middle East. Sheikh Johnny soon despatches the animal. *Harum Scarum (Harem Holiday* in Britain) (1965)

paralyses a fearsome tiger with a single karate chop. On being presented by the Ambassador to Prince Dragna (Michael Anzara) and his partner Aishah (Fran Jeffries), Johnny is invited to be the first American ever to be the guest of the Prince's brother, King Toranshah (Philip Reed) of Lunakhan – an offer he can hardly refuse. The plane is waiting for him next morning to fly him over the Mountains of the Moon. Passing through the desert, they touch down and set up camp and Johnny finds himself being entertained by Aishah after the Prince has retired. She lets her hair down, offers him a glass of wine and that is the last thing he remembers. He is kidnapped by the King's deadly enemies, the Assassins, and awakens to find himself surrounded by beautiful young houris in the Palace of the Garden of Paradise. The dream is rudely interrupted when Johnny is dragged off to be confronted by Sinan, Lord of the Assassins (Theo Marcuse), who turns out to be the master of Aishah, who arranged the kidnapping. Both apologize for the unceremonious way in which Johnny has been abducted, and Sinan explains that the star's deadly karate skills are required for him to execute a very important person. Johnny angers Sinan by not only refusing to help, but making fun of him as well. Johnny is again dragged off, this time to be whipped, after which the houris are again on hand to tend his wounds. At the same time the leader of the Honourable Guild of Market Place Thieves, Zacha (Jay Novello), who tries to pick his pocket, turns out not only to be working for Sinan, but also more than willing to double-cross him and help Johnny to escape in return for ten thousand American dollars. They hide in a pool of water lilies until Johnny can overpower the guard, when they climb a tree and jump over the palace wall, arranging to meet later. Johnny thinks he has escaped to freedom, but finds himself in the pool of the quarters of Princess Shalimar (Mary Ann Mobley).

She pretends to be a slave girl and agrees to find him horses to assist his get-away. They meet up again with Zacha at the Pool of Omar where they quote 'Omar Khayyam' to each other before sharing an embrace. When he tells her the reason for his being kidnapped – 'They want me to assassinate a very important man' – she runs away from him, taking the three Arabian horses she had brought with her. She hurries into the palace to warn her father, the King, of the danger he is in and finds him playing chess with his brother, Prince Dragna.

Zacha comes up with another plan for Johnny's escape, via the musicians who are due to entertain to celebrate the end of the Fast of Ramadan, but in the meantime he is recaptured and Aishah tells him he must agree to kill the King, or his friends, the jugglers and clowns who risked their lives in helping him to get away, will be killed. The assassination is due to take place at the palace while the entertainment has diverted attention from the royal security. Johnny pretends to go along with the plot and sits out of the way, heavily cloaked and hooded. As he advances towards the King, the Princess recognizes him. He is arrested and locked up with his friends the jugglers and clowns in a dungeon underneath the palace. Once again he is helped to escape by the loyalty of his friends, in particular the pickpocket dwarf, Baba (Billy Barty), who creates a great diversion by evading his pursuers and eventually gets into the prison with a rope by which they all climb to safety. Johnny manages to find Shalimar's room, where she is with her father, confessing her love for the man she cannot believe had willingly plotted to kill him. Aided by Baba, Johnny lets himself down into the royal presence on the rope and persuades King Toranshah of his good intentions. Supported by Shalimar, they enter into a plan to unmask the real villain, Prince Dragna. When the King's quarters are searched they find his bed bloodied and slashed with knives,

putting the blame for his murder on Johnny. On hearing this the King of the Assassins takes action to usurp the throne, which Dragna has already taken over. In effect he will continue to be called king but as a puppet ruler under the dominance of Sinan, with Aishah at his side. With the help of Zacha, Johnny creates yet another diversion: in the ensuing chaos he overpowers Sinan, gags him just after he has given orders for the assassination of all the court clowns and jesters with their nimble girl helpers. The ever-resourceful Zacha comes up with a plan to find willing helpers with old scores to settle against the Assassins. Sinan dies from a well-aimed arrow in the chest. The King interrupts his plotting brother in the middle of a game of chess with Aishah, challenges him to a duel which he wins and banishes him from his kingdom, with his favourite chess player, Aishah, for consolation. He then gives his blessing to the Princess and Johnny during the spectacular finale at the Galaxy Hotel, Las Vegas, where he is starring, surrounded by colourfully clad Harem Holiday beauties.

Sam Katzman's (*qv*) second cheap but cheerful quickie, directed, like the first, *Kissin' Cousins* (*qv*), by Gene Nelson, marked a crucial stage in the public's regard for Elvis. The 'summit meeting' between himself and the Beatles was held in the same year, 1965. His fans, as ever, were loyal, apart from mutinous rumblings among the readers of the British fan club magazine, *Elvis Monthly*. His films were still showing profits, his records still selling, but in both cases there was a falling off. His more mature fans dutifully went to see every film and bought every disc, but the Beatles had taken over the affections of the very young – and the teenagers. *Harum Scarum* has family appeal aplenty with enjoyable slapstick elements when Elvis disguises himself as a water lily before emerging from the pool to dispose of the palace guard in expert karate style and when Billy Barty snips off the money purses hanging beneath the stomachs of the fat merchants in the market place. The apparently opulent palace sets of the Shangri-La-like kingdom of Lunakhan, 'protected from the encroachments of so-called Western civilization for a thousand years' are very easy on the eye apart from some strange-coloured mountains and backdrops. The obligatory beauties sport revealing and attractive costumes (though uncredited) and William Tuttle as always lavishly paints myriads of lovely faces while the Sydney Guilaroff hairstyles seem the peak of Hollywood chic. So what more could anyone want? For starters, a less frankly ludicrous storyline. The elements of *Ali Baba and the Forty Thieves* are blended with *Kismet* (cue for song), *Aladdin* and any Maria Montez–Sabu–Jon Hall fantasy you care to mention.

Give Katzman his due; the effects of penny-pinching are not visible to the non-professional eye and the musical numbers are panto-style entertaining, thanks to the pretty dancers and the choreographical skills of Earl Barton and director Gene Nelson, himself no slouch in the terpsichorean field. The opening scene, with tuxedoed film star Johnny, moving stiffly and gravely among the heads of state, princes and ambassadors, pictures Elvis with an expression of quizzical boredom, which could equally be ascribed to subtle acting or a comment on the film itself.

Mary Ann Mobley, reputedly one of the Elvis's favourite leading ladies, portrays the sweetness and simplicity required of her prettily and with grace, but the distaff side of the plot is effortlessly stolen by glamorous villainess Fran Jeffries, who injects welcome bite and depth into her role as Aishah. Philip Reed, an ex-husband of Joan Crawford, plays against his usual menacing type as the saintly and other-worldly king in what appears to be his last film role to date, while Michael Ansara injects the baddie with the requisite suave duplicity.

The climax is predictable with the kindly king retaining his throne, thanks to Elvis and friends, and forgiving his wicked brother though banishing him from the kingdom, with his favourite chess partner, the lovely Fran Jeffries for consolation. Indeed a kindly king, observes Elvis, but 'Do us a favour – don't banish him to the U.S. of A!'
(See also: Elvis and the Beatles; Katzman, Sam; Kissin' Cousins)

HARUM SCARUM
(RCA LPM 1468) October 1965

HAREM HOLIDAY *
Written by Peter Androili, Vince Poncia Jr.
After the MGM Lion's roar, up come the film titles over a blue papier mâché mountain peak, Elvis's voice backed by guitars, drums and saxophones. With background vocals by The Jordanaires, Elvis declares, as so often, that he wants to travel while he's free, with the great big world calling him to kiss all the pretty girls, because he's on a Harem Holiday.

MY DESERT SERENADE * *
Written by Stan Gebler.
No sooner has Sheikh Johnny killed the threatening tiger with one bare hand and untied the maiden tethered to a post as the potential victim, than he kisses her, sweeps her into his arms and launches throatily and emotionally into his Serenade. Those of us with long enough memories are back to 1933 with Sheikh Ramon Novarro singing 'Love Songs of the Nile' to Myrna Loy, among the lotus blossoms in *That Night in Cairo*, (*The Barbarian* in the US) – charming, but one can see why the younger members of the audience were apt to snigger. Drums, guitars and strings well to the fore, with The Jordanaires helping the melody along manfully.

GO EAST, YOUNG MAN * * *
Written by Bill Giant, Bernie Baum, Florence Kaye.

Johnny Tyrone sings a song, 'especially written' for the distinguished gathering at the Premiere. Again, it's an expression of his hedonist philosophy (for Johnny read Elvis), a call to foray into the desert, take love where he can find it, eat, drink and be merry. Dancing girls and desert drums, open tents, all beckon him to be a sheikh in paradise, to the rhythmic beat of guitars, strings and the usual desert accompaniment, with no discernable vocal backing by The Jordanaires.

MIRAGE * * *
Written by Bill Giant, Bernie Baum, Florence Kaye.
When Johnny Tyrone awakens from the drugged drink that enabled him to be transported unaware to the Palace of Lunakhan, a beautiful girl is kissing him. As he opens his eyes he begins to sing, thinking she must be a mirage, a trick of his imagination. As he sings, two other young lovelies drift in to sit adoringly at his feet, followed by two more, one bearing a tray of exotic fruits. As the song ends he closes his eyes and lies back, thinking to return to his dream. The first lovely kisses him again and he starts up, looking around him, saying, 'Hey, you're real!' Another lush, plangent melody, in tune with the mood of the story. It is difficult to fault these songs, as they are so much part of the action, but easy to see why Elvis felt at a disadvantage when answering the Beatles' (*qv*) question as to why he was not making more records in the style which swept him to the top of the Hit Parade (as it was still called). So much smoochy piano, so many twanging guitars, violins and mandolins, all eased along by The Jordanaires vocal backing were perfectly in context but not something to send the fans rushing to the record shops. As ever, Johnny/Elvis is spoiled for choice, telling each girl that his search for love had come true.

KISMET * * *

Written by Sid Tepper, Roy C. Bennet.
After Johnny has been helped to escape from duress and fallen – literally – into the quarters of the Princess Shalimar, she pretends to be a slave girl called Janni and they agree to meet at the Pool of Omar where she brings horses to further aid his escape. Having quoted the 'loaf of bread, jug of wine and thou' at each other – *The Rubaiyat of Omar Khayyam* was required reading for every well-brought up slave girl – they settle by the pool and Johnny launches into 'Kismet'. He thanks Kismet for bringing him his one true love at last. The Jordanaires and orchestral backing are a constant.

SHAKE THAT TAMBOURINE * * *

Written by Bill Giant, Bernie Baum, Florence Kaye.
Johnny, complete with tambourine, executes this fast, up-tempo song and dance number in the market square at the feast to celebrate the end of the fast of Ramadan as part of another ingenious plot, by Zacha, leader of the Market Place Thieves, to help Johnny to escape during the havoc caused by various cute tricks by the nimble dwarf Baba. To divert attention three dancing girls gyrate while Johnny manipulates his tambourine and the band plays along, with plenty of drums, bells and guitars. During the fight which ensues Johnny is active with his karate kicks, while Baba throws stones and a young girl called Sari proves herself an adept with a sling.

HEY, LITTLE GIRL * * * *

Written by Joy Byers.
Sari is as adept a dancer as she is in her aim with a sling: she starts an Eastern-type dance with Johnny as her partner, while he sings, telling her how cute she is and that she should be a movie star. Here is another instance of how effective Elvis is in his numbers with children. At first it seemed a cute gimmick but later, as he complained, it became almost an in-built feature of the plots. It is tempting to read this into a post-Lolita syndrome as a little titillation to the knowledgable in an otherwise bland and seemingly innocent romantic setting, e.g. the glamorous slave girls ('We are entirely at your disposal, Master!'). The little dancer, whom he calls either 'Lola' or 'Little One' according to ones interpretation of Elvis's accent, sits affectionately on his knee till she slides off and tells him that she, too, will be a slave girl, 'and a most accomplished one'. She invites him to watch as she places a drum into the hands of a muscular character who appears to be one of the family and goes into the sensual dance, with embryo bumps and grinds, in which Elvis joins her. Fanciful? Maybe.

GOLDEN COINS * * *

Written by Bill Giant, Bernie Baum, Florence Kaye.
As the Princess sits dreaming of the lover she thinks she will never see again, he comes to her in a vision through the waters of the pool. The vision sings of the wealth and luxury he will bring to her, including wonderful gowns and Persian rugs that will enhance her floor. All he asks in return are the delights of love. The Princess looks understandably misty-eyed before she tickles her pool and the image disappears as her understanding hand-maiden comes to comfort her. The trio of writers in charge of the most romantic songs in the movie go into dream mode with Elvis's ballad conjuring up everything she could wish for from him. Wistful yearning abounds, accompanied by drumbeats, cymbals, strings and mandolins.

SO CLOSE, YET SO FAR (FROM PARADISE) * * *

Written by Joy Byers.
Johnny sings this at the window of his prison cell – more yearning for the Princess, dreaming of the kisses they shared: he wants to see her and sweep her off to Paradise, yet when he reaches out for her she turns out to be just a mirage. Insistent drums swell to a climax with the equally insistent vocal backing of The Jordanaires, just prior to the beginning of another spectacular escape on a rope with Johnny scaling the walls of the palace to gain access to the Princess's quarters, helped by Baba. They both climb down into her bedchamber, where she is talking to her father, King Toranshah, about her love for the American. With Shalimar's help, Johnny is able to persuade him that he means him no harm and tells him of Prince Dragna's plot to assassinate his brother and usurp the throne. Elvis' powerful baritone reaches up to tenor at one point.
LP: 'Mahalo from Elvis' – the only song from the film *Harem Scarum* repeated on another LP.

ANIMAL INSTINCT (Bonus) * * *

Written by Bill Giant, Bernie Baum, Florence Kay.
Recorded for the film but not used. This is a strange one for *Harem Scarum* – very beaty, almost in the tempo of 'Yoga Is As Yoga Does' from *Easy Come, Easy Go*, perhaps designed for the beginning of the film within a film before the Sheikh fells the tiger. Flutes make an intriguing counterpoint and it is surprisingly not included on any other LP.

WISDOM OF THE AGE (Bonus) * *

Written by Bill Giant, Bernie Baum, Florence Kaye.
Recorded for the film but not used. More sandy wisdom of the 'Kismet' variety, possibly omitted on account of being in similar mood to Sid Tepper and Roy C. Bennet's song of the same name. All the songs on the LP are very much in 'The Love Songs of the Nile' mode with the exception of 'Animal Instinct'.

Critics have dismissed the LP as the nadir of Elvis's recording career, and the absence of chart entries indicated that the buying public concurred. Personally, I have always had a sneaking affection for the disc associated with the film, daft story and all. Significantly, this was the last Sam Katzman (*qv*) production, reputedly turned out – LP included – in under three weeks.

HOLLYWOOD: THE TEST

Veteran producer Hal B. Wallis (*qv*) may not have been the first to recognize the film potential in Elvis Presley, but he was well placed to judge the new star's incredible marketability, being both publicity director for Warner for several years as well as a top producer of movies for his own Hal Wallis Productions, released by Paramount. He had a reputation for quality as well as commercial know-how and many of his films won Academy Awards. In 1956, Presley's great breakthrough year, Wallis was about to film *The Rainmaker*, starring Katharine Hepburn and Burt Lancaster, and it was a scene from that film which was chosen for Elvis's screen test. The date was April 1st, a week after the first meeting between Wallis and Presley.

Elvis sang 'Blue Suede Shoes' and did a scene opposite Frank Faylen, the actor whose most famous part was probably that of the sadistic male nurse opposite Ray Milland in *The Lost Weekend* in 1945. Wallis was impressed, saying 'It was quite extraordinary. Presley walked onto the set to do his test with Frank – an actor with many years of experience: I hadn't a clue how he would do: he might have been quite awful. But after a few minutes I knew he was a natural, in the way that Sinatra was. And with just as much personality.' For his part Elvis was full of confidence and so sure that his first film would be *The Rainmaker* that he said in an interview 'It was a dream come true. I have a movie coming out in June with Katharine Hepburn and Burt Lancaster.'

He reckoned without Colonel Parker (*qv*), with whom he had recently signed a long-term management contract, under which Parker would get 25% commission on everything Presley did in public.

When asked if he would perform in the film, Elvis ill-advisedly said he wouldn't care about singing in the movie. He wanted to be a serious actor and had been studying the work of Brando, Dean and Rod Steiger. There was the rub: the Colonel rejected the idea as unsuitable thus starting a dichotomy between Presley's ambitions and what his mentor decreed he would do. From then on he sang in every movie, even when there was no logical reason for him to do so. That the Colonel's judgement was not always infallible became apparent just three weeks after the film test when he booked his protégé into his first Las Vegas gig at the New Frontier Hotel's Venus Room and found the Casino sophisticates were just not ready for Presley. The Colonel cut his four week engagement to two and he did not return to Vegas for thirteen years.

Hal Wallis had nothing ready for Elvis's debut, so he was loaned to Twentieth Century Fox for a black and white western called *The Reno Brothers*, already in production, starring Richard Egan and Debra Paget. Songs were inserted in two scenes where Elvis sings to his family on the front porch and also at a picnic. When one of them, 'Love Me Tender', became a huge success the film's producer, David Weisbart, saw the wisdom of changing the title to incorporate the hit. Weisbart had been responsible for James Dean's *Rebel Without a Cause*, so knew a thing or two about how to appeal to the young. He, like the cast, was pleasantly surprised, not only by Presley's inherent politeness, but also his professional handling of his scenes. Meanwhile Elvis had signed a seven-year deal with Paramount to do three films a year with Hal B. Wallis producing, on a rising scale starting at $100,000 and going up to $200,000 each.

(See also: Parker, Colonel Tom)

9

INSULTS

The BBC's *Burger and the King* programme predictably provoked a rash of letters to the press: a lady who expressed herself particularly succinctly was Trudi Taylor of Edgar Road, Hounslow. Headed 'An Insult to the King' (*Evening Standard* 5/1/96) she wrote 'It is enough of an insult to Elvis Presley fans to show an hour's television last weekend on what he became in later years – a receptacle for fast food, according to his hangers-on. But for Victor Lewis-Smith to devote a whole review to the same topic only makes it worse. Lewis-Smith's column can be quite amusing. It is all right to make fun of egos with little talent who consider themselves important, but to ridicule a man who gave a lot of pleasure to millions through his music, and had a great sense of humour and was never involved in any sort of scandal is despicable.'

Nearly forty years before, another lady was insulted by a diametrically different cause. Anne Lockerstone, of Taranaki, New Zealand, wrote to *Picturegoer*, 3.1.57, 'I am horrified to hear that Elvis Presley is a possible for *The James Dean Story*. What an insult to the memory of a remarkable actor.' The banner headline calling attention to the letter was 'OH, NO! – NOT Presley as Dean', between cut-out heads of both stars. She need not have worried: like countless other Presley film projects, it was not to be.

(See also: Menus; The Films That Got Away – And Some That Didn't)

IT HAPPENED AT THE WORLD'S FAIR * *

Released by: Metro-Goldwyn-Mayer (Metrocolor, Panavision); **Producer:** Ted Richmond; **Director:** Norman Taurog; **Screenplay:** Sim Rose and Seaman Jacobs; **Art Director:** George W. Davis; **Director of photography:** Joseph Ruttenberg; **Technical Advisor:** Colonel Tom Parker; **Music:** Leith Evans; vocal background by The Jordanaires and The Mello Men; **Running Time:** 105 mins; **Opened:** April 10, 1963.

Cast: Elvis, Joan O'Brien, Gary Lockwood, Vicky Tiu, H.M. Wynant, Edith Atwater, Guy Raymond, Dorothy Green, Kam Tong, Yvonne Craig, Red West, Kurt Russell.

Bush pilots Mike Edwards (Elvis) and Danny Burke (Gary Lockwood) are scraping a meagre living by dusting endless potato fields in Washington State. Mike's gambling mania lands them in fights and eats into their small earnings. Their debts far outweigh their income and the local sheriff serves papers attaching their plane, Bessie, leaving them no reason to stay. After a daunting experience when a pretty girl slows down her car, apparently to give them a lift, borrows Danny's gold cigarette lighter and makes off with it, they thumb a ride from

a Chinese farmer (Kam Tong) and his small niece Sue-Lin (Vicky Tiu) who are on their way to the Seattle World's Fair. Since her uncle has business to attend to, Mike finds himself volunteering to take Sue-Lin to the fair, while Danny goes to look for a buddy who might be able to help them out of their financial jam.

Sue-Lin has a full day on the rides and gorges herself to such an extent she gets an upset stomach and Mike takes her to the dispensary. The nurse, Diane Warren (Joan O'Brien), is so pretty that Mike feigns something in his eye to lure her into close proximity. She is not convinced and orders him out of the surgery. Mike finds a small boy who walks into him and offers the child (Kurt Russell) a nice inducement to kick him hard in the shin. After asking him if he is drunk the boy accepts the inducement and gives him a good hard kick so effectively that he has good reason to limp back to Diane's surgery. She refuses to believe he has a leg injury until the matron (Edith Atwater) comes in and asks why she is not attending to the patient. She finds he has an abrasion and the skin is broken. After attending to the wound and bandaging his leg the Matron directs Diane to see him safely home. Unwillingly, Diane helps him into the passenger seat of one of the fairground's tricycles. Leaning on her heavily as he hobbles out of the carriage, Mike pretends to be faint from lack of food and Diane sees it as her duty to take him for a meal

Elvis as Mike Edwards marvels at the
eating capacity of his young charge Sue-
Lin (Vickey Tiu). *It happened At The World's
Fair* (1963)

in the restaurant at the top of the space needle. He talks his way into her good books by showing sudden interest in her enthusiasm over the space programme. After they have ordered, a hidden organ swells into spontaneous action as Mike sings 'I'm Falling in Love Tonight', looking into her eyes. She allows him to hold her hand and at the end of the song they share a kiss. Just as spontaneously as the organ materialized, the other diners break into applause.

As Diane helps him away from the restaurant they run into the small boy who kicked Mike in the shin: he asks if he would like another kick – 'I could use another quarter.' Mike gives him half a dollar and the boy promptly kicks him again. The spell is broken and Diane storms off. At that moment Sue-Lin appears, in tears, saying that her uncle went off in a truck in the morning and disappeared. Mike promises to help Sue-Lin find him and takes her back to the trailer Danny had found for them as temporary accommodation, breaks up a crap game in which Danny is involved and settles the child to sleep with a lullaby 'Cotton Candy Land'. He rings Diane but she hangs up immediately. Sue-Lin, on hearing this, decides to play cupid and pretends to have a fever by putting her forehead near the electric heater. She then gets Mike to phone Diane and takes over the receiver, begging her to come and care for her.

Diane drives over, finds the child in bed with a feverish brow and asks Mike to fix a cold compress. In the meantime Sue-Lin gives herself a temperature with another visit to the fire and Diane leaves her in Mike's care, praising his kindness, but advising him he should notify the Child Welfare Board. They kiss and make-up, but the atmosphere is disrupted when partner Danny comes home drunk and all set to make a pass at Diane. In the meantime, Danny contacts an old friend who offers him a lot of cash if he and Mike will fly a load of freight to Canada that night. Mike has to tell Sue-Lin her

uncle Walter has not turned up and to cheer her up he sings a duet with her 'How Would You Like To Be'. Mike agrees to undertake the flight and Sue-Lin agrees to stay with their friend, Barney, for a couple of hours, but a Child Welfare Officer, Miss Ettinger, appears at the door to say Sue-Lin will have to accompany her as a trailer with two bachelors is not the right environment for an 'abandoned' child. To make matters worse, Danny's gambling friends turn up, ready for a crap game. The tearful Sue-Lin gets in the car with Miss Ettinger, who tells Mike that it was Diane Warren who filed the complaint to the Welfare Board.

The two pilots bail out their plane with their newly acquired cash, but before leaving Mike calls the Welfare Office to talk to Sue-Lin, only to be told by Miss Ettinger that she has run away. He leaves Danny with his fuming friend, Vince, who had put up the money, locates the child asleep in a car in the fairground and hurries back with her to the airport where Danny is loading up the freight and preparing to leave without him. Diane hurries over to assure Mike it was not she who filed the complaint, but Vince butts in to say the kid can't go on the flight with Mike and Danny, as they don't want the police 'sniffing around'. Mike's suspicions are aroused; he opens one of the containers and finds it full of illegal furs. Vince threatens them with a gun, takes Diane and Sue-Lin hostage, but a sharp bite from the moppet redresses the balance and after a fight Mike gets the smuggler arrested. Danny admits it was he who notified the Welfare Board about Sue-Lin, just in time for them to join the big parade, singing 'Happy Ending', while Sue-Lin is reunited with her uncle, whose van was involved in an accident, in which he was unhurt.

This wafer-thin storyline is played out against what is basically a conducted tour of the World's Fair in Seattle, to which master lighting cameraman Joseph Ruttenberg does full justice, but it is

something of a comedown for the man who won Academy Awards for the black and white war drama *Mrs Miniver* (1942) and *The Great Waltz* (1938) and for the classic colour musical, *Gigi*, in 1958, all of them also for MGM. The characters are sketchily drawn, with most of the emphasis, apart from Presley's upright but girl-chasing bush pilot Mike Edwards, on seven-year old Chinese moppet Vicky Tiu, a formidable little actress but whose winsome ways soon begin to pall. Elvis plays with cheerful insouciance and is always ready with his guitar or with a smoochy ballad when the action threatens to drag – which is all too often.

Joan O'Brien looks attractive in her nurse's uniform, the cap fixed perilously at the back of her Sidney Guilaroff coiffure and acts her conventional part as Diane Warren with charm and conviction, alternating between indignant rejection of Mike's advances and melting yieldingly into his arms at the drop of a sentimental ballad. Gary Lockwood as Danny Burke has a strong personality and is a fitting contrast, with his ruthless streak, to Elvis's ever-gallant and caring persona in the role of Mike Edwards.

Director Norman Taurog (*qv*), an excellent craftsman, who specialized in film musicals and was responsible for several early Bing Crosbys, was an adept at turning even the most unpromising themes into entertaining box-office propositions and handled Presley so well in his come-back movie after army service, *G.I. Blues* (*qv*) in 1960 that he directed a further eight Elvis subjects, of which *World's Fair* was the third. Even Taurog's expertise could do little to maintain the standard he had achieved before Colonel Parker (*qv*) adopted his cut price policy towards the end of the Presley career; the last he handled, *Live a Little, Love a Little* in 1968 was a dismal affair, apart from one delightfully bizarre duet with, of all people, Elsa Lanchester (*qv*).
(See also: Crooners for Swooners: G.I. Blues; Lanchester, Elsa; Live a Little,

Love a Little; Parker, Colonel Tom; Taurog, Norman)

IT HAPPENED AT THE WORLD'S FAIR
(RCA LPM 2697) 1963

BEYOND THE BEND * *
Written by Fred Wise, Ben Weisman, Dolores Fuller.
Introductory song as bush cropper Mike Edwards and his co-pilot Danny Burke are on their way to nowhere, happy to be free, except that Mike hopes to find a girlfriend. The fast, carefree song features the higher pitch timbre of Elvis's voice. He's backed by light guitar and heavy drum music, with background voices of the Mello Men group.

RELAX * *
Written by Sid Tepper, Roy C. Bennett.
Here Elvis uses a low, throaty, seductive voice, reminiscent of his 'Fever' recording, snapping his fingers to the beat to ensnare a casually encountered girl called Shirley. He coaxes her to relax. He is backed by sultry guitar music and The Jordanaires are credited with being in the background, but you'd have to listen very carefully. Before he has purred her into the total relaxation he desires, the girl's parents discover them in a clinch and the father goes for his gun. End of romance.
LP: 'Mahalo From Elvis'

TAKE ME TO THE FAIR * *
Written by Sid Tepper, Roy C. Bennett.
A short, fast number about Elvis's happy anticipation of going to the fair. Behind him is a big chorus of male and female voices and a guitar and drums backing.

THEY REMIND ME TOO MUCH OF YOU * * *
Written by Don Robertson.
Elvis in a sentimental, reminiscent mood as he takes a gentle ride on a roundabout with the little Chinese girl Sue-Lin he is looking after, whose uncle drove them to the fair. Sue-Lin, worn out by the exitement of the fair, is sleeping soundly while the song goes through his head of his absent love, reminded of her by the stars and the moonlight. He begs her to return to him. He sings tenderly, his famous tremolo much in evidence, backed by the Mello Men and an evocative piano.
Single B/W: 'One Broken Heart For Sale'
LPs: 'Elvis Aaron Presley'; 'Elvis in Hollywood'; 'Elvis Sings Hits From His Movies – Vol. 1'; 'Elvis – The Other Sides – Worldwide Gold Award Hits – Vol. 2'

ONE BROKEN HEART FOR SALE * * *
Written by Otis Blackwell, Winfield Scott.
Elvis sings this fast rocker to his pilot buddy while pondering how to win the sympathy of the nurse who has caught his fancy. He accompanies himself on his guitar, ending by walking out of their trailer and strolling around the fair, accompanied by the Mello Men who sing along with him.

I'M FALLING IN LOVE TONIGHT * * * *
Written by Don Robertson.
A slow tender ballad sung by Elvis to Joan O'Brien in the restaurant at the top of the space needle: his low, vibrant voice is exploited to the full as he tells his girl how he is falling in love with her. There is effective backing from an organ and only Elvis's voice can be heard.

COTTON CANDY LAND * * * *
Written by Ruth Batchelor, Bob Roberts.
Lullaby sung by Elvis to Vicky Tiu to try and send her to sleep; he conjures up a cotton candy land where you ride on a white swan on clouds of pink ice-cream and the moon is made of marshmallow. A backing of guitar, piano and drums keeps a solid beat and Elvis seems genuinely to be enjoying the lyrics; he is at his most tender with children, which is probably why he had to do it so often, leading to his later wry comment, 'I'm tired of singing to children, animals and walls!'

LP: 'Elvis Sings For Children and Grownups Too'

A WORLD OF OUR OWN * * *
Written by Bill Giant, Bernie Baum, Florence Kaye.
Another ballad sung by Elvis to Joan O'Brien after they have settled his small Chinese protégée to rest for the night. He sings of two lovers building a world for themselves when they are in each others' embrace. The tempo is mid-paced, with an upbeat air and a backing that swells up to encourage Elvis to sing out over it. The spell is broken when Gary Lockwood comes in drunk.

HOW WOULD YOU LIKE TO BE * * *
Written by Ben Raleigh, Mark Barkan.
Another novelty song, aimed at cheering up Vicky Tiu when her uncle fails to return from a trip. A catchy rhythm and lyric, in which Vicky joins Elvis to a background of merry-go-round music played on a Winifred Atwell type jangling piano, with military style drumming. Elvis asks her how she'd like to be various circus characters. Again, his tenderness with children is quite obvious – embarrassing though it undoubtedly is for some of his less sentimental fans.
Single B/W: 'If Every Day Was Like Christmas'
LPs: 'Elvis Sings For Children and Grownups Too'; 'Elvis Sings Hits From His Movies – Vol. 1'

HAPPY ENDING * *
(Film duet with Joan O'Brien)
Written by Ben Weisman, Sid Wayne
The Jordanaires join in a zippy, fast finale song rocker with male and female singers and a military band – Elvis adds a cute dance step as they march along.
LP: 'Mahalo From Elvis'

JAILHOUSE ROCK * * * * *

Released by: Metro-Goldwyn-Mayer, an
Avon Production (black and white,
Cinemascope); **Producer:** Pandro S.
Berman; **Director:** Richard Thorpe;
Screenplay: Guy Trosper from a story by
Ned Young; **Art Directors:** William A.
Horning, Randall Duell; **Director of
Photography:** Robert Bonner, QSC;
Technical Advisor: Colonel Tom Parker;
Music: Jeff Alexaner, vocal background by
The Jordanaires; **Running Time:** 96
mins; **Opened:** October 17, 1957, re-
released March 9, 1960 (after Elvis's
discharge from army).

Cast: Elvis, Judy Tyler, Mickey
Shaughnessy, Vaughn Taylor, Jennifer
Gorden, Dean Jones, Anne Neyland,
Hugh Sanders, Grandon Rhodes,
Katherine Warren, William Forrest.

Vince Everett (Elvis) is a truck driver on a
housing site. He's doing well at his job, is
a wow with the girls and can look after
himself in a fight. On pay-day the
paymaster asks him what he's going to do
with all his money. 'I'm going to buy me
a herd of dancing girls and make them
dance on my bed', he tosses over his
shoulder as he heads for the
neighbourhood bar where the bartender is
an old buddy. Vince challenges him to
arm-wrestle, which he knows will make
him the centre of attention – too much,

as it turns out. The local floosie sidles up
and asks him to buy her a drink. After
looking her over he says, 'Sure, I'm
buying. Jake, draw one for the lady',
having already ordered drinks all round.

Suddenly a man rushes over and
pushes the girl off her stool. Vince tries to
restrain him, saying, 'Hey, she didn't
mean anything – I just bought a round
for the house'. The man turns on him
with, 'Keep out of this. Look Buster – if
you want some teeth knocked down your
throat, keep it up.' Vince taunts him, 'You
scare me, women-beaters always scare me.'
As a final insult the man says, 'Why don't
you run away, before I muss up your
hair'; picks up a drink and pours it over
Vince's shirt.

Vince hits him hard and in the
resulting fight gives him a good beating.
He goes on hitting him until he is
restrained. 'Vince, he's had enough. He's
had enough.' More than enough; the man
is dead. Vince is arrested and sentenced to
from one to ten years for manslaughter. In
the State Penitentiary the warden warns
him they don't discipline prisoners with
bare hands – they use guns. And the
whip. Vince's cellmate is Hunk Houghton
(Mickey Shaughnessy), a former Country
and Western singer, who rules the inmates
by doing them favours in return for packs
of cigarettes. Hunk is the prison fixer,
who can pacify unruly inmates by playing
his guitar and singing to them. Hunk

lets Vince play his guitar and senses his
raw talent.

He tells him, 'You play ball with me
and I'll stake you. I can't have my cellmate
walking around and looking like a bum.
Another thing is your job. You been
assigned yet?' 'Not yet'. 'You'll probably
draw the coalyard. Fresh fish always do. I
can probably get you out of it'. Vince
who is catching on fast, asks 'For how
many packs?' Hunk tells him five – and
he'll loan them to him – for which he gets
charged interest on each pack with
another. Vince says 'I haven't got five
packs. I'll take my chances.'

So he ends up in the coalyard, where
it is indeed dirty and hard work, with a
sadistic warder who keeps the men short
of drinking water. In the cell Hunk
reminisces about his days as a hillbilly
singer in vaudeville and how he could
easily earn $200 a week. Vince is seriously
interested and Hunk lets him practise on
his guitar, with the admonition, 'Don't
break any strings.' One day Vince lets his
finger glide over the guitar and sings a
song his uncle taught him 'You're So
Young and Beautiful': at the end the silent
cell block erupts into the clatter of pots
and pans against iron bars – the way the
convicts show their approval. Hunk is
impressed and, although insisting Vince
still doesn't play well, grudgingly admits
'Maybe you're learning'. He has his own
plans for him. Then one day some

**Elvis as Vince Everett performs the title
song in a TV re-enactment of his
incarceration – choreography by Pandro S.
Berman.** *Jailhouse Rock* (1957)

producers get the idea to do a live
television show from the prison: Hunk is
appointed to handle it, from his old
connection with show business, and tells
Vince he had fixed a spot for him. Vince
only shows interest when told the show
is to go out on television.

Vince makes an incredible
impression on the viewers and the jail is
flooded with fan mail for him, but Hunk
jealously makes sure it does not get to
him by bribing the post officials with
packs of cigarettes to keep the letters
from reaching Vince until after his
discharge. Meanwhile, he persuades his
unsuspecting protégé to sign a 50-50
agreement to split whatever Vince makes
when he gets out of jail. (Not even
Colonel Parker (*qv*) had the temerity to
propose such a contract!) 'Let me worry
about the business end. Here, I've made

a contract for us. We split everything
right down the middle.' It was one thing
to get enthusiastic applause from what
Hunk called 'The captive audience' who
packed the rows in front of the stage as
Vince plays his guitar and sings 'I Want
To Be Free' – what else would they be
likely to do? – but their applause has
already convinced him that the stage is
where he wants to be more than
anywhere else.

Prison life becomes more and more
irksome, as Vince crosses off the days on
the calendar. The nadir is reached after a
riot in the mess hall, into which Vince
gets drawn as fists are flying and he
lashes out at a prison warder. He learns
that the warden's statement that the whip
was used to punish offenders was no idle
threat, when he is hauled off to be
whipped on his bare back – the guards
have not held their blows and he is
bleeding from their lashes when he is
pushed into the cell. He gets scant
sympathy from Hunk, who says he tried

to get him off the sentence but could not
afford it. He goes on, 'It's a lesson to be
remembered. Without money you might
as well be dead. You'll get no sympathy
from me. Pity's a commodity in here.
You buy it and sell it like anything else.'
'What are you, man?' shouts Vince:
'Some kind of animal?' Hank replies,
'That's right, Buddy. I'm an animal in a
jungle and I got a motto. Do unto others
as they would unto you. Only do it first.'
Vince realizes how true Hunk has been
to his theory when on his release he
receives the sack of mail that had been
withheld from him. He reads them over
and over and his bitterness knows no
end. He feels he must do something to
try and justify the complimentary letters
and goes to a pawnshop to buy a guitar,
then he wanders into a small bar.

A pretty girl comes in and sits next
to him: they get talking after he has
asked her about the lists of figures she is
writing down. Although he refuses to
buy her a drink, she seems to like him

and tells him she works on exploitation for a major record company. Her name is Peggy Van Alden. Her main charge is Mickey Alba, a new recording star. Hoping to impress her, although the manager refuses to give him a job as a singer, Vince jumps up onto the stage and sings a song, but the customers are not impressed and continue talking. One laughs loudly and repeatedly. Vince jumps down from the stage and smashes his guitar against a table before stalking out. Peggy follows him, convinces him she has faith in his potential and arranges for him to make a demo disc. After he has recorded 'Don't Leave Me Now' the musicians congratulate him; he has sung the song in his own way, having previously done it the way Hunk Houghton had taught him – a style ten years out of date. They take the record to the boss of Geneva Records, who seems not to be impressed, but agrees to try and sell it to New York. He then steals Vince's song and brings it out as a record for Mickey Alba. There is nothing legally Peggy and Vince can do about it. After a lovers quarrel over Vince's boorish manner and the way he had insulted Peggy's parents (Grandon Rhodes, Katharine Warren) and their guests at a party, they make it up and it is Vince who suggests they form their own record company. They call it Laurel Records and a lawyer friend of Peggy's, Mr. Shores (Vaughan Taylor), agrees to be Vince's manager.

With Peggy's promotional talents hard at work, their first record 'Treat Me Nice' (*qv*) is a hit. Money rolls in and Vince is able to buy the red convertible he'd always wanted. There are lots of parties and an offer for a major TV show. Peggy sees that success has changed Vince and she insists they put their relationship on a purely business level. At that moment, Hunk, released from prison, comes back into his life, eager to claim his share of the deal they had signed. Resentful at the way Hunk had used and double-crossed him, Vince

nevertheless talks the TV company in New York into letting Houghton sing a song on the show. At rehearsals it becomes apparent that Hunk's style is sadly dated and he is ruthlessly cut from the TV Spectacular, on which Vince makes his biggest hit yet singing 'Jailhouse Rock' (*qv*). Meanwhile, Vince has had their original contract vetted and discovered that it is not legally binding.

For the sake of their one time friendship he proposes to allow Hunk 10 per cent of his earnings and to be his minder and right hand man: he needs someone to look after him, now that Peggy is not around. With his records topping the charts, Hollywood coaxes him out to the coast with a million dollar contract and a blonde leading lady called Sherry Wilson (Jennifer Holden), who is at first bored with Vince but soon responds to his ardour during their first love scene together. His Hollywood home is always plentifully stocked with starlets who are ready, willing and able, but at the back of his mind it is always Peggy he longs for. He is delighted when she turns up at the pool side, only to be disappointed when she makes it clear she has only come to persuade him to cut some new discs. 'Nobody gets so big they can ignore the records, Vince,' she says. 'Not even you.'

When his lawyer – manager, Mr. Shores, arrives with a proposal from Geneva Records (the company that had 'stolen' Vince's first song) offering a small fortune to buy up Peggy and Vince's record company and to put him under exclusive contract, Vince is delighted but puts off telling Peggy until after a studio party. She takes it very badly and leaves in tears. Hunk, already drunk and resentful at the menial position Vince had reduced him to, starts laying into him with his fists, saying 'It's not just the record company that's bothering her, sonny. Tramping on me is one thing, but hurting a sweet little girl like Peggy is another.' Vince refuses to hit him back and a hard blow to the larynx puts him

out for the count. It also nearly kills him, causing it to swell, cutting off his windpipe.

He wakes up in hospital after an operation, which has been successful, but the doctor warns him he might not be able to sing again. He puts off the moment for as long as he can, but Hunk and Peggy bring along a bunch of musicians to encourage him to try out his voice. As the pianist strikes up the first few bars of 'Young and Beautiful', looking straight at Peggy, Vince begins to sing...............

Elvis's third movie was a strange one to come out of the usually glossy Metro Goldwyn production line. Richard Thorpe's fast-moving, gritty, unsubtle prison musical was more the type that Warner Brothers turned out with such proficiency and seemed set to steer the star into the mould of the sullen, bitter, ungracious tough guy whose fists and quick temper land him in serious trouble. But it was not to be. After *King Creole* (*qv*) and army service, he was transformed into the likeable, easy-going, all-American nice guy, though still handy with his fists and, as a bonus from the army, terrific with his karate gymnastics. The highlight of the *Jailhouse Rock* TV spectacular, with its staccato choreography, introducing an uptempo, gyrating Elvis for the first time, is far more effective in black and white than it would have been in colour and here the hand of producer Pandro S. Berman, responsible for the best of the Astaire–Rogers musicals, is most evidently in control. The songs by Jerry Lieber and Mike Stoller fit the mood of the film and its star admirably and in Judy Tyler, a warmly sympathetic leading lady, whose career was so soon to be tragically brought to an end by a fatal road accident, there was an actress whose style complemented Elvis's to perfection. The complex character of Presley's prison cellmate, by turns callous and bullying, ruthless, loyal and caring, is fleshed out by Mickey Shaugnessy with a depth somewhat lacking in Guy Trosper's script. A young Dean Jones makes the most of slender opportunities as an amiable disc jockey. Stereotypes abound: all the prison staff are sneering and sadistic; the girls, apart from Judy Tyler, cardboard cut-out bimbos; Judy's parents' rich friends are cuttingly patronizing and so on.

Elvis rises above all this with his sincerity, switching from arrogant surliness to touching vulnerability with instinctive ease; although the ending is predictable, he and Judy Tyler make it genuinely touching.

(See also: King Creole)

JAILHOUSE ROCK (EP released 1957)

JAILHOUSE ROCK * * * * *

Written by Jerry Lieber, Mike Stoller.
Vince Everett features this in a special programme recorded live from the prison where he has been incarcerated after accidentally killing a man in a bar room fight.

This, the musical highlight of the movie, is spectacularly sung and danced by Elvis, to Pandros S. Berman's powerfully staccato choreography – light years away from the terpsichorian effects he used to produce for the Astaire–Rogers musicals and for Ginger Rogers herself. Lieber and Stoller wrote all but two of the songs for *Jailhouse Rock* and Mike Stoller actually played piano, in place of the usual backing pianist, Dudley Brooks, along with D.J. Fontana on drums, Scotty Moore on guitar and Bill Black on double bass. They also appeared in the movie, with vocal backing by The Jordanaires.
Single B/W: 'Treat Me Nice'
EPs: 'Dealers Preview'; 'Extended Play Sampler'
LPs: 'Elvis, Elvis – a Canadian Tribute'; 'Elvis – A Legendary Performer – Vol. 2'; 'Elvis – Golden Records'; 'Elvis In Concert'; 'Elvis In Hollywood'; 'The Elvis Medley'; 'Elvis Recorded Live in

Memphis'; 'Elvis – TV Special'; 'Elvis – Worldwide 50 Golden Hits – Vol. 1'; 'Essential Elvis – The First Movies'; 'The Number One Hits'; 'Pure Gold'; 'This Is Elvis'; 'The Top Ten Hits'

YOUNG AND BEAUTIFUL * * *

Written by Abner Silver, Aaron Schroeder.
Vince, in his prison cell with Hunk, an ex-Country and Western singer, listens as he sings an old trad song 'One More Day', accompanying himself on guitar. He is moved to ask him to let him borrow it to try a song himself, though he does not really know how to play. This is the song, sung gently in a tenor register and with tender feeling, expressing his love for a girl and telling her she means everything to him. The other prisoners rattle their mugs in applause; Hunk, though jealous and grouchy, agrees to show Vince how to play guitar. The delicately understated theme of their relationship is that the bullying but tender-hearted Hunk sees Vince as his 'punk' – the love object for hardened prisoners, deprived of female company. Later he tries to protect his friend from being involved in a prison brawl over food but Vince is caught and beaten severely.
LPs: 'A Date With Elvis'; 'Elvis: The Other Sides – Worldwide Gold Award Hits – Vol. 2'; 'Essential Elvis – The First Movies'; 'I Was The One'; 'A Valentine Gift For You'

I WANT TO BE FREE * * * *

Written by Jerry Lieber, Mike Stoller.
This is the song Vince sings at the original prison concert – it tells of longing to be like the bird he can see from his cell window and is just right for the occasion, the time and the place: brilliant lyrics and Elvis truly expresses youthful optimism, tunefully supported by The Jordanaires. The song delights the viewers in their homes and angers Hunk, when all the post-show fan mail is for his cellmate. He sees Vince's

potential and draws up a contract for them to team up after their release, bribing the trustees to withhold the letters.
LPs: 'A Date With Elvis'; 'Elvis – The Other Sides – Worldwide Gold Award Hits – Vol. 2'; 'Essential Elvis – The First Movies'

DON'T LEAVE ME NOW * * *

Written by Aaron Schroeder, Ben Weisman.
The song chosen by Vince for his first demo disc, with Peggy's encouragement. He sings it twice – first time accompanying himself on guitar and is disappointed when he hears the result. He says he sounds like so many others: Peggy persuades him to sing it the way he feels it – from the heart. He agrees and lays aside his guitar, saying he doesn't play much – his distinguished musicians provide the backing and he sings with all the spirit Elvis was capable of: result in the movie – a hit record for another singer. Perfectly convincing for the storyline but lacking the Lieber/Stoller touch that might have done the trick in real life.

Interestingly, though Elvis joked that he only knew three chords on the guitar, he had learned to play as a child from his uncle, Travis Smith, and during his career had spent hours with the legendary guitarist, Chet Atkins, working on his technique.

TREAT ME NICE (not featured on EP) * * * *

Written by Jerry Lieber, Mike Stoller.
Vince's new record for his Laurel label is a major hit, thanks to DJ promotion by Peggy's friend Teddy Talbot.
Single B/W: 'Jailhouse Rock'
LPs: 'Dealers Preview'; 'A Touch of Gold – Vol. 2'; 'Elvis's Golden Records'; 'Elvis Worldwide 50 Gold Award Hits – Vol.

KATZMAN, SAM

Sam Katzman, nicknamed 'King of the Quickies', has been pinpointed by many as the start of the noticeable decline in the Presley vehicles. Lance Gefault, who was responsible for the choreography in several of the musicals, told Jerry Hopkins, one of the best early Presley biographers, talking about the first film produced by Sam Katzman, *Kissin' Cousins* (*qv*), 'We shot the film in 17 days and I think that was the turning point in Presley films – up until that time, certain standards had been maintained, but that was where we noticed that there was no rehearsal for all the numbers.'

Katzman had entered films as a prop boy at the age of thirteen, working his way up to producer via numerous studio positions. One of his most money-spinning productions was the 1956 *Rock Around the Clock* with Bill Haley. At the time Katzman met Colonel Parker (*qv*) he had been working on *Your Cheating Heart*, the story of the late Hank Williams, which starred George Hamilton and was shot in fifteen days. It seems that Katzman was so impressed by the amount of money the Hank Williams film had made, partly as a result of the way the Colonel advised MGM how to distribute the movie, that he and the Colonel sat down over a cup of coffee and struck a deal, cigars firmly in place, as was the wont among tycoons such as they. Parker asked Katzman to

produce his forthcoming *Kissin' Cousins* in the economical way for which he was famous. He told him they had been spending $4,000,000 a picture and he wanted Katzman to do this one his way. The Colonel figured that way he could save a few dollars and, no doubt, he was right, but the toll on everyone's nerves was considerable because of the tight schedule. Gene Nelson, the blond and amiable song and dance man, who had made movies with Doris Day among others and started his career as a skater in Sonja Henie's ice show, going on to be a director, told Jerry Hopkins that Elvis returned from a brief holiday in Memphis to record at the RCA Studios in Nashville and got down to recording the songs for the film with his friends The Jordanaires from 9pm. They worked through the night and eight hours later all nine songs that Elvis was to feature in *Kissin' Cousins* had been recorded. The director said that Presley, although as always business-like and professional, was practically throwing the songs away as he sang them. They went straight back to Hollywood to start filming and Nelson says, 'Things got tense. Elvis had never worked this way before. The Colonel explained that Elvis would make more money on the 50% of profit deal he had, in addition to $750,000 in salary. When I said it was like shooting a television show and to pretend it was that instead of a film, Elvis went along. There were times when Sam leaned very,

very hard. He was always on the set and I hadn't learned the patience and control I think I have now and I'd get uptight. This upset Elvis. He came to me the last week and said he didn't like to work this way, it wasn't worth it. He said he knew what pressure I was under and he volunteered to get sick or show up late if it would help. I said to hang in – it was my problem, not his.'

Here is an instance of just how caring Presley could be. He and Nelson were to do another film with Katzman, *Harum Scarum* (*qv*) the following year, 1965. Both that and *Kissin' Cousins* were written by Gerald Drayson Adams, who said, 'There never were any story conferences. They consisted of money, first act, second act money. And all were conducted by Colonel Parker; he would go to almost any lengths to avoid a fight, so in the end everyone suffered. Except the Colonel. When they finished *Harum Scarum* Elvis said to Gene Nelson, "Maybe one day we'll do one right"'.

Sam Katzman went on producing tightly scheduled movies including one called *How To Succeed With Sex*, of which he was executive producer, in 1972, the year before his death at 71.
(See also: Harum Scarum; Kissin' Cousins; Parker, Colonel Tom)

KID GALAHAD * * * * *

Released by: United Artists, a Mirisch Company Production (De Luxe Color);
Producer: David Weisbart; **Director:**

A reluctant boxing champion, Walter Gulick (Elvis), recently out of the service, finds himself up against unscrupulous opposition, wins the girl and the big fight and quits the ring for ever. *Kid Galahad* **(1962)**

Phil Karlson; **Screenplay:** William Fay, based on a story by Francis Wallace; **Art Director:** Gary Odell; **Director of Photography:** Burnett Guffey ASC; **Technical Advisor:** Colonel Tom Parker; **Music:** Jeff Alexander; **Running Time:** 95 mins; **Opened:** August 29, 1962.

Cast: Elvis, Gig Young, Lola Albright, Joan Blackman, Charles Bronson, Liam Redmond, Ned Glass, Robert Ernhardt, David Lewis, Michael Dante, Judson Pratt, George Mitchell, Roy Roberts, Richard Devon, Jeffrey Morris, Ed Asner.

Just demobbed, Walter Gulick (Elvis) hitches a lift on the back of a lorry to the hick town where he was born, Cream Valley. Looking for work as a mechanic he is introduced, through the good graces of Dolly Fletcher (Lola Albright) ex-singer and girlfriend of Willy Grogan (Gig Young), to the tough and indigent Willy, who runs a training camp for boxers. The camp, which once had a good reputation, is run down due to Willy's obsession with gambling, which has brought him into debt not only with government departments but also with a crooked boxing promoter, Otto Danzig (David Lewis). Danzig is attended by thugs with nasty habits: Maynard, his right-hand man (Richard Ernhardt), along with Marvin and Ralphie (Richard Devon and Jeffrey Morris). They are happy to put the frighteners on Willy and move in to keep an eye on him. He phones his sister, Rose (Joan Blackman), co-owner of the training camp, and asks her for money. Rose comes over to take charge, deciding she is grown-up enough to put a curb on his expensive excesses.

The cheapskate boxing promoter from the neighbouring camp, Howie Zimmerman (Judson Pratt), walks in while Walter is asking Willy for a job and sees him as a good potential punching-bag for his own local champion, Joe Shakes (Michael Dante), but insists he can only afford to pay him

five dollars a round. Walter accepts the offer, despite the protests of Dolly, who has taken him under her wing, along with Willy's gentle giant of a manager, trainer Lew Nyzack (Charles Bronson). Walter, nicknamed 'Kid Galahad' by Willy when he knocks out a hoodlum trying to get fresh with Dolly, insists he needs the money and goes into the ring with Zimmerman's champ, who is a fearsome puncher. Against him Walter (Kid Galahad), whose only boxing experience has been in the army, initially takes a terrible beating, but then suddenly delivers a knock-out punch and Joe is out for the count. Willy sees great potential in Walter and Lew puts him into rigorous training. Inventing spurious knockouts for Kid Galahad in Australia, Willy insists on a $1,000 price from promoter Jerry Sperling (George Mitchell) to put him in the ring for his first professional fight on television before he is ready for the big time. Lew, Dolly and Rose are filled with misgivings – Dolly says Willy should be arrested and wants the fight stopped as Kid Galahad is knocked all round the ring and at one point can barely get up to continue. Suddenly, as before, the Kid delivers the coup de grâce.

The Kid and Rose have fallen for each other and he insists on driving her to a big county picnic in an ancient jalopy he had refurbished and painted a vivid red – a car, he insists, that has more character than any other. Be that as it may, after a great time at the picnic and a romantic interlude in the country afterwards, the engine breaks down and the delay while he fixes it makes them late home to Willy's fury. He threatens Galahad, tells him to keep away from his sister and becomes so belligerent when the boy tells him that he and Rose are going to get married that Dolly has to step in to part them. She also tells Willy exactly what she thinks of him for keeping her hanging around for years without proposing the marriage he promised when they first became lovers.

She packs to leave and returns to Lieberman's (Ned Glass) restaurant as a singer. Willy realizes what he has lost and goes after her.

Kid Galahad agrees to take part in the big fight sponsored by the Cream Valley Chamber of Commerce in the hope that the big prize money will enable him to quit the fight game, go into partnership with the local garage owner and eventually own a chain of garages. He confides this to Rose when she asks him why he is going to put his health in jeopardy again against the reigning champion, Kid Sugarboy, well-known as a killer. Otto Danzig, willing to go to any lengths for his man to win the fight with the big money involved, offers Lew Nyzack $500 to quit as Galahad's second so he can put his own henchman in the corner to cut Galahad up if he shows any sign of winning the fight. Lew throws the money away contemptuously and for his pains has his hands broken by Otto's thugs, Marvin and Ralphie. Willy comes into the locker room before they can do any further damage and with Kid Galahad's help knocks them out cold. Before the big fight Willy intercepts Danzig's man, who is ready to go into the ring in place of the incapacitated Lew to make sure the Kid gets injured for real. Willy quickly despatches the substitute, who is carrying a bag of lethal-looking cutting instruments. Outside interference ousted, Kid Galahad wins the big fight legitimately. Dolly returns to the fold, full of admiration for Willy's part in worsting Otto and his boys, makes her own proposal of marriage and Grogan gives his blessing to his sister's union with the now retired champ, Kid Galahad.

A fascinating film in many ways, not least because it represents the final real attempt to provide Presley with a substantial story line with a challenging character to play, under the production team of David Weisbart, who had done so well by Elvis in three previous movies

and director Phil Karlson, so adept at handling action subjects. *Kid Galahad* was a remake of the film, directed in black and white by Michael Curtiz in 1937, starring Edward G. Robinson and Bette Davis, and making a star of Wayne Morris in the title role, as well as featuring Warner Brothers contract ingénue, Jayne Bryan as Rose. *The property* was a typically gutsy subject for Warners and Curtiz with their stars, Robinson and Davis, both in fighting mood as Willy and his long-suffering mistress, and Morris, whose second film this was, in a part he played with great conviction and was never again able to match. His promising career was nipped in the bud after his call-up into action in World War II, during which he won several decorations for Distinguished Service.

The performances in Karlson's remake compare respectably with those of the original apart from Gig Young, who is too light-weight an actor to be entirely convincing in the duplicitous, cynical character of Willy. Presley acquits himself well in the boxing scenes, punching and taking punishment with considerable conviction, though he is not helped by the make-up – mostly small strips of sticking plaster to convey the effects of the terrific hammerings he takes from his opponents before delivering the victorious K.O. Unfortunately also, when stripped in the ring, a certain avoirdupois is apparent, especially when matched against his first sparring partner in the story, the lithe and muscular Michael Dante, who at 27 was the same age as Elvis. The songs – no less than six, although catchy, and in one case pleasantly romantic, inevitably lessen the impact of the drama and the climax, inevitable though the conclusion was bound to be. Elvis overcomes these disadvantages with his usual sincerity and charm, but the best male performance in the movie is Charles Bronson's beautifully judged boxing coach, Lew Nyzack, one of the most subtle portrayals of his career.

Lola Albright, inevitably less mannered than Bette Davis as Dolly Fletcher, brings a touching reality to her scenes with Willy and contrasts strongly in her naturalness with the over wide-eyed innocence of Joan Blackman as Rose, lovely though she be. The late Liam Redmond unexpectedly turns up as the Irish Catholic priest, Father Higgins, who is happy to unite Walter and Rose in marriage, and turning out to be, of course, a boxing fan. Quite why this distinguished Abbey Theatre actor crossed the Atlantic to take this role is not readily apparent; he brings to the cameo role a glowing bonhomie, but would have posed no threat to Hollywood's resident Irish player of Catholic priests, Barry Fitzgerald, who died the year before *Kid Galahad* was released. He may well have been pencilled in for the part during the midsummer pre-planning of the boxing story in 1961.

Hairdresser Alice Monte devised a strangely elaborate, highly waved coiffure for the Kid topped by a dark cherry tint, fetching, but odd in the context of his role. Be that as it may, the film reached nine in *Variety*'s list of Top Grossing films for the year with a total gross of $1.75 million.

KID GALAHAD
(EP Released 1962)
KING OF THE WHOLE WIDE WORLD * *
Written by Ruth Batchelor, Bob Roberts. Sitting on the back of a lorry on which he has hitched a ride on the way home after his release from the army, Walter Gulick tells of a man who can sing about being king of the whole wide world, even though he owns nothing. Cute lyrics and the travelling beat which opens so many Elvis films. Guitars, drums, saxophones, piano and and unidentified vocal chorus accompany Elvis as he beats time on the tailboard of the truck.
Single B/W: 'Home Is Where The Heart Is'

LPs: 'C'mon Everbody', 'Return of the Rocker'

THIS IS LIVING * *

Written by by Fred Wise, Ben Weisman. The training camp's quartet, with guitars, busk along to those oh-so-familiar lyrics about 'this is the life for me', joined by the boxer Joe Shakes whom Walter knocked out at the end of their first bout. They shake hands, become the best of friends and Joe invites Walter to join him and the boys in their singalong. Walter not only improvises the words, but beats time with the rest of them.
LP: 'C'mon Everybody'

RIDING THE RAINBOW * *

Written by Fred Wise, Ben Weisman. Walter drives Willy and his trainer Lew Nyack to participate in a boxing match being shown on TV. He turns up the radio in the old refurbished vehicle and happily sings yet another Wise – Weisman travelling jingle. Lew hopes he'll be as happy on the way home after the fight.

HOME IS WHERE THE HEART IS * * *

Written by by Sherman Edwards, Hal David.
Walter sings the one romantic ballad in the film to Rose before they set out on a picnic in his beloved old car, painted red for the occasion. Strings and a vocal chorus are predominant in the backing of a sweet, if hardly original love song.
Single B/W: 'King Of The Whole Wide World'
LP: 'I Got Lucky'

I GOT LUCKY * * *

Written by Dolores Fuller, Fred Wise, Ben Weisman.
A gentle twist number sung and danced by Elvis and Joan Blackman with the other young people at the picnic. Guitars, vocal chorus, drums, saxes and clarinets play along with the dancers.

The lyrics beg the girl to give him a chance and marry him, then he'll know his luck has not run out. Later they get stranded when the jalopy breaks down and share a kiss while he is repairing the engine. When they return late Kid Galahad, threatened by Willy, tells him a few home truths.
LP: 'I Got Lucky'

A WHISTLING TUNE * * *

Written by Sherman Edwards, Hal David.
Galahad, dressed smartly in a dark jacket and slacks, walks along towards the church arm in arm with Rose to see the Padre to make the final arrangements for their wedding a month's hence. Gentle guitars accompany Elvis's whistling while he sings of June and moon, just like Bing Crosby used to. Light years away from the atmosphere of the first, strictly unromantic Kid Galahad, but entertaining in its anodyne way.

*KING CREOLE * * * * **

Released by: Paramount Pictures (Black and White); **Producer:** Hal B. Wallis; **Director:** Michael Curtis; **Screenplay:** Hubert Baker and Michael Vincente Guzzo from the novel 'A Stone for Danny Fisher' by Harold Robbins; **Art Directors:** Hal Perriea and Joseph

MacMillan Johnson; **Director of Photography:** Russell Harlan; **Technical Advisor:** Colonel Tom Parker; **Music:** Walter Scharf, vocal background by The Jordanaires; **Running Time:** 116 mins; **Opened:** July 2, 1958.

Cast: Elvis, Carolyn Jones, Walter Matthau, Dolores Hart, Dean Jagger, Liliane Montevecchi, Vic Morrow, Paul Stewart, Jan Shepard, Brian Hutton, Jack Grinnage, Dick Winslow, Raymond Bailey.

Danny Fisher (Elvis) supports himself, his sister Mimi (Jan Shepard) and his often unemployed father (Dean Jagger) by doing odd jobs at the sleazy nighteries of the French quarter of New Orleans before and after school, where he is having a second try at graduation, having flunked out the first time. One morning, going to clear up at the Blue Shades night club, he finds a drunken party still in progress. The place is run by Maxie Fields (Walter Matthau), local big shot

Elvis as Danny Fisher, star attraction at the King Creole club, with Forty Nina (Liliane Montevecchi), the club's previous favourite entertainer. She assures him there are no ill-feelings.
***King Creole* (1958)**

Danny Fisher attracts the attention of Bonnie (Carolyn Jones), girlfriend of gangland leader Maxie Fields and lays himself open to a load of trouble. *King Creole* (1958)

and gang king, whose girlfriend Ronnie (Carolyn Jones), is still at the party being mauled by a drunk. She was once a well-known singer, whose career Maxie took over and in effect destroyed by his sadistic treatment, causing her to become an alcoholic. Danny gets her away from the drunk and takes her to the gates of his school, where he is late for his last day at school. In gratitude Ronnie kisses him from the taxi, a scene witnessed by his classmates. They jeer and he gets into

a fight which leads to his suspension from school and the denial of his right to graduate.

On the way home he is set upon by thugs in a dark alley, the leader of whom is Shark (Vic Morrow), the brother of the boy he punched at school. He proves more that able to take care of himself with his fists (this is pre-karate Presley); the three boys are bested and Shark gasping in admiration, 'You sure fight dirty!', asks him to join the gang. At first he refuses contemptuously, but as the proposition only entails singing at the 5 & 10 cent store to distract the customers and counterman while they rob the joint, he agrees. Though the girl in

charge of the soda fountain, Nellie (Dolores Hart), notices what he is up to, she finds him so attractive that she does not give him away, having no particular love for the place, and agrees to go on a date with him after. True to his nature – and his experience of girls – he takes her to a cheap hotel on the pretext that they are going to a party, tricks the clerk into giving him the key to the room where the party is supposed to be held and is dismayed at her innocence when she cottons on to the ruse and hesitates to go in with him. With an unexpected burst of respect, he leads her away and they take a romantic boat trip instead. She tells him she loved him from the start and hopes he likes her and says she now regrets not giving in to him in the hotel room. He assures her it's because she is a genuinely good girl and he's sorry for the cheap trick he played on her.

Danny is clearing up at the Blue Shade on Bourbon Street when Ronnie walks in with Maxie and makes the mistake of pretending she doesn't know Danny when he greets her. She tries to explain that she's just heard him sing and Maxie hoists her with her own petard by ordering Danny to perform. He creates a sensation with a couple of songs, Maxie admits his mistake in doubting his singing ability and is put out when his long-time rival, Charlie LeGrand (Paul Stewart), who owns the King Creole club down the road, offers Danny a job. Ronnie tells Danny that LeGrand is an honourable man, who once used to manage her career and that he's the only person on the street who is not afraid of Maxie. Danny hesitates about accepting the offer, as his father is anxious for him to go back to school, having talked to the principal who has faith in his talent, but disapproves of his hoodlum side. Mr. Fisher wants to celebrate the fact that he is hopeful of being offered a job in his original trade as a pharmacist and he insists that from now on he will earn the money to keep the family, while Danny returns to take his graduation next term. Danny, sceptical of his father's ability to hold down a job, insists he wants to take up LeGrand's offer to sing at the King Creole; they strike a bargain that if his father gets the job he had applied for he will return to his education, otherwise he will go on with his ambition to be a singer. At the pharmacy, Fisher is at first turned down by the arrogant chemist, but is eventually taken on at the insistence of his boss. Danny stops by to see his father at work and is humiliated to see how the chemist, resentful at having been made to hire Fisher, demeans him at every opportunity. However, he does not let his father know he had witnessed the scene and seizes the opportunity to give the chemist a glowing reference for the new employee.

Meanwhile, Charlie LeGrand persuades Danny to invite him home to dinner to give him a chance to persuade his father to let his son fulfil his genuine talent as a singer. Enraged, Fisher orders his guest from the house and Danny hits back by telling his father how he had witnessed the way he allowed himself to be used and insulted by his employer and goes ahead to accept LeGrand's offer to work at his club. He is a huge success and Charlie, who has fallen for his sister, Mimi, who is present at the opening, gives him a generous fee and his name in lights. The King Creole, which had fallen on hard times, is again a success to the disgust of his rival, Maxie Fields. Fields has taken Shark and his henchmen into his employ and deputes him to bring Danny to see him, who only agrees after veiled threats against Mimi, who returns LeGrand's affections. Danny is admitted by Ronnie, who Maxie treats like a slave and mocks the fact that she is drinking heavily. Danny again refuses to leave LeGrand to work for Fields, who warns him that he is used to getting his own way. Ronnie advises him to get away from that house for his own good. Maxie summons Shark to come up with a plan to make Danny change his mind and he, still smarting from the beating he received in the alley, is only too happy to comply.

At the King Creole, the hitherto star attraction, Forty Nina, (Liliane Montevecchi) (*qv*), whose act includes a sizzling dance routine with bananas, followed by a strip-tease (unseen), complains that the customers now only want to hear Danny sing and have even started calling out 'Keep them on!' as she starts to disrobe. She likes Danny, however, and bears no grudge. After Maxie's scheme to compromise Ronnie with Danny fails – at first she tells him that Maxie, apparently lying drunk in the next room, will punish her if he does not spend the night with her: eventually her better nature asserts itself and she tells Danny to say 'no' to Maxie's offer. At Shark's suggestion, Maxie's next ploy is to involve Fisher Senior by robbing his employer when he goes to the bank with the takings. Heavy rain causes the chemist to send Fisher instead, and it is he who takes the vicious beating from Maxie's thugs, thus playing straight into Fields' hands. Fisher lies at death's door and only an expensive operation can save him.

Maxie takes over and pays for the operation, which is successful. Danny has no option but to sign a contract to work for him. After a final show at the King Creole Danny makes a curtain speech and tells Charlie he is walking out on him. Charlie is understandably hurt and Mimi, now engaged to marry him, even more so. She tells her brother, with whom she has never previously had a cross word, that he belongs out in the streets with the other hoodlums. As if this were not enough, the dumb boy Sol (Brian Hutton), one of Shark's gang, whom Danny had befriended after the raid on the 5 & 10, is waiting with a written warning that Maxie is with the convalescent Mr. Fisher. Maxie has told him falsely that Danny actually took part in the robbery that nearly cost him his life, but intended to punish the chemist. In the circumstances, his son's protest, 'I did it for you, father', rings more than a little hollow and Fisher leaves him without a word.

Danny bursts in on Maxie and Ronnie and gives Fields the beating of his life, telling Ronnie to get away while she can – Maxie has just hit her and snarled that she was his property. Ronnie runs out and Danny leaves Maxie unconscious on the floor. As he comes to he phones his boys to go after Danny, who is viciously savaged and left for dead. Ronnie finds him and takes him to a secret hideaway at the end of a ramshackle wooden jetty where she has been able to get away from Maxie in the past and nurses him back to health. She begs him to pretend he loves her so she can enjoy just one day of happiness before she is found and destroyed by her nemesis. Danny, having already hurt Nellie by telling her he can no longer go along with their plans for marriage until he has sorted himself out, realizes that he also loves Ronnie and there would be no pretence if he made love to her.

Maxie, crazy for revenge, somehow discovers their whereabouts and arrives in his car, accompanied by Sol, Danny's dumb friend, whom he deputes to wait by the rickety door at the beginning of the jetty. When Sol sees that Maxie has a gun he follows, intent on warning Danny and Ronnie, but is unable to make himself heard. Maxie fires and the first shot hits Ronnie, who collapses into Danny's arms. Meanwhile Sol has caught up with Maxie and is able to deflect his aim as he fires at Danny. He wrestles Maxie off the rickety pier and into the water. As they fall, Maxie's gun goes off and he himself is despatched by the bullet he had earmarked for Danny. Ronnie dies in his arms, murmuring 'It was a lovely day for a little while'.

Danny returns to Charlie's King Creole club. Nellie comes to his dressing room before the show, embraces him and says 'Maybe now', but he interrupts her with 'Not now Nellie; maybe in a little while, when the time is right.' She tells him she has plenty of time and will wait for him. He goes on stage to sing 'As Long As I Have You' as Nellie and his sister Mimi watch. When his father comes in through the door, Danny notices him and directs the words of the songs towards him. Father beams, Mimi and Nellie beam. Fade out on a happy ending.

Never was a happy ending more richly merited, or more of a relief. For all that Danny Fisher's problems are really brought about by his own rebellious nature, he does have more than his fair share to put up with in a part reputedly designed for James Dean. This is one of

the few instances when Elvis had the benefit of a more that competent director – Michael Curtiz has been called one of the greats – even though it was towards the end of his prolific career. The result shows us a vibrant, caring Presley, in one of the truest and most moving performances he ever gave. It is, in fact, an extremely violent movie – the stark mood of the sleazy New Orleans back waters, with garish night-spots and dark alleyways, is sharply etched in Russell Harlan's black and white photography: colour could only have muted the impact of dramatic character clashes. Danny, struggling to escape from his sordid environment by trying to please his idealistic father (Dean Jagger) by graduating from school when his heart is set on making his name as a singer; the father, kind and well-meaning, but weak; the innocent and trusting waitress, Nellie (Dolores Hart), who falls immediately for Danny's charms, but is not prepared to fall straight into bed with him in the cheap hotel room into which he has tricked her; Ronnie, the glamorous ex-singer (Carolyn Jones), now alcoholic and a kept woman, who sees in Danny a dream of escape from the sordid life into which she has drifted; Maxie Fields (Walter Matthau), a sadistic gangland king and Ronnie's keeper, callous, uncaring, but insanely jealous; Mimi, Danny's elder sister (Jan Shepard), devoted to her family, but only too happy to seize an opportunity to make a life of her own when the straight-dealing owner of the King Creole night-club (Paul Stewart) offers her his hand in marriage: these are the pivotal characters around whom the plot revolves and all are admirably well characterized. Curtiz, who brought out the best in such stars as Errol Flynn, John Garfield, James Cagney, Bette Davis, Ingrid Bergman, Humphrey Bogart and Joan Crawford, works his alchemy among his players here. Elvis was never more sensitive or dynamic; Walter Matthau, in his pre-

comedy days, never more dislikeably villainous, nor Paul Stewart, an unjustly underpraised actor more toughly sympathetic as Matthau's deadly rival in the night-club business. One of the most off-beat and unusual actresses of her day, Carolyn Jones, is both hard-surfaced and touchingly vulnerable: that she never reached the ultimate heights of stardom could be due to her mannerisms being too reminiscent of Bette Davis', admirably suited though they were to Carolyn's most popular role in the mid-sixties as Morticia in *The Addams Family*. Dolores Hart, totally convincing as an innocent girl who falls romantically in love, has an inner radiance lacking in most Hollywood ladies – or can that be hindsight, considering she gave up her career in the mid-sixties to become a Roman Catholic nun, and is now known as Mother Dolores? Presumably here is one ex-star who will not be selling her story to the tabloids about a steamy relationship off-set with her co-star! Jan Shepard's role is hardly demanding: filial and sisterly devotion are what are called for in the main, but she handles her discovery of love and one explosive outburst effectively. Dean Jagger excels as always in portraying other-wordly sincerity as effectively in these later character roles as he did earlier as leading man to such stars as Dame Anna Neagle and Linda Darnell.

Critics on both sides of the Atlantic were cautiously enthusiastic over the discovery that Presley could act. *Picturegoer*'s Margaret Hinxman, most damning of the films magazine critics over *Love Me Tender* (qv), wrote 'Stop the laughs – now it's perfect Presley.' American *Variety* raved – even more than usual about 'thespian tops' – and Paul Dehn, originally one of the severest critics announced in the *News Chronicle*:

Mr. Presley has a new admirer – me! ...... completely won over to Mr. Elvis Presley, the ranks of whose billion admirers I now gratefully swell. (He) has suddenly learnt to act very well indeed, curbed his convulsions (he even sings one number sitting down) and cut off his sideburns (qv)....the part gives him scope to stop behaving like an electrocuted baboon and to act like a human being, which he does with a new skill, a new restraint and a new charm....the bad thing about the picture is that the hero's indecisions are all resolved by recourse to physical violence ......brisk, exciting pace set by director Michael Curtiz which never lets up, except for the admirably spaced production numbers, in which Mr. Presley gives us, at some length, his musical all. His very singing has actually improved with his other attainments and the voice, which used to resemble a repeatedly butted goat's is now beginning to sound like a new-born lamb.'

Born again critic, indeed. My only complaint is with one facet of the story-line, which is probably down to writer Harold Robbins in the first place: when Danny Stone has to announce the conclusion of his engagement at the King Creole night-club, he does it without warning his benefactor, Charlie LeGrand, and understandably quizzed by 'What was that all about?' says 'I'm walking out on you, Charlie – you never did produce that contract and you can't very well tear up a handshake' – or words to that effect. Whereas he could have saved hurting his sympathetic employer and his sister with the simple explanation that he'd been blackmailed into it by Charlie's rival Maxie Fields, who'd been the only one able to pay for the operation that saved Danny's father's life. Much simpler, but less dramatic. *(See also: Love Me Tender; Montevecchi, Liliane)*

KING CREOLE
12(RCA LPM 1884) August 1958
KING CREOLE * * * * *
Written by Jerry Lieber, Mike Stoller. The title song of the film features Danny Fisher in jubilant mood, having received the news from the hospital that his father has successfully undergone a crucial operation that saves his life after enduring a vicious beating. Lieber and Stoller at their peak provide Elvis with probably the trickiest phrasing job he ever tackled and this is a brilliant achievement – the ideal fusion of lyricists, musical content and singer. Elvis expresses sheer *joie de vivre* as he dances in frenetic tempo to demonstrate the activity of the hip-shaking King Creole, swinging his guitar like a tommy gun. Just behind him, in matching happy mood, Orleans-style, The Jordanaires sing and play clarinet, sax and trombone.
EP: 'King Creole – Vol. 1'
LPs: 'Elvis in Hollywood'; 'Elvis – The Other Sides – Worldwide Gold Award Hits – Vol. 2 King Creole'

AS LONG AS I HAVE YOU * * * *
Written by Fred Wise, Ben Weisman. Effectively, the climax to the story – the happy ending that all the good people have been waiting for (the bad ones having been disposed of). Danny, back working for Charlie LeGrand at the King Creole, sings one of the most evocative slow ballads he has ever recorded, expressing his feelings that, come rain or high water, he's happy as long as he has the people he cares for around him, including his sister Mimi, now engaged to Charlie, the faithful Nellie, and, most of all, the father from whom he has been estranged.

HARD HEADED WOMAN * * * * *
Written by Claude Demitrius. One of the fastest rockers Danny Stone sings at the King Creole club. It's about a mean but infinitely attractive woman. An exciting number, delivered with the electricity Elvis can generate like no other, aided by the backing of tailgate trombones and screaming Dixieland trumpets.
Single B/W: 'Don't Ask Me Why'
EPs: 'A Touch of Gold – Vol. 1'

LPs: 'Elvis – The Elvis Medley'; 'Elvis – Worldwide Gold Award Hits – Vol. 1 King Creole'; 'The Number One Hits'; 'The Top Ten Hits'

TROUBLE * * * * *
Written by Jerry Lieber, Mike Stoller. Sung at the command of Maxie Fields as busboy Danny is clearing up at his club, the Blue Shades. Fields walks in with Ronnie and Danny comes to greet her. She cuts him dead and Maxie wants to know how she knows him. She says she heard him sing a song. 'Boy – I hear you can sing,' says the Big Bossman, 'Then sing: if you don't, then I know the lady's lying.' So Danny, with the club's backing band, including a black trumpeter, goes into this Lieber–Stoller masterpiece, admirably suited to express just what he thinks of the gangland boss who has made Ronnie's life such a living hell. After a Dixieland opening, Elvis talks the first four lines then swings into a Dixieland songslide, then back to four more spoken lines and so on. Towards the end the song is swung furiously, with Elvis ripping through the lyrics which emphasize how evil he is and not to be messed around with – the sentiment repeated, leading into a quick and cute climax. This is a prime example of singing with acting – Elvis expresses sheer contempt with every timbre of his voice and expression. Great swing background – every musical instrument going at full blast.
EP: 'King Creole – Vol. 2'
LPs: 'Elvis – The Other Sides – Worldwide Gold Award Hits – Vol. 2'; 'Elvis – TV Special'

DIXIELAND ROCK
(not on record)
Written by Aaron Schroeder, Rachel Frank.
At Charlie LeGrand's King Creole nightclub – Danny had decided to accept his offer of a job on the recommendation of Ronnie, whose agent he once was – he has to go on after the

sensational strip number 'Bananas' by Forty Nina, the top attraction at the club. This could have been a bonus number on the 'King Creole' LP, but, alas, there is no room for bonuses, so it has to be seen to be believed. This song is Danny's try-out and is such a triumph that Charlie engages him forthwith, on the gentleman's agreement of a handshake. The song is an entirely successful blending of trad jazz and rock, thanks not only to Elvis's interpretation of the words, but also to the fantastic singing and dancing pace he manages to keep up. From then on his name is in lights.

EP: 'King Creole -Vol. 2'
LP: 'Elvis – The Other Sides – Worldwide Gold Award Hits – Vol. 2'

DON'T ASK ME WHY * * *

Written by Fred Wise, Ben Weisman. Another sad song, coming after Maxie has blackmailed Danny into signing a contract with him, having persuaded Ronnie to talk him into it. Danny realizes that she is bad for him, that the attraction is mainly physical, though there's more to it than that. He sings this with a slight edge to his voice, which prevents the song becoming a mere dirge. The full-blooded instrumental backing to Elvis and his guitar is counterpointed by The Jordanaires echoing of the lyrics. The Wise–Weisman team have had more than their share of detractors, but they are tops when it comes to wringing the heart strings. It is after this that Danny tells Nellie he can't go through with their planned marriage: another reason for the ballad to be a sad one.

Single B/W: 'Hard Headed Woman'
EP: 'A Touch of Gold – Vol. 3'
LPs: 'Elvis – The Other Sides – Worldwide Gold Award Hits – Vol. 2'

LOVER DOLL * * * *

Written by Sid Wayne, Abner Silver. Danny sings this song in the 5 & 10 stores to deflect attention from his

hoodlum associates who are helping themselves from the counters. Customers and staff listen to him with rapt attention. Simple, sweet lyrics concern the lover doll he adores. One for the kiddies, really. It certainly makes soda fountain girl Nellie fall for him, to the extent that she does not report him for his part in the theft. It's all twanging guitars, with The Jordanaires singing softly but gaily along. It is an up-dated version of the kind of song Britain's top film stars in pre-war years, Gracie Fields (*qv*) and George Formby with his ukelele, used to sing in stores while the customers jigged around them.

EP: 'King Creole – Vol. 1'
LP: 'Elvis – The Other Sides – Worldwide Gold Award Hits – Vol. 2'

CRAWFISH * * * * *

Written by Fred Wise, Ben Weisman. (Duet with Kitty White). A wonderful opening to the movie, taking in the sights and sounds of New Orleans, with the fish vendors crying their wares. The camera picks out one of them: Kitty White, singing of the crawfish in the basket on her head, as she drives through the street with her horse and cart, under a large parasol to keep the sun away. This introduces Elvis on a close-up as he joins in with her and sings of how he caught one of these fishes down in the Bayou and looks forward to how good it will be when cooked. A unique recording, not only for being the first time Elvis sang with a girl vocalist, but for the content and the extraordinary range it calls for in his voice. Drum beats predominate in the best opening to any Presley movie and one of my own personal favourite songs, admirably setting the tone for the whole film. Strictly an uncommercial, but a beauty.

YOUNG DREAMS * * * *

Written by Aaron Schroeder, Martin Kalmanof.
Sung by Danny to Nellie and obviously dedicated to her youth and innocence.

Strong melody line and great backing, charming sentiments charmingly sung, but for some reason not entireley satisfactory despite The Jordanaires best endeavours.

EP: 'King Creole – Vol. 2'
LP: 'Elvis – The Other Sides – Worldwide Gold Award Hits – Vol. 2'

STEADFAST, LOYAL AND TRUE * * * *

Written by Jerry Lieber, Mike Stoller. A variation on the Hail, Alma Mater theme, sung ad lib by Danny at Ronnie's request to keep the rowdies at the Blue Shades club quiet after Danny, cleaning up has rescued her from the advances of one of them trying to get off with her. A scarcely perceptible male chorus backing is redundant: Elvis sings the lyrics simply, sadly and beautifully, despite the attempts of one of the drunks to make him 'rock it up'. Uncharacteristic Lieber–Stoller but worthwhile; only on 'King Creole' EP.

NEW ORLEANS * * * * *

Written by Sid Tepper, Roy C. Bennet. A blues vocal with Dixieland backing at a tense moment for Danny, having just turned down Maxie Field's pressing insistence he join his club as a singer. This builds up to the near death of Danny's father at the hands of Maxie's hoodlums. Saxophone introduction leads Elvis into some real blues phrasing, combined with hip swinging – literally, either way you want it – producing a great beat unlike anything else in the movie. The Jordanaires join in predominantly and with evident relish, adding up to one of the best Presley numbers ever.

EPs: 'King Creole – Vol. 1'; 'See the USA the Elvis Way'
LPs: 'Elvis – The Other Sides – Worldwide Gold Award Hits – Vol. 2'

DANNY

2(not included in movie)
Written by Fred Wise, Ben Weisman.

Recorded for film King Creole but not used.

EP: KING CREOLE

B/W: As Long As I Have You, Lover Doll
LP: 'Elvis – A Legendary Performer – Vol. 3'
EP: 'King Creole – Vol. 2: Trouble, Young Dreams'
B/W: 'Crawfish', 'Dixieland Rock'

THE KING IS DEAD – VIVAT REX

Elvis's world fell apart after his divorce. He went on working and never lost his rapport with his audiences but that and Lisa Marie (*qv*) were all he had to live for and he certainly was not taking care of his health. Although already a sick man, his intake of forbidden substances – drugs and fatty foods had reached inordinate proportions. According to Dee Stanley in her book, 'After he and 'Cilla broke up, he lost control'.

Ginger Alden, the last girl to share Graceland (*qv*) with him, moved in at the time Lisa Marie was enjoying her longest – and last – visit with her father since she and Priscilla moved out in 1972. Lisa had been staying with Elvis on a fairly regular basis, but never for as long as this. After waking for breakfast at four in the afternoon of August 15, 1977, Elvis played with Lisa Marie for the last time, until he left on his motorbike with Ginger to visit his dentist, Dr. Lester Hoffman, to have two teeth filled. On returning he asked Ginger and his cousin Billy and wife Jo Smith to play racquet ball with him, which they did until 6 a.m. the next morning, when he and Ginger retired to bed. Unable to sleep, he read for a while before asking Rick Stanley for his usual medication, which was brought to him by Aunt Delta. Ginger stayed up with him until 9 a.m. when she went to bed, telling him not to fall asleep over his book, *The Face of Jesus* which he took with him to his dressing

room/bathroom, as was his wont. He answered, 'All right, I won't', which were the last words anyone heard him speak.

When Ginger awoke at 2 p.m. and found she was alone in the bed she went to look for him and found him still in the bathroom, lying doubled up face downwards. Unable to wake him, she went to summon help and returned to find Aunt Delta trying to give him mouth-to-mouth resuscitation. Then Ginger heard Lisa climbing the stairs, asking what was wrong. She told her 'nothing' and shouted to Al Strada, the Memphis Mafia (*qv*) member who had been on duty that evening, that Lisa was trying to get in. Meanwhile Ginger tried to stop the child rushing round to the other end of the landing to get into the bathroom from the other side. Al quickly locked the door and Lisa was mercifully spared from seeing what had happened. Joe Esposito (*qv*) had called the ambulance and joined Aunt Delta in trying to revive Elvis. But the King was already dead.

(See also: Elvis and the Face of Jesus; Girls, Girls, Girls (not the movie); Presley, Lisa Marie; Memphis Mafia; Narcotics)

KISSIN' COUSINS * * * *

Released by: Metro-Goldwyn-Mayer, a Four Leaf Production (Metrocolor, Panavision); **Producer:** Sam Katzman; **Director:** Gene Nelson; **Screenplay:** Gerald Drayson Adams from a story by Gerald Adams; **Art Director:** George W. Davis; **Director of Photography:** Ellis W. Carter, ASC; **Technical Advisor:** Colonel Tom Parker; **Music:** supervised and conducted by Fred Karger, vocal background by The Jordanaires;
Running Time: 96 mins; **Opened:** March 6, 1963.

Cast: Elvis, Arthur O'Connell, Glenda Farrell, Jack Albertson, Pam Austin, Yvonne Craig, Cynthia Pepper, Donald Woods, Tommy Farrell, Beverley Powers, Hortense Petra, Robert Stone, Hezekiah.

The US Air Force plan to build a missile base atop a Tennessee mountain, Big Smokey, but the General (Donald Woods) (*qv*) points out that the mountain is private property, owned for the past hundred years by the Tatum family, headed by Pappy Tatum, a moonshiner whose family are a pretty wild bunch. The General deputes Captain Robert Jason Salbo (Jack Albertson) to overcome the opposition to the building of the missile base on the mountain, on pain of being posted to the Air Forces North Pole base in the event of failure. The Captain passes the onus onto Lt. Josh Morgan (Elvis) to persuade the Tatum family to grant the lease of their mountain as a missile base. When Josh and his platoon set out to find the Tatums they are met with some sharp shooting from behind the rocks. The sharp shooters turn out to be two extremely pretty young girls, Selena and Azalea Tatum (Pam Austin and Yvonne Craig) who, hearing from Josh that he is a distant cousin, descended from his Great Aunt who married a Tatum, put away their guns and leap at him. In the twinkling of a possum's tail the three of them have fallen into a convenient haystack while he sings to them. Jodie, a boisterous young hillbilly, their blond brother, strolls up with a murderous gleam in his eye, which turns to wonder when he realizes he is looking at someone who is almost his double. Jodie is also played by Elvis Presley in blond mode: Josh is Presley with his usual gleaming black hair.

He and his platoon are invited back to the Tatum ranch and made welcome by Ma (Glenda Farrell) (*qv*) over a memorable meal. When the Captain congratulates her on her cooking and asks what it is, she explains, 'It's just possum tails and gizzards and grits, fried with batter grease and that there gravy. That's just goats' milk with vulture eggs and mashed catfish eyes.' 'The cat fish eyes bring out the flavour of the possum's tails' adds Pappy, helpfully. This sounds for all the world like one of Elvis's favourite snacks. The Captain turns green, excuses himself and hurries out. Unfortunately, even Josh is unable to talk Pappy into signing an agreement, although Ma and her daughters are intrigued with what they could buy with the money from the lease. After vacillating between the charms of Selena and Azalea, both of whom do all but rape him, he tries to please them both by singing 'One Boy, Two Little Girls'. When a gang of girls, The Kittyhawks, starved of male company, hear there are men in the vicinity they come screeching up, having converged upon the platoon. To the enlisted mens' disappointment the Tatums beat off these mountain groupies. In the meantime, Jodie falls head over heels for a pretty blonde stenographer Midge Riley (Cynthia Pepper), imported into the camp by the Air Force. Josh persuades the Captain that it would be good strategy to provide the girls with pretty clothes: he drives the Tatum sisters into town and they come back loaded with eye-catching garments, including some for the Kittyhawks in return for their promising to stay away from Josh and Jodie. While on their shopping spree, the girls tell everyone about the proposed missile site and the story gets into the papers. While Pappy is on a hunting trip, Ma orders Josh to get the soldiers away from Smokey Mountain as the girls are neglecting their household chores by playing around with their new dresses.

While Josh is in the officer's tent, the General phones to say the story has hit the headlines in Washington and he is setting out for the Tatum ranch. While on an exercise the entire platoon is ambushed and, one by one, the men are abducted by the Kittyhawks. The Captain rounds up his men, prizing them from the insatiable Kittyhawks' arms and the girls agree to misdirect the General to delay his arrival at the Tatum homestead. Ma Tatum is deeply distressed when their bloodhound,

Hezekiah, comes back without Pappy, realizing that he must be in serious trouble. She relents about expelling the enlisted men from the mountain and they go in search of the missing head of the household, eventually locating him stuck up a tree, hitched to a branch that is in imminent danger of breaking and depositing him in Howling Devil's Gorge and certain death. Josh and his friends rescue him in the nick of time and they go back to the homestead to celebrate.

When the General arrives in his jeep, the Kittyhawks having set him on so many false trails that he is six hours later than anticipated, he is confronted with a whirling, colourful barbecue–cum square dance, headed by Pappy, dispensing copious quantities of Ma's lethal home brew of Mountain Maidens' Breath, of which he has partaken so generously that he is virtually wide-eyed and legless. Ma defuses the General's fury by taking him off to enjoy some of her home cooking washed down by her home brew. After much dithering, Pappy is persuaded by Josh to let the Force have their site. The General agrees to pay $1,000 a month for the land; also that the army will build a new and direct route to Porcupine Flats on the other side of the mountain and that no Government personnel should trespass on the Tatum's side of the mountain – which delights Pappy, as revenue men are part of Government personnel. Josh has settled for Azalea, Selena has been paired off with Master Sgt. Bailey (Tommy Farrell) and Jodie, after being thrown several times by the athletic stenographer, Midge, had persuaded her to accept his embraces. Signal for the entire cast, including the General, to join the celebration with a final reprise of the title song.

Considering that the film was a watershed for Colonel Parker's (*qv*) new economy drive in the production of Presley musicals under the production methods of Katzman (*qv*), the result is

remarkably entertaining, with Elvis convincingly differentiating his dual role of elegant lieutenant in his smart blue uniform and his hillbilly cousin in checked shirts and tight jeans. In his introduction to the TV showing of the film, David Stanley, Elvis's stepbrother, said that the blond wig worn by the hillbilly Jodie – which Elvis hated wearing and having to be reluctantly persuaded from his dressing room to face the cameras – is an approximation of his real hair colour before he dyed it black after meeting Roy Orbison at the Sun studios in Memphis. Elvis's asides are thrown away with just the right underplaying to get laughs, in contrast to the rough-and-tumble of the mountain nymphomaniacs hurling themselves at anything in trousers, Lieutenant Morgan's Forces' training in karate standing him in good stead with his cousin 'the Mountain's Champion Wrestler'. The doubling work here with Lance LeGault is extremely effective. 'What are you doing with my face?' is Jodie's response on meeting his cousin for the first time. After the Captain's hurried exit from table after hearing the ingredients of the meal he has just eaten with such relish described to him, Pappy asks why he was in such a hurry: 'Did something come up?' and Josh's reply is, 'Not yet, but I think it's about to!' Whether these lines can be ascribed to story writer Gerald Drayson Adams or director Gene Nelson, who re-wrote the script, is difficult to gauge, but I suspect the latter, who does such an effective job of co-ordinating the fast action and the choreography, ascribed to Hal Belfer. This is all the more remarkable as it appeared that there was often no time for proper rehearsals of the musical numbers. Everything was left to Nelson, an accomplished dancer himself, as he proved in so many musicals. The Colonel told him; 'We don't know how to make pictures. We have you for that. All we want is songs for an album.'

A bonus was the excellent

supporting cast, with the brilliant Arthur O'Connell again playing father to Elvis. He makes a real character out of Pappy Tatum and is matched for excellent characterization by the witty star of so many early talkies, Glenda Farrell (*qv*), who turned to character work from the Fifties onwards. Frank Albertson gives full value to his comedy lines as the Captain, while Donald Woods, a handsome juvenile through the Thirties, makes an imposing figure of the General, looking, at 60, some fifteen years younger and investing a stock character with authority.

All the girls, of course, are pretty and voluptuous: Yvonne Craig, who was sung to by Elvis the previous year in *It Happened at the World's Fair* (*qv*), is the most outstanding as Azalea Tatum, the sister Josh finally chooses for his own. Hortense Petra contributes an incisive portrait as go-getting reporter Dixie, and Beverley Powers the most impressive cleavage as Tracy, leader of the Kittyhawks. Total gross on the film was about $2.5 million, so presumably most people were delighted. Particularly Colonel Tom Parker.

In Britain, the film was released heading a double bill. The other half was *Never Put it in Writing*, starring Pat Boone (*qv*) and made in the UK. Presumably the reasoning was to counterbalance a Presley film, for those who still felt uneasy about rock 'n' roll, with the squeaky clean, ever-wholesome and famously religious Boone, whose records also sold in millions.

(See also: Boone versus Presley; Dogs; Farrell, Glenda; It Happened at the World's Fair; Katzman, Sam; Parker, Colonel Tom.)

KISSIN' COUSINS

(RCA LPM-2894. 1964) (Complete Soundtrack)

KISSIN' COUSINS (No. 2) * * *

Written by Fred Wise, Randy Starr. Introductory number, sung over credit titles. A racy beater, with amusing lyrics, accompanied by drums, guitars and an insistent piano.

Single B/W: It Hurts me.

SMOKEY MOUNTAIN BOY

(Bonus) (not included in movie) Written by Leonore Rosenblatt, Victor Millrose. Not heard in the film. A new beat for Elvis – a swing march tempo which is highly effective.

THERE'S GOLD IN THE MOUNTAIN * *

Written by Bill Giant, Bernie Baum and Florence Kaye. Describes the setting for the plot of the film – a remote hillbilly section of the Big Smokey Mountains. Jangling guitars accompany Lieutenant Josh Morgan as he serenades Selena and Azalea Tatum who sing along with him.

ONE BOY, TWO LITTLE GIRLS * * *

Written by Bill Giant, Bernie Baum and Florence Kaye. A romantic ballad, sung by Josh to the Tatum sisters as they stroll together in the woods near the family homestead. Piano and guitar accompany Josh, who explains he's having too much fun at the moment to give up either one of them. This is Elvis in wistful, teasing mood, singing of the joys of keeping his options open, clad in one of his most sexy outfits – a skintight white jumpsuit, open to the waist to reveal a scarlet shirt. If he was having weight problems, it's certainly not visible here.

CATCHIN' ON FAST * * * *

Written by Bill Giant, Bernie Baum and Florence Kaye. Sung by Jodie and the entire cast, including the Kittyhawks, at a party to celebrate Pappy's rescue from near death – a real hillbilly song and dance.

TENDER FEELING * * *

Written by Bill Giant, Bernie Baum and Florence Kaye. A slow ballad, sung by Jodie, with which he romances PFC Midge Riley (Cynthia Pepper), stenographer on loan to the unit. She has already shown him she is not to be won over easily, flipping him with ease over her shoulder when his advances become too boisterous. Guitars are again predominant, the beat slow, in accordance with the mood of the song, by which she appears to be visibly moved. But the kiss at the end is too much. Again she throws him and he scrambles to his feet and gives chase, saying 'You're going to get tired some time and say you'll marry me.'

LP: 'Burning Love'; Hits from His Movies

ANYONE (COULD FALL IN LOVE WITH YOU) * *

Written by Bennie Benjamin, Sol Marcus, Louis A. Dejusu. Another romantic ballad, sung to Azalea, when Josh has made up his mind that she's the one for him. Guitars, strings and drums.

BAREFOOT BALLAD * * * *

Written by Delores Fuller, Lee Morris. Another big 'jump' number, sung by Jodie with the whole cast singing and dancing along to a country/hillbilly flavoured song, while the Tatum family celebrate.

ONCE IS ENOUGH * * *

Written by Sid Tepper, Roy C. Bennett. Another rocker, in which Elvis lets loose with everything in his vocal battery, backed by twanging banjos, drums, piano and double bass. The cast again participate and Yvonne Craig executes some nifty high kicks. The song switches from one Elvis to the other, 'Hey Josh, you sing pretty well for a city boy.' Pappy leads into the number, signifying his assent to the union of Azalea and Josh.

Cliff Richard, Britain's answer to Elvis Presley, displays his Golden Disc from his hit movie. *The Young Ones (Wonderful To Be Young* in the **US). (1961)**

KISSIN' COUSINS

(No.1) as above (reprise) * * *
Concluding number, with Elvis's famous duet with himself. With him as Josh is Azalea, with Jodie is Midge, still in her uniform. They all collapse into each other's arms, conveniently separated by the ubiquitous haystack. Mysteriously absent from the action is Selena Tatum, though she can be glimpsed in the background with other cast personnel as Pappy and the Captain hold up THE END signs.

The rest of the LP is taken up with three bonus songs: (not included in movie)

ECHOES OF LOVE

Written by Bob Roberts, Paddy McMains.
This is nostalgia, sung with the yearning Elvis expressed so potently.

IT'S A LONG, LONELY HIGHWAY

Written by Doc Pomus and Mort Schuman.
Variation on the nostalgia theme – this time with a beat.

IT HURTS ME

Written by Joe Byers, Charlie Daniels.
Single B/W: Kissin' Cousins
LPs: 'Elvis – A Legendary Performer – Vol. 13'; 'Elvis Gold Records Vol. 4'; 'Elvis: The Other Sides'; 'Worldwide Gold Award Hits – Vol. 2'.

KNIGHT, KING AND MOVIES

Sir Cliff Richard, since 1958 Britain's most enduring teenage rave has emerged, nearly forty years later, into what Julie Mundy, President of the Official Elvis Presley Fan Club of Great Britain, called in an article in the *Monthly Magazine* the 'Peter Pan of Pop'.

Born Harry Webb in Lucknow, India, October 14, 1940, five years later than Elvis Presley, he was heavily influenced by him and when he formed his first group, 'The Quintones', at the church youth club in Cheshunt where he then lived, he would spend hours in front of the mirror, practicing the curl of the lip, the hip swivel and leg gyrating, while miming to Elvis records. His first manager, John Foster, booked him into the 2 i's Coffee Club in Old Compton Street, Soho, the virtual birth place of British rock 'n' roll, after Tommy Steele's (*qv*) smash hit there. He made his first TV appearance as Cliff Richard and the Drifters on September 13, 1958, in Jack Good and Josephine Douglas's *Oh Boy*. It was Good who first recognized the amazing audience reaction to Cliff's looks and voice, made him shave off his sideburns, took away his guitar and encouraged him to steer clear of the Presley image.

The next year, 1959, after his first no. 1 hit record 'Move It', he was 'introduced' to movies in Terence Young's *Serious Charge* (*Immoral Charge* in the US) – a heavy drama in which a vicar (the late Sir Anthony Quayle) is accused of seducing a young boy (Andrew Ray) by an embittered spinster parishoner (Sarah Churchill) who resents the vicar's indifference to her charms. It did well on two counts – an early treatment of the theme of homosexuality, two years before Dirk Bogarde's more famous *Victim* and the introduction of Cliff Richard as a singing friend of Andrew Ray in the coffee bar frequented by teenagers. The name of Sarah Churchill (daughter of Sir Winston) gained it an American showing. She had recently been to Hollywood for Fred Astaire's *Royal Wedding*. Elvis had then been called into the army.

Cliff's first starring role was in the film musical *Expresso Bongo*, directed and produced by Val Guest and co-starring his wife Yolande Donlan, which was released in 1960, the same year as Elvis's *G.I. Blues*. It did not rival the latter in popularity but did very respectably in Britain. The story, of a young singer's rise to rock 'n' roll stardom, was adapted by Wolf Mankowitz from his play *Expresso Bongo*, a major hit on the West End Stage, with a plot reminiscent of Presley's 1957 *Loving You*: such a theme at that time, was an almost certain passport to success. Cliff's next two movies in colour, *The Young Ones* (*Wonderful To Be Young* in the US), directed by Sidney Furie, already at 28 a cult director, and in 1961 *Summer Holiday*, two years later, directed by Peter Yates, were, along with their theme songs, 'Top of the Pops' in Britain. The next, in 1964, the year of Elvis's *Viva Las Vegas*, was *Wonderful Life* (*Swingers' Paradise* in the US) also directed by Sidney Furie, though slightly less popular. After this Cliff concentrated with enduring success on his recording career, cleverly adapting his style to suit with the times. He has, to date, made three more movies, *Finders Keepers* (1966), *Two A Penny* (1968) and *Hot Property* in 1973.

In 1996 Cliff realized his long-cherished dream to play Heathcliff in the musical version of Emily Bronte's *Wuthering Heights*, investing a good deal of his own money in the project and reaching the West End after a long pre-booked out tour. Critics may scoff, but the profits may well take him back to the movies, in a role the Elvis could have been born to play in his film heyday.

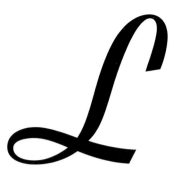

LANCHESTER, ELSA (1902–1986)

Eccentric English comedienne Elsa Lanchester made history in the Elvis Presley annals by being the only mature female to accompany him in a comedy song and dance scene. Married to the great Charles Laughton, who had introduced the first *Ed Sullivan Show* that Elvis ever appeared on (September 9th, 1956), Elsa had cornered the Hollywood market in playing zany grande dames and out-and-out weirdoes, for which her extraordinary features and physique made her uniquely fitted. She brightened up the otherwise undistinguished Presley film of 1967, *Easy Come, Easy Go* (qv) with her appearance as Madame Neherina, who runs yoga classes for the artistic set at the home of Jo Symington (Dodie Marshall). During a very funny scene Madame leads him in a dance entitled 'Yoga Is As Yoga Does', enveloping him in her vast flowing kaftan. The song, written by Gerald Nelson and Fred Burch, made a distinct departure for Elvis, as unusual as was his partner in the duet. Such comedy antics used to be a familiar scene for Elsa during her early career as a cabaret artiste in London's Soho, where she herself had her own band of off-beat followers in the Twenties. Two of her most memorable roles in films were as Queen Anne of Cleves, opposite Laughton's *Henry VIII* in 1933 and again opposite him as his bullying nurse in *Witness For The*

Prosecution with Dietrich, for which she received one of her two Oscar nominations – the other was *Come To The Stable* as a nun in 1949. People still talk about her terrifying appearance in the 1935 *Bride Of Frankenstein*.

On being introduced to her by director John Rich on the set of *Easy Come, Easy Go*, Elvis surprised her by having seen all of these films, as well as the George Cukor version of *David Copperfield*, her first Hollywood film, in which she played the maid, Clickett. 'How sweet of you to say so,' she said, 'but I don't believe a word of it – after all, they were mostly made before you were born.' 'Well ma'am,' he replied, 'I used to work as a cinema usher and I caught some of them then: now I hire the local movie hall if I want to see movies with my buddies and you'd be surprised at the range we can get.' He told her that after meeting Charles Laughton on the *Ed Sullivan Show* he made a point of seeing *Witness For The Prosecution* several times, 'You see ma'am, I had an ambition to be a proper actor myself, once.' 'Oh, but you are, my dear, you are. Your own performances always have a touch of magic, even in the most trying of circumstances.' Their duet was a wow.

Before she died she wrote a warts and all account of her life with her late husband, Charles Laughton.
(See also: Easy Come, Easy Go)

LIVE A LITTLE, LOVE A LITTLE *

Released by: Metro-Goldwyn-Mayer (Panavision, Metrocolor) **Producer:** Douglas Laurence; **Director:** Norman Taurog; **Screenplay:** Michael A. Hoey, Dan Greenberg, based on Greenberg's novel *Kiss My Firm But Pliant Lips*, **Art Directors:** George W. Davis, Preston Ames; **Director of Photography:** Ted Koencamp, ASC; **Running Time:** 90 mins; **Opened:** October 23, 1968.

Cast: Elvis, Michele Carey, Don Porter, Rudy Vallee, Dick Sargent, Sterling Holloway, Celeste Yarnall, Eddie Hodges, Joan Shawlee, Morgan Winbeal, Benjie Bancroft, Mary Grover, Emily Bandy, Merri Ashley, Phyllis Davis, Ursula Menzel, Susan Shute, Gabrielle, Eddie Baskin, Ginny Laneen, Susan Hennessy, Red West and Albert.

Greg Nolan (Elvis), a photographer on an LA paper, heads for the beach, intent on taking some shots of the ocean and getting a little peace. Within seconds his beach blanket is being shared by Albert, a massive Great Dane and his young and irresponsible mistress, Bernice (Michele Carey), an artist, who also goes by several other names as the mood and the man of the moment strike her. Alice, Betty, Mrs. Baby and Susie are some of her aliases. She asks Greg if he would like to make love to her and when he proves apprehensive and unresponsive she tells

Photographer Greg Nolan (Elvis) is not too sure he welcomes the advances of Bernice (Michele Carey) and her Great Dane, Albert, who is frankly bored with the whole situation. *Live A Little, Love A Little* (1968)

Albert to chase him into the sea and keep him there until the sun sets over the Atlantic, when she takes him home with her, dazed and shivering with cold. He is too weak to resist when she puts him to bed and medicates him: unsurprisingly he is running a temperature.

Surprises are in store: the tradesmen, including the redheaded grocery delivery boy (Eddie Hodges) and milkman (Sterling Holloway) seem to have the run of the house and each has his own name for her. There is also a 'dead' husband, Harry (Dick Sargent), who turns out to be neither dead, nor her husband. When Greg returns to his newspaper he finds he has been fired and the city editor tells some of his men to throw him out – one of them, inevitably, is Red West, throwing punches as to the manner born. He also discovers that Bernice had moved him out of his apartment, claiming to be his sister, 'Mrs. Baby', and paid the back rent. He has been moved in with Bernice and the prospect does not appeal. People come and go at will and Harry still has a key to the apartment where he hangs around for no apparent reason and has to be despatched with a punch when Greg arrives for a dinner date with Bernice and finds Harry there too, ready to dispense champagne. Greg is convinced he's losing his mind and has to get himself a job – quickly. He has no difficulty with his combination of aggressive approach, talent and charm, in landing not just one job, but two, in advertising agencies on alternative floors, for men with diametrically opposing outlooks on the advertising game. Mike Lansdown (Don Porter) is a progressive, leery bon viveur, who dresses all his female staff bunny-girl style and lives a life of partying. He also hates formality in dress and orders Greg never to wear a tie – 'It restricts the circulation'. One floor below, Louis Penlow (Rudy Vallee) is an old stick-in-the-mud traditionalist who insists on sartorial correctness.

Lansdown's starting time for employees is 9.30 a.m., Penlow's 9 a.m., giving the dynamic Greg just time to change from his immaculates to his casuals in the men's room and run up or down the stairs to do his photography. So excellent is his work and time-keeping that nothing is suspected until the two directors meet face to face during one of Lansdown's photo sessions for a centre spread. Greg is fired but almost immediately reinstated.

Meanwhile, Bernice has picked out an elegant one-bedroom flat for Greg, with whom she is increasingly besotted. He is shocked to find her a guest at one of Mike Lansdown's almost all-girl parties. When he brings home a beautiful model from the party, Ellen, (Celeste Yarnell), Bernice bustles in, doing the vacuuming, and the girl angrily asks Greg to take her home. There is a crash – Bernice is collapsed on the floor, with Albert by her side. Greg calls the doctor, but it appears she only has a lump on her head from hitting the table. She is put in Mike's bed to recover, 'too ill to move', and insists she is too ill to molest him. Her next ploy is to erect a wooden wall of Jericho (See Gable/Colbert in *It Happened One Night*) down the centre of the double bed. After one night of this Greg throws the wall through the window and 'makes a woman of her'. This apparently confuses her so much she goes back to Harry. Greg confronts him angrily in the beach house that had been Harry's all along. He lets the 'best man win', tells Greg where to find her and throws a half-hearted punch at him in retaliation for the one he had received at the dinner party earlier. Greg finds Bernice back on the beach where they first met with Albert, who is so attuned to their dialogue that he evens up the score by chasing Bernice into the sea when she tells Greg that his kiss means nothing to her. He runs after her into the sea, fully clad as before, to share a passionate embrace while the waves wash over

them. Albert gets the final close-up, looking into camera and showing a fang to express his attitude to the strange ways of the two-legged species.

This has to be the nadir of Elvis's film career – three to go, but none so absurd. It's a sad tale of opportunity missed. Norman Taurog (*qv*) simply did not have the style to make the most of what was obviously intended to be a soufflé of crazy comedy inconsequentiality. To invite comparison with Frank Capra's all-time witty comedy handling of *It Happened One Night* by pinching the 'Wall of Jericho' gag was a fatal mistake. The dialogue by Michael Hoey and co-writer Dan Greenberg, from the latter's novel *Kiss My Firm But Pliant Lips* – now there was a more effective title – is trite in the extreme and entirely misses the goal of sophisticated humour which was evidently the aim. Nor has Michele Carey the experience to make something out of the cooky nymphomaniac role with which she is saddled – it would have needed a Carole Lombard. The kidnapping of Presley's Greg Nolan effectively to be her sex slave needs the most delicate sensitivity to make it work as a theme. Maybe the Capra touch could have coaxed the requisite performance out of Elvis, who is here thrown back on his own resources and familiar reactions: also there's nothing really worthwhile to sing. The most the part does for him is to provide an effective mannequin parade of contrasting clothing styles as he changes from chic casual to mostly elegant fancy suitings, all of which he models with considerable aplomb. Perhaps the incessant running up and down stairs helped keep his physique in trim, though one wonders why Frank Tuttle's make-up department have given him flesh tones that recall his occasional American Indian characterizations.

Albert the Great Dane inevitably steals the film – and the final close-up, for which he's been provided with a

Dracula-like fang which maybe, as he's such a super performer, he keeps out of sight for the rest of the time. Or can we again blame Frank Tuttle's department? Interestingly, one of Elvis's co-stars is Rudy Vallee, at 67 some thirty-five years on from his swoon-crooner days of the late Twenties and early Thirties and well into his third career as an elderly character actor. His is an amazing portrayal of the staid and stodgy advertising executive, nicely contrasted with Don Porter's as the raunchy Lansdown: silver-haired but both still recognizable from their heyday when inter alia Porter was a handsome co-star of Constance Bennett in 1941 in *Madame Spy*. Another character actor from the Thirties and Forties, Sterling Holloway, reappeared at 63, still blond and hillbilly voiced, playing the milkman in Michele Carey's life – obviously an in-joke of the director's, for whom he must have played scores of milkmen and delivery boys in the early talkies.

(See also: Taurog, Norman)

LIVE A LITTLE, LOVE A LITTLE

(1968) (Singles from the movie)

WONDERFUL WORLD * *

Written by Guy Fletcher, Doug Fett. Greg Nolan's voice is heard over the credit titles as he makes his way in his beach buggy to the shore. Everything is wonderful. A full orchestral accompaniment, with vocal echoes, produces a hurdy-gurdy effect in which Elvis sensibly doesn't attempt to give utterance, considering the rough terrain over which the vehicle bumps and glides – even flying over a hillock at one point. Perfectly appropriate as a 'travelling' opening number, interchangeable with many others in the Presley annals.

LPs: 'Elvis Sings Flaming Star'; 'Singer Presents Elvis Sings Flaming Star'

EDGE OF REALITY * * * * *

Written by Bill Giant, Bernie Baum, Florence Kaye.
The second song in the movie, out of a mere four, comes during one of Greg's dreams – nightmares when he is Bernice's prisoner, sharing a room with her Great Dane, Albert. In a fantasy scene choreographed by Jack Regan, Greg is winkled out of bed by Albert, talking and in almost human, upright form saying he'll help take him to the hills, to get away from Bernice: instead he pushes him into an Alice in Wonderland fall through the air to a psychedelic-coloured wonderland, where he starts to sing the words of the 'Edge of Reality', which is where he finds himself surrounded by dancing figures from his recent life, like Albert, Bernice, her boyfriend Harry, the grocer's boy, the milkman, all of whom appear to mock him, while he joins their dance. Greg, in song expresses his fears that Bernice is destroying his sense of equilibrium with her constant change of names and personae. He faces the borderline of sanity as she sits tormenting him – the figures fade and he wakes up to find Albert snoring away on his cot. The number is a strange fusion of ballet, intimate revue and stylized dramatics, quite unlike anything else by the Giant–Baum–Kaye team, and calls for considerable range from Elvis's singing, to which he rises effortlessly, to a background of echoing vocal gymnastics, with an insistent beat, including drums, saxophone, violins, piano and tympany. One senses that Presley finds here something unusual to which he can respond: if only the theme of the movie, so impressively encapsulated here, could have been expressed as stylishly in the film.
Single B/W: 'If I Can Dream'
LP: 'Almost In Love'

IF I CAN DREAM

Written by W. Earl Brown.
Single B/W: 'The Edge of Reality'
LPs: 'Elvis – A Legendary Performer –

Vol. 2'; 'Elvis – TV Special'; 'Elvis: Worldwide 50 Award Hits – Vol. 1'; 'He Walks Beside Me'

A LITTLE LESS CONVERSATION * * *

Written by Billy Strange, Mac Davis. Greg sings this plot-illustrating ditty, as a party piece at one of his advertising jamborees, over a gadget invented by his employer, Mike Lansdown – a 'nothing box', which does absolutely nothing, but is a great conversation opener. He borrows it to impress a lovely blonde model, Ellen, to entice her away from the party after she has learned he is a Sagittarian and they are 'not compatible'. He says the gadget is much more reliable than the stars. She complains that all it does is go round and make noises as he leads her away from the party with some fast lyrics about a little less talk and a little more action being necessary. Quite appropriate to the circumstances. Guitars and female chorus predominate.
Single B/W: 'Almost In Love'
LP: 'Almost In Love'

ALMOST IN LOVE * * * *

Written by Rick Bonfa, Randy Star. Bernice strums a few chords on a guitar, saying, 'What about a little cocktail music?' and Greg starts to sing as he takes her in his arms to dance cheek to cheek, intoning just the kind of smoochy romantic lyrics that Bing Crosby, Dick Haymes et al always sang towards the end of a film. Lots of strings, violin, piano, drums – pretty, but not up to the mark for Elvis.
Single B/W: 'A Little Less Conversation'
LP: 'Almost In Love'

LOVE ME TENDER * * *

Released by: 20th Century-Fox; (Black and White, Cinemascope); **Producer:** David Weisbart; **Director:** Robert D. Webb; **Screenplay:** Robert Buckner, based on a story 'The Reno Brothers' by Maurice Geraghty; **Director of Photography:** Leo Tover ASC; **Music:**

Lionel Newman; **Running Time:** 89 mins; **Opened:** November 15 1956.

Cast: Richard Egan, Debra Paget, Elvis Presley, Robert Middleton, William Campbell, Neville Brand, Mildred Dunnock, Bruce Bennett, James Drury, Russ Conway, Ken Clark, Barry Coe.

At the end of the Civil War, Confederate Lieutenant Vance Reno (Richard Egan), with his brothers, Brett (William Campbell) and Ray (James Drury), hijack a Union payroll. Their mother Martha (Mildred Dunnock) and young brother, Clint (Elvis), waiting back home, have received a false report that Vance had been killed in action. Grieving with his Texas rose girlfriend Cathy (Debra Paget), Martha and Clint are inconsolable, less so in Clint's case as he then makes haste to marry Cathy for whom he has always had a yen.

Meanwhile, hearing that the Armistice had preceded the heist by twenty-four hours, Vance, Brett and Reno decide that the money can be considered the legitimate spoils of war, so they split the proceeds and head back to civilian life. After the first shock of discovery that his intended has married, the understanding Vance, who inherited his high principles from the grieving Martha, decides that the honourable thing to do is to give Clint and Cathy his blessing and leave to make his own life elsewhere. He plans to take his leave during a family party.

However, the festivities are interrupted by the arrival of Major Kincaid (Bruce Bennett) with a Pinkerton detective and warrants for the arrest of the three elder Reno brothers. They are arrested and taken to the county jail to await trial. Vance decides to return the payroll and get on with his own life, but, unaware of this, Clint enlists the help of Vance's old platoon and breaks his brothers out of prison. Vance tries to persuade the others to give up the payroll, but they refuse and he

takes it from them by force, intending to return it to Major Kincaid. Vance is pursued by the Sheriff with his posse, manages to evade capture and get back to Cathy, whom he asks to look after the money until it can be returned to the Major.

Cathy has found that marriage to Clint is not a bed of roses – he actually hits her in a jealous scene – and she realizes she still loves Vance. She persuades him to return to her after riding back to town to return the money and face the consequences. The now jealous Clint, persuaded by Vance's old platoon sergeant to hunt Vance down and take his revenge, shoots him when he returns to explain everything and as he lies helpless, seeing the sergeant moving in for the kill. Clint, stricken with remorse, covers his brother's body and takes the bullet that was intended for Vance. Clint dies in Cathy's arms having made his peace with them both.

This scene reputedly upset Gladys Presley considerably at the film's Memphis premiere; not only that, but studio tests showed that audiences were distressed at Elvis's dying at the end of the film. He was therefore called back to Hollywood at the beginning of October to add footage showing Clint as a ghostly presence singing the title song as the credits rolled. The critics were scathing on both sides of the Atlantic. *Time* magazine mocked, comparing the voice to a 'rusty foghorn ... or a noise produced like the voice of a cricket, by the violent stridulation of the legs.' *Picturegoer*, gunning for Presley from the start, said 'His screen debut is a crashing bore. That is, when it isn't being unintentionally riotously funny.' Margaret Hinxman went so far as to say, 'Can Presley survive this film?' She pointed out that the character is unsympathetic, with hero Richard Egan getting all the sympathy. 'Presley is bad-tempered and snarling, he beats his wife and, horror of horrors, he dies in the end.'

Actually the film is not that bad: these attacks smack of a vendetta and the fans were not at all put off. They adored it and box office receipts reflected their adoration. Elvis's first scene is handling the ploughshare on his ma's farmstead as he responds to her call when she has just welcomed back the sons she'd given up for dead. His puzzled look turns to delight when he recognizes his brothers: the scene cuts to brother Vance rushing to sweep the girl he planned to marry into his arms. Clint turns from welcoming Brett and Ray to embrace Vance, with a strangled, 'They told us you were dead.' He then has to break the news that he and Cathy were married about three months before. After a brief scene of the family sitting down to supper and the still boyish Clint fencing with the sword his brothers have brought home from the war and exulting over the new 'Sunday go to meeting' suit that Vance passes off as his young brother's special present, Elvis goes into the obligatory homecoming song fest, with guitar.

Presley handles theses mood changes with remarkable dexterity, supported by the superb Mildred Dunnock, whose most memorable film role was the wife in the 1951 *Death of a Salesman*, based on Arthur Miller's Pulitzer Prize winning play.

The nominal stars of the film, Richard Egan and Debra Paget, play their colourless parts as if they really believed in them: as members of Fox's B team they always turned in dependable performances, without being given much of a chance to shine. Egan's nadir was perhaps as King Ahasuerus of Persia opposite Joan Collins as the eponymous Queen in *Esther and the King* – not one of the films which Collins either would be likely to acclaim as her finest hour.

The obvious way would have been to introduce Elvis in, as the great film critic C.A. Lejeune once described, 'a close up of song', but either director Robert T. Webb or, more likely, producer

David Weisbart gave him a chance to ease in by showing his mettle as an instinctive actor. Weisbart was to be responsible for three of Presley's more imaginative subjects, *Flaming Star* (*qv*), 1960, *Follow That Dream* (*qv*), 1962 and *Kid Galahad* (*qv*), 1963. The folksy song 'This Old House' which followed gave Elvis the opportunity to execute a few of the notorious wiggles which so incensed the Establishment, and, before his 'conversion', TV mogul Ed Sullivan.

The death scene is touchingly played and in the ghostly reprise of the title song, ending with a reassuring smile – that curl of the lip which Presley imitators have been trying to emulate since the beginning – another presence lurks unseen: Colonel Parker (*qv*) is there affirming to his public 'You see, my boy can never really die.' Even he could not have suspected how right he was.

One of the more interesting members of the cast, eighth-billed as Major Kincaid, is Bruce Bennett, a few years before his retirement from the screen to go into real estate. This was a move prompted, one imagines, by nonentity roles like this after one of the most colourful – if not always the most successful – careers in Hollywood.
(See also: Bennett, Bruce; Flaming Star; Follow That Dream; Kid Galahad: Parker, Colonel Tom)

LOVE ME TENDER (EP Released 1956)

THIS OLD HOUSE * * *
Traditional (Not recorded)
The first song ever sung in a movie by Elvis Presley is this traditional rocker with which Clint Reno entertains his family on the back porch of their home. It would have been a great start to this EP – right in the family tradition.

LOVE ME TENDER * * * * *
Written by Ken Darby (Based on 'Aura Lee' – 1861)
Clint sings this to his mother and it also expresses his feelings for Cathy the girl he married while his brother was away, reported dead. Elvis sings this gentle ballad with unique feeling, straight from the heart. Full marks to Ken Darby for bringing the old song 'Aura Lee' back to life after almost a century. Clint accompanies himself on his guitar while his brother supplies the vocal background. In fact, the Ken Darby Singers handled the vocals, disappointingly to Elvis who had hoped for his old associates, The Jordanaires.

Single B/W: 'Any Way You Want Me'
EPs: 'DJ 7 Great Country and Western Hits'
LPs: 'Elvis, Elvis – A Legendary Performer – Vol. 1'; 'Elvis as Recorded at Madison Square Garden'; 'Elvis Golden Records'; 'Elvis TV Special'; 'Elvis: Worldwide 50 Gold Award Hits – Vol. 1'; 'Essential Elvis – The First Movies'; 'A Golden Celebration'; 'The Number One Hits';'Pure Gold'; 'This is Elvis'; 'The Top Ten Hits'

ANYWAY YOU WANT ME (THAT'S HOW I'LL BE)
(not included in movie)
Written by Aaron Schroeder, Cliff Owen.
Single B/W: 'Love Me Tender'
LPs: 'Elvis Golden Records'; 'Elvis Worldwide 50 Gold Award Hits – Vol. 1'

LET ME * * *
Written by Elvis Presley, Vera Matson, Ken Darby.
First of the jolly party songs delighting lassies who jig and scream in a ladylike way as they watch him do his stint on the platform with his guitar. He is wearing his 'Sunday go to meeting' suit which Vance had hoped to wear at his marriage to Cathy. The lyrics are fairly unambiguous as he makes it clear what he wants to do, but Elvis sings what he really wants is merely another dance. He is accompanied by two other guitars and a drummer; as the song comes to a climax he does some of the leg gyrations that had caused such scandal among the establishment at his concerts – toned down as far as possible for the screen. The trouble with trying to mute Elvis's performances is that he exudes sex in every gesture and every line in the same way that, some twenty years earlier, Mae West (*qv*) would make a nonsense of censorship with a look or an intonation. All's pure to the pure. Presley's party songs can be taken as good clean fun, though not even he could have imparted a double meaing to 'This Old House'.
LPs: 'Elvis: The Other Sides – Worldwide Gold Award Hits – Vol. 2'; 'Essential Elvis – the First Movies'

POOR BOY * *
Written by Ken Darby (Credited to Elvis Presley and Vera Matson).
More picnic capers: though credited with the song, Elvis was not happy to have to sing it. He felt, as so often in later years, that songs had been foisted on him. Maybe this 'authorship' was to placate him.
Single B/W: 'An American Trilogy'

WE'RE GONNA MOVE * *
Written by Ken Darby (Credited to Elvis Presley and Vera Matson)
The fourth song on the EP seems to get swallowed up in the dramatics when Cathy begs Vance not to leave home because she loves him. Another pot boiler as above, with the same drummers and guitarists.
LPs: 'A Date with Elvis'; 'Elvis – The Other Sides'; 'Worldwide Gold Award Hits – Vol. 2'; 'Essential Elvis – The First Movies'

LOVING YOU * * *
Released by: Paramount Pictures (Vistavision, Technicolor); **Producer:** Hal B. Wallis; **Director:** Hal Kanter; **Screenplay:** Herbert Baker and Hal Kanter from a story by Mary Agnes Thompson; **Art Directors:** Hal Pereira, Albert Noza, **Director of photography:** Charles Lang Jnr; **Technical Advisor:** Colonel Tom Parker; **Music:** arranged

Elvis in his first colour film as Deke
Rivers, a trucker whose talent as a rock
singer has been discovered by press agent
Glenda Markle (Lizabeth Scott) and band
leader Tex Warner (Wendell Corey).
Loving You (1957)

and conducted by Walter Scharf, vocal accompaniment by The Jordanaires; **Running Time:** 101 mins; **Opened:** July 9, 1957.

Cast: Elvis, Lizabeth Scott, Wendell Corey, Dolores Hart, James Gleason, The Jordanaires, Ralph Dumke, Paul Smith, Ken Becker, Jana Lund, Vernon and Gladys Presley.

Band leader Walter 'Tex' Warner (Wendell Corey) and his boys are doing a gig at an outdoor rally on behalf of Jim Nelson (Ralph Dumke), an ambitious politician cum phoney medicine man. Tex's ex-wife, press agent Glenda Markle (Lizabeth Scott), is handling the publicity for the event and has just been told they won't be paid until the would-be governor can raise the necessary. She breaks the news to Tex and he suggests they walk out on their two-timing employer in search of a gimmick that will put them back on top again. On cue Deke Rivers (Elvis), a local boy, drives up to deliver a few kegs of beer and while they're jigging to the rhythm of Tex's band Glenda asks his friend to dance and liven up the show with a touch of local talent. The guy says he's no dancer but that Deke is a great singer. Glenda persuades him, much against his will, to do a rock number with the band. The crowd and particularly the girls go wild. Glenda spots her potential gimmick and insists Deke give her a ride in his do-it-yourself jalopy to show her what the car can do. In reality she wants to get him on his own to propose signing him for Tex's band. Reluctantly he signs up with her, mainly because with the band is a pretty young singer, Susan Jessup (Dolores Hart). However Glenda's offer of 50 dollars a week to start with was also an inducement, compared with the 18 dollars he earned making deliveries. Any lingering doubts are dispelled when he is fired for making a late delivery. He arrives in the nick of time to join the tour on which Tex and

Glenda are embarking. From the start he is a wild success and is promoted into being on stage with the band instead of being an apparent 'plant' from the audience.

Things start to go really well. Glenda's publicity ideas are fantastically successful – for instance she engineers a riot when two elderly ladies are persuaded to say how appalling Deke is in the hearing of teenage fans, needless to say there is a carefully planted photographer at the scene. Then there's the white Cadillac which a rich widow had apparently donated out of sheer admiration, occasioning more nation-wide publicity, when in fact Tex has bought it by realizing his life insurance policy. Glenda, fond though she is of her ex-husband who is still deeply in love with her, is attracted to Deke and, being jealous of his obvious love for Susan, goes along with booking agent Earl (James Gleason) when he suggests that she and the backing group be excluded from the deal that will take Deke into the big time. He is booked for a breakthrough concert to be broadcast from just outside Dallas. Not knowing that Susan has been let out of her contract without anything being said to him, Deke goes to her family's farm, intent on bringing her back. Glenda follows in the white Cadillac and persuades him he owes it to his backers to return and honour his agreement to appear as the star of the show. She does, in fact, make her attraction for him obvious with an impassioned kiss and it is only when Tex lets out the fact that Glenda is his ex-wife and he has hopes of one day winning her back that Deke feels used and betrayed and is sure that her show of affection was merely a ploy to get him back to honour the contract.

With the broadcast set, featuring nation-wide interviews with people who have been pivotal in Deke's life, including Susan, he drives off in a fury in his old jalopy. Glenda follows, determined to get him back for the show

on which all their futures could depend, and finds him with his wrecked car by the roadside. He is uninjured, but still angry and hurt at what he sees as her duplicity. Realizing that his true love is for Susan – however carried away he had been by Glenda's glamour and power – she tears up their contract and says he is free to do whatever he chooses. Meanwhile the distraught Susan has revealed to the studio audience that their star is not there. Deke, impressed at last with Glenda's honesty, dashes back in time to make the show a great success. Embraces all round – fade out.

Loving You has been unfairly dismissed as a time-filler between Presley's first movie, *Love Me Tender*, and his third and fourth, all three serious subjects in black and white, marking the initial development of a potentially significant actor in the Brando–Dean mould, who happened to have a unique singing voice into the bargain. His second film, setting the pattern for the future by being in colour, was much more than an adequate stop-gap. It was based, very loosely, on his own early career in the character of Deke Rivers, from truck driver to megastar, with some moving dialogue by Herbert Mason and Hal Kanter. Elvis acts the dramatic scenes with a touching truth and at the end of the story, after various traumatic setbacks, we see him reunited with the friends for whom his young life has been a search, leaving aside the talent that brings him great worldly success. The drive to canalize that talent comes across from the pivotal character in the film, press agent Glenda Markle, who fulfills the Colonel Parker (*qv*) role in her protégé's career. Lizabeth Scott, who epitomized the Forties and Fifties Hollywood dream girl: blonde, husky voiced and with an androgynous quality of the ilk of Veronica Lake and Lauren Bacall, was, in fact, groomed as Paramount's answer to the sultry Warner star. An excellent actress, she had the right quality of steel combined with glamour as a career woman who will stop at nothing to promote her star – well, almost nothing; she is convincing in her devotion to the young singer whilst still caring for her ex-husband, band leader 'Tex' Warner, and in having sufficient heart to tear up her contract when she realizes that it is sweet, innocent Susan Jessup who Deke really loves. This was effectively the end of Scott's Hollywood career, which had never quite recovered from her suing the scandal magazine *Confidential* in 1955 over their allegations concerning her sexual preferences. In those days the implication of lesbianism was sufficient to put paid to a career. The rest of the casting is equally right: Wendell Corey has the requisite touch of dogged devotion to his ruthless ex-wife hidden beneath a nice measure of cynicism to make him credible. Dolores Hart, in her film debut, is the perfect ingénue – wide-eyed and with an innately innocent quality, which she retained during her second movie with Elvis, *King Creole*. James Gleason's gravel-voiced comedy is wasted here as an agent go-between who fires Susan from the band.

Charles O'Curran's handling of the musical numbers exactly hits the mark and The Jordanaires' expert vocal backing here begins a long-standing and happy association with Presley as far as films are concerned, though he had long been an admirer of their work and always gave them credit for having a hand in his early success. *Loving You* came seventh in *Variety*'s weekly list; Elvis's new-found ease before the cameras caused one of his most virulent early detractors, Britain's *Picturegoer*, to admit, 'Elvis gets his break at last!' The article goes on to damn with faint praise, but grants him 'attack, sex appeal'. Little credit is given to his rounded heart-felt performance as a shy, lonely youngster who only finds confidence in himself when he discover his trust in those near to him has not been misplaced. Kanter's script and direction must take some of

the credit, but it is Elvis's own firm grip on the character so akin to his own that makes his every scene ring true.
(See also: King Creole; Love Me Tender; Parker, Colonel Tom)

LOVING YOU
(RCA LPM – 1515) July 1957
(Complete Soundtrack)

MEAN WOMAN BLUES 7* * * *
Written by Claude DeMetrius.
Elvis as Deke Rivers sings DeMetrius's fast rocker to a juke box in a diner in Amarillo, where the band and Deke are headlining. Elaine, a girl from another of his gigs, recognizes him and raves to her big, leery boyfriend, who challenges Deke to show that he can sing. He does, with full leg movements and handclaps, getting the whole joint rocking. The discomfited Wayne picks a fight with Deke who finally knocks him out by the juke box. The police are called and in the resultant trial Deke is acquitted, the boy who started the fight is fined and more local headlines created for the concert.
Single B/W: 'Have I Told You Lately That I Love You?'
EP: 'Loving You – Vol. 2'
LPs: 'Elvis Aaron Presley – Forever', 'Elvis – The Other Sides', Worldwide Gold Award Hits – Vol 2', 'Essential Elvis -Vol. 2', 'This is Elvis'

HAVE I TOLD YOU LATELY THAT I LOVE YOU?
(Not included in movie)
Written by Scott Wiseman (1944), Tex Ritter.
Single B/W: 'Mean Woman Blues'
EP: 'Just For You'
LP: 'Essential Elvis – Vol. 2'

TEDDY BEAR (LET ME BE YOUR) * * * * *
Written by by Kal Mann, Bernie Lowe.
Elvis as Deke Rivers, starting out on the road to fame, first sings this as a snatch in a montage sequence, standing on the

highway as the coach zooms on through the various signposted gigs. Further snatches build up to the big airing at their first important booking at a concert hall in Amarillo, Texas, where he wears the outstanding Country and Western outfit with a white top, red embroidery and red trousers bought for him by Glenda and plays the new guitar that goes with it, a present from Jess. A sweet and simple rocker, sung at breakneck speed – ditto the flailing limbs – guitars working overtime, The Jordanaires zipping along in time with Elvis. The pace hots up, orchestra in a crescendo of instruments, until the final repetition of 'I Just Want to be Your Teddy Bear', having run through the gamut of animals he doesn't want to be, including lions and tigers. His voice growls along the ultimate bass notes, before a final convulsive leg thrust heralds the last chord – then silence, followed by deafening applause. Easy to understand why this sparkler topped all the charts, especially coupled with 'Loving You'.
Single B/W: 'Loving You'
EPs: 'Dealers', 'Prevue! Loving You'
LPs: 'Elvis, Elvis – A Canadian Tribute'; 'Elvis Aaron Presley', 'Elvis as Recorded at Madison Square; Garden'; 'Elvis's Golden Records', 'Elvis in Concert', The Elvis Medley'; 'Elvis Sings for Children and Grown-ups Too'; 'Elvis: Worldwide 50 Golden Award Hits – Vol. 1'. 'the Number One Hits'; 'This is Elvis'; 'The Top Ten Hits'

PUPPET ON A STRING
Written by Sid Tepper, Roy C. Bennet.
See *Girl Crazy*

LOVING YOU * * * * *
Written by Jerry Lieber, Mike Stoller.
Theme song to the movie – a tender, romantic ballad, taken here as an introductory number with a rolling beat, piano, drums, sax and guitars to the fore while a tiny red heart, sketched over Wendell Corey's billing, wanders off to the right of screen – why, we wonder?

Elvis stops singing after the first few bars and the orchestra plays on to the end of the credits. The song is repeated during the action, sung by Deke Rivers to Susan Jessup at her farm, after she has told him that she and the group have been discharged from backing him. This time he sings it with real meaning, causing her to say, 'You've never sung it like that before'. Finally the music is repeated at the end, over the credits, after the various partners have been paired off fittingly.

Single B/W: 'Teddy Bear'
EPs: 'Dealers Prevue'; 'Loving You – Vol. 1'
LPs: 'Elvis, Elvis – A Canadian Tribute'; Elvis's Golden Records'; 'Elvis – 50 Worldwide Golde Award Hits – Vol. 1', 'Essential Elvis – the First Movies', 'Pure Gold'

GOT A LOT OF LIVIN' TO DO
* * * * *

First song in the movie: Deke Rivers is persuaded by press agent Glenda Markle to get on the rostrum and sing a song to inject a little local interest into a dismal rally to promote an unpopular politician, Jim Tallman. With guitar borrowed from a bandsman, Skeeter, he goes into this frenetic rocker, with leg gyrations to match, vocals by The Jordanaires. The effect is electric, especially on the women, and Glenda is inspired to hire him to join Tex's band. Deke repeats the rocker at the finale of his broadcast.
EP: 'Loving You'
LPs: 'Elvis – The Other Sides – Worldwide Gold Award Hits – Vol. 2'; 'Essential Elvis – The First Movies'; 'Elvis Aaron Presley – Forever'; 'Essential Elvis – Vol. 2' (Compact Disc)

LONESOME COWBOY * * *
Written by Sid Tepper, Roy C. Bennet. Deke, promoted to solo status in Tex's band, sings this as a set piece on stage, pinpointed by a spotlight, to a clip-clop cowboy rhythm, backed by piano, drums and bass to full dramatic effect. Elvis

laments his loneliness prompting a girl to stand up and shout , with full southern accent, 'What's your number, honey? Ah'll give you a call!' – shocking Deke, but delighting Glenda.
EPs: 'Loving You – Vol. 2'
LPs: 'Elvis – Gold Records'; 'Elvis – The Other Sides – Worldwide Gold Award Hits – Vol. 2'; 'Essential Elvis – The First Movies'

HOT DOG * * * *
Written by Jerry Lieber, Mike Stoller. Lieber and Stoller's pacey rocker, first sung by Deke in a road montage sequence to the rhythm of wheels, gets its real workout in a concert gig where the ever-resourceful Glenda engineers a riot.
EP: 'Loving You – Vol. 2'.
LPs: 'Elvis – The Other Sides – Worldwide Gold Award Hits – Vol. 2'; 'Essential Elvis – The First Movies'

PARTY * * * *
Written by Jessie Mae Robinson. When Deke joins Tex's outfit he is called up from the audience as a gimmick – he borrows Skeeter's guitar, inevitably breaking a string with his energetic strumming. The song is a party rocker, calling everyone to join in, to rock 'n' roll, do whatever they fancy: guitars, piano, drums, bass, The Jordanaires' vocalizing, Elvis's legs, frenetic action.

BLUEBERRY HILL
(not included in movie)
Written by Al Lewis, Larry Stock, Vincent Rose (1940)
EP: 'Just For You'
LPs: 'Elvis Aaron Presley – Forever'; 'Elvis Recorded Live on Stage in Memphis'; 'Essential Elvis – Vol. 2'

TRUE LOVE
(not included in movie)
Written by Cole Porter.
EP: 'Loving You'

DON'T LEAVE ME NOW
(not included in movie)
Written by Aaron Schroeder, Ben Weisman See 'Jailhouse Rock' EP

HAVE I TOLD YOU LATELY THAT I LOVE YOU
(not included in movie)

I NEED YOU SO
(not included in movie)

M

MEMPHIS MAFIA AND OTHER INTIMATES

'El's Angels' was probably a term Elvis infinitely preferred to the Memphis Mafia tag which grew up because he remained loyal to his original buddies from his home town of Memphis; he hung out with them in preference to the Hollywood crowd his producers were anxious for him to involve himself with. He had few star friends – Natalie Wood was one of them, introduced by a mutual friend, actor Nick Adams, and they had a brief affair in 1956 – but most of his intimate circle were strictly non-Hollywood guys and dolls, who were named 'El's Angels' because they were noted for riding powerful Harley-Davidson motorcycles. Natalie Wood was included because she enjoyed riding around Memphis on Elvis's Harley and long after passion between them cooled, they remained friends and kept in touch.

Nick Adams (1931-1968)

Nick Adams had been a close friend of James Dean in whichever capacity the troubled young actor required him; it seems likely that he saw Elvis as a viable substitute after Dean's death and made sure of meeting him, introducing himself on the set of *Love Me Tender* (*qv*). The generous rising star befriended him and in return got to know young actors like Natalie Wood and Russ Tamblyn. But it was always his 'Angels' who went everywhere with him, including film sets

Nick Adams – Elvis's first actor friend, who introduced him to Natalie Wood and others of Hollywood's young set. He died in 1968, of an overdose, aged 37. (Photo circa 1955).

– he had to have friends around him all the time – and gradually the Mafia legend grew. There were usually about ten of them and they lived in Graceland with their wives and girlfriends. Each one of the Guys – another term preferable to Mafia – had his own prescribed job around the King and in return had a roof over their head and unlimited access to parties, free food and drink, and a constant stream of eager young girls anxious to be friendly with anyone who could introduce them to Elvis. The disadvantages were being on constant call night and day and poor pay, though Elvis was always liable to surprise them with the present of a costly car.

Alan Fortas

Some of the boys came and went several times, but one of the longest stayers was Alan Fortas, who was with Elvis as assistant and bodyguard from 1958 to 1969. He was an all-star Memphis football player and looked after Elvis's travel arrangements. He also sometimes played the tambourine on stage and appeared in the NBC 1968 TV Special. He was an especial friend and confidant and loyal to a degree.

Lamar Fike

Fat man Lamar Fike – he weighed in at about 300 pounds – met Elvis at the Sun Studios, was attracted by his colourful way of dressing and they became friends: by 1957 he was a charter member of the Memphis Mafia and needed his strong sense of humour as the frequent butt of Elvis's jokes. Two of the names he called him were 'The Great Speckled Bird' and 'Buddha'. When his weight prevented him joining up with Elvis, he nevertheless went with him to Germany and stayed with him during his time with the Army. He was of great assistance in building up an extensive network of music business contacts. One of the hits he found for Elvis was 'Kentucky Rain'. He was a pallbearer at the funeral and went on to a career of his own, with his wife Mary, as personal manager, producer and talent scout. They live and work in Nashville, Tennessee.

Red (Robert) West

Elvis met Red (Robert) West at Hume's High School, where he was outstanding as a boxer and footballer, always taking his side in school fights. He became Elvis's driver when he started out on the road with the Blue Moon Boys in 1955. He enlisted in the Marines in 1955 and caught up with Presley again in 1960 on his discharge from the Army. He went to Hollywood with Elvis as bodyguard and started a career of his own, with parts in almost all the Presley films. One of the most prominent was *Wild in the Country* (*qv*) as his brother and hated rival: the film starts with a fist fight between them. Another movie in which Red was the recipient of Elvis's punches was *Tickle Me* (*qv*). He was not only strong man, stuntman and actor, but wrote several songs for Elvis, including 'Separate Ways'.

Sonny (Delbert) West

Red's cousin, Sonny (Delbert), also had hit parts in several films and was in charge of Elvis's numerous motorized vehicles, being rewarded with several Cadillacs, Harley Davidsons and pickup trucks. When he and Red, together with Dave Hebley were fired after a fight with Vernon (*qv*), all three got together to write the notorious *Elvis: What Happened?* which made Elvis's drug dependency public knowledge and ended their relationship for the short time that he had to live.

Marvin Gamble

Marvin Gamble combined the position of chauffeur and valet.

Larry Geller

Another prominent Mafia member was Larry Geller who became Elvis's personal hairstylist after 1964. He had a special hold over Elvis because of his preoccupation with religion and the occult. Colonel Parker saw him as a threat and tried unsuccessfully to get rid of him. He was perhaps the only friend with whom Elvis could talk about religion and psychology and had a special fascination with the supernatural. Elvis relied on Geller to contact his dead twin, Jesse, who really was his alter ego and the clue to so much that was seemingly inexplicable in Elvis's life.

Cliff Greaves

Elvis's long-time friend, Cliff Greaves, who was an early member of the Guys, used to hang out with the singer in the Fifties, and went with him to Hollywood for the filming of *Love Me Tender*. The things that stand out in his association with Elvis are that he introduced him to his girlfriend, Anita Wood, and that he was in the studio for the impromptu 'Million Dollar Quartet' recording session between Elvis, Jerry Lee Lewis, Carl Perkins and Johnny Cash.

Charlie Hodge

Charlie Hodge, guitarist and singer, was with Elvis from the beginning to the end; riding in the ambulance with him on his last journey to the Baptist Hospital in Memphis. Charlie lived for more than seventeen years at Graceland, where he took care of personal business for Elvis: later it was he who handed out the scarves the singer used to toss to the audience. It would be fascinating to know how many survive as revered relics. Hodge and Presley joined the Army at the same time, did basic training together at Fort Hood, were on the same steamer to Europe and were stationed together in Germany.

Marty Lacker

Marty Lacker was another schoolfriend from Hume's High, but did not join the Mafia until 1960 after which he worked for Elvis for seven years. As bookkeeper and personal secretary to the King, he was the recipient of several cars and some jewellery, but his wife, Patsy, feels that it was Elvis who introduced him to drug abuse. Although, with Joe Esposito (*qv*), he was best man at Elvis's wedding, he received his notice soon after. Their exact relationship remains one of the imponderables.

The personal histories of several of these men indicate that they were genuinely devoted to Elvis and were ready, willing and able to offer friendship and/or guidance when he needed it. The snag was that no one was expected to criticise or quibble with his wishes; it would be the worse for them if they did. His wife Priscilla (*qv*) tried, especially in respect of the constant presence of his male friends and their female dependants. She was not allowed companions of her own, nor, for that matter a life of her own, which made the widening rift between them as inevitable as it was tragic. The King's insistence on his own positively papal infallibility had the effect of exiling him from human companionship; he loved his animals, but in the end even his beloved chimpanzee, Scatter (*qv*), at first always party to Elvis's personal pranks on his friends – particularly those of a sexual nature – lost his position as court jester and was exiled to an isolated air-conditioned cage. He pined, grew vicious and, it has been suggested, died of a broken heart. Priscilla was of sterner mettle and found her own way out of her unhappiness. She, too, had tried to warn Elvis of his increasing drug dependence, with as little effect as Red West and the others.

Perhaps the only person who could have saved him from that fate might have been his mother: her loss left him, in effect, only half a person. It is tempting to speculate that, had she lived, his own life could have been prolonged to at least its normal span. His music and his public were his only consolation and in the end they took their own inevitable toll. Natalie Wood died in 1981 in a tragic boating accident , aged 43: she had known the best of Elvis. (*See also: Presley, Priscilla Beaulieu; Elvis: The Movie; Esposito, Joe; Girls, Girls, Girls (not the movie); Love Me*

Tender; Parker, Colonel Tom; Presley, Gladys Love Smith; Presley, Vernon Elvis; Scatter; Tickle Me; Wild in the Country)

MENUS

In 1995 concentration on Elvis Presley's bizarre, indeed grotesque, eating habits and capacity became all the rage, prompted by two books published in the second half of the year. The first, David Adler's *The Life and Cuisine of Elvis Presley* goes into details of an indulgence which the author believes, all too credibly, led to the King's early death on

the pan, weighing in at 250lbs. Elvis's stepbrother, David Stanley, who grew up with him from the age of four and later became his valet and friend, writes with loyalty and affection but considerable frankness in *The Elvis Encyclopedia*, and comes to virtually the same conclusion: that his stepbrother's gluttony was at least a major contributory factor to his untimely end: 'If you knew Elvis like I did, grew up with him like I did and walked into a bathroom to find him dead from a drug overdose like I did – and still love him – *then* call yourself a fan.'

A strategically placed guitar masks the King's thickening girth. *Elvis On Tour* **(1972)**

The books sparked off in-depth reviews in many of the papers, serious as well as tabloid, and a BBC programme called *The Burger and the King* inevitably went with unctuous relish into close-up detail, with the King's own cooks holding out platters of his favourite gastronomic delights and waffling away lovingly in mostly deep Southern accents. The press notices inclined to the view that the programme treated a tragic subject with tasteless levity liable to enrage Presley's fans.

Elvis's early eating habits were recalled by his great-aunt, Annie. The Presley family, then poor whites living in the black district of Tupelo, Mississippi, existed on a diet of greens, sweet potatoes, deep-fried squirrel and boiled or baked possum, a small bush-dwelling animal hunted in the south for its lean, dark meat. Even then, according to his great-aunt, Elvis had a really big appetite.

By 1956, when he was a millionaire and living on the fat of the land in Memphis, Tennessee, he had progressed to 'sweet treats' provided by his mother, Gladys (*qv*), who herself was no sylph. They included hamburgers – 500 calories each – and the house special, the jelly sandwich. This was toasted white bread, filled with strawberry jam and peanut butter and then deep fried – about 800 calories each – a snack that would be repeated several times a day. In 1960, when he was in Nevada, dating Tuesday Weld with whom he was to co-star in *Wild in the Country* (*qv*), no less an authority than columnist Louella Parsons reported he had two portions of strawberry shortcake 'to try and gain weight'. That was in public – the great lady was not permitted a peep behind the scenes.

By the early 1970's, with his personal relationships way up the creek and an increasing load of touring and concert work, Elvis told his head cook, Mary Jenkins, who managed a relay team of cooks at Gracelands, that the only

thing he got any enjoyment out of was eating. His 'day' would start with breakfast in bed at 5 p.m. consisting of six large eggs, overcooked in butter and lashings of salt, 1lb of burnt bacon, 1/2lb of sausages and 12 buttermilk biscuits, all served on a specially designed bed tray. This alone accounted for 5000 calories.

By midnight he would be hungry again. He would fly to Denver, Colorado, where his friend, Buck Scott, owned a restaurant, order a dozen of his 'Fool's Gold' sandwiches and fly home again. The recipe for 'Fool's Gold' was a jar of strawberry jam, a jar of peanut butter and 1lb of crisp fried bacon all contained in three thick, crusty slices of bread: two of these comprised dinner. Supper (4–5 a.m.): five double hamburgers and a heap of deep fried peanut butter and mashed banana butter-fried sandwiches: day's total intake – more than a typical Asian elephant, according to a report in the London *Sunday Times*, December 24, 1995. (*See also: The Burger & The King; Wild in the Country*)

MONTEVECCHI, LILIANE
(b. 1931)

Picturegoer and Disc Parade, September 13, 1958, featured a picture of a stunning girl, clad in wisps of chiffon adorned with what looked like bananas, slightly evocative of the great Josephine Baker at the Folies Begere in the Twenties, with the caption 'The Girl Who Said NO to Presley'. In smaller print 'Liliane Montevecchi did not take to Presley – neither did her poodle'. The second caption was something of an exaggeration. The story went:

'Presley with the girls doesn't do too badly. But now comes a tale of a young miss that he just couldn't date – Liliane Montevecchi, who has a role in his King Creole (qv). She does a sensuous song and dance number and on set aroused

the interest of the boys. Presley too.' A 'friend' had reported, exclusively of course, that 'The Memphis Lothario' tried every trick he had used so successfully in dating girls from his other pictures. 'He didn't even get a chance with 'The Eyes', as everyone calls her. He tried to impress her with presents, but when she returned the first one, he was wise enough to call off his order for a small German car.'

This informant went on that Miss Montevecchi's poodle refused to make friends with Elvis – strange, as he was such a dog lover and had several of his own – but concludes that Miss Montevecchi was, nevertheless, 'Very nice, very polite and very aloof – she just doesn't mix with the Hollywood crowd.'

Daily Mail, May 7th, 1996: Jack Tinker's theatre review is headed by a photo of a stunning girl, 'swathed in small slithers of velvet' with the caption 'Liliane Montevecchi is a class act.' Along with every other national critic, he positively exudes superlatives of her performance at London's Jermyn Street Theatre, tracing her career from star of the Folies Bergère to stunning prima ballerina, through her Hollywood contract to the Tony Award she won on Broadway for Tommy Tune's Eighties erotic production of the musical *Nine*. He speaks of 'the hauteur of the true Parisienne' and an 'explosive cocktail of smokey sophistication, Gallic wit and irrepressible charm'. All this and more comes through from the lady in person, who gives the lie to the film magazine story. She says she and Elvis had 'an adorable relationship – very platonic, very healthy.' She used to pick him up in her car, dodging the hysterical girls who were ever on the trail and they would go swimming together, with her 'unfriendly' dog in attendance. She had made several recordings that Elvis did not know about, and he sent for them and gave them to all his friends. They did not meet at all in later life.

N

(See also: Dogs; King Creole)

THE NAKED TRUTH: 'ELVIS'S SPERM'

American TV series. Producer Nancy Haas; Director: Ted Bessell; Script Laurie Parres; Created by Chris Thompson.

Of all the crazy themes to come out of American sit-coms, this has to be the wildest – and one of the funniest. The *Daily Mail* on Wednesday July 10th, 1996, listed it as the day's best comedy, with the rider, 'Very funny but very, very American'. Starring Tea Leoni as Nora Wilde, girl reporter on a sleazy tabloid thirsting for the big scoop of her life, and Larry Drake as a somewhat eccentric scientist who hands it to her on a plate or, rather, in a phial. He just happens to be carrying around a phial of Elvis Presley's frozen sperm – to be specific 400cc's 'donated' in 1973. Nora barges into her editor's office with the news and the usually laconic Camilla Dane – a highly amusing performance by Holland Taylor – plies the scientist, an understandably jejune Larry Drake, with such questions as 'What prompted this 'donation' of – er – nectar?' Most of the dialogue is on that level – to be sure, not for the squeamish – but if one can accept the flagrantly appalling bad taste of the subject, the laughs are practically non-stop and punched across with positively Wimbledon standard of thrust and parry. Imagine Lucille Ball in her *I Love Lucy* days (if such a premise could even have been dreamt of then) and you get the idea.

Even she could not have bettered Tea Leoni's reaction when the doctor makes it clear that he would be gratified if she would agree to be impregnated in order to give birth to the future 'King'. Her editor jumps practically over the moon with enthusiasm at the prospect that her newspaper will be the foster-parent of such a world-shattering scoop, plying Nora with offers of limitless financial remuneration if she agrees to the proposition. Nora retorts that the disposal of her own womb is entirely hers to dispense as she sees fitting – certainly not from 'some twenty-five year-old Elvis popsicle!'

Apart from a dream sequence, with a monstrous baby in a high chair with a black Elvis wig and deep Memphis voice that is not as funny as it seems to think it is, the half hour spoof is a riot, and there's a tiny bonus for fans of *The Golden Girls* with an opening vignette from Betty White. The ending is, literally, explosive.

NARCOTICS

Elvis's attitude to drugs was unique unto himself. As he grew older he took more and more – for sleeping, waking up, depression and so on – all of them perfectly legal because they were on prescription by his personal physician, Dr. George Constantine Nichopoulos (*qv*): 'Dr. Nick' to Elvis, to whom he was a close friend. Too close for comfort, in fact: over the years he wrote thousands of prescriptions for highly addictive narcotics and has been widely considered to be largely responsible for Elvis's drug dependancy. Whatever the King wanted he could get from Dr. Nick. Elvis rationalized his use of prescribed drugs as a necessary adjunct to his way of life and expressed deep concern for the rock performers on hard drugs like cocaine and heroin, which gave him the idea that if he had an official narcotics badge his example could exercise a potent influence over them to alter their habits. In December, 1970, he went to the Deputy Director of the Federal Narcotics Bureau to offer his services and was dismayed and astonished to be turned down; he was so convinced of the rightness of his mission that he drove to the White House to deliver a hand-written request to President Nixon to grant him an audience. His confidence was justified when the President rang him at his hotel and invited him to a meeting.

Elvis was dressed for the meeting, which was held in the Oval Office, in a purple velvet suit with a gold belt and took with him his two aides, Terry Schilling and Sonny West. Earnestly the King told the President that he wanted to help in the war on drugs and asked if he could have a Federal Narcotics agent's badge and ID. The request was extremely unusual, but Nixon was a far from conventional President. Nixon made a phone call and instructed someone to get them from Deputy Director John Findlater, who had already refused the request. Elvis was then sworn in as a

Federal Narcotics Officer. Photographs were taken which went round the world and one of the strangest meetings in history was officially recorded. It has been suggested that Elvis only did this because he wanted to add a badge of the Bureau of Narcotic and Dangerous Drugs to his collection of police badges, of which he had been an obsessive collector since his boyhood, and the only way he could collect one was by becoming an honorary deputy. But this does not take into account his passion for law enforcement and what he sincerely believed to be the decline of American values through the use of illegal drugs and the related drug culture.

The irony of the situation entirely eluded him. For all his own bizarre life-style, he sincerely believed in himself as exemplifying the conservative values of the rural South from which he came. Later he sent for his step-brothers Billy and David and gave them a pep-talk about stopping drug trafficking in the US. He said 'I'm tired of John Lennon talking about drugs. They're destroying our youth. They're going straight to hell because of rock 'n' roll stars.' He believed every word that he was saying.

(See also: Elvis and the Beatles; Memphis Mafia; Nichopolous, Dr. George Constantine ['Dr. Nick'])

NEWLEY, ANTHONY
(b. 1931)

Among the least likely of stars to have been given a big career boost by Elvis Presley is Britain's Anthony Newley, who first came to prominence as a child star at the age of 16 in the film version of the famous novel *Vice Versa* by F. Anstey. Newley played the schoolboy who swaps personae with Roger Livesey, as his pompous father, by means of one of those magic devices which abound in fantasy – in this case a magic skull. Tony's girlfriend was the young Petula Clark. After another big hit as the Artful Dodger in *Oliver Twist* he went into something of a decline, often

The British film which launched Anthony Newley as an international star. Playing a pop singer who's drafted into the army, he impersonates Elvis, even to the songs, including 'Idle Rock-a-Boogie', 'Sat' Day Night Rocka Boogie' and 'So Long'. The film and Newley as singer were an immediate hit, tying in with Elvis' call-up to the Services. In the still, Newley with his girlfriend, (Anne Aubrey) and manager (Sid James), hears news of his own call-up into the Forces.

experienced by youngsters when they pass the age of playing children and played a string of often small character roles. He was even Dame Anna Neagle's jive partner in her last film, *The Lady Is A Square*, co-starring with one of Elvis's favourite British singers, Frankie Vaughan in 1959. In the same year Newley made the film that kick-started his career back into the big time, *Idle On Parade*. This was an Elvis spoof cashing in on his induction into the army, which proved immensely popular.

The theme was based on a pop singer drafted into the army, whose fans chase him everywhere ; Newley re-wrote it with John Antrobus as a swipe at the world of pop music. Conceived as a satire, Newley bought all Elvis's records and set out to imitate them. Then it was decided that his own voice would be better than an imitation and four of the songs from the film were issued to coincide with the release. They were 'Rock-A-Boogie', 'Idle On Parade', 'Saturday Night Rock-A-Boogie' and 'So Long'. Another song from the film – he usually had a hand in his songs as co-author – that got him into the Top Ten, wistfully entitled 'I've Waited So Long', not only started a run of chart entries for him, but made a lie of the statement he made to *Picturegoer*'s Tom Hutchinson at the end of his interview, 'What they should do is put me in a musical.... but you know what studios are. I suppose I'll be back to character roles again.'

He did better than that – with Leslie Bricusse he co-authored, co-produced, directed and starred in one of the most innovative musicals of the early sixties, *Stop The World, I Want To Get Off*. The LP gave him another hit with the plaintive 'What Kind Of Fool Am I?' – which could have been great for Elvis. The play was a big hit on both sides of the Atlantic. Another notable collaboration with Bricusse was *The Smell Of The Crowd, The Roar Of The Greasepaint*. In 1971 Newley introduced his evergreen, *The Good Old Bad Old Days* in the musical of that name.

The Bricusse–Newley partnership endures; Christmas, 1996 saw the London opening of *Scrooge*, starring Anthony Newley in the title role, following a prolonged national tour: music by Leslie Bricusse.

NICHOPOULOS, Dr. GEORGE CONSTANTINE (Dr. Nick)

The doctor who was to become a close friend, confidant and personal physician to Elvis had only been practising for seven years when they met, quite by chance, in 1967. Elvis had bought the ranch in Mississippi and was suffering from saddle sores. His regular physician was not available and Mafia regular George Klein consulted his wife, who worked for a doctor. She recommended her boss 'Dr. Nick' and so started a relationship that was to become one of the most crucial in Elvis's life, one that would only be severed by his death ten years later. Dr. Nick was appointed the singer's personal physician and it was through him that the amount of prescriptions for medication escalated so violently. In the Seventies Elvis bought his physician a house in Memphis costing $350,000.

After Elvis and Priscilla were divorced Elvis went into a period of monumental depression. The amount of drugs he was taking to help him through caused concern in Dr. Nichopoulos, who at last was beginning to realize that he had created a Frankenstein's monster by prescribing so many in the first place. He persuaded his patient to check into Memphis Baptist Memorial Hospital for treatment for 'recurring pneumonia' though in fact it was an attempt to 'detoxify him from everything he was taking', according to the doctor.

The attempt was a forlorn one. Elvis was surrounded by people who were ready to supply him with everything he wanted in defiance of the special diet sheets the Graceland (*qv*) cooks had been given. It was more than their jobs were worth to deny him, for instance, his favourite cheeseburgers.

After the King's final fatal collapse, Dr. Nick came racing up as the ambulance was about to leave Graceland for the Baptist Memorial Hospital. Having been told by Joe Esposito (*qv*) on the phone that Elvis was still breathing, he climbed into the ambulance and started massaging Elvis's heart. All the way to the hospital he kept shouting, 'Elvis, breathe... come on breathe for me!' Half an hour later, when a team of doctors and technicians in the operating theatre had failed to revive his patient, Dr. Nick had to return to Graceland to break the news to the family – a particularly traumatic task as he was not sure whether Vernon (*qv*) would survive the news of his son's death. He did, however, until two years later, when he died of a heart attack in 1979.

That same year a TV reporter named Geraldo Rivers alleged on the ABC Network *20/20 Show* that Presley's death had been due to drug abuse, rather that the accepted 'heart attack'. This led to Dr. Nick being charged along with two other doctors of over-prescribing drugs in fantastic quantities between the start of 1976 and Elvis's death: on that day alone he wrote eight separate prescriptions. In 1977 he prescribed an average of 25 narcotic and amphetamine pills a day for Elvis. The doctor was sentenced to be suspended for three months and to a similar term of probation. In 1980 he was suspended for a period of months by the Tennessee Board of Medical Examiners for over-prescribing drugs in ten cases, including Elvis, Jerry Lee Lewis and Marty Lacker, but at the subsequent trial relating to the charge he was acquitted of malpractice.

Many fans hold him responsible for Elvis's death and at least one reported attempt on his life has been recorded. He did, indeed, seem to get off remarkably lightly. But to blame one person or one cause seems altogether too simplistic. *(See also: Graceland; Memphis Mafia)*

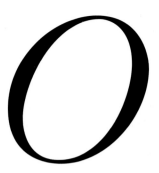

OF LOOKALIKES AND SIGHTINGS

There are two groups of what can justifiably be called 'Specialist' Elvis fans: both could probably fill a book on their own, but space and time preclude any kind of detailed listings of either. The first group are the legion of Elvis 'lookalikes' or 'wannabes' or 'soundalikes'. In this category come several professionals already mentioned in this book, who have done outstanding work impersonating the King on stage, screen, TV and radio. Then there are a surprising number of impressionists, in many countries, who earn a respectable living simply by spending their lives emulating Presley in the media. Two, in my capacity as a theatre critic, I have evaluated, met and admired – one American, the other British, performing on stage to considerable popular and critical acclaim. The American, Liberty Mountain, in looks, stature and costuming, is remarkable in the effect he creates on both sides of the Atlantic. The second, Johnny Earle, is British, slighter in build, but nonetheless brilliantly successful in creating an ambience of Elvis. Johnny started this part of his career under his own name of Johnny Dumper, changed to Earle, then back – at the time of writing he is Earle again.

The second group of 'Specialists' are those who deal in Elvis sightings; just occasionally the two groups come together, sometimes uncomfortably. A

newspaper report mentioned that Presley 'last seen stacking shelves at the Deal branch of Tesco' in July, 1996, had had a hectic summer. First there was the body reported under a bridge in Settle, Yorkshire, closely resembling the King. On closer inspection it turned out to be a life-size papier mâché model: the police deduced this when they noticed, according to a spokesman, that 'the blue suede shoes were missing'. Then, from Crondell in Hampshire, an unfortunate accident overtook lookalike Dave Hurrell, who had been giving an Elvisian rendition of 'Teddy Bear' at the Fleet carnival. Sporting a mountainous black coiffure and a jewel-encrusted Las Vegas type costume, Dave was on his way home in his $40,000 open-topped Cadillac when the sighting was obviously too much for a non-believer and an accurately aimed waterbomb exploded on Mr Hurrell. He leapt into the crowd to exact retribution. After a fracas he went back to his Cadillac and picked up his wet microphone. He ended up in hospital: all he can remember was an electric shock going through his lips to his feet. His wife, Dee, who wore a bouffant wig and was dressed as Priscilla, was driving the car and took him to Frimley Park hospital. Although he didn't say so, he must have felt all shook up.

Since then an advert has appeared on television, featuring a lookalike, referred to only as 'the King'. Seated in an armchair is the back view of a large

black pompadour hairdo. Facing the chair is a bank of TV sets: a white clad, bejewelled arm reaches out from the chair and picks up a remote control: the man in the chair flicks from set to set, all reporting Elvis sightings: he chuckles to himself until a headline on the screen proclaims THE KING IS DEAD! Elvis's voice says 'I'm not dead baby, I'm just having a break'. He adds, 'Have a break – have a Kit Kat!' Several worlds merge through the modern miracle of television. So that's what he was stacking in Tesco's.

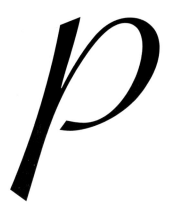

PARADISE, HAWAIIAN STYLE **

Released by: Paramount Pictures (Technicolor); **Producer:** Hal B. Wallis; **Director:** Michael Moore; **Screenplay:** Allan Weiss, Anthony Laurence, from a story by Allan Weiss; **Art Directors:** Hal Pereira, Walter Tyler; **Director of Photography:** Kelley Wallace ASC; **Aerial Photography:** Nelson Tyler; **Technical Advisor:** Colonel Tom Parker; **Music:** Joseph J. Lilley, vocal background by The Jordanaires, The Mellomen; **Running Time:** 91 mins; **Opened:** July 6, 1966.

Cast: Elvis, Susanna Leigh, James Shigeta, Donna Butterworth, Mariann Hill, Irene Tsu, Linda Wong, Julie Parrish, Jan Shepard, John Doucette, Mary Treen, Edy Williams, Robert Ito, Grady Sutton.

Pilot Rick Richards (Elvis) flies back to Hawaii – out of work again from the usual cause – stewardess trouble. At the airport he meets an old friend, Danny Kohana (James Shigeta), who's flying an executive, Mr. Coverson (Grady Sutton), who is promoting alligator shoes to a convention at the Maui Sheraton. He arrives at the wrong hotel – he'd been given the wrong name – and blunders into a meeting of the RSPCA – a society for the prevention of cruelty to alligators,

who remove his shoes forthwith. He arrives back at the plane with bound feet. Rick suggests they go into partnership to start a helicopter charter service. Danny at first does not think there's enough customer potential but changes his mind when Rick gets to work contacting various girlfriends on the islands to persuade customers to use Danrick Airways. The first is Lehua (Linda Wong), a hostess at the Sheraton, and soon customers are lining up in sufficient numbers to change Danny's mind about backing the airline. Other willing representatives to put passengers their way are Pua (Irene Tsu) at the Polynesian Culture Centre, whom Danny accompanies on stage as an extra inducement. He meanwhile has engaged a secretary, Judy Hudson (Suzanna Leigh), who is a flyer herself. For self-protection, she wears a wedding ring at Danny's suggestion. Joanna (Julie Parrish) needs more convincing to put her recommendations around at the Kahala Hilton, so Rick takes her on a flight to deliver a consignment of pedigree dogs to a rich woman to show at an important dog show. The dogs get out of hand and so does the helicopter: trying to regain control, he forces a car beneath him off the road and into a ditch. The driver, Donald Belden (John Doucette), is an important member of the FAA (Federal Aviation Authority);

his wife (Mary Treen) injures her back and he lodges a complaint with Danny about Rick's dangerous piloting. So does the owner of the dogs and Rick finds himself grounded for a week. He is already in bad trouble with Danny, whose daughter January (Donna Butterworth) he had taken for a flight but she buries the ignition key, so they get stuck on a remote beach until daylight. Danny furiously dissolves their partnership when he lands to collect his daughter.

On his return, Rick finds Judy relieved to see him, but anxious because Danny and Jan have not come back. She insists on searching for them and Rick takes them up in his helicopter, risking having his licence permanently revoked. Judy spots Danny's plane grounded on a small island. On landing they find Jan unharmed, but Danny has broken his leg – he slipped while investigating a minor fault on the plane. Rick and Danny make up their quarrel, but fear they are both in danger of losing their licences which would be the end of Danrick Airways.

Visiting Danny in hospital, Rick reads that Belden is going to be guest of honour at a big Polynesian festival at which Jan is going to sing. Rick attends with Judy and decides to take the bull by the horns by approaching the magnate when he is being made up for TV. When he hears Rick's side of the story, Belden relents. Impressed by the skill he showed in rescuing Danny, he assures Rick he will make sure he will be permitted to fly again, after the FAA's next meeting. Judy tells the truth about her wedding ring and finds that Rick knew all along – preparing the way for a happy ending, while she and Danny watch the spectacular finale as Rick sings 'Drums of the Island'.

PARADISE, HAWAIIAN STYLE

(RCA LPM 4643) June 1966
(Complete Soundtrack plus bonus cuts)

PARADISE, HAWAIIAN STYLE * *

Written by Bill Giant, Bernie Baum, Florence Kaye.

Pilot Rick Richards, fired from his airline for unseemly behaviour with a stewardess, sings over the credit titles another paen of lush praises for the islands, accompanied by The Jordanaires and The Mellomen, to Hawaiin guitars. Dreamy, not to say soporific.

QUEENIE WAHINI'S PAPAYA

(Duet with Donna Butterworth) * * *
Written by Bill Giant, Bernie Baum, Florence Kaye.

Rick is entertained at the home of his pilot friend, Danny Kohana, and his wife Betty with their five children, the eldest of whom, Jan, puts on her leis and starts to pose as Queenie Wahini. Rick tells her she looks like a little queen and sits on the verandah steps with the children around him. He sings to them about the virtues of Queenie's cooking. Jan starts to join in with him and the tempo gets faster and faster until they end, kneeling on the sand, foreheads touching. Hawaiin guitars accompany them in a cute and simple song – strictly for the kiddies.

SCRATCH MY BACK (THEN I'LL SCRATCH YOURS) * *

Written by Bill Giant, Bernie Baum, Florence Kaye.

Rick contacts an old flame, Lani, who entertains at the Sheraton Hotel – the second girl he persuades to put customers his way for the airline he plans to start up with Danny. They swan down together in a car running along rails right into the lounge of the hotel, where the band is set up for Lahua's song, the words of which express *double entendres*, all to a rhumba beat. Bass bassoon, drums, guitars accompany them as Rick joins her in song and dance, entailing a bout of backscratching.

DRUMS OF THE ISLANDS * * *

Written by Sid Tepper, Roy C. Bennet (based on a Tongan chant).

Rick joins Pua of the Polynesian Culture Centre – another willing recruiting officer for his airline, in a canoe parade along a river past a line-up of colourfully dressed Polynesians, swaying in grass skirts and wearing leis. He leads the Tongan chant 'Drums of the Islands' on stage: bongo drums, Hawaiian guitars accompany Elvis and the male choristers in basic lyrics concerning the drums beating in their hearts.

DATIN' * *

Written by Fred Wise, Randy Starr. (Duet with Donna Butterworth). Rick takes Jan up in a helicopter for a ride and they sing about the oddities of grown-ups dating, doing things that lead to a 'baby carriage'. This plane is equipped with full orchestral effects including piano, guitars and drums.
LP: 'Elvis Aaron Presley'

A DOG'S LIFE * *

Written by Sid Wayne, Ben Weisman. Rick flies a consignment of pedigree dogs to the Kaui Hilton to be exhibited in a dog show. Joanna, whom he picked up on the way, goes along for the ride and to help look after their canine passengers. Another of those ridiculous scenes with which Elvis was being lumbered with increasing regularity – this time he sings

to four dogs of assorted breeds. When he stops singing and mentions a steak as a reward for her dog-sitting chore, they go beserk, scrambling all over the place. A red setter blocks his view and he narrowly misses a car on the highway below, running the occupants into an irrigation ditch. The lyrics are, predictably, about the dogs, with asides referring to Joanna. When they hand their passengers over, Mrs. Daisy Barrington is horrified to discover her dogs covered in bandages and sticking plaster. Learning that they had been given plebian dog biscuits to quieten them down she attacks Rick with her umbrella. Drums, guitars, piano and barking dogs liven things up.
LP: 'Elvis Aaron Presley'

A HOUSE OF SAND *

Written by Bill Giant, Bernie Baum, Florence Kaye.

Rick and Jan land on a beach, where cavorting bathing-suited floosies materialize, not to mention beach boys beating bongo drums; all romp around the beach in rhythm with the guitars etc., while Rick sings some meaningless lyrics. Jan beats with wooden spoons on cooking pots. She spots an elaborate sandcastle and sets about gleefully demolishing it, aided by Rick and the maidens.

STOP WHERE YOU ARE * *

Written by Bill Giant, Bernie Baum, Florence Kaye.

The evening of reckoning, when all the girls Rick has enlisted as recruitment officers for the airline converge in the restaurant where Rick is dining with his secretary/Girl Friday. The girls confront Rick, quoting his 'Scratch my back' motto and demand to know how he's going to keep his promise to pay them all back, finally agreeing to a financial settlement. To get away Rick joins some garlanded girls with grass skirts, all swaying in rhythm, in a dance where he hopes they will hide him. Small chance, as he breaks into song advising the girls to stop where they are – freeze frame. Another plot filler, and amusing as far as it goes.

THIS IS MY HEAVEN * * *

Written by Bill Giant, Bernie Baum, Florence Kaye.

Rick is swept away from a clinch with his Girl Friday by boys and girls eager to sing of the joys of his island paradise; may it last forever – starting with frenzied drum beats and a male chorus line executing an energetic native dance: dusky maidens in ballet skirts pirouette daintily around him, while he beats time with drum sticks. All this activity leads into a reprise of 'Drums of the Islands', complete with waterfalls, heralded by a summons on conch shells for the entire cast, vividly choreographed by Jack Regas.

SAND CASTLES

(not included in movie)
Written by Herb Goldberg, Davis Hess.

PARKER, COLONEL TOM (1909–1997): RISE AND FALL OF AN 'ÉMINENCE GRISE'

Tom Parker died in Las Vegas on January 21, 1997, aged 87, following a stroke. His death released the floodgates of resentment felt by 'Elvis's fans worldwide through the years after his death in 1977. Music critic and composer Ray Connolly writing in the *Daily Mail* the following day encapsulated these feelings with the headline 'Conman who killed the King', adding, 'He may have discovered Elvis, but Colonel Tom Parker was a greedy, low-life huckster who pushed Presley towards drugs and the brink of artistic suicide'.

Harsh words indeed, but justifiable, insofar as by setting box office profits ahead of any other consideration, Parker effectively condemned Presley to a diet of repetitive and often shoddy musicals. Parker was quoted as saying that 'no one who pays Elvis $1 million a movie is

going to give him a bad script' and therefore subjected him to material such as the flimsy *G.I. Blues* after turning down a starring role in the epic *West Side Story*, stating that he was not going to allow 'his boy to play second fiddle to Natalie Wood'. The latter was an enormous success without Presley; who is to say how much better the film might haved fared (let alone what it would have done for his acting career) with the added attraction of Elvis in a dramatic role he would have filled brilliantly. Thereafter, the few good movies which followed were due to luck and, sometimes, good direction, and always to Elvis's professionalism.

Throughout this time and up until three years after his death the Colonel was taking between 25 and 50 per cent of Elvis's earnings. When Elvis died in 1977, after selling more records than any other performer in history, he left only a million dollars in his estate. Parker had failed to create any tax shelters, profit-sharing schemes or other long-term investments that an artist of Elvis's stature should have had. It is currently estimated that Lisa Marie Presley will shortly inherit $100 million from record sales since Elvis's death combined with proceeds from the opening of Gracelands.

Parker had already invented a mythology for himself by the time he met Elvis Presley. He claims to have been born in Huntingdon, West Virginia, but Presley biographer Albert Goldman says otherwise. His book, probably the best-selling of all the hundreds written about Elvis, set out not only to re-examine all previously published facts but also to discredit all the precautions that Parker had taken to sanitize both his client and himself. Goldman states that the 'Colonel', an honorary title, was born in Breda, Holland, as Cornelius van Kuijk, one of nine children, and known as Andre. He inherited his interest in the circus – his skills as technical advisor were put to good use in *Roustabout* (*qv*)

– from his mother, of French ancestry, who had travelled with a carnival, while his father, having been in the army for many years, was skilled with horses. After a long trip to the US at the age of eighteen, he returned with presents for all his family and went back to America in 1930, joining the US army and changing his name to Tom Parker. For two years he sent letters and money home. After that they heard no more. It seems that with America in the throes of the Great Depression, he became involved with a circus and acquired a great flair for publicity which he put to good use in promoting his show business clients like Eddy Arnold and Hank Snow. Parker acquired his title of 'Colonel' from the Governor of the State of Tennessee, for whom he had done some useful promotion.

Prior to Parker's involvement with Presley, Elvis had visited Sam Phillips' Memphis Recording Service, where he made an acetate record of himself playing guitar and singing 'My Happiness' and 'That's When Your Heartaches Begin'. The first song had been made famous by the Ink Spots, the popular black group who had done record business on both sides of the Atlantic, including the London Palladium. The second, a country ballad, was also recorded by the Ink Spots. Sam Phillips was out when Elvis called and it was his secretary, Marion Keisker, who dealt with him. The usual arrangement was to pay four dollars to cut a single one-sided acetate, but Elvis asked if he could record two songs as a birthday present for his mother. He was also influenced by wanting to be heard singing by a representative of the Sun record label, which was Sam Phillips' main interest. Marion was so impressed by what she heard that she taped part of the recording (in the normal course of

A still taken during one of his 1957 tours showing the emotion Elvis put into his performances.

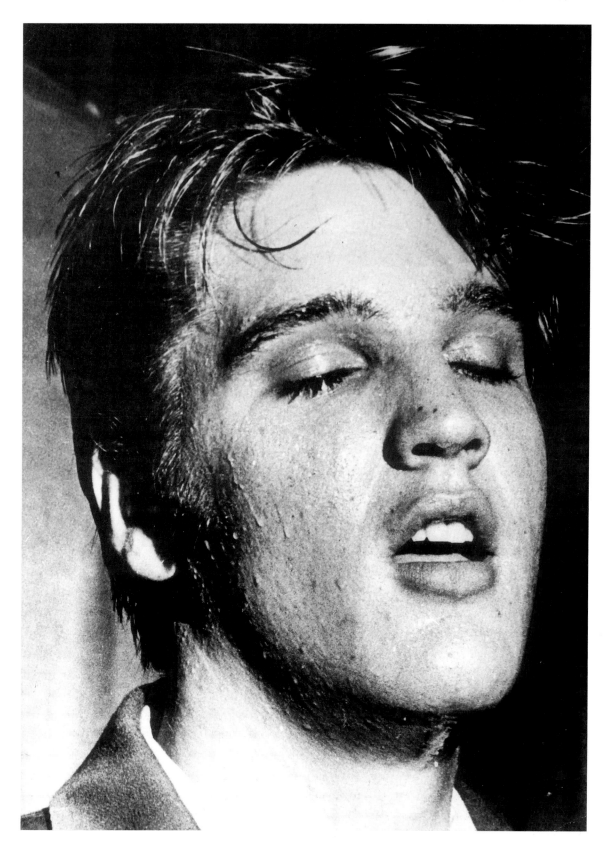

events there would have been no copy of the original acetate recording) and noted the Presley address in Alabama Street and the phone number of the upstairs neighbours, as the Presley's had no phone.

Due to Marion's persistence this eventually led to the famous impromptu blues session with Elvis, bassist Bill Black and guitarist Scotty Moore, on black singer Arthur 'Big Boy' Crudup's 'That's All Right, (Mama)'. This was to crystallize into Elvis's first commercial release for the Sun label, backed by 'Blue Moon of Kentucky'. Thus the real credit for Elvis's discovery belongs to Marion Keisker. If there isn't a plaque, there should be! After repeated air plugs by DJ Dewy Phillips, Scotty Moore was signed, fairly reluctantly, as Elvis's first manager. This arrangement came to an end when Scotty, unhappy about being a manager as well as guitarist, was replaced by Bob Neal, a popular DJ well known on the Memphis music scene. Bob restyled Elvis, for some time billed as the 'Hillbilly Cat', and his band of Scotty, Bill and drummer D.J. Fontana, as Elvis and the Blue Moon Boys. He had become a regular on the *Louisiana Hayride Radio Show* following the good reaction to his first appearance in October, 1954. With growing fame, albeit of the local kind, some of the stresses that were later to take over his life were beginning to surface. He had so much nervous energy on stage, contrasting with his totally quiet and polite demeanour off-stage, that Scotty recalls, 'We had to sit up nights to wear him out so that he could sleep!' Eventually his inability to sleep would lead to him taking drugs – with the inevitable result that he had to take others to wake him up. Gladys (qv) was increasingly concerned with the amount of time his gigs would keep him from home and at the increasingly demonstrative nature of his girl fans, 'tearing and clawing like animals' said his friend Red West who had begun touring

with the band to protect him from them and their increasingly jealous boyfriends.

Which is when the 'Colonel' really began to sit up and take notice. When Elvis performed with country artists he was never the headline attraction and always went on stage last as his act attracted audience attention that was impossible to follow. Parker began to co-operate with Bob Neal and he sought the opinion of those who worked with Elvis, like country entertainer Whitey Ford, known as the 'Duke of Paducah' who was on a tour Parker organized which included Hank Snow. After the release of Elvis's fourth Sun recording, 'Baby Let's Play House' and 'I'm Left, You're Right, She's Gone', entered the national country charts in July, 1955, eventually reaching the Top Ten, Parker decided to strike while the iron was hot and take over the Presley career himself. He became friendly with Gladys and Vernon Presley (qv) as well as Bob Neal and Sam Phillips. When Gladys was finally convinced by her friend, singer Whitey Ford, that the Colonel had the boy's best interests at heart, plus the power to implement them, deals were struck. Parker negotiated a payment of $40,000 with RCA – his original target was $50,000 – for Elvis's recording contract. Sam Phillips received $35,000 and Elvis himself $5,000 to cover royalties owing from his Sun recordings. His final record for them, 'Mystery Train' which was released with 'I Forgot To Remember To Forget' in August 1955, became his biggest hit and seller for Sun recordings. During November it topped the country charts. After the end of the year Sam Phillips ceased to have rights to any Presley recordings: RCA reissued all Sun singles years later.

Bob Neal subsequently became Johnny Cash's manager before moving to Nashville where he guided the careers of several country music stars. Sam Phillips used his $35,000 to good effect to promote the careers of several young rock 'n' rollers, especially Carl Perkins,

whose recording of 'Blue Suede Shoes' finally got Sun Records into the National Charts.

Although hardly a philanthropist, Colonel Tom Parker certainly gave entertainers other than Elvis Presley a boost in their careers.
(See also: Presley, Gladys Love Smith; Presley, Vernon Elvis; Roustabout)

PEARL AND TONY

The White Hart at Hampton Wick has a separate outbuilding where the Middlesex Branch of the official Elvis Presley Fan Club has meetings every two months. Pearl, who with her ex-husband Tony Cattemull, has run the club for the past thirteen years goes along in the afternoon to set the scene for an Elvis disco. Portraits and posters are liberally displayed: there is an entrance fee of £3 and a bar which charges standard pub prices. Presley records play throughout the evening, with a sound level which does not preclude conversation. Pearl – she prefers to be referred to by her Christian name – explains how her branch of the club, run from her home at 30, Addison Road, Teddington, Middlesex, came into being. The club was only blessed with the 'Official' title eight years ago and I attended their third Elvis disco since they moved to the current venue, whose landlord Syd is what Pearl refers to as a 'closet Presley fan' with a large collection of world-wide Elvis stamps. 'It took something like this to make him and his wife come out of the closet and be counted. There's an awful lot of closet fans, wherever you go in the world: everyone knows about Elvis and you can always have a conversation about him. So many people have at least one record or CD at home.'

Pearl, who is blonde and bouncy and looks twenty years younger than her age of 48, owns not to have started as a Presley fan: 'I was always into Cliff (qv) when I was in my teens – didn't think much of Elvis at all – it was Tony, seven years younger than I, who was the 100%

Elvis fan. When we met up, Tony had just been divorced and was feeling very fed up. I knew he'd always liked Elvis and I said to him "Stop feeling sorry for yourself, get off your butt and start a fan club." He said, "but I don't know how." I said "Neither do I, but, come on, let's do it: I enjoy Elvis and you love Elvis, so lets do something to bring him to other people." Then we hired the back of the Lion public house; it was only a very small venue in those days. We started there on Tony's dole cheque – he was unemployed at the time – fourteen people turned up and we showed two films with a disco in the evening. It built from there.'

There are now some forty other branches run from the headquarters of the Official Elvis Presley Fan Club in Leicester (qv). The Secretary is Julie Mundy, who took over from Todd Slaughter, now retired, having run the Club for nearly thirty years. Julie was previously Club Branch Leader of the Bucks and Northants Counties. There were many more branches but, in the words of Pearl, they have been 'whittled down' as far as the British Isles are concerned. She lists her phone number as 0181 977 9610, Elvis fans are free to ring her and she never refuses to chat to them, provide information or, if they're feeling a bit down, she will do her best to lend cheer.

The branch's resident Elvis interpreter, 27 year-old Neil Horan from Chiswick, has been a fan since childhood. As an early teenager he turned his back on his records to follow the music trends of the time. From seventeen onwards he returned to appreciate the music of Elvis, collecting every available record and CD. He has some thirty books, into which he likes to dip from time to time: rarely reading one right through, like many Presley fans.

Neil travels all over the country to attend Presley conventions. 'It's my hobby' he says 'and I love it.' He says he enjoys doing what he can to 'keep the

Elvis spirit alive' and impressive sideburns are part of his day-to-day persona. His speciality is miming to the discs, although he sings a bit, despite being, in his own words 'not too hot at it'. His Presley outfit, fairly sober dark suit, with a black and white chequered shirt and a belt with an enormous gold buckle, is his pride and joy. It is an exact replica of the one Presley wore when he was received by President Nixon.

1 (*See also Fan Clubs of Great Britain; Of Lookalikes and Sightings; Sideburns*)

PHYSIQUE AND PERSONAL APPEAL

Elvis's stepbrother, David Stanley, in his book lists some vital statistics that chart Presley's development, from the 'Greek God' of his halcyon days to the final overweight battle of the bulge of his Las Vegas years, as definitively as do the photos from cute Jackie Coogan-like kid onwards.

His height of 6 ft gave him the stature, from puberty onwards, always to be able to wear his clothes with style, even when the outfits themselves were the antithesis of stylish; his fighting weight of 168lbs rose after 1975 to 250lbs: his waist from 30 to 42 inches; his hair, originally the 'dishwater blond' described so unflatteringly by Stanley and on display in his 1956 debut in *Love Me Tender* (qv), later became – and remained – jet black. The constant application of dye and increasing use of lacquer seemed never to affect the luxurious abundance of his crowning glory.

Elvis's physique, though solid, lacked definition: Elvis clearly did not go in for the weight training of so many screen Adonises, or if he dabbled, the effect did not show on the screen, despite the film moguls' decree that he should be photographed without his shirt whenever possible, notably in *Flaming Star* (qv). To heighten the effect, the posters for that movie depict him in his 'Pacer' role as positively bulging with

muscles, etched in by enthusiastic scenic artists around his own modest outline. Similar liberties were taken by Paramount with Mae West (qv), nipping and tucking to give her the required *Belle Of The Nineties* hourglass figure and to disguise what some ungallant people described as a 'middle-aged spread'. Elvis continued to strip, often to good effect, in his musicals, but in *Blue Hawaii*, in particular, there is more than a hint of excess flesh visible.

It is noticeable that muscular male co-stars are as conspicuous by their absence as the female variety abound in outstanding definition. Strangely enough, it seems that Elvis was embarrassed by having to show his legs, which were notably well-shaped and muscular.

He photographed at his best in well-cut shirts and trousers of contrasting colours. Well-styled suits, sometimes of strikingly original design – courtesy of costumier Edith Head – and service uniforms always became him and he could get away with quite extreme and fanciful hairstyles, presumably under the supervision of make-up genius Wally Westmore. Some of his fringes could be more extreme than those of his leading ladies, but to the end of his film career, with the exception of his one bearded role, Jess Wade, in the 1968 *Charro!* (qv), he always looked immaculately well-groomed and young. In his last documentary, however, *Elvis on Tour* (qv) (1972), his increasingly elaborate stage costumes failed, in some shots, to conceal his increasing girth. Photographer Robert Thomas had to be very selective with his lighting and colour tones.

A list of the King's favourite goods may give a clue as to what contributed towards his overweight: peanut butter, mashed potatoes, sauerkraut, cheeseburgers, pork chops and grape jelly. Taken in conjunction with his special menus, the whole thing becomes a nightmare.

To end on a more delicate note: 'Brute', quoted as his favourite aftershave, recalls Cybill Shepherd's (*qv*) TV interview on her memories of Elvis and their first meeting in a darkened movie theatre – 'He smelled so good.' When asked what did he smell of she said 'Some sort of special Elvis smell.' Have we the key to the mystery?

(See also: Charro!; Blue Hawaii: Elvis on Tour; Flaming Star; Love Me Tender; Shepherd Cybill; West, Mae)

POST MORTEM

The sad subject of Elvis Presley's death has been analysed ad nauseum: the conflicting reports of exact times and of how many drugs were or were not discovered have filled pages of literally hundreds of books. The mourners at his funeral have variously been estimated at between 75,000 and 80,000: the exact cause of his death has never been definitely established and published; the complete autopsy report which Vernon Presley (*qv*) asked for must remain private until 2027. There it is best to leave the subject and try to find out why it happened instead of the interminable hows, whens and wheres.

The fact that Elvis's twin brother, Jesse, was stillborn seems to have preyed on his mind all his life. Even if he accepted his mother's theory that all the good qualities of the dead twin would have gone into his own psyche, thus making him twice as noble, good and wise, that was one hell of a burden to carry around. If he did not accept the premise, the thought that he was only 'half a person' would have been even more of a worry. Then, the death of Gladys (*qv*) at the early age of 46 surely further diminished his faith in himself. He had always said she was more than a mother to him and his anguished cry by the graveside 'Oh God, everything I have is gone' confirms this almost mystic relationship. If it had been Vernon who died at an early age Elvis would have undoubtedly grieved for his 'daddy', but

the grief would have been containable.

Even in the early days of his inaugural Fan Club, originally run by his first girlfriend, Dixie Locke, there were signs of problems with his sleeping and weight. In his letter of July, 1956, to the Elvis Presley National Fan Club (*qv*) he wrote that at six-feet tall he weighed 195 pounds and had gained about 20 pounds during the past year, although his appetite was not as good as it had been earlier. He went on to say that he never seemed to be able to relax and had the greatest difficulty falling asleep at night; at the most getting two or three hours of unbroken sleep. All of this prefigured the escalating cycle of uppers and downers to bring about the desired effects and the never-ending cascade of pills to relieve the anxieties of day and night living. Enter Dr. Nichopoulos (*qv*) with his prescriptions unlimited.

From the moment Elvis met his dream girl, Priscilla Beaulieu, in Germany, he had a romantic ideal on which to set his heart; a fairy-tale that was lived out when he first persuaded Vernon and his second wife Dee to allow Priscilla's father to let her visit Graceland for Christmas and stay in their exclusive care, with not a word to be leaked to the ever-hungry media. Eventually this became a permanent arrangement, except for the rare occasions when those same media let slip that Elvis was blotting his copybook with this or that lovely co-star, at which point Priscilla usually went home to father until the always persuasive fiancé persuaded her that it was all a dirty lie. Marriage to her at 24 seemed the ideal solution for all of Elvis's problems of loneliness. The birth of Lisa Marie (*qv*) appeared to set the seal on this bliss; fans and friends alike hoped that Prince Charming had met his Cinderella and would live happily ever after.

There was only one bad fairy lurking in the wings to destroy this familial happiness – the Presley personal fairy of many appetites; of possessiveness;

of insatiable cravings for sexual and gastronomic satisfaction; for ever more potent drugs and an ambition for recognition of his genius as performer and musician. This canker in the bud was to destroy his marriage, as Priscilla was denied her own friends and forced to accept her husband's. More and more she was required to function as an ever-decorative and compliant doll, even being sent out to palliate her boredom by taking lessons in one of Elvis's favourite sports, karate. It was here she met the instructor Mike Stone and found him happy to supply the affection that Elvis had been rationing as far as his wife was concerned. This led eventually to divorce and the final severing of a relationship which began with such promise. If he had been able to listen to Priscilla's pleas to cut down his drug intake and his dietary excesses; if he had allowed her to tour with him and look after him during those tours, he would not have made life so impossible for her. For a long time she strove to keep up at least the semblance of a relationship. It took over three years for her to confess her relationship with Mike Stone and only then because she had discovered the numerous occasions when Elvis had been unfaithful to her. From afar she still tried to influence him over the way he was hurtling to his own destruction: his only consolation seemed to be the visits from Lisa Marie – on the night of his death one of his last actions had been to play games with her.

The loss of probably the one person he loved most after his mother was a final blow to his already shattered self-esteem. The other girls who moved in with him after the divorce were probably devoted and Linda Thompson only left after she could take no more. She has her detractors, but David Stanley seems convinced of her loyalty and good intentions, although she certainly benefited from Elvis's generosity with innumerable expensive gifts, including new homes for her parents and brother.

Ginger Alden, the last girl in his life and the one who probably found him dead, had put about rumours of their impending marriage, but it would appear he never really recovered from the loss of Priscilla, just as he was unable to come to terms successfully with Gladys Presley's death, or even, in his heart, of his twin brother.

(See also: Girls, Girls, Girls (not the movie); Graceland; Presley, Gladys Love Smith; Presley, Lisa Marie; Presley, Priscilla Beaulieu; Presley, Vernon Elvis)

PRESLEY, GLADYS LOVE SMITH (1912–1968) AND ELVIS'S EARLY DAYS

Elvis's mother was born in Pontotoc County, Mississippi, into a family of sharecroppers and migrant workers. Gladys Love Smith met Vernon Presley when she was 21 and working as a machinist in the Tupelo garment factory. He was 17 and working for a dairy farmer named Orville S. Bean, driving a truck and delivering milk to homes in East Tupelo, Mississippi, where they both lived, quite near to each other. At their wedding in Pontotoc Church, in the county where she was born, they gave false ages, which were entered on the marriage licence, Vernon claiming to be 22 and Gladys 19 – a white lie deemed necessary for church-going working folk in those days. Vernon's parents, Jessie and Minnie Presley, and his brother, Vester, and their three sisters lived in a two-roomed house in Old Saltillo Road and the young couple moved in with them; in those years of the Great Depression people living in rural areas had little opportunity of escaping from the extreme poverty which was their lot.

The initial borrowed finance for the young couple's first home was repaid to Orville Bean in the form of rent. This move was essential as Gladys found herself to be pregnant after a year of marriage. She soon had to give up work and Vernon's salary became their sole source of income. The prospect of one or, as she hoped, two mouths to feed – from the start she knew she was bearing twins – was a daunting one; in the event Gladys gave her surviving son as much as she could afford, but brought him up strictly. The manners she inculcated from the beginning were to stay with him into stardom: he always stood up when adults entered the room and addressed them as 'sir' or 'ma'am'. Vernon worked hard, long hours for little remuneration, but was always scrimping and saving along with his wife to provide the best they could for their only child – Gladys had learned she would not be able to have any more children after the birth of Elvis and his stillborn twin, Jesse Garon.

This poverty was a motivation for a minor crime involving the changing of a sum on a cheque made out to Orville Bean, which resulted in Vernon and two companions, Gladys's brother Travis

Elvis kisses his mother Gladys goodbye as he prepares to enter the army on National Service. (1958)

Smith and a man called Lether Gable, being sentenced to three years in the state prison of Mississippi, the notorious Parchman Penitentiary, although in the event Vernon was discharged after serving less than one year. Nevertheless, Orville Bean, unsurprisingly not brimming over with the milk of human kindness, turned Gladys and three-year old Elvis out of the family home. They moved back in with Jessie and Minnie Mae Presley and Gladys went back to her work as a seamstress.

Elvis and his mother were virtually inseparable and at the First Assembly of God Church, with its Pentecostal leanings, he assimilated his affection for and closeness to gospel music, which he said, 'became such a part of my life that it was as natural as dancing. I loved to hear the choir – my mother told me that when I was two years-old I would slide off her lap and stand there singing. I could carry a tune, even though I didn't know the words – maybe I wasn't always in tune, but you could sure hear me above the rest!' From the age of four or five he looked forward most of all to Sundays, when they all went to church. He said, 'I loved the old church, filled with sunlight and the security of my mother and father beside me. That was the only singing training I had – I never took lessons.' It seems his controversial wiggle was something he saw the preachers do at 'religious revivals', where 'the preachers used to cut up all over the place. That was how I was introduced to the on-stage wiggle – the preachers did it!'

From age five he was an unremarkable pupil at the school premises across Highway 78 – the only incident of any moment was the time he sang 'Old Shep' at the 1945 Fair and Dairy Show, broadcast on the local station WELO, which thus formed the setting for his broadcasting debut. For the next few years the Presleys' poverty increased; Vernon went from one poorly paid job to another with the family having to move house frequently, again

sometimes depending on relatives.

The occasion when his parents bought him a guitar, which cost about 12 bucks, because they could not afford a bicycle is movingly recreated in *Elvis: The Movie* (*qv*), with Randy Gray as the young Elvis, Shelley Winters as Gladys and Bing Russell as Vernon. Things went from bad to worse and the family quit Tupelo for Memphis, 100 miles away in the neighbouring state of Tennessee, into the most depressing and run-down of all their dwellings. It was a slum property divided into 16 units where the bathroom was shared with several other families and the main room was shared with a variety of bugs. Elvis attended the nearest school, Hume High, a three storey building accommodating 1600 pupils (now that really can be called a comprehensive!) At first he ran away, but eventually got used to it.

His mother used to take him to school until he was 15 and nothing spoiled their close relationship: he knew if he had any problems, even in the middle of the night, he could call on her to try and help him.

Things improved when Vernon got a job as a packer for $40 a week – not a fortune, but an improvement on what he had been earning in Tupelo. They were accepted for a dwelling in Lauderdale Courts, a federally funded Housing project for needy families with an income below a certain level, costing them $35 a month, the same as they had paid in their previous ghastly 'home'. It was to be their residence from 1949 to 1953 and was a great improvement, with a sitting room, two bedrooms, kitchen and a bathroom. Vernon's mother, Minnie Mae, moved in with them.

Elvis's work as an usher at Loew's State Cinema on South Main Street was pleasurable but of short duration, when he found it detracted from his schoolwork. The $12. 75 cents per week for which he worked from 5 p.m. to 10 p.m. had come in very handy and the bonus was the time he could spend

watching his idol Tony Curtis, with his controversial 'ducktail' haircut. In the summer of 1951 he emulated his hero by growing his hair longer; the jet black quality Elvis later ascribed to the influence of Roy Orbison was another characteristic of the Curtis style, so it took more than one example to contribute to the definitive Presley persona. As Dietrich in *Shanghai Express* said in quite another context, 'It took more than one man to change my name to Shanghai Lilly!'

Elvis's admiration was not confined to any one group or class; 'Truck drivers were my idols', he said, ' and in Tupelo and Memphis I'd see lots of truckers with sideburns (*qv*) , and it was my ambition at that time to look like them.' Another strong factor that weighed with him were the clothes exhibited in the window display of Lansky Brothers on Beale Street, Memphis – brightly coloured outfits of assorted types – the kind of eye-catching clothes black entertainers loved to wear. Black musicians and singers, to whom the young Presley loved to listen by the hour, despite or perhaps because of the 'sinful' aspect of their music, markedly helped form the Elvis sound recognized by Sam Phillips' assistant at Sun Records, Marion Keisker, when she turned on the tape recorder to capture his first demo discs, 'My Happiness' (*qv*) and 'That's When Your Heartaches Begin' (*qv*). She knew Sam Phillips had long been looking for a white man who had 'a negro sound and a negro feel': 'With such a combination I could make a billion dollars!'

Meanwhile, after the cinema usher episode, Elvis got another job at the Marl Metal Manufacturing Company on Georgia Avenue, where he worked shifts from 3 p.m. to 11.30 p.m. – all this after his daily school hours. Not unnaturally, he used to fall asleep during classes. Discovering this, Vernon and Gladys made him resign from the manufacturers' and he found another, less time-consuming part-time job mowing the neighbours' grass after his parents were able to scrape together enough money to buy a lawnmower.

At that time the whole family were working extremely hard. Elvis said, 'When my father hurt his back, my mother went to work on the wards in St. Joseph's Hospital. She bathed patients, made beds, scrubbed floors and worked harder than ever before, and in the evening she would come home and cook supper, do the housework and then mend other people's clothes.' By the time Elvis left school at eighteen the family had been made to leave their subsidized home at Lauderdale Courts: the scene is faithfully recorded in *Elvis: The Movie*, when Shelley Winters' Gladys, told that the Presleys have marginally exceeded their joint income allowable by the Memphis Housing Authority, departs from her customary deferential attitude to the official, asks is the house still theirs at that moment, and when he reluctantly agrees that it is, turns into a home-defending virago and bundles him out of the door. They had to move to a smaller apartment, at increased rent, at 398, Cypress Street. Despite these constant setbacks, when Elvis wound up at the Crown Electrical where his boss, a Mr. Tipler, liked him and gave him the job of driving a Ford truck around Memphis delivering supplies, he was able to indulge his dreams. After all, one ambition had come to pass – he was a truck driver, with sideburns and a Tony Curtis hair style. When shiny new cars went by, he says, 'I always felt that some day something would change for me. I didn't know exactly what, but there was this feeling that the future looked kinda bright'. For those with faith in planetary influences, Capricorn (*qv*) was right in there, representing cheerfulness in adversity and ambition, as yet unformulated.

His musical aspirations were not looked upon with favour by his parents;

Vernon was keen that his son should concentrate on being an electrician, as 'He'd never seen a guitar player who was worth a damn!' Nevertheless, Elvis took his battered guitar everywhere with him, hoping for an opportunity to sing. He said, 'I used to go down to the fire station and sing to the boys there, because they were the only people who seemed to have time to listen!'

After his breakthrough with Sun's Sam Phillips, a contract was signed on July 12th, 1954, in which Scotty Moore became his manager, on 10 per cent of all earning from engagements, appearances and bookings made by him for Elvis Presley. Vernon and Gladys also signed, as Elvis was under 21. After Scotty's 10 per cent, the rest of Hillbilly Cat Trio's earnings were split three ways, Elvis taking half and Scotty and Bill Black sharing equally the remaining half. At the end of the month in which the contract was signed, they were booked to appear on a country package show headlined by Slim Whitman, Webb Pierce and Marty Robbins at the Overton Park Shell in Memphis – the first time they had played to a large audience. This was the first time Elvis used his notorious 'wiggle'. Webb Pierce said later he remembered hearing Elvis say that he was not only scared stiff, but that he might faint in the intense heat on stage, so that he had begun to flap his legs against passing out. Sam Phillips had another version: 'The audience hadn't warmed to him as much as we hoped – he looked cramped when he sang and I told him "You've really got to move". Well, he went back out there and it was as though he'd released all the tension. That left leg of his really took off!'

After that first important concert the Trio began playing more and more dates around Memphis, although Elvis, Scotty and Bill still had day jobs. They failed to make an impression on the *Grand Ole Opry Show* live radio broadcast from Station WSM, Nashville,

attracting an audience of several million in the Midwest and American South. The show's booker, Jim Denny, went so far as to suggest Elvis should return to driving trucks. Undaunted, Sam Phillips booked Elvis for another big radio show, *Louisiana Hayride*, broadcast on Saturdays from Shreveport, Louisiana. This was the show on which the likes of Hank Williams, Slim Whitman and Webb Pierce gained their early breaks: on October 19th, 1954, Elvis was presented to the listening public by booker/announcer Frank Page, with the words, 'Just a few weeks ago a young man from Memphis, Tennessee, recorded a song on the Sun Label and in just a matter of weeks that record has skyrocketed up the charts and it's really doing well all over the country. He's only 19 years old, he's a singer who's forging a new style – Elvis Presley!' Elvis was eventually signed to a one-year contract to make regular appearances on the *Hayride*.

In November of that year Elvis gave up his job with Crown Electric to devote himself full-time to his musical career. He retained the original Trio of himself, Scotty Moore and Bill Black for recordings, but engaged drummer, D.J. Fontana, a musician regularly on *Louisiana Hayride*, for live appearances. In 1955 Bob Neal, a popular DJ on the Memphis music scene for WMPS, replaced Scotty as Elvis's manager and renamed the trio Elvis and the Blue Moon Boys, receiving fifteen per cent as his management fee and another ten per cent of Elvis's income towards promotion. During this time Elvis's closest companion was his girlfriend, Dixie Locke, with whom he was close until the end of 1955.

After Colonel Parker (*qv*) took over the entire control of the Presley career – a move largely engineered by Mae Boren Axton mother of country singer Hoyt Axton (she and Tommy Durden had written 'Heartbreak Hotel' (*qv*) for Elvis) life changed conclusively and consistently. Mae was a schoolteacher in Jacksonville, Florida, combining this activity with songwriting and handling publicity work for Colonel Parker whenever his acts came to town; she became friendly with Elvis, advising him to join the Colonel and forecasted that she would write his first million selling hit, which, of course, is what 'Heartbreak Hotel' became – several times over.

It was in May 1956 that Elvis was at last able to buy Gladys the house of her dreams. He said, 'It was something she'd always wanted, but never talked about, but I knew and I wanted to get my mother a home.' It was at 1034 Audubon Drive, Memphis. The photo of Vernon, Gladys and Elvis outside the house, which cost him $40,000, shows them looking more bewildered than ecstatic; a forecast of the day in March 1957 when they had to move from Audubon Drive, which had become a nightmare place, where they were constantly pestered by fans. He found a new home in the countryside, Graceland, a twenty-three room mansion built on two storeys in the Memphis suburb of Whitehaven. He paid $100,000 for it and had the interior extensively redecorated in bright colours, with opulent furniture and added a swimming pool and carport. Grandmother Minnie Mae Presley moved in with them. Among his 'minders' at that time were his schoolfriends, Red West and Bitsy Mott and his cousins Gene and Junior Smith.

Gladys' feelings about all these extreme changes were mixed – thrilled that her son had achieved wealth and fame beyond all their wildest expectations – and increasing desolation that he was constantly being taken away from her, firstly by the tours and concerts, then by Hollywood and, the most bitter blow of all, by his call-up for the army. She had turned increasingly to vodka and pills to deal with the deep depression that had become increasingly

part of her life. After filming *King Creole* (*qv*), Elvis returned from Memphis to spend a final weekend with his family and bid a tearful farewell to his adored parents. Gladys, who from early days had nightmares about what calamities might be going to befall her son, grew ever more despondent. Though she never let him know, she longed for him to give up his music career: she confided to Minnie Mae that Elvis could afford to acquire a business – perhaps a hamburger palace – where he could settle down with a wife of his own. She was constantly trying to conceal the internal pain she endured, and despite the bond between mother and son it is unlikely that he was aware that something was terribly wrong with her.

Elvis's two weeks of army leave was occupied by frequent recording sessions and by spending as much time as he could manage either at Graceland with his parents or with his new girlfriend, Anita Wood, a Memphis celebrity, singer and DJ – Dixie Locke had been unable to take the pace and found another beau. Elvis having given Anita a diamond ring, rumours were rife that the couple had become engaged; Anita did not exactly quench the flames by making a record for Sun, 'I'll Wait Forever'.

When his leave was up Elvis made arrangements for his parents to live close to his base at Fort Hood, Texas, in a mobile home, but in the event they moved to a three-bedroomed house where Elvis was allowed to live. Gladys's health was steadily worsening and she was having difficulty in walking; she was also constantly tired. Vernon decided she should return to Memphis to be near the family doctor: then in a private ward at the new Methodist Hospital, the doctors diagnosed hepatitis. Elvis was granted compassionate leave to be near her and during the early hours of Thursday, August 4th she died of a heart attack. Elvis, asleep at Graceland, was awoken with the terrible news, which he was unable, at first, to comprehend. The

umbilical chord had never really been broken and to the end he was completely dependant on her for many things. 'I was the only child and Mama was always right with me' he said: when they were apart he was constantly on the telephone to her.

This ending is at variance with the *Elvis* film, in which both he and Vernon were at her bedside when she slipped peacefully away. No doubt the fans would have wanted it that way. Three thousand of them stood silently outside the funeral home in Memphis. She was buried at the Forest Lawn cemetery, with a ten foot-high marble monument – a statue of Christ with two angels kneeling at either side. The inscription reads, 'Gladys Smith Presley, April 25, 1912–August 14, 1958. Beloved wife of Vernon Presley and mother of Elvis Presley. She was the sunshine of our home.' Elvis was devastated at the funeral and was heard to say, 'Oh God, everything I have is gone.'

(See also: Capricorn; Elvis: The Movie; Girls, Girls, Girls (not the movie); King Creole; Parker, Colonel Tom; Presley, Vernon Elvis)

PRESLEY, LISA MARIE (b. 1968)

Elvis's only child, a daughter, was born at 5 p.m. at Baptist Memorial Hospital, Memphis, on February 1, 1968, weighing 6lb 14oz. Lisa Marie and her mother Priscilla (*qv*) were driven home to Graceland (*qv*) on February 5 by Elvis in a stretch limo. These were the best times for their marriage; both parents adored the baby who was inevitably the centre of attention at Graceland. This was a time when Elvis was being rushed from one movie to another to fulfil a contract with which he was becoming increasingly disenchanted. When he went west to get ready to film *Live a Little, Love a Little* (*qv*) at the end of February, Priscilla and Lisa Marie followed in the care of Joe Esposito. Filming began on March 11, three days

The first photograph of Lisa Marie Presley, with Priscilla and Elvis. The baby was born at Baptist Memorial Hospital, Memphis, weighing six pounds, fourteen ounces, nine months after her parents' wedding, May 1, 1967.

after his comedy western, *Stay Away Joe* (*qv*), with Joan Blondell and Burgess Meredith, opened in the USA. The proud parents still found time to lead a busy social life, with visits to Tom Jones' show at the Flamingo, Las Vegas, visiting his dressing room after the show en-route to the studios to continue Elvis's

role in the new movie next day. The day the film was finished Elvis and Priscilla flew with the gang to Hawaii to relax. Next day, May 25, Presley found time to indulge his passion for karate by attending the karate tournament of Champions in Honolulu. One of the participants was Mike Stone, who was later to fall in love with Priscilla. Early the next month, Elvis and his wife went to Los Angeles for him to prepare the show on which he had really set his heart – his first TV special, *Elvis on NBC.*

He was to film another western,

Charro!, in July. In the meantime he spent as much time as possible with Lisa Marie. After yet another movie, *The Trouble With Girls* (*qv*), was finished in mid-December, Elvis, Priscilla and Lisa Marie travelled from Los Angeles to Memphis to prepare for the baby's first Christmas at Graceland. Elvis never outgrew the magic and excitement of that season. It may well be that Lisa Marie's earliest memories are of this time when Graceland was alive with coloured lights and a very special tree by which Elvis waited with intense anticipation for her to awaken and be shown her presents. A compulsive giver, the sky was the limit at Christmas when Elvis would always remember the poor of the world and wish he could help them all. The Christmases of Lisa Marie's early years were the happiest times for the family.

As Priscilla grew more and more disappointed by her life – or lack of it – as Mrs. Elvis Presley, she had more time on her hands to take stock of Elvis's increasingly erratic life-style and the pressure she felt from the constant presence of the Memphis Mafia (*qv*) and their wives. She was also concerned by the effect his nightly capers might be having on the three year-old child, whom he always wanted to stay up to be with him. When the final break occurred, with divorce between Elvis and Priscilla finalized on October 9, 1973, she was given custody of Lisa Marie, then aged five: happy photographs were taken of the couple arm in arm outside the Santa Monica Superior Court, although in fact, Elvis was very far from happy. His life had virtually fallen apart.

After the divorce Elvis regularly sent his private jet to bring Lisa Marie to his concerts. It is reported that he once flew her to Utah and back at a cost of $30,000 because she told him she had never seen snow. As young as four years-old she was being showered with diamonds and furs and rings that were all too big for her and Priscilla refused to let her have them until she was eighteen. At Graceland she had a special yellow bedroom with a fur bed, which she had to climb up stairs to get into.

The last of many visits Lisa Marie made to Graceland to stay with her father began on August 8, 1977, the day he rented the Libertyland Amusement Park for her entertainment. With Ginger Alden they arrived at the Park after 1 a.m. for an all-night session at the funfair, leaving at dawn. Another all-night entertainment was at the local movie theatre, where the three of them sat together until nearly 6 a.m.. There

were two such visits, after which Elvis, due to start another tour in three days, went on one of his drastic crash diets to lose weight. He had not left enough time to achieve the desired result and was frustrated and angry: the publication of the book *Elvis: What Happened?* at the beginning of the month had also cast him further into the slough of despondency. Nine year-old Lisa Marie was staying at Graceland when Elvis died.

She was left $5,000,000 in trust for her 25th birthday, which she has moved back until she is 30 (1998). By her own admission she became a spoilt brat at the various exclusive private schools she attended, which is hardly surprising. When she was 12 her mother enrolled her in a Scientology-run establishment called the Apple School, by which time Priscilla had entered into a six year liaison with a model called Michael Edwards, who moved out when, according to his autobiography *Priscilla, Elvis and Me*, he began to have 'inappropriate' feelings for the 12 year-old child. Commented Lisa Marie to *Life* magazine 'That one lasted too long. He was sick'. At 14 Lisa Marie was smoking marijuana, by 17 she was well on the way to kicking the habit when Priscilla entered her into the Scientology facility called the Celebrity Centre. Her mother, for some time established as a television actress, was herself interested in the scientology cult.

In 1986 Lisa Marie decided to move out of Priscilla's house and have a go at life on her own. She did not find this to her liking and leapt at the chance when the pragmatic Priscilla offered to build her a house in the garden. In 1988 Lisa Marie married a musician called Danny Keogh at the Scientology Celebrity Centre where they met. Their first child, Danielle, was born the following year and the second, Benjamin, in 1992. By 1994 Danny and Lisa Marie had discovered that 'friendship was more suitable for us than

marriage' and they were amicably divorced.

She first met Michael Jackson in 1974. Elvis took her to see the Jackson Five at the age of six. Jackson was 16 at the time and she was escorted backstage to chat with him and his family. It was nine years before their unlikely friendship blossomed when mutual friends brought them together again, first at a private dinner and then at a more formal meeting, when Jackson hoped to secure songs from the Elvis Presley catalogue. They began to phone each other regularly and discovered that they were soulmates, both having felt robbed of their childhoods. In August 1993 at the age of 34 Michael Jackson was accused of molesting a 12 year-old boy, Jordy Chandler. He began phoning Lisa Marie desperately, protesting his innocence, as he did when he appeared on television to answer to and vehemently deny the molestation charges. He proposed to her on the phone in September, 1993. She said, 'Of course' – just like that – and in November he cancelled the remainder of his world tour, checking into London's Charter Nightingale Hospital at Lisa Marie's suggestion. It has been suggested that he finally won her heart during his television appearance, protesting his innocence with more that a little dignity.

Jackson began dating Lisa Marie and twenty days after her divorce from Danny Keogh was made final, they were married at a civil ceremony in the Dominican Republic, first in Spanish, then in English, on May 26. On August 1 Lisa Marie issued a statement confirming her married name and saying she intended to dedicate her life to being Jackson's wife. Priscilla's own statement went as follows: 'I totally support everything my daughter does. I have nothing further to say!' An undisclosed sum was paid to Chandler's family and Jackson's attorney apparently settled the matter once and for all. After the wedding the police investigation into

Jackson was dropped, although the Los Angeles district attorney's office said the case could be re-opened if any more children came forward with allegations.

Speculation as to the reason for the marriage, leaving aside their evident affinity in some respects, has put forward Jackson's need to provide evidence of his heterosexuality and, on her side, associates have suggested that she may have subconsciously realized that the resultant publicity of such a marriage would establish her in the music business. Earlier she had recorded four songs, all produced by Danny Keogh under the aegis of her manager, Jerry Schilling, who had been a member of the Memphis Mafia. He played them to some record company executives and the verdict seems to have been that she had a voice but no experience. After that she had her son and temporarily abandoned the idea. But for all her diffidence and denials it seems she is still wanting to prove herself with a record career which she says is 'artistically important' to her. She has built a recording studio in her Los Angeles home and is writing songs.

Her marriage to Jacko foundered after some 20 months with Lisa Marie refusing to discuss the matter. It has been said that they had an agreement that he should bring his talent and music industry know-how to help her with her own plans to form an entertainment company when she came into her inheritance. But it seems that he has failed in his side of the agreement, except to get her to appear naked in his *You Are Not Alone* video. What the future will bring remains to be seen but in the meantime she concentrates on her own plans – or her trainers – to keep perfectly fit through going on special diets such as the six week cleansing programme called Cleanse Thyself – a course for cleansing intestines; details are not for the squeamish. In view of the way her father went it is only logical that she should be concerned about looking after her weight. It seems that this dichotomy of

interests is present, understandably, in other facets of Lisa Marie's life.

A part of her makes heroic attempts to lead an ordinary, normal life – as in 'Mrs. Young Everywoman, USA'. She has been seen on a Saturday afternoon shopping spree in a Los Angeles grocery store, where every week she hands in the discount vouchers she has collected from daily papers, along with cans and bottles that are redeemable for hard cash. She lives in the suburb of Hidden Hills, 30 miles north of Los Angeles, among the modest homes – some 500 of them – situated behind obligatory 3 feet high fences. Lisa's house, however, has its own special fence some four feet behind the first one: an 8 feet high metal security fence. The community – 1.65 square miles of it – is protected by security officers at each of three gated entrances. Another security guard lives in the home of Lisa Marie and her two children in guest quarters off the kitchen. Their huge house is a four bedroom, three bathroom building, some 300 feet from the end of the main street and is forbidden to all-comers without special passes and permission arranged by the resident – which goes for all the houses in the exclusive community. Hidden Hills, indeed. People who have visited say that the furnishings inside are mainly modestly priced, bought by Lisa Marie from discount stores – a reflection of her determination to lead her own life in contrast to film-star mother Priscilla's grander *modus operandi*, one might say through Elvis-coloured spectacles, which led her to buy her daughter a multi-million dollar mansion in Beverley Hills after her marriage in 1988 to Danny Keogh. After living there for less than a month the couple moved to a modest ranch home in Tarzana, a suburb of Los Angeles. It seems that Lisa Marie finds proximity to her mother daunting, though they seem devoted to each other in their own off-beat way.

Lisa spends most of her time with her children, playing in their swimming

pool, often taking walks around the neighbourhood with friends but always with two bodyguards in attendance. When she goes to see a film, it is usually to a matinée, when the prices are cheapest. Perhaps Lisa Marie inherited some of her business sense from her mother since it was Priscilla's business acumen which not only saved Graceland from the shabby and impecunious state to which it was drifting, but recouped the original investment within 38 days and made nearly fifty million dollars in the first year, so that Graceland now ranks among the top half-dozen tourist attractions in the USA. Lisa Marie has said she dreads being 30, which is when she will come into the first part of her inheritance. Eventually it is estimated that the empire she will come into will be $200,000 million and she cannot but be aware that this breath-taking amount will be largely due to Priscilla.

At the time Mrs. Jackson first asked for a separation from her husband he was in New York's Beth Israel North Medical Centre, having collapsed from low blood pressure and other unspecified causes in December, 1995. The press had a field day, one headline reporting that she had sued for divorce at a time when he was fighting for his life. The term AIDS was bandied about with unbecoming glee. She asked only for the restitution of her maiden name and for Jackson to pay her legal bills. It has been reported that she still regards him with affection and hopes to make a film with him. Certainly he gave her a $250,000 diamond necklace at the end of January, 1996, to prove that there were no hard feelings.

When she dyed her hair black and had it cut short, she resembled uncannily the young Elvis. Whichever way the pendulum swings, it seems likely that one way or another she will perpetuate the name and fame of her two unique parents.

(See also: Girls, Girls, Girls (not the movie); Graceland; Live a Little, Love a

Little; Memphis Mafia; Presley, Priscilla Beaulieu; Stay Away Joe; The Trouble With Girls)

PRESLEY, PRISCILLA BEAULIEU (b. 1943)

During Elvis's army service the press were given little access to him, with the predictable result that the *Stars and Stripes*, a newspaper designed for the Armed Forces, was reduced to printing persistent stories about his love life. One romance that escaped the notice of the press, however, at least in the beginning, was his meeting in November, 1959, with Priscilla Beaulieu, the step-daughter of Air Force Captain Beaulieu, stationed in Wiesbaden. They were introduced at a party by Elvis's friend US Airman James Curry, when Priscilla was only 14. The scene is one of several graphically re-created in *Elvis – The Movie*. Kurt Russell (*qv*) and Season Hubley enact a touching and convincing depiction of love at first sight; although she does not look 14 she does have a tremulous innocence about her. In any case, it is probable that Priscilla looked older than her years. He was smitten by her well-mannered ways, sophisticated yet unspoiled, and by her pretty face and long curly brown hair. One of the most attractive things about her was that, unlike most of the other girls he met in Germany, she seemed unaffected by his star status and behaved completely normally. This sudden relationship had the effect of cooling what had been perhaps his strongest attachment to date, with Anita Wood, a talented and beautiful nineteen year-old DJ from Memphis and host of the TV show *Top Ten Dance Party* whom Elvis met in 1957. He took her to Graceland to meet his parents – she was well-liked and many of those close to him thought that marriage was on the cards. They did, indeed, discuss the matter, which was promptly negated by Colonel

Parker (*qv*), who did not want his protégé tied up with any one girl.

Priscilla and Elvis were able to meet quite often; right-hand man and friend Lamar Fike would motor several miles to pick her up in the early evening and take her back later. In January, 1960, Elvis was promoted to sergeant and put in command of a three-man reconnaissance team earning the praise of his platoon leader, as he did of everyone who had anything to do with him in the army. In December Elvis threw a lavish party, attended by Vernon (*qv*) and the regulars. Also present were Army Sergeant Bill Stanley, who had fought in World War II. Priscilla was the centre of attention at the party; Elvis having given her a solid gold watch studded with diamonds.

When Elvis's imminent discharge was announced for March, the Colonel laid his plans. In the interim he had made sure the Presley industry kept moving: five very successful singles had been issued and each topped the million sales; LP's were repackaged and the fans kept buying, despite the lack of new material. On March 3rd Elvis attended a Press Conference at Fort Dix; with him were Colonel Parker and Nancy Sinatra. He arrived back in Memphis on March 7 in full dress uniform and the fans went wild. By March 20 he was back to work in the studios at RCA in Nashville. During the session he recorded 'Stuck on You', 'Fame and Fortune', 'Make Me Know It', 'It Feels So Right' and 'A Mess of the Blues'. The Colonel had fixed Elvis's TV comeback for the Frank Sinatra *Timex Show*. Both wearing tuxedos, they did a duet of 'Witchcraft' which has passed into showbusiness history; on his own Elvis sang 'Fame and Fortune' and 'Stuck on You'. The show was aired on May 8 and by May 12, obviously feeling bereft of Priscilla who had remained behind in Germany, Anita Wood was back on the scene, sporting a diamond necklace given to her by Elvis. They were photographed riding on a

roundabout in the Memphis Funfair. He had already started filming his comeback vehicle *G.I. Blues* (*qv*), and now had another interest to fill the empty space created by the absence of Priscilla – his leading lady, Juliet Prowse. The affair seems to have been brief but intense and did not please Frank Sinatra, whose interest in her had made headlines internationally and even the word marriage had been mooted. Mooted but not consummated, despite the rumours reputedly circulated by the lady herself.

By December Elvis had begun a campaign to get Priscilla over to Graceland for the holidays. He enlisted the help of Vernon and Dee, who had been married in July 1960, after her divorce became final. Although Elvis was conspicuous by his absence from their wedding, the campaign was successful and Priscilla came over from Germany on December 8 for a discreet, low-key visit, chaperoned by grandmother Presley, Minnie Mae. Elvis's devotion was total: he even went to the length of asking his 'Boys' if they liked her. They all said the right things and by the end of her original two-week stay an extension was secured from her stepfather and she finally returned reluctantly to Germany in the New Year. It was clear that Elvis did not intend to live without her and by October 1962, her stepfather had agreed to her moving to Graceland; she would finish her schooling at the Immaculate Conception Highschool in Memphis, with Elvis responsible for her education and well-being. She moved in with Vernon and Dee at their house in Hermitage. She was then seventeen and David Stanley regarded her as a big and very kind sister.

She delighted him and his brothers by dressing up as a vampire, very convincingly, he recalls. Even at that early age it seems that Priscilla was not only very resourceful but already had a sense of the dramatic that was to stand her in good stead in her career years later. She was already having a markedly good influence on Elvis; during her first real Christmas at Graceland he had assembled his family and friends in the dining room and presented her with a diamond ring. Anita Wood had finally called it a day, after seeing him through several other romantic associations and flings. At the time he was going from film to film and recording the soundtracks; during the long periods that he was absent Priscilla took good car of her surrogate family, even though she was still at school.

In Elvis's rented house in Perugia, LA which Elvis used when he was filming in Hollywood, it was party time, with lights on all night and rock around the clock. Rumours were rife about himself and his sultry new co-star, Ursula Andress. *Fun in Acapulco* (*qv*) was the title of their film together and it soon became clear that the fun was not confined to Acapulco. The major filming was done in the Paramount studios, while a second unit went to Mexico where the action was set. The shooting began at the end of January and continued to the end of March: this would be the last but one movie in Elvis's film career to enjoy a normal length schedule. Elvis hung around in Perugia until the beginning of April, the month in which RCA announced that he had sold over 100 million records. The 'Elvismobile' – his travelling luxury hotel – returned to Memphis on April 6, when a month was spent in recording sessions which continued into May. In June Priscilla graduated from the Convent of the Immaculate Conception and went on to attend Memphis's Patricia Stevens Finishing School. In July Elvis began work on *Viva Las Vegas* (*qv*) opposite Ann-Margret (*qv*).

During his long periods away in Hollywood, Priscilla spent most of her time with Vernon, Dee and grandmother, Minnie Mae: Joseph Beaulieu had allowed his daughter to move to Memphis on condition that the senior Presleys become virtually her

guardians. Dee's biography of Elvis, *We Love You Tender*, outraged the fans; for marrying Vernon she could do no right in their eyes; the more rabid of them have always considered her a rank outsider and it was inevitable that Elvis, for all his natural courtesy and his affection for his father, could hardly avoid resenting her for attempting to supplant his beloved Gladys (*qv*). Writing about the relationship between Elvis and his mother, she has stepped in where angels fear to tread; her innuendoes, in the eyes of the worshippers, have qualified Dee for burning at the stake. Whatever she had said, she was treading on sacred ground, but where Priscilla is concerned her conclusions seem fair and reasonable. She says,

She did things that most normal teenagers do, except when Elvis was home, when she would do the things he wanted to do – parties, movies, riding. But she wasn't in any way a normal teenager, because it was always assumed that one day she and Elvis would get married .... she came to Graceland to see how we lived, and she proved that she could stay there with the family ...... and she did really well. She was everything he really wanted.

In other words she was being tested for her future role as queen consort, which might have been considered the ideal way for a young princess to be groomed for stardom. The snag was that King Elvis was no ordinary monarch. What she could not know was that she would be marrying the whole court as well: if such a thing came to mind, she could dismiss it as an unwelcome spectre that would be banished by their mutual love and togetherness.

Elvis was still on the crest of a wave until this year of change – 1963: his films and records were money-spinners, with every single and LP reaching the Top Ten. *Viva Las Vegas* was the last film

to be made before Sam Katzman (*qv*) moved into court as putative Lord Chancellor and overseer of the royal coffers. A minor spectre materialized in the nubile form of co-star Ann Margret, who was indiscreet enough to hint at possible wedding plans. Priscilla left Graceland to stay with her parents , who were now living in San Francisco. But the romance with Ann-Margret petered out and Elvis sweet-talked Priscilla into accepting that rumour – and the media – were lying jades and Graceland again became the background for Elvis's great love. He and Ann-Margret remained friends after her marriage to Roger Smith: one of the advantages she possessed over most of his ladies was that she knew how to ride a motorbike.

At the end of 1963, after the lightning schedule on *Kissin' Cousins* in October, Elvis went back to Memphis in November to be with Priscilla and the Mafia (*qv*) – a term he hated, as much as he had loathed being called 'Elvis the Pelvis'. He spent his time riding around the grounds of Graceland in his golf carts and around Memphis on his Harley Davidsons. The world was still reeling from the assassination of President Kennedy.

A personal watershed for the Presleys was Christmas Day, 1967, when Elvis announced his engagement to Priscilla in front of family and friends; another diamond ring marked the occasion. The wedding followed in a private ceremony in Las Vegas at the Aladdin Hotel on May 1, 1964, at 9.41 a.m., by justice of the Nevada Supreme Court. In attendance were the best man, Joe Esposito (*qv*), Elvis's friend from the days in West Germany and Marty Lacker, whose relationship with Elvis went back to high school at Hume: the maid and matron of honour were Michelle Beaulieu, sister of the bride and Joe's wife, Joan. Marty Lacker designed Elvis's elegant black tuxedo, while Priscilla's gown was of white chiffon, with a six-foot train. The ceremony lasted only eight minutes and there were eleven guests, all close family, except for Elvis's schoolfriend, George Klein, while Joe Esposito and Marty Lacker were the only members of the Memphis Mafia present. Marty, who had organized the ceremony, knew nothing about the subsequent arrangements and was shocked to find that most of the groom's friends had not been invited to the wedding or the reception. It has never been made clear whose decision this was but Marty, in his book *Elvis: Portrait of a Friend*, did not believe it was Elvis's. In any case it was, at the very least, a tactless decision and left most of the guys 'Mad as hell', according to Marty, who was, in fact, fired by Elvis the following year. *Elvis: The Movie* depicts the scene where Red West (Robert Gray) receives the news that he has not been invited with hurt bewilderment. Red had known Elvis longer that anyone, with the possible exception of George Klein, also at Hume High, and had stuck up for him in playground fights. He looked after Elvis most of his life, wrote songs for him and had roles in most Presley movies. There was a second wedding reception at Graceland for friends and relatives who had not been at the wedding, the Stanley boys, Billy, Ricky and David included, but the hurt was never healed, particularly for Red West, who was fired in 1976.

The honeymoon in Palm Springs was interrupted on May 2 when Elvis had to return to United Artists to do some extra dubbing on *Clambake* (*qv*). Two days later the bride and groom and their various families returned to Memphis. The rest of the year for Elvis was spent mainly in filming *Speedway* (*qv*) with Nancy Sinatra, and *Stay Away Joe* (*qv*) with Burgess Meredith and Joan Blondell. On September 29 Governor Bufors proclaimed Elvis Presley Day in the state of Tennessee. The end of the year, with Priscilla eight months pregnant, was a stay-at-home time for the Presleys.

Lisa Marie Presley was born at the Baptist Memorial Hospital on February 1, 1968, weighing in at 6lb 14oz and mother and daughter came through well. The marriage entered into its happiest phase and Elvis was a doting father. He had seemingly ceased to care that his films were receiving worse and worse reviews and that the songs were becoming more and more stereotyped – probably because he had already made up his mind to return to performances before real, live audiences as soon as he could wrap up his film commitments.

In effect his first TV special, *Elvis*, taped between June 27 and 30 for NBC at Burbank in front of a live audience, was his first public appearance as a singer for more than ten years. He appeared radiantly cool, calm and collected – his nerves were acute but in no way apparent. The audience responded with warm enthusiasm and he confirmed his own belief that live performance was what he loved best. Ironically, his next movie, *Charro!*, which began shooting on location on July 22, gave him a really strong and serious part, which some of his fans regard as his best. The critics, however, were apathetic.

After the first careless rapture of fatherhood, tensions began to surface in the Presley marriage, many of them to do with the omnipresent Memphis Mafia. The situation is neatly summed up in *Elvis: The Movie*. Priscilla asks her husband if he has to have all his friends with him *all* the time. That goes, too, for their wives and girlfriends; they were not her choice of companions and she seems to have had no life of her own. Elvis had spent endless sums of money on new homes, including a ranch at Walls, Mississippi, where there were mobile homes for his entourage, pick-up trucks galore and stables stocked with prize-winning horses. There was a luxurious home in Beverley Hills, California, complete with swimming pool and a magnificent view over Los Angeles: the house, at 1164, Hillcrest Road, being

high on a hill. The ranch was really one of many presents for Priscilla, who loved horse riding; it was named Flying Circle G; there was already a Circle G in Texas. Elvis's love of horses equalled his love of human company; Rising Sun was a particular favourite whom he delighted in riding at Graceland.

Vernon, in charge of the payment of bills, was aghast at the never-ending expenditure, including cars for the entourage – the giving of which had always been a particular pleasure to Elvis, as well as an extra staff of ten at Graceland. Desperately Presley senior invoked the help of the Colonel, who insisted that some of the paid companions be made redundant, telling them that Elvis had gone beyond what he could afford and that things had to change. The Flying Circle G, which Elvis could barely find time to visit, was sold in 1969, after which Elvis and Priscilla divided their time between their Memphis and California homes. She became virtually a prisoner in her own home. He did not encourage her to have friends and would not allow her to tour with him. To alleviate her boredom she took up first dancing, then karate, of which he approved as it was his favourite sport. Her instructor was Mike Stone; the two were mutually attracted and subsequently became lovers.

Elvis triumphantly returned to the stage at the International Hotel, Las Vegas, on July 26, 1969. He had definitely justified the Colonel's billing of 'The World's Greatest Entertainer'. He was away from home more and more often with the result that the affair between Mike Stone and Priscilla was kept from him for three and a half years. After discovering that her husband had been unfaithful to her on innumerable occasions, Priscilla decided to tell him the truth late in 1971; furthermore, she revealed that she was leaving him and going to live with Mike Stone. The divorce was finalized in October, 1973 – for technical reasons Elvis was the one who filed the petition. Deep depression was added to his increasingly bad health; his dependence on drugs – all legally prescribed by doctors who were making millions by satisfying his craving – escalated disastrously, as did his inordinate eating binges. Even before their divorce Priscilla had become increasingly unable to curb his excesses. She requested, to keep herself and Lisa Marie, $750,000 plus $6,000 a month, half the proceeds of the sale of one of their Los Angeles houses and five per cent of two of Elvis's publishing companies. He complied willingly, but his self-destructive urge set him on a course from which there was only one way out.

After Elvis's death, the income of the Presley estate became substantially depleted, due to Vernon Presley's inability to control Colonel Parker's stranglehold on the late singer's finances. Vernon's death from a heart attack in 1979 caused control of the Estate, as Grandmother Minnie Mae was in her late eighties, to pass officially to Lisa Marie and thus to Priscilla, as queen regnant of the regnant to be. Priscilla's relationship with the Colonel was by no means as easygoing as had been that of the ever-pliant Vernon, especially when she insisted on money being spent on facilities for visiting fans. The gardens of Graceland had been previously available to the public but in 1982 the mansion was turned into a memorial museum, with guided tours around the house and grounds, at $5 for adults and $3 for children. The *Daily Mirror* in London carried a report some weeks before the tours began that the Presley Estate needed extra finance to meet running costs.

An attorney appointed by the Memphis Probate Court prepared an involved report on the way the Presley Estate had been managed, prior to the establishment of a Trust Fund to which all the Estate assets would be transferred. The proceedings brought to light the

enormous amounts of money that had been paid by the Estate to Colonel Parker. In his counter Patker asked the Court to ratify all his agreements with Presley and to stop investigations into them, to prevent the Estate's remaining value being whittled away by litigation.

Divorce brought out hidden depths in Priscilla, which were not limited to her business acumen. Having joined the long-running soap opera Dallas in the latter half of the Eighties, she went on to a successful film career, notably in the spoof crime series The Naked Gun: although in her forties, looking incredibly young and delicate. She now has a son from Brazilian Marco Garibaldi called Navarone and career-wise has proved more than capable of managing the Presley Estate: her relations with Lisa Marie have always been cordial even if their lifestyles have diverged. Graceland thrives as never before and looks likely to do so, due in no small measure to her level-headedness and common sense. *(See also: Ann-Margret; Charro!; Clambake; Elvis: The Movie; Fun in Acapulco; G.I. Blues; Girls, Girls, Girls (not the movie); Katzman, Sam; Kissin' Cousins; Parker, Colonel Tom; Presley, Gladys Love Smith; Presley, Vernon Elvis; Speedway; Stay Away Joe; Viva Las Vegas)*

PRESLEY, VERNON ELVIS (1916–1979)

Elvis's father was born in Fulton, Mississippi, on April 19, 1916, where the family had lived for generations. He has, in general, suffered from a less than sympathetic press, including the unfair and simplistic description, 'Gladys was a worker, Vernon, a shirker.' Although she was undoubtedly the stronger character and more able to turn her hand to a diversity of hard-grafting and poorly paid jobs during their struggles to bring up their son and give him the best they could afford, there can be no suggestion that Vernon shirked any of the myriad occupations that came his way in those

days of the Great Depression. The couple made a handsome pair in the early days before Gladys put on weight – her dark and slightly continental features contrasting with his blond and open-faced image. There was a hint of the young Van Johnson about him – the MGM star was, coincidentally, born the same year as Vernon. The couple were undoubtedly devoted to each other and to their only surviving child.

As the family fortunes improved dramatically when Elvis's career began to take off, Vernon had virtually retired, and by the time of Gladys' death in 1958, was devoting himself entirely to looking after his son's interests. He did this with the blessing of Colonel Parker, who realized that Vernon was neither experienced enough nor knowledgeable in the ways of big business to be any threat to his control. When Elvis was drafted Vernon went with him to Germany, along with Lamar Fike, a friend of Sam Phillips, who had met Elvis in the early days in the Sun offices and been impressed with his distinctive style of dressing and manner of comportment. By 1957 Fike was a charter member of the Memphis Mafia (qv) and Elvis's right hand man, taking care of travel arrangements and the ins and outs of tours and public appearances. They all stayed there during Elvis's term of duty.

In West Germany Vernon met Tennessee born Dee Elliott, at that time married to Army Sergeant William Stanley from whom she was divorced in 1960. After her decree nisi she and Vernon were married in her home town of Huntsville, Alabama. Elvis could hardly have welcomed the match but his devotion to his 'Daddy' outweighed his feeling that his beloved mother's memory had been betrayed a mere two years after her death. He behaved with his customary courtesy when Vernon brought his bride Davada (known as Dee) with her three sons to live at Graceland. They were Stanley William, born in 1953, Richard Earl, born the same year and David Edward, born 1955. When Elvis could no longer overcome his instinctive antipathy to Dee, the family moved to a house outside the grounds of Graceland, in Hermitage Street. In his book *The Elvis Encyclopedia* David writes of how welcome his stepbrother made him as a scared and rather lonely five year-old. In 1972, as a 17 year-old teenager, David started working for Elvis as a personal aide, against his mothers wishes and later became a personal bodyguard. The other boys also worked for Elvis. Billy, the eldest, dubbed 'Charlie Manson' because he thought he looked sinister, became a personal aide and Richard (Restless Ricky), who seems to have been something of a problem brother also became an aide and personal bodyguard. He was arrested in 1975 for trying to use a forged prescription for amphetamines at a local hospital and has been quoted as one of Elvis's drug suppliers, though, God knows, his own doctors provided him with more than enough. He was fired after an argument with one of Elvis's girlfriends, Linda Thompson, but reinstated after she left Elvis.

Vernon was kept busy as his son's business manager and, in the process, cost him considerable sums of money in taxes that could have been avoided by judicious investments that would have benefited the estate. He was blinkered in other ways, too, being seemingly unaware of the tragic toll that his son's massive drug intake and eating binges were having on his health and mental capacity, added to the gruelling pressures of the tours. On what turned out to be Elvis's swan song, June 26th, 1977, at Market Square in Indianapolis, he did an uncharacteristic thing, by calling Vernon on stage to take a bow with him. They stood together for a long and moving ovation from 18,000 lustily cheering fans – a fitting curtain call to many years of devoted togetherness.

In 1977, Dee divorced Vernon; she was one of several wives of Presley's close circle who left their husbands due to the pressures of close attendance on the King. The reason – or at least the main reason – in every case was the time the husbands were away from home; the result, in Vernon's case, was that he suffered a near-fatal heart attack. When he recovered, still upset from the loss of the son who had been the focus of his life for so long, plus the departure of Dee, Vernon – the only person who might have been able to place some sort of curb on Colonel Parker's money-making proclivities – showed little inclination to do so. The fact that he was a main beneficiary in Elvis's will, along with grandmother Minnie Mae Presley and Lisa Marie (*qv*), who was to inherit the bulk when she reached the age of 25, may also have been a major factor.

Vernon Presley died in 1979 of the heart attack that had been waiting in the wings for two years. He was 63. Dee and the other survivors of the clan Presley have been reaping the whirlwind ever since in the form of interminable exposés by family, associates, friends et al. Perhaps the most ironic title of all is *Elvis, We Love You Tender* by Dee Presley, Billy, Rick and David Stanley. Dee, in particular, has earned the disapprobrium of Presley fans. The one family member who has been accorded less than her true recognition is Priscilla (*qv*), whose devotion during his life was sorely tried, and who since his death has worked ceaselessly to put to rights the tangle of affairs that were at one time threatening to run Graceland financially into the ground. Elvis's more bigoted admirers tend to feel bitter over the fact that she eventually left him for karate instructor Mike Stone, but the provocation was astronomical.

(See also: Memphis Mafia; Parker, Colonel Tom; Presley, Gladys Love Smith; Presley, Lisa Marie; Presley, Priscilla Beaulieu)

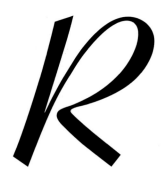

ROCK 'N ROLL TEDDY BEAR KING

By August 1956 Elvis, the Rock 'n Roll phenomenon, was being headlined in the media as just a child at heart, for all his ex-truck driver persona. He was portrayed as a real 'mother's boy' – an all too accurate description – devoted to his parents, whom he had bought a palatial house in Memphis, complete with swimming pool. Despite having four Cadillacs, it was recorded that he neither smoked nor drank and night clubs bored him. His favourite pastimes were going to funfairs or 'carnis' and trying to win more teddy bears and toy dogs. Sitting on his bedroom floor among them was his favourite form of relaxation and to prove it there were pictures of him doing just that. After this news got out and his fans were let into the secret of what made him happiest, the teddies had to have a special wing built for them and a rota of minders to cater for their welfare.

Letters poured in, often accompanying yet another teddy, asking how could the King be accused of corrupting the morals of the young when he had such sweet and simple pleasures? Further, when his second film was released the following year, the song 'Teddy Bear (Let Me Be Your)' (*qv*) became one of the year's hits and topped the *Billboard* charts for seven weeks. So many furry toys flowed in from all over the world that, fittingly, Elvis donated a truckload full to a Christmas children's charity.

(See also: Loving You; 'Teddy Bear'; Roustabout)

ROUSTABOUT * * *

Released by: Paramount Pictures (Technicolor, Techniscope); **Producer:** Hal B. Wallis; **Director:** John Rich; **Screenplay:** Anthony Lawrence and Allan Weiss; **Director of Photography:** Lucien Ballard; **Music:** Joseph J. Lilley; **Running Time:** 101 mins; **Opened:** November 11, 1964.

Cast: Elvis, Barbara Stanwyck, Joan Freeman, Leif Erikson, Sue Anne Langdon, Pat Buttram, Joan Stanley, Dabbs Greer, Steve Brodie, Jack Albertson, Billy Barty, Richard Kiel, Red West, Raquel Welch.

Barbara Stanwyck as Maggie Morgan, carni circus owner, Elvis as part-time fairground hand Charlie Rogers, and Joan Freeman as Cathy Lean, daughter of Maggie's assistant and sometime lover. *Roustabout* (1964)

Charlie Rogers drops by the tent of fortune-teller Madame Mijanou (Sue Ann Langdon) to see what she has in store for him. *Roustabout* (1964)

While singing at the Teahouse Roadhouse, Charlie Rogers (Elvis) is needled by arrogant college students; when he answers back they ask him outside and start to throw punches, but are felled by his knowledge of karate. Meanwhile waitress Marge (Joan Stanley), whose affections for Charlie are not reciprocated, calls the police. Charlie's hot temper loses him yet another job and he is put in the county jail. Bailed out by Marge, he refuses to take her with him on his motorbike. Heading for parts unknown, he gets into an argument with the grouchy driver of a jeep, Joe Lean (Leif Erikson), who runs him off the road, smashing his bike and his guitar. Passengers in the jeep are Joe's daughter, Cathy (Joan Freeman) and his girlfriend, Maggie Moran (Barbara Stanwyck (qv), the owner of a travelling carnival. Charlie, falling for Cathy, agrees to Maggie's offer to take him on as a temporary roustabout, doing odd jobs around the 'carni'.

Business is not exactly booming and Maggie owes money to the bank. A few songs from Charlie, (accompanied by the ubiquitous Jordanaires) and word gets around: soon crowds of screaming teenagers are flocking to the fairground and Maggie's show starts to do well again. Gradually Cathy begins to return his affection, although Joe's heavy drinking and antagonistic attitude is a constant liability and Charlie's casual affection for the carnival's resident fortune-teller Madame Mijanou (Sue Anne Langdon) infuriates Cathy. When Maggie finds rival owner Harry Carver (Pat Buttram) hanging around and taking stock of the way Charlie's singing is packing in the public she warns him off, having prior experience of him as a smooth operator and ruthless to a degree, which is what has kept him in the big time. Charlie turns down Carver's offer to pay him more than Maggie can afford, but he picks a fight with a customer who persists in throwing a ball to dunk Cathy in a water tank.

When the man mislays his wallet he accuses the carnival people of stealing it and Joe is arrested.

Meanwhile Charlie finds the wallet caught up on one of the tent ropes, turns down Mijanou's offer to split the proceeds and decides to take his time about bailing out Joe. After an accident on the Wall of Death, Charlie falls from his bike and Maggie finds the wallet: when Joe gets out of jail, Mijanou tells him that Charlie deliberately withheld the money that could have got him out earlier. Joe knocks him over and orders him out of their carnival. He heads for Harry Carver's circus to take up his offer to provide a rival attraction.

This he does so effectively that Maggie's carnival again hits the doldrums and the bank refuses her any more time to pay. Mijanou persuades Cathy to swallow her pride and go to Charlie and beg him to return to save their livelihood. He agrees, paying off the bank with money he earned at Carver's, then takes another beating from Joe, who relents when he realizes Charlie is back for good. Encouraged by Maggie, who tells him just for once to stop pretending to be a louse, Charlie declares his love to Cathy and is at last accepted by Joe as the credits roll.

At 30, Elvis is in good shape and Lucien Ballard photographs him with the knowledge one would expect from a cameraman who had worked with that master of lighting, Joseph Von Sternberg. There is a special glow to Ballard's use of colour photography which lends itself well to the carnival set-up, one of the few original touches of this routine Presley vehicle, which lifts chip-on-shoulder attitudes from his earlier films, including the obligatory karate expertise used to such amusing effect two years previously in Follow That Dream (qv) and the tough pose concealing a heart of gold from almost any Presley story line. It is heart warming to watch such a past-mistress of style as Barbara Stanwyck investing her carnival owner role with

warmth to such a degree that even her affection for the bear-with-a-sore-head character played on one surly note by Leif Erikson becomes credible. No one wore blue jeans with as much chic as Stanwyck, even though her grand starring roles in the past showed an impeccable dress-sense, which she claimed to find unimportant. Here Elvis's outfits really did him credit: apart from wearing black leather as to the manner born, he sticks to pale blue, black and white, wearing black crew necks under blue shirts or sweater shirts under loose cardigans – pants mainly hipsters, usually black.

While Joan Freeman's 'nice girl' role as Leif Erikson's daughter is played with more spirit than many Presley heroines, it is Sue Anne Langdon as the flirtatious fortune-teller, Madame Mijanou, who has some of the best lines and draws forth most rapport from Elvis. For example, as he is passing her tent she just happens to be smoothing down her tights to reveal quite stunningly symmetrical legs. He takes a look and says 'Marlene Dietrich does it better.' His intentionally flat delivery of that line provokes the perky rejoinder, 'But she's not here.'

Other interesting cast members are Pat Buttram as Maggie Moran's successful rival carnival owner, Harry Carver, who played the villain in several westerns with singing cowboy Gene Autry, and 7 ft 2 in Richard Kiel as the strong man, who was to make his memorable mark some thirteen years later as the villainous shark-biting Jaws in two James Bond Movies, *The Spy Who Loved Me* and *Moonraker*. Red West, one of Elvis's life-long school friends, bodyguard and member of the Memphis Mafia, makes one of his many appearances in a Presley film as a carnival worker. Summing up: as Deanna Durbin sang, 'It's foolish, but it's fun.'
(See also: Stanwyck, Barbara; Welch, Raquel)

ROUSTABOUT

2(RCA LPM 2999) October 1964
(Complete Soundtrack)

ROUSTABOUT * * *

Written by Bill Giant, Bernie Baum, Florence Kaye.

Charlie Rogers sings this over the credit titles as a car bowls along the highway – a favourite start for an Elvis musical – with the twist that the car is not driven by him and contains students on their way to the roadhouse where he is singing. The theme of the song is that he is free to roam the roads as he chooses; even if he sees an attractive girl, he'll just say a quick hello then leave. It's the wandering life for him – a fast number, with guitars, drums, piano, saxes making an ideal opening.

Single B/W: 'One Track Heart'

LITTLE EGYPT * * * * *

Written by Jerry Lieber, Mike Stoller.
The outstanding song of the soundtrack recording. Lieber and Stoller's steamy number, previously a hit for the Coasters, is given a special quality by Elvis's rendering: as rock writer Dave Marsh pointed out: 'He seized every song that possessed a glimmer of worth and wrung out its full potential.' It is the number chosen for Charlie's debut at the rival carnival run by Harry Carver and is distinguished, apart from Elvis's sexual feeling for the words, by the sensuous gyrations of Wylda Taylor, the dancer portraying 'Little Egypt', accompanied by curious hiccupy repetitions of the words 'A, A, A – *Men*' while she weaves her way among the other dancers on stage. Earl Barton's choreography is exemplary and the vocal accompaniment complements the tambourines, drums and flutes to give the requisite oriental flavour.

EP: 'Elvis TV Special'

POISON IVY LEAGUE * * * *

Written by Bill Giant, Bernie Baum, Florence Kaye.

This is the song in the roadhouse that gets Elvis into trouble with the college louts who have settled noisily at a nearby table. The lyrics tell of rich layabouts who tempt him to punch them. The song begins as a serious college song about his 'Alma Mater' and develops into a fast rocker, backed by piano, saxophone, drums and vocal chorus: the last note from Elvis is one of his effective high ones.

HARD KNOCKS * * * *

Written by Joy Byers.
The sheer good humour of Joy Byer's rocker, backed by saxophone, drums, piano and guitars, plus vocals by The Jordanaires, belies the lyrics that lament that all Charlie ever gets is hard knocks. The applause and delivery of the song attracts the interest of the rival carnival owner, Harry Carver, who tries to get Charlie away from Maggie by offering more money. He refuses.

IT'S A WONDERFUL WORLD * * *

Written by Sid Tepper, Roy C. Bennet.
Charlie sings to Cathy as they go round on the Big Wheel about the sheer joy of living. A hurdy-gurdy rhythm backed by guitars and vocals.

BIG LOVE, BIG HEARTACHE
* * * * *

Written by Dolores Fuller, Lew Morris, Sonny Hendrix.
Cathy, encouraged by Mijanou, who tells her that there was never anything between her and Charlie – she was willing, but he cared only for Cathy – goes to see him at the Harry Carver carnival. Charlie's singing has taken away all the trade from Maggie's circus, after she and Joe had virtually thrown him out, following a big punch-up between the two men. Charlie sings with all the yearning only Elvis can impart to a sad lyric. As she listens she realizes she loves him and he is only too happy to return to help out Maggie, though he has to endure another attack from the jealous Joe. Maggie tells Charlie to stop acting

like a tough guy and tell the truth for once – he admits he loves Cathy and there's nothing Joe can do about it. Elvis is backed by The Jordanaires, with guitars, strings, piano and alto sax – a scene beautifully sung, played and acted.

ONE TRACK HEART * * *

Written by Bill Giant, Bernie Baum, Florence Kaye.

Charlie's singing of this to Cathy is calculated to win her affection after the animosity she has shown for his attitude to her father, who has told him to stay away from her. It's a hard-sell number, with insistent drumbeats, guitar, piano and saxophone, telling her he's made up his mind, he loves her and won't be diverted.

Single B/W: 'Roustabout'

IT'S CARNIVAL TIME * * * *

Written by Ben Weisman, Sid Wayne.
Elvis puts over this fairground-type number with such infectious *joie de vivre* that it's little wonder the lads and lasses come flocking in the direction of Maggie's carnival show. An amusing coda to this song is that it caused some controversy over Ruby Murray's summer revue *The Grand Show of 1965* when an enthusiastic publicist put out the story that the sweet and wholesome Ruby – the only girl to have had five hits in the Top Twenty at the same time – was to sing a Presley number. Her then husband, Bernard Burgess, who had left the Jones Boys' singing group to manage his wife's career, objected that such a move would tarnish his wife's image. Bernie, a die-hard musician of the old school, was against rock 'n' roll and all that it stood for: in particular, Presley of the *Jailhouse Rock* era was associated with teenage riots and the throwing of unseemly garments onto the stage. Bernie had avoided Presley movies like the plague and was unaware that Elvis's image, since his army service, was as clean-living as Ruby's herself.

I suggested he listen to the

soundtrack of *Roustabout* before the director set about finding a replacement song. The lyrics concerning lemonade and candy and inviting people to hurry to buy a ticket won him over to the view that the song was as innocent as could be and ideal for a closing number to the first half of the show, with Ruby stepping gingerly among the toy creatures on a slowly revolving roundabout to gentle hurdy-gurdy music.

CARNY TOWN * * *
Written by Fred Wise, Ben Weisman.
Charlie Rogers sings some more sweet music and simple lyrics to a fairground beat, accompanying himself on guitar, to attract the public into the wonders of the show inside the tent. More of the same kind of innocence.

THERE'S A BRAND NEW DAY ON THE HORIZON * * * *
Written by Joy Byers.
Joy Byer's catchy and optimistic final song has the entire cast joining in, including the strong man and the Bearded Lady. Cathy and Charlie leap on stage for the final clinch. It's the kind of jigging number that brought down the curtain on film musicals back in the days of George Formby in the Thirties and before.

Earl Barton stages the musical numbers with a certain flair but is only allowed to be inventive in the 'Little Egypt' routine. As usual, Colonel Parker (*qv*) is credited as Technical Advisor: his early days as a circus promoter undoubtedly qualifying him as an authority on the carnival team. In any event he would get his share of the profits.
LP: 'Elvis in Hollwood'

WHEELS ON MY HEELS * *
Written by Sid Tepper, Roy C. Bennet.
Charlie rides his motorbike away from the roadhouse from which he has been fired for fighting. More rolling wheel rhythms with guitars and saxes underlining the action; drums and piano join in while he sings of the wanderlust that makes him keep travelling along. He overtakes a station wagon driven by Jim Lean, the bad-tempered second-in-command to Maggie Morgan who owns the local carnival show. She and Joe's daughter Cathy are passengers in the car and when Charlie shouts to Cathy how pretty she is, her hung-over father crowds him and his motorbike off the road. The bike is badly damaged and Maggie offers Charlie a job at her carnival to keep him going until repairs have been carried out.

RUSSELL, KURT (b. 1951)
The 12 year-old Kurt Russell, who so enjoyed kicking Elvis (professionally) in *It Happened at the World's Fair* (*qv*) had been in movies for three years, so he knew how to pull his kicks. Elvis would not have that; 'Go on, Kid', he said 'Do it for real.' So he had to – several times. His film career debut was in Walt Disney's *The Absent-Minded Professor*. As a Disney contract artist he starred in 10 films as 'an adorable Disney moppet' – days he looks back to fondly, during the Sixties.

Russell was 28 when he made *Elvis* for Dick Clark, the legendary rock 'n' roll promoter for ABC Television, in 1979, which was such a success it went into the cinemas as *Elvis: The Movie*, with Kurt playing Elvis from youth up to the time of his Las Vegas comeback. His father Bing was Vernon Presley (*qv*). At the time Kurt Russell was married to Season Hubley who made a convincing Priscilla (*qv*), even if she did not actually look 14 in the scene where she and Elvis first met in Germany. The film and his performance have been reviewed elsewhere, but Kurt says he did feel the presence of the King. 'Elvis wasn't actually guiding me through the role, but he was there all right, and weird things did happen.'

His versatility has been proven through a diversity of films, including John Carpenter's sci-fi horror *The Thing* and riveting performances in *Silkwood* and *Backdraft*, but his favourite is the 1983 flop comedy *Swing Shift* simply because he met the number one person in his life, Goldie Hawn. They were subsequently married and remained happily so up to the time of writing.

(See also: *Elvis: The Movie, It Happened at the World's Fair*; Presley, Priscilla Beaulieu; Presley, Vernon, Elvis)

S

SCATTER

The London *Daily Mail*, in an answer to a reader's letter, supplies a sad PS to the legend of Scatter, arguably the most famous chimp in the world apart from Tarzan's Cheetah, who is alive and well and living in luxury in the USA at the grand old age of 64. Seemingly, he is partial to a drop of the hard stuff, which does not seem to have done him any harm, unlike Scatter, who lived with Elvis both in Graceland and Los Angeles. Scatter was reported in the book *All About Elvis* by Fred L. Worth and Steve D. Tamerius to have acquired a taste for whisky and bourbon, which used to amuse his master and some of the Mafia (*qv*) who used to encourage him to get legless. This eventually led to his death from cirrhosis of the liver, which does not necessarily contradict Albert Goldman's view in *Elvis* (*qv*) that he died from pining for the master who had previously made him the focus of everyone's attention, especially when egged on to become horny with one or more of Elvis's young female playthings. This situation is neatly diffused in Priscilla's coy reference in Graceland to Scatter being a 'great one for chasing the ladies'. By the time she did the commentary for the film in 1985, Priscilla, could have been in no doubt as to the nature of some of her husband's little frolics.

Scatter was a 40 lb 3 oz, 3 ft tall chimpanzee who had been trained by his first owner, a Memphis cartoonist who used him in his TV show, to dress up in clothes, drink whiskey and chase women. When Elvis took him to Hollywood he would carry him around on his shoulders, show him off to friends and treat him like a baby, even changing his nappies. He even used him to play tricks on dignitaries like the illustrious Sam Goldwyn. Scatter climbed up the drainpipe and got into the great man's office, having sent his secretary screaming off in terror. He leapt onto the desk and created mayhem among his contracts and family pictures. No wonder the poor beast went into a decline when put out to grass.
(See also: *Animals; Graceland; Memphis Mafia; Presley, Priscilla Beaulieu*)

SEX AND ELVIS

In his early movies Elvis Presley portrayed the embodiment of male aggression – the young rebel always clashing with establishment morality and so handy with his fists that in one of them, *Jailhouse Rock* (*qv*), he was sent to prison for manslaughter. In *King Creole* (*qv*) he engaged in what was, in effect, a war to the death with the Mafia-type gangland king played by Walter Matthau, whose girl, Carolyn Jones, throws herself at the Presley character who represents, in her mind, the gentleness and gallantry so conspicuously lacking in the Matthau character. Even in his first musical, *Loving You* (*qv*), Elvis

has a fight with a bully who makes the mistake of calling him 'yellow' and ends up in court. He is acquitted, as his adversary was the one who provoked the fight; later, on a matter of principle, he is ready to walk out on his press agent Lizabeth Scott, who is working hard to transform him from an impecunious truck driver into an adored world figure with fame and fortune.

After his army service, under the guidance of his éminence grise, Colonel Tom Parker (*qv*), the young Presley character was refined into the kind of upright young man acceptable to family audiences, with the exception of two 'experimental' movies, *Wild in the Country* (*qv*) and *Flaming Star* (*qv*): in the latter he is a half-breed country boy whose quest for vengeance on the white men instrumental in bringing about his mother's death ends with him riding off, mortally wounded, to face a lonely death himself. In the first film he starts by fighting a no-holds-barred battle with his violent brother, whom he wrongly assumes he has killed, but ends up on his way to an academic career through the good graces of a philanthropic psychologist, played by Hope Lange. These two films, however, were less financially profitable than the musicals *Loving You* and *G.I. Blues*, so the pattern was set for an endless succession of light-weight coloured musicals, mostly of a repetitive and anodyne nature, with the exception of the brilliant *Follow That*

Dream and the boxing drama *Kid Galahad*, which gave him a meaty part to play, but was marred by being weighed down with songs. In virtually all his films his virility was established by the character he played being involved in inevitably victorious battles with no-good hombres, often to defend the honour of females. After his army training he was able to add spectacular karate exhibitions to his repertoire.

For all this the enormous sexual excitement purveyed in Presley's work, especially in regard to his cinematic persona, was not without an androgynous quality. The remarkable combination brought about on one of Elvis's first TV appearances after he left the army, *Frank Sinatra's Welcome Home Party for Elvis Presley*, showed the subtle change that had come about in the formerly self-confident aura Elvis displayed in public. Not only was his screen image the 'acceptable' one the Colonel had decided was the way things would be for the future, but there was an appreciable change in his demeanour, probably brought about by his apparently happy acceptance of life in the services, but certainly by the mortal blow of his mother's early death and the subsequent remarriage of his father, along with Elvis's anxiety about whether he would be able to relaunch a successful career. There was a vulnerability in his even more handsome looks and the duet with Sinatra, much smaller but wiry and unmistakably masculine, is the nearest thing to 'camp' Presley became in public performance. His Little Richard pompadour, combined with limp wrists and shy, diffident smile did contrast markedly with Frank's assured poise – even if not qualifying for what Albert Goldman described as 'outrageously gay' – his body language flashing 'I surrender dear' as they combined forces for 'Love Me Tender' (Frank) and 'Witchcraft' (Elvis) while together they duetted 'Teddy Bear'.

It is a bizarre fusion of styles,

vocally and physically, but the show achieved the largest audience in history when it was screened in the States on May 12, 1960. Elvis's apparent diffidence may well have been brought about by calling to mind some of the incredibly offensive remarks Sinatra had made to the press about rock 'n' roll, as 'the most brutal, ugly, degenerate, vicious form of expression it has ever been my displeasure to hear'. He had dismissed Elvis's music as a rancid-smelling aphrodisiac. Elvis's life-style had, indeed, changed from the almost puritanical outlook he had inherited from Gladys Presley (*qv*). After a frankly orgiastic two week-long furlough in Paris with some of his boys at the Hotel Prince de Galles, named after the high-living Prince of Wales, who came to the British throne as Edward VII, Elvis emulated the royal devotee of night life by watching the two evening shows by the Bluebelle Girls at the Lido, then taking them back to supper at the hotel and dallying with the favoured ones until dawn, his Guys following the example of their leader. For a while after his return to the States these kinds of capers were discontinued, until one rowdy night in an hotel, when the boyish pranks of Elvis and his cronies – such as squirting each other with water pistols and rugger-style fights – got out of hand and an elderly lady, nearly hit by a guitar hurled by Elvis at two of his playmates, complained to the management and they were asked to leave. Here Colonel Parker took a hand, not to try and inhibit their behaviour, by purchasing a residence in Bel Air that had belonged to the Shah of Iran. Here they were able to indulge their pranks without interference and to party to their hearts content, the selection of available young women who were only too eager to gain access to the Presley residence being virtually unlimited.

His tastes for partying along with his range of drug taking grew more esoteric as the years passed: his houses in Hollywood having two-way mirrors and

other devices to enable the Guys to watch the girls undressing or doing what comes naturally in the course of an evening's relaxation. Eventually, after Hollywood was no longer the central point of Elvis's professional activity, party-time spread to Graceland (*qv*): the routine was that the host would indicate his preference for whichever of the guests turned him on and those that were left over were the prizes for the Guys. On occasion Elvis's room would be crowded with eager voyeurs looking at what went on in the bedroom next door through the two way mirror which had been installed in the wallspace behind a section of the floor to ceiling bookcases that lined the opposite wall. If there was no activity on offer Elvis would arrange for a couple of his friends to get girls into the room and have sex with them. For his own delectation the King would take two or three beauties of his choice to his room for group sex: something which had become a habit when the joys of one to one intercourse began to pale. This would normally be about 2 a.m., after they had all watched the late movie. His delight was for the girls to strip down to their panties and wrestle with each other.

With the development of Sony videotape machines for 'home use' there entered a new and exiting element into these bedroom follies: he would become director and occasional guest star of a series of fantasies that would act out his erotic ideals, particularly young women grappling together and simulating lesbian sex. A later development was the introduction on to the market of what were known as 'cat movies' featuring young women who fought each other, tearing off items of clothing and handfuls of hair, revealing panties – white was the favourite shade – until both wrestlers were reduced to a shambles.

This predilection for violence, especially among young women and as a spectator, suggests, especially when bolstered by the presence of his favourite Guys, an inherent dislike of the female sex, other than as mother figures or pure young madonnas who could be put on a pedestal and venerated. These objects of veneration were to be nurtured and protected, until they could be prepared to bear a child in holy wedlock. This was the role enacted by young Priscilla Beaulieu (*qv*), the girl who was actually only 14 when Elvis was smitten by her and who was gradually inducted into Graceland, protected by respectable guardians Vernon (*qv*) and Dee Presley, to be prepared and cosseted as the future consort of the young King. Nothing kinky or voyeuristic was to be countenanced for this young lady. Heretical whispers have ascribed the final wedding date to have been urged by the Colonel, who was torn between not wanting 'his Boy' to be the legal spouse of any one woman and an awareness that Priscilla's continued presence in Graceland after so many years might begin to smack of moral turpitude among Elvis's female admirers.

At the risk of sounding sacrilegious, there was in Elvis Presley's attitude towards the female sex something akin to that of the world's senior practitioner of the romantic novel, Barbara Cartland; there are 'good gels', inviolate before marriage, and there are 'tarts', prepared to fulfil masculine lusts without the benefit of clergy.

Returning to the video scene, there came a point when Elvis's private collection was ceremonially consigned to the flames, but it seems that a few escaped destruction. Which leads to the story about the Colonel, which may well be apocryphal. It has been rumoured that Tom Parker came into possession of one or more of these rarities and that they were kept in safe custody, to be produced if his client objected to any proposition put forward by himself. Certainly, the Colonel occasionally was on the receiving end of one of Elvis's notoriously short-fused bursts of temper, but in public

Presley continued to state solemnly that he owed the Colonel everything – a statement in which there was, in fact, a good deal of uncomfortable and ironic truth.

As for ambivalence in Presley's sexual tastes, to date no one has come out in print, stating, in an exclusive hot flash, 'I was Elvis's male lover', despite the growth of public tolerance in these matters. However when photographs of Elvis with Liberace hit the presses there were raised eyebrows and pursed lips, even though at that time the renowned pianist – surely the most overtly gay entertainer ever other than the world's celebrated drag artistes – was awarded substantial damages against a London newspaper which made allegations about his sexuality. The truth about those photos was undoubtedly the Colonel's way of firstly casting a glow over Elvis's ill-fated Las Vegas cabaret debut in April 1956 at the New Frontier's Vienna Room, which was such a disaster that it closed two weeks early, and secondly introducing his protégé to the family audiences of America, to whom Liberace was a god.

Elvis's only close male actor friend of his early film days was Nick Adams, four years his senior, who introduced himself on the set of *Love Me Tender*, shortly after the death of his best friend, James Dean, from whom he was inseparable, and with whom he had played in *Rebel Without a Cause*. Natalie Wood was friendly with both young actors and it was Nick who introduced her to Elvis and also to other young up and coming stars like Sal Mineo and Dennis Hopper, with whom Nick shared a flat. He thus widened Elvis's circle of acquaintances and found other things to do than eat his supper in his hotel, the Knickerbocker, where he shared a suite with his cousins Gene and Junior Smith. Now with Nick and Natalie and others of the gang, Elvis would cruise the city on the Harley Davidsons he bought for himself and his friends.

Nick had been a lover of Dean and he saw in Elvis the same kind of rebel, searching for an identity. They shared a closeness that Natalie, who was supposedly enjoying with Elvis what the press called 'A motorcycle romance', found akin to Nick's relationship with his buddy James Dean. Whenever he could, Nick would visit the sets where Elvis was working: his own career really took off when he starred in the TV series *The Rebel*. He supported Doris Day in a couple of films, *Teacher's Pet* and *Pillow Talk*, and was nominated for an Oscar in *Twilight of Honour* in 1963. He died tragically of an overdose in Los Angeles on February 6, 1968, five days after Lisa Marie Presley (*qv*) was born in Memphis. Overjoyed as he was at becoming a father, Elvis grieved deeply for his friend, who had touched in him a chord that even his cronies had not discovered, with the possible exception of his 'guru' Larry Geller, who appealed to the deeply religious side of Elvis, especially the supernatural aspects, right up to the end. *(See also: Follow That Dream; Flaming Star; G.I. Blues; Graceland; Jailhouse Rock; Kid Galahad; King Creole; Loving You; Memphis Mafia; Parker, Colonel Tom; Presley, Gladys Love Smith; Presley, Lisa Marie; Presley, Priscilla Beaulieu; Presley, Vernon Elvis; Wild in the Country)*

SHEPHERD, CYBILL

Actress Cybill Shepherd, talking to the *Daily Mail* in January, 1996, about 'her bumpy career and why she needs a man' claimed it had taken forty-five years to sort herself out, quoting two disastrous marriages, an ill-fated affair with director Peter Bogdanov and being turned down flat by Bruce Willis, her co-star in the popular TV series *Moonlighting*. She refers to him as a 'talented jerk' and is clearly someone who expects to get her own way with the opposite sex. So when she encountered Presley in her home town, Memphis, it seems likely they were twin minds with but a single thought.

She became a star at the age of twenty-one when she made a big hit as the teenage sexpot in Peter Bogdanov's *The Last Picture Show*, the same age as Elvis's film debut in *Love Me Tender* (*qv*). When she parted from Bogdanov, after he piloted her through several films, ending with the musical *At Long Last Love*, which flopped, she started dating Elvis, her senior by fifteen years. The romance was short-lived: his way of courting did not appeal to her. She says when he greeted her with 'an emerald ring in one hand and a bottle of sleeping pills in the other, it wasn't my scene – so I returned both.'

Shepherd was interviewed on *The Gaby Roslin Show* on Channel 4 television on Saturday May 11, 1996 and she explained how she came to meet Elvis after winning Miss Teenage Memphis. The moderator of the pageant was a good friend of Elvis who rang up and said he wanted to meet her. She was terrified and said she would have to bring along some friends. Elvis rented out the local movie theatre from midnight where about fifty of his best friends were gathered. A third of the way through the movie Elvis arrived and sat down next to her. 'It was dark in the theatre', but she says 'he smelled so good'.

When Gaby Roslin asked – What did he smell of? – with an expansive gesture Cybill replied that it was some sort of special Elvis smell. (Elvis's favourite after shave was reputed to be Brut). Asked what style he was wearing, Cybill replied that it was '73 and he hadn't gotten obese yet'. She says he was still 'the most gorgeous man that ever walked the face of the earth', but commented that he loved to eat. He could sit down and eat 'a plate of Chicken-fried steak this big' – and Cybill threw her hands wide apart. The relationship she says, was on and off for only about six weeks but was close. Asked what Elvis was like, Cybill answered that he was very kind – a very

sweet man – but the people around him were very boring. Also, he had the drug problem. It was legal; the doctors gave him all those drugs. But it just wasn't her scene. Also he wanted her just to go out with him and that wasn't going to work for her. She wanted to see Bogdanov, whom she was living with. But when Elvis told her to get rid of this 'Dogbanovitch' guy she had to chose one or the other and it was bye-bye Elvis. She felt very bad about it, because he was so very lonely. His song 'Are You Lonesome Tonight?' is her Elvis number and she always felt that he was so very lonesome.

SHAW, SID

On 18 March 1997 a London High Court judge effectively ruled that 'Elvis Presley Belongs to the World'. Thus ended a six-year legal battle when souvenir seller Sid Shaw of Shoreditch triumphed against the multi-million dollar might of the Elvis Presley Estate in Memphis to trade under the name of Elvisly Yours in Britain. Shaw, an ex-school teacher and barrowboy had been running his business since 1978 in London's Shoreditch, when he began his company selling memorabilia of the King of Rock n' Roll, expanding to toiletries in 1986 and producing a turnover in excess of £3 million between 1978 and 1992.

Then the Memphis-based Graceland Organisation appealed to the Trade Marks registry for the exclusive right to merchandise soaps, perfumes, deodorants and toothpaste under the Elvis name and signature. Shaw objected strongly and took his case to the Trade Marks Tribunal, claiming that the American trustees were trying to put him out of business. He explained that he had built up a substantial reputation over a long period. "They claim to have a monopoly of someone who has been dead since 1977 and they can't do that just because they are the Elvis Estate."

The whole issue was finally resolved

by Mr Justice Laddie when told that for more or less anything he could think of, there is an Elvis item - even toenail clippers. "That about gallows?" asked the judge, who was obviously in merry mood. The outcome is that Sid Shaw can continue marketing all his heart desires under the Elvis insignia. His annual turnover from his souvenirs has never exceeded £250,000, while the Presley estate earns an estimated £20 million a year from its tours of the singer's Graceland home, which attracts 700,000 visitors a year, while their control of the souvenir industry in America means they make millions more from merchandise through licensing deals.

David slays Goliath again!

SIDEBURNS

Towards the end of Presley's career his heavily pronounced sideburns became as much of a feature of his persona as his jewel encrusted suits and increasingly wide and ornamented belts. His first publicity shot, at the age of eighteen, shows him with fairly long sideburns, which he was to retain during his early days on stage and in the movies up to *Jailhouse Rock* (*qv*) in 1957, when the plot sent him into prison, where of course they had to disappear. The following year, in 1958, prior to his induction into the Army, they were absent in *King Creole* (*qv*).

The US version of 'short back and sides' left no margin at all for sideburns, which were conspicuous by their absence when he returned to the screen in *G.I. Blues* (*qv*) in 1961. From then on he remained clean-shaven even for his Valentino spoof in the 1965 *Harum Scarum* (*qv*) when sideburns might have been apposite, until *Live a Little, Love a Little* (*qv*) when they made a modified reappearance in 1968. They were back with a vengeance in his two final musicals, *The Trouble With Girls* (*qv*) and *Change of Habit* (*qv*), both released in 1969. Las Vegas was beckoning and Elvis was only too happy to shake the dust of

Hollywood from his shoes. Sideburns were definitely 'in' for his Las Vegas come-back on January 26th, 1970. He was to refer to them, jocularly but with undoubted affection, from time to time saying he wore them 'truck driver' style. The vogue inevitably caught on like wildfire.

The public once again became interested in how the name sideburns came about. The term was originally burnsiders, signifying mutton chop or sidebar whiskers. The style was popularized in the American Civil War by General Ambrose Everett Burnside (1824–1881), although he wore them with a full moustache. His spectacular failures and equally spectacular victories kept his picture in the press. It was he who commanded the main Union Force, the Army of the Potomac, at the battle of Fredericksburg in December 1862 and had a bridge named after him following the Battle of Antietam in September of the same year when his troops spent more than two hours trying to cross a bridge over Antietam Creek.
(See also: Change of Habit; G.I. Blues; Harum Scarum; Live a Little, Love a Little; Pearl and Tony; The Trouble With Girls)

SIEGEL, DON (1912–1991)

How Elvis became involved with a 'cult' director like Don Siegel remained a puzzlement for years. However, the fact that they only made one movie together, *Flaming Star* (qv) in 1960, is easily explained by the fact that, apart from *Wild in the Country* (qv) the following year, the remainder of the Presley output were light-hearted musicals, a genre far removed from Siegel's main body of work. In Presley's first movie after he came out of the army, there was a chance that he might have been allowed to diversify and grow in his ambitions to become a straight actor, but the overwhelming success of the light-weight *G.I. Blues* sealed his fate as it were. As

Siegel tended to specialize in dealing with loners, there is just a chance that if he had been able to direct *Kid Galahad* (1962) the hero would have been more convincing than Phil Karlson's portrait of a boxer, overloaded as he was with songs. And there lies the rub: Technical Advisor Colonel Tom Parker (qv) versus the Director.

Which brings us back to *Flaming Star*. In his interview with *Films and Filming*'s Gordon Gow in 1973, Don Siegel discussed his elevation to a cult figure; Gow's was a perceptive and penetrating article, in which Siegel said 'Most of the populace are pods ... they have no cultural aspirations....they feel nothing.' *Flaming Star* was originally written for Marlon Brando as a half-breed, which would have suited Siegel very well: the previous year of 1959 he had been involved with pop singer Fabian in *The Hound Dog Man*, a hard-hitting tale of the West, which Gordon Gow criticized as a film he must have made to earn a living, rather than because he was inspired by the material. Siegel agreed, but added, 'I don't think it should be criticized because it is different from most of my films. It could have been very good, it could have been done by Sam Peckinpah, who is of the West and knows it well. Unfortunately, 20th Century Fox bought it and did it very artificially, starring Fabian ..... I did everything possible to stop him from singing. So I just had fun with the film. Same thing happened when I did *Flaming Star* with Elvis Presley. I tried very hard not to have Elvis sing: I thought Elvis was very good in it. The studio, of course, was very upset when I didn't want him to sing. What they do is miscast and then they make you live with it.' He almost had his way, but didn't think the film itself was very good. There were only two songs, but as it turned out the title song was a hit and rose to No. 3 in Elvis's Top 40 Hits, remaining there for 14 weeks.

Latterly, with the Clint Eastwood

movies, Siegel had his own way much more: they hit new heights together, artistically, with *The Beguiled* in 1971 and at the box office with *Dirty Harry*. In 1977 *The Shootist* was John Wayne's last and greatest film, called by David Quinlan in *The Illustrated Guide to Film Directors* 'one of the great films of our time.' Siegel's final film, *Jinxed*, with Bette Midler in 1982 was an unhappy experience all round – they did not get on.
(See also: Flaming Star; Follow That Dream; G.I. Blues; Gordon, Douglas; Kid Galahad; Parker, Colonel Tom; Wild in the Country)

SPEEDWAY * *

Released by: Metro-Goldwyn-Mayer (Panavision, Metrocolor); **Producer:** Douglas Laurence; **Director:** Norman Taurog; **Screenplay:** Philip Shuken; **Art Director:** Leroy Colema, George W. Davis; **Director of Photography:** Joseph Ruttenberg; **Music:** Jeff Alexander; **Running Time:** 94 mins; **Opened:** June 12, 1968.

Cast: Elvis, Nancy Sinatra, Bill Bixby, William Schallert, Victoria Mayerink, Ross Hagen, Carl Ballantine, Poncie Ponce, Harry Hickox, Christopher West, Miss Beverley Hills, Harper Carter, Bob Harris, Michele Newman, Courtney Brown, Dana Brown, Patti Jean Keith, Carl Reindek, Cari Hardy, Charlotte Considine, Sandy Reed. Stock-car racers: Richard Petty, Budd Baker, Gale Yarborough, Dick Hutcherson, Tony Lund, G.C. Spencer, Roy Mayne.

Steve Grayson (Elvis) and his partner, Kenny Donford (Bill Bixby), travel their racecar around the country to wherever

Elvis as Steve Grayson trips the light fantastic with Income Tax Assessor Susan Jacks (Nancy Sinatra), who is after him for tax evasion. Their business association does not preclude a ripening friendship. *Speedway* (1968)

there is stock-car racing, almost invariably winning the races and earning a great deal of money which they then dispense philanthropically to needy people. They also allow themselves generous expenses, which run to a trailer full of gimmicks, including a tape recorder which plays a realistic zoo escape soundtrack, handy for driving gullible maidens into male arms for protection. One day, out of the blue, Steve receives an invoice for $100,000 from the I.R.S. Kenny, who is supposed to be keeping account of their finances, is totally feckless and unable to understand official forms. Steve is equally feckless and recklessly generous, so it is no surprise they end up in trouble. Steve hires a business management firm to help and the Revenue boss, R.W. Hepworth (Gale Gordon), assigns an agent called Susan Jacks (Nancy Sinatra) to keep track of their earning and make sure the government gets its dues. In the beginning Susan is almost impervious to Steve's charms, but eventually they arrange a truce and Susan appropriates his latest large earnings cheque as security. Summoned before Hepworth, Steve and Kenny await the verdict on Kenny's book-keeping, which is catastrophically disorganized and unrealistic. Among the expenses disallowed is the trailer with its expensive gadgets. Susan calls on Steve and tells him his maximum allowance for living expenses is one $100 a week with $50 for Kenny. He is outraged and goes to Susan's hotel with a bouquet of red roses to try and bribe her. His ploy fails dismally and Susan visits Steve to return the roses and tell him that his weekly allowance has gone down to sixty-five dollars, as she has found out Kenny put the flowers on the account. Steve is so furious he lets his dinner burn and puts out the flames with the ill-fated bouquet. Furthermore, he discovers that all the charitable distributions have been similarly put on the account – so they

are all being repossessed, including the station wagon Steve had presented to the father (William Schalbert) of the four little girls. In fact Kenny had gambled away all their hoard destined for the government over a kiss and a song.

Steve and Susan become close and she agrees to ring her boss to persuade him to let Steve keep some of the money promised to the government to help him meet his personal obligations. At first Hepworth refuses indignantly but Susan says if he does not agree to let him keep his winnings from the big race on Sunday, not only will Steve not race but he'll also sell his stock-car. She reasons with him that Steve could earn the government a great deal of money, plus all the winnings from future races. Worn down by her arguments, plus the fact that she is phoning him at four o'clock in the morning, Hepworth gives in and Susan and Steve seal the deal with another kiss.

The only problem now is to win the race, but during the qualifying run he blows a tyre and the car is seriously *hors de combat* with no money to get the parts to fix it in time. The ever-resourceful Susan suggests he borrows new parts from his friends and they all give a hand to help him fix the car in time for the race. Steve is well ahead when he finds out that one of the mechanics has fallen asleep in the car after working all night. The extra weight is a serious liability and Steve has to stop to get him lifted out of the car. He gets back into the lead until a further mishap spins his car off the track and it turns over and over. Steve is able to climb out, unharmed, before it bursts into flames. All is not lost: coming in third place he still wins enough money to pay his debts and give the Inland Revenue its first instalment. He and Susan celebrate with a party and a duet.

It's still the silly season for Presley films: the same sort of plot, another demon racing driver – stock-car this time – the same generous nature – he

takes a motherless family of little girls and their father under his wing. The novelty here is Nancy Sinatra as an Internal Revenue agent with a handy way with a song and the will – after initial misgivings – to help him out of his financial difficulties and enable him to win the big race – the stock-car Charlotte 600 in this case. Well, almost.

Norman Taurog (*qv*) directs this ridiculous plot zestfully and a familiar face in Elvisland is Bill Bixby, improbably cast as his manager. He's an inveterate gambler, liar and cheat, but Elvis keeps forgiving him. There's a certain fascination in watching Bixby's hair change from black one side up to the parting, then to titian, then back again to overall russet: it quite takes one's mind off the story. Nancy Sinatra's charms are notably brittle, but it may nonetheless have been her popularity at this time that helped to lump the total gross up to $3 million and No. 40 in *Variety*'s list of top-grossing films. What more is there to say other than that she and Elvis team well and he looks relaxed and at ease, even in the most trying circumstances.

(See also: Clambake (re Bill Bixby); Girls, Girls, Girls (not the movie); Taurog, Norman)

SPEEDWAY
2(RCA LPM – 3989) June 1968 (Original Soundtrack album)
SPEEDWAY * * *
Written by Mel Glazer, Stephen Schlacks.
Fast tempo credit song for Elvis, singing about the application needed to be a successful driver. An effective introductory number. Drums, piano, cymbals and male voice chorus.

LET YOURSELF GO * * * *
Written by Joy Byers.
Steve Grayson, for all his busy life as a stock-car racer, is always ready to jump in with a rocker like this with guitars, drums, piano and saxophone extolling

the necessity of letting yourself go. Elvis's second song in the film, no relation to Berlin's Astaire/Rogers number.
Single B/W: 'Your Time Hasn't Come Yet Baby'
LPs: 'Elvis – A Legendary Performer – Vol. 3'

YOUR TIME HASN'T COME YET BABY * *

Written by Joel Hirschorn, Al Kasher. Steve sings this gentle song to Ellie Mayerlink, eldest of the four little girls to whose father he has given a brand new car, stocked with groceries. The child says she wishes she were old enough to marry him and he explains how she will turn into a beautiful woman in due course. Drums, guitars, piano and chimes ease the lyrics along.
Single B/W: 'Let Yourself Go'

HE'S YOUR UNCLE, NOT YOUR DAD *

Written by Sid Wayne, Ben Weisman. Steve and Kenny Donforth are called to the I.R.S. headquarters to account for their expenditure. As they wait in an outer office with desks full of soberly-suited officials, Steve gets on a desk in front of the Stars and Stripes flag and sings a song about how Uncle Sam will look after you – all he needs is your money. The officials jump up and join him and Kenny in a song and dance around the room to military music, while the other men waiting for interviews leap up to the drum beats and execute a few high kicks. When the boss, H.W. Hepburn, comes out of his office to see what the rumpus is about, he is swept up, protesting, into the male chorus line. He disengages himself and takes Steve and Kenny into the office for interrogation. This number has to join the line-up for the most stupid and embarrassing routine Elvis ever had to undergo. It must be said he joins in with professionalism and good humour – high kicks and all.

WHO ARE YOU (WHO AM I) * *

Written by Sid Wayne, Ben Weisman. The sixth and penultimate number in the film. At last Steve breaks down Inland Revenue girl Susan's resistance and they dance together while he explains that it would only take one kiss to answer the question in the title. Saxophone, strings, piano and drums back the dreamy theme to some mundane lyrics.

THERE AIN'T NOTHING LIKE A SONG * * *

Written by Joy Byers, William Johnston. The final song in the movie. Steve has made enough money from the big race to pay off his debts and satisfy the I.R.S. as well. The entire cast join him in a song and dance scene in which Elvis duets with Nancy Sinatra's Susan Jacks to close the film. He starts off on the drums, then beats time with the drumsticks – guitars and saxophone back words that keep repeating the title.

YOUR GROOVY SELF (Bonus) * * *

Nancy Sinatra's solo. She gives it plenty of oomph, but it doesn't amount to much.

FIVE SLEEPY HEADS

(not included in movie)
Written by Sid Tepper, Roy C. Bennet.
LP: 'Elvis Sings for Children and Grown-ups Too'

WESTERN UNION

(Bonus) (not included in movie)
Written by Sid Tepper, Roy C. Bennet

MINE

(Bonus) (not included in movie)
Written by Sid Tepper, Roy C. Bennet.

GOIN' HOME

(not included in movie)
Written by Joy Byers.

Elvis as bandleader Rusty Wells in *Girl Happy* with Shelley Fabares as his employer's daughter (1985)

Mike McCoy in his band leader persona in
Speedway **sings 'Let Yourself Go' (1968)**

Recorded for film *Stay Away Joe*.

SUPPOSE
(not included in movie)
Written by Sylvia Dee, George Goehring.
Recorded for film *Speedway* (not used)
This was the last soundtrack LP Elvis recorded.

SPINOUT (CALIFORNIA HOLIDAY in Britain) *

Released by: Metro-Goldwyn-Mayer, a Eutrope Production (Panavision, Metrocolor); **Producer:** Joe Pasternack; **Director:** Norman Taurog; **Screenplay:** Theodora J. Flicker, George Kirgo; **Art Directors:** George W. Davis, Edward Garfagno; **Director of Photography:** Daniel L. Fapp; **Technical Advisor:** Colonel Tom Parker; **Music:** George Stoll, vocal background by the Jordanaires; **Running Time:** 90 mins; **Opened:** November 23, 1966.

Cast: Elvis, Shelley Fabares, Diane McBain, Deborah Walley, Dodie Marshall, Jack Mullaney, Will Hutchins, Warren Berlinger, Jimmy Hawkins, Carl Betz, Una Merkel, Cecil Kellaway, Frederic Worlock, Dave Barry, Red West.

Mike McCoy (Elvis) is leader of a touring rock 'n' roll band, whose love of women matches his love of racing formula cars. He earns a good living as a singer, but motor racing is an expensive hobby so he has a problem when he is run off the road in his Cobra by a beautiful young woman whom he could not resist racing. He and his car land in a river and to add insult to injury he is submerged in a hidden pit when he sets out to teach her a lesson. She goes on laughing and drives off, implying they'll be meeting again soon.

When he gets his car out of the mud, he heads for a gig at a local club to raise the cash to get his car repaired in time for the big race in Santa Fe. After the final show at the club he is approached by a man who offers him a good deal of money to sing at his daughter's birthday party. Though he keeps raising the price Mike refuses, to the dismay of his fellow musicians: Curly (Jack Mullaney – still doing his Jerry Lewis impersonation), Larry (Jimmy Hawkins) and Les, their girl drummer (Deborah Walley), who is secretly in love with Mike. Mike is a man of principle and the birthday party clashes with a previous engagement for the band. They decide to camp along the road and while they prepare their tents and table with candelabra, Les, who is a gourmet cook, prepares a meal. Suddenly Mike notices a mysterious blonde who has been following him for some time, peering through binoculars and making notes. When he challenges her she introduces herself as Diana St. Clair (Diane McBain), a best-selling writer who is preparing a book on the perfect American male, a role in which she has cast him. Furthermore she declares that if he wins the title, she is going to marry him. 'Over my dead body!' snorts Les, creating a loud rumpus with her drums.

During rehearsals Mike is told by the promoter that the tour is to be cancelled by the man who tried to persuade Mike to sing at his daughters birthday party unless they agree to accept the $5,000 singing fee enclosed in the letter, which turns out to be from millionaire Howard Foxhugh (Carl Betz), the designer of formula racing cars, whose models Mike has always admired. Mike agrees to perform at the birthday party because if he does so his band's tour will be reinstated. The birthday girl is none other than Cynthia Foxhugh, the woman who drove him off the road and left him in a jam, laughing. He sticks to his bargain and sings the song she requests, before telling her what he thinks of her. After crying a little she declares that she is going to marry him, to the distress of her father's young secretary Philip Short (Warren Berlinger), who loves her himself. He is a sensitive soul much given to fainting fits. The next day Mike agrees to drive Howard's car in the big race, having tested its qualities, but changes his mind when Howard tells him to lay off Cynthia and on no account to marry her. Insulted, Mike tells him he will marry whom he pleases, and as Howard thinks he's good enough to ride in his car but not marry his daughter, he can drive it himself in the race.

Howard complains to the police that Mike and his friends are creating a nuisance by camping in the area and says he wants them sent away from the district. Lt. Tracy Richard (Will Hutchins) is deputed to ask them not to camp in the district, but he takes a liking to them – especially Les – and agrees they can stay until morning. Meanwhile Mike decides no big shot is going to move him around and to get even and show his independence they will move into the house next door to the Foxhughs. He introduces himself to their neighbours, a nice old couple called Violet and Bernard Cranley (Una Merkel and Cecil Kellaway) and by subtle flattery persuades them to leave on a second honeymoon to recapture the excitement that used to be in their marriage. They are happy to leave Mike to look after the house in their absence. Worried that if Mike decides to marry either Diane or Cynthia it will be bad for the future of their combo, Les, Curly and Larry decide to give a big party with lots of girls to distract his attention and the Cranley's mansion is an ideal place to hold it.

The party is wild; both Diane and Cynthia turn up, uninvited, the latter escorted by Philip Short, whose affection for her has cured him of his fainting spells. The next arrival is Howard, unable to sleep because of the noise of the party. Diane introduces herself and is thrilled to find he has read all of her books. Her resolution to marry Mike begins to waver and soon her affections have been transferred to the more mature man. Not to be outdone by the glamour of Cynthia and Diane, Les takes off her pinafore and puts on a startling red evening dress. At last she captures Mike's attention and they are soon in each others arms. But not for long; Lt. Tracy Richards, whose love of cooking matches Les's own, has found in her a soul mate. He separates them and declares his love to her.

Next day at the race Violet and Bernard arrive back rejuvenated and delighted with Mike. He jumps into his Dusenbaker he has lent them for their holiday and sets off for the race, but the battery runs out. By a miracle one of the drivers is disqualified, Mike takes over his car and wins the race in a car that is not even his own. He then puts on his wedding gear and marries off each of the three beauties who were after him: Cynthia to Philip, Diane to Howard and Les to Tracy. Mike remains a batchelor guy, with his combo, but flailing away on the drums is a new girl, Susan (Dodie Marshall) whom he met at the party and who stated she would not be ready for marriage until 50 – or even 55. She is watched by the three newly-wed couples, who are soon jiving like demented dervishes to the music.

The story says it all, and surprisingly gleaned some enthusiastic reviews. For myself, I am allergic to racing cars and suffered from a surfeit of Elvis's jiving bimbos. He himself appears happy in the milieu and is supported by some excellent players. Outstanding is Warren Berlinger as the secretary with the vapours, who almost bumbles his way through to winning the big race until his boss, Carl Betz, resents being overtaken and snaps at him 'You're fired!', which brings on a final faint. Berlinger made a big success on the West End stage in the hit musical *How To Succeed in Business Without Really Trying* in the part Robert Horse played in New York and in the 1965 film version, again as a timid youngster who succeeds in spite of

himself. The role of Philip Short runs almost parallel in that he marries the bosses daughter, against no less a rival than Elvis. Producer Pasternak always had a flair for light musicals and Jack Backer's staging of the musical numbers achieves maximum cinematic effect. It was good to welcome back veteran comedians Cecil Kellaway and Una Merkel as the lady who recaptures her zest for life in a second honeymoon. She is the third outstanding comedy blonde of the Thirties and Forties to give good accounts of themselves in Presley films – the other two being Glenda Farrell (*qv*) and Joan Blondell. Elvis's three main leading ladies are well contrasted and Deborah Walley especially amusing as the girl drummer. Norman Taurog (*qv*) again does a professional job – but, oh, those noisy cars.
(See also: Farrell, Glenda; Taurog, Norman)

SPINOUT (CALIFORNIA HOLIDAY in Britain)
(Original Soundtrack Recording) (SLP 3702) October 1966

STOP, LOOK AND LISTEN * *
Written by Joy Byers.
Mike McCoy performs at one of the gigs on the tour with his combo – Mike, Curly and Larry all on guitars, with Les on drums – are undertaking to raise the money to indulge his favourite pastime: racing formula cars. A mystery blonde, who follows him everywhere with her binoculars, making notes, is in the audience. Joy Byers's words deal with the advice his pappa gave him when he was a child – if he sees a pretty woman he was to follow the words of the title. Brief and a lead up to his second song.

ADAM AND EVIL * *
Written by Fred Wise, Randy Starr.
The bible story rewritten by Wise and Starr to suit Elvis as Mike, who is more than ready to accept Ev-il, even if she is wicked. To underline it's not to be taken

too seriously, guitarists Larry and Curly are 'menaced' by a large and rather rubbery serpent. Mike, thanking the Santa Barbara audience for giving him a great time, receives suggestive winks from an assortment of bimbos.

ALL THAT I AM * * *
Written by Sid Tepper, Roy C. Bennett.
After their midnight picnic Mike notices the blonde with her binoculars still peeping. He challenges her and asks if she is a member of the P.T.A. – Peeping Toms' Association. She introduces herself as Diana St. Clair, an authoress writing a study on the perfect American male. If he qualifies he gets her as a prize. Which brings on the romantic declaration implied in the title, despite a display of fury from Les, glaring out of her tent. During the song Curly and Larry accompany him, apparently on guitars from their tents: the mystery is, where do the drums come from? Certainly not from Les, who interrupts their kiss by shouting that, 'People are trying to get some sleep around here!'
Single B/W: 'Spinout'

NEVER SAY YES * * *
Written by Doc Pomus, Mort Shuman.
Mike entertains with a fast rocker, explaining his hedonistic philosophy, the secret of his success. This is the last rehearsal before Foxhugh has their tour cancelled.

AM I READY * * *
Written by Sid Tepper, Roy C. Bennett.
The romantic song requested by Cynthia Foxhugh on her birthday when Mike and his group are bought and brought back by her millionaire faither at the cost of cancelling their tour plus $5,000. The birthday girl declares her intention of marrying Mike. He is not at all sure he is ready to fall in love with her. His trusty combo, Les, Larry and Jim are on hand to supply the backing.

BEACH SHACK * * *

Written by Bill Giant, Bernie Baum, Florence Kaye.

Mike, at the party in the house he has been loaned by the grateful Cranleys is surrounded by jiving youngsters as swim-suited girls are thrown into the pool; more of his hedonist attitude to life: anyone who visits his beach shack will be made comfortable and entertained – maybe they'll be alone. On the other hand as the song ends he is seen ushering a bevy of lovelies into the shack. His group are backing the jollifications – to a rumba beat.

SPINOUT * * * *

Written by Ben Weisman, Sid Wayne, Dolores Fuller.

First sung over the credit titles, but finally performed for the camera, Mike's group supplying the backing while he is free to sway among the jiving floozies. The words are sheer *double entendre* – this is the party his friends have arranged to let him loose among lots of girls to take his mind off marriage. It is clear that the lyrics are not referring only to car motors when they refer to revving up, getting hot etc. At this party, playing his guitar, Mike meets the gyrating Susan.

B/W: 'All That I Am'
LP: 'Elvis in Hollywood'

SMORGASBORD * * *

Written by Sid Tepper, Roy C. Bennet. Mike, still at the party, moves among the guests with his guitar, singing about his passion for smorgasbord referring, of course, to a buffet meal of assorted dishes but implying he's referring to girls. At one point in the rocker, while Mike's serenading Susan, Larry appears, blowing like crazy on his alto saxophone (apparently). The song tails away as Mike forgets his words at the vision of Les walking down the stairs all glamoured up.

I'LL BE BACK *

Written by Sid Wayne, Ben Weisman. Mike's final song with his combo – same boys with guitars, but a new drummer in Susan. He's celebrating his freedom, but hopes the door will remain open. Just the right song for the occasion, but doesn't go anywhere.

TOMORROW IS A LONG TIME

(not included in movie)
Written by Bob Dylan.
LP: 'A Valentine Gift For You'

DOWN IN THE ALLEY

(not included in movie)
Written by Jesse Stone.
LP: 'Reconsider, Baby'

I'LL REMEMBER YOU

(Not included in movie)
Written by Kuickalani Lee.
LPs: 'Elvis – A Legendary Performer – Vol. 4'; 'Aloha From Hawaii Via Satellite'; 'The Alternate Aloha'; 'Elvis Aaron Presley'

STANWYCK, BARBARA (1908–1990)

Barbara Stanwyck, who had been inactive in movies since her comeback in *A Walk on the Wildside* in 1962, was ready, willing and able to step into the part turned down by Mae West (*qv*), that of Maggie Moran, owner of the travelling Carni in *Roustabout* (*qv*). At 57, Stanwyck had been one of the Hollywood Greats for years since starring in *Lady of Leisure* in 1930, after a career on the Broadway stage which began in 1926 in *Noose*, a thriller which ran for nine months. She started her film career in a silent called *Broadway Nights* and rose to become one of the most versatile and dependable stars on the screen, with such great directors as Frank Capra and William Wellman to help guide her career.

Among her great movies were *The Lady Eve, Meet John Doe* and *Ball of Fire* (both opposite Gary Cooper) and *Double Indemnity*, all in the mid-Forties.

By 1944 she was reported by the Inland Revenue Service to be the highest paid woman in the United States, slightly ahead of Bette Davis. Among the leading men they had in common were Henry Fonda, Errol Flynn and Humphrey Bogart. Her career foundered in the mid-Fifties in a series of B movies and after *Forty Guns* in 1957 she was absent from the screen for five years. Perhaps one of the reasons for her decline was her refusal to dye her hair – in which she was unique among Hollywood stars – so her iron grey locks, at first taken in black and white movies as blonde streaks, became impossible to disguise, though they belied her strikingly unlined and photogenic features. Always a fighter she would not compromise but later became a leading star of television in *The Barbara Stanwyck Show* and the long-running series *The Big Valley*, a western, in which, billed as Miss Barbara Stanwyck, she was the head of a large family of young sons and daughters, including Doug McClure and Linda Evans.

For this she compromised to the extent of wearing a blonde wig, persuaded by the producer's insistence that the young generation of fans would not readily accept a grey-haired heroine. The *Big Valley* is often repeated on TV screens world-wide. In the meantime, she stuck to her guns in *Roustabout* and very fetching she looked in her Edith Head designed jeans. 'Mr Presley' she found 'wonderful and very professional.' Given that her role is hardly demanding for an actress of her talent, she performs with a degree of conviction that gives a depth that few other stars could have brought to the sketchily written character of Maggie Moran. Inevitably Mae West would have rounded her out in her uniquely different style. Stanwyck's next film, in 1965, *The Night Walker*, opposite her ex-husband, Robert Taylor, proved to be her last for the big screen.

She made a remarkable comeback as a star of television in *The Thorn Birds* in the early Seventies in the adaptation of Colleen McCullough's sensational novel, as the rich matriarch who lusts for a Catholic Priest, played by Richard Chamberlain, and who tries to buy his favours by munificent donations to the Church. She fought serious illness to go on working, notably in the off-shoot of *Dynasty, The Colbys*. She was still not pulling her punches: of her co-star, Charlton Heston, in *The Colbys* she said 'The trouble with him is he still thinks he's Moses parting the Red Sea.' Stanwyck died June 28, 1990, aged 82. *(See also: Roustabout; West, Mae)*

STAY AWAY, JOE * * *

Released by: Metro-Goldwyn-Mayer (Panavision, Metrocolor); **Producer:** Douglas Laurence; **Director:** Peter Tewkesbury; **Screenplay:** Michael A. Hoey, based on the novel by Dan Cushman; **Art Directors:** George W. Davis and Carl Anderson; **Director of Photography:** Fred Koencamp; **Music:** Jack Marshal; **Running Time:** 102 mins; **Opened:** March 8, 1968.

Cast: Elvis, Burgess Meredith, Joan Blondell, Katy Jurado, Thomas Gomez, Henry Jones, I.Q. Jones, Quentin Dean, Anne Seymour, Douglas Henderson, Angus Duncan, Michael Lane, Susan Trustman, Warren Vanders, Buck Martalian, Maurishka, Caitlin Wyles, Marya Christen, Del 'Sonny' West, Jennifer Peak, Brett Parker, Michael Keller.

Elvis as Joe Lightcloud is an indefatigably hearty, hell-raising, hard-drinking young stud, son of indigent Indian, Charlie Lightfoot (Burgess Meredith), who has been away from home for an appreciable time. However, he makes his noisy way back to meet a congressman (Douglas Henderson) whom he has conned into giving him twenty cows and a bull so he can become a cattle baron, thanks to a new government management project. Having run his car into a river, he

returns on the back of the bull in question with a gang of noisy, boisterous cowboys and their girls. He seizes his stepmother, Annie (Katie Jurado), and swings her around disrespectfully, to her simulated annoyance, before she breaks loose to go and see to the work around the house that both Charlie and Grandpa, Chief Lightcloud (Thomas Gomez) are too idle to do anything about. After all leaping into a muddy river just for the hell of it, Joe throws a wild party for the gang. Among the guests are his sister Mary (Susan Trustman), who has moved into town to work in an office, and a young newspaper owner, Lorne Hawkins (Angus Duncan), to whom she has become engaged. Joe engineers a fight, so he can have it away with the new girlfriend of one of his more violent buddies, Frank Hawk (Michael Lane). Annie refuses to cook for the drunken rowdies and defiantly takes a bath in the living room. The shindig gets so out of hand that not only does the herd of cows get loose, but the bull ends up as dinner for the hungry roisterers.

Charlie and Joe wake up from beneath piles of beer cans and Annie belabours them with her broom when the full results of the evening's carousel become apparent. Joe undertakes to get a prize stud bull, borrows a dollar from his father and heads off for his old flame Glenda Callaghan (Joan Blondell), sweet-talking her into change for the phone and a can of beer. The effect of his overtures is ruined when Glenda comes back unexpectedly and finds him trying to get intimate with her 19 year-old daughter, Mamie (Quentin Dean). She aims her shotgun at his vitals and Joe hurries on his way to con a local dealer into exchanging a car for an old horse – the man is anxious to do a quick deal. He returns to Glenda's store to tell her the law is on its way to arrest her for selling illegal liquor and tells her she's the one he's after, not Mamie: 'I need a woman of real maturity'. He persuades

her to drive to safety in the new car and takes the opportunity of her absence to throw another party at Glenda's store, so he can get to know Mamie better. Glenda returns unexpectedly and finds them together. She tries to shoot him but her aim is bad. In the meantime he is in potential real trouble for selling the cows given him by the government to buy a new bull.

The bull arrives to the family's great joy, which turns to grief when the bull only wants to sleep and shows no interest whatever in the cow, which Joe schemes to bring back. Joe exhausts himself trying to get the bull to move – even his song 'Dominick' fails to arouse him from his torpor. Meanwhile up at the ranch, Annie has sold the old station wagon to raise the money to buy an indoor toilet for the visit of Mary's fiancé's up-market mother, Mrs. Hawkins (Anne Seymour). By the time the lady arrives with her son Lorne and Mary, Charlie has made heroic efforts to improve the interior of their shack. Their five unruly dogs surge into the place ahead of Mrs. Hawkins, rather spoiling her glowing impression of 'the lovely home'. Further shocks are in store when Lorne's leg goes through the unrepaired hole in the floor and shots rain through the walls as Glenda arrives with her shotgun, pumping lead, aimed at Joe, who has ridden off with Mamie on his motorbike. Mrs. Hawkins leaves with Lorne – in shock but still keeping her brave smile intact.

When Dominick's original owner visits Joe he lets drop the fact that the bull is not a stud bull, but a bucking

Joe Lightcloud (Elvis) is a hard-living, hard-drinking young man with aims to become a cattle baron, but spends most of his time chasing the teenage daughter, of his old flame, Glenda Callahan (Joan Blondell). Here Mamie is angrily spirited away by her mother after being found with Joe. *Stay Away, Joe* **(1968)**

show animal who is only longing to be ridden, which gives Joe the idea of taking him to the rodeo to make easy money. He challenges riders to keep on the bull, which only he can ride. When the congressman comes to arrest Charlie for selling the herd, Joe drives up with the news that he has been able to make enough cash to increase the herd of 20 to 100. At the same time Glenda drives up with Mamie, all dressed up for a shotgun wedding with the judge in tow. The judge is reluctant to go ahead, particularly after Joe has persuaded them that all he did to Mamie was to kiss her. The still innocent girl thought that meant she was in the family way. Glenda takes her away to teach her the facts of life. Lorne finally forces his way into the old homestead to make Mary see reason and marry him – the events of his mother's visit having convinced her that she did not belong in his world. While they embrace the Lightfoot home finally disintegrates – the result of one wild fight too many between Joe and his cronies.

This is a follow-up to the soft porn carryings on in *Tickle Me*, taken to the nth degree with Presley's super-stud part Indian, Joe Lightcloud, bedding all the girls in sight – even, it seems, in the past, dear old Joan Blondell, looking amazingly well-preserved in her 60th year, with stunning legs and a profusion of Sydney Guilaroff-styled blonde hair. She does not take kindly to him trying to have his wicked way with her nineteen year-old daughter Mamie, who she has apparently failed to enlighten about how the birds and the bees actually function. For Memphis Mafia read cowhand buddies, who spend their time leaping on each other and rolling around, prior to turning their attention to the floozies in their entourage.

Director Peter Tewkesbury noted for his stylish direction on such TV series as *Father Knows Best* and *My Three Sons*, was understandably dismayed by the poor material he was given to handle

in the few big-screen subjects that came his way and, after one more Presley film in 1969, he returned to television. Here he obviously settled for out and out farce which in the main works well, thanks to the enthusiastic participation of a superior cast, headed by Elvis at his most fist-wielding. He seems to enjoy the constant rough-and-tumbles thoroughly – unless, of course, that was just an instance of what a good actor he could be. Macho run riot is what he purveys with such gusto, but even he is defeated by having to sing to a dozy bull and the plot permutations make it unclear just how he is managing to con all of the people all of the time. Poetic justice has him ending up girl-less, but apparently satisfied by having reduced the old homestead to rubble by one punch-up too many.

Blondell apart, and she was always great value for money, there is much enjoyment to be had by the splendid Katy Jurado, noticeably heavier than in the days when she was Brando's favourite girl in the 1961 *One-Eyed Jacks*, dispensing rough justice to her wimpish Indian husband Charlie, another no-holds-barred performance by Burgess Meredith. There is one delightfully subtle performance that doesn't really belong in the rumbustuous gallery, that of Anne Seymour as Mrs. Hawkins, the blue-blooded mother of juvenile lead Angus Duncan – a pallid young actor, among all these butch hombres. Her well-bred politeness and social smile survive much starling elements as the crudity of Grandpa Chief Lightfoot and the tactless insensitivity of his son and even the apparition of Joan Blondell taking wildly inaccurate pot-shots at Elvis.

It says a lot for Elvis's enduring appeal that *Stay Away Joe* came 68th in *Variety*'s list of top grossing films for 1968. It might have risen higher, had it not been for the flagrantly racist slant of portraying the Indians as lazy, incompetent fools.

(See also: Tickle Me)

STAY AWAY JOE (RCA Singles) 1968 * * *

Written by Sid Wayne, Ben Weisman. Hillbilly background to Joe's return party with his noisy buddies and his sister Mary, visiting with her fiancé Lorne. Drums predominate.
LPs: 'Almost In Love; 'Let's Be Friends'

STAY AWAY (Based on 'Greensleeves') * * *

Written by Sid Tepper, Roy C. Bennet. Elvis sings this adaptation of the old Greensleeves classic, dating back to the time of Elizabeth I, as Fred Koenecamp's camera roves through the mountains and valleys of the Wild West which are calling him home – he has been away too long. Elvis's sings with feeling against a gentle guitar background.
B/W: 'US Male' LPs: 'Stay Away

Two numbers sung by Elvis in this film were, unsurprisingly, not recorded:

LOVELY MAMIE ** – a few bars sung on the way to a petrol station, to the tune of French standard 'Alouette – Gentil Aloutte' forming the background theme for Mamie the 19 year-old daughter of Glenda Callaghan whom she tries to marry to Joe Lightfoot at the point of a shotgun.

DOMINICK *

Written probably either by Messrs Wayne and Weisman, or Tepper and Bennett. Sung by Joe (Elvis) to the bull, Dominick, who only wants to sleep, not sire a herd, for the simple reason he's a rodeo bull.

ALL I NEEDED WAS THE RAIN *

Written by Sid Wayne, Ben Weisman. Almost as silly as 'Dominick' is Joe's lament to his five shaggy dogs when his car breaks down in pouring rain and they all shelter under a blanket.
LPs: 'Elvis Sings Flaming Star'; 'Singer Presents Ditto and Others'

J

TAUROG, NORMAN (1899–1981)

The director of ten Presley films, who maintained consistently that if Elvis had been given better scripts he could have proved himself a great actor. With the exception of *G.I. Blues*, and possibly *Blue Hawaii*, most of their movies together were scraping the bottom of the barrel, but they worked together well and in harmony, often lamenting the dross they were expected to spin into box-office gold. They often did, too, which could only have confirmed Colonel Parker of the rightness of his policy. It was also what attracted the Colonel to Taurog initially.

Born in 1899 he was on the stage from childhood and entered movies in 1913 as a boy actor at the Ince studios (Thomas Ince was a dynamic director, producer, scriptwriter whose break came when he directed Mary Pickford, probably silent films' greatest star; his studios were known as Inceville) In 1919 he began directing Larry Semon shorts at Vitagraph: Semon was a comedian whose work has sometimes been compared with that of Chaplin, Keaton and Harold Lloyd. From 1928 his work as a feature director was prolific and diverse: in 1931 he won the best director Academy Award for *Skippy*, a film starring his nephew, boy actor Jackie Cooper.

Among the delightful entertainment films Taurog turned out, some of the ones which have stayed in the mind are the W.C. Fields episode in *If I Had a Million* (1932), several Bing Crosby musicals, *Mad About Music* (1938), one of Deanna Durbin's best, that year he was nominated for an Oscar for *Boys' Town*, with Mickey Rooney and Spencer Tracy, who won the Best Actor award; another with Mickey Rooney was *Girl Crazy* with Judy Garland and *Bundle of Joy* (1956) with Debbie Reynolds. He was known as the ideal director of entertainers as opposed to actors – not one of the greats , but consistently reliable and almost always a money spinner. Which brings us back to Colonel Parker.

(See also: Blue Hawaii; G.I. Blues; Double Trouble: Girls, Girls, Girls!; It Happened at the Worlds Fair; Live a Little, Love a Little; Speedway; Spinout; Tickle Me; Parker, Colonel Tom)

TRIBUTE CONCERT

This is a fascinatingly thorough updating of Elvis's music and career from the beginning, with clips of live performances and interviews with sympathetic contemporaries, including his best song writers Jerry Lieber and Mike Stoller, Scotty Moore, D.J. Fontana, George Klein, Allan Weiss, Hal Kanter and actress Jan Shepard, who was in two Presley films, *King Creole* (1958) and *Paradise, Hawaiian Style* (1966). She speaks with obvious affection for Elvis and asserts, like the majority of the interviewees mentioned that he had the potential to be a great actor, rather that having to settle, increasingly for second best.

An assortment of stars pay tribute, in their own way, to Elvis's music: perhaps the most interesting is his old friend, Carl Perkins, distinguished and acquiline, with iron grey hair, performing his original hit of 'Blue Suede Shoes', which he says Elvis was generous enough not to record until his own version was no longer a potential threat. Tony Bennett deals gently and feelingly with 'Love Me Tender', whose authorship he ascribes to Presley and, still among the survivors of those days, Jerry Lee Lewis has lost none of his old dashing keyboard style. Among the younger generation to give good account of themselves are Wet, Wet, Wet, U2 and Dwight Yoakam.

Some of the documentary footage is familiar, but, with Priscilla handling a moving introduction, there is another combination that has already receeded into history – from the equivalent of the Royal Box, 'Lisa Marie Presley Jackson' is introduced with her husband Michael and his sister, Janet. All in all, a real family occasion.

THE TROUBLE WITH GIRLS
＊＊＊＊

Released by: Metro-Goldwyn-Mayer (Panavision, Metrocolor); **Producer:** Lester Welch; **Director:** Peter Tewkesbury; **Screenplay:** Arnold Lois Payser, adapted from novel by Dex

875-34

Charlene (Marilyn Mason), Johnny
(Edward Andrews), Walter Hale's
assistant in the travelling Chautauna
Tent Show, and Walter himself (Elvis)
share a joke over the entries to the
carnival show talent contest. *The Trouble
With Girls* (1969)

Keene; **Art Directors:** George W. Davis, Edward Carpagne; **Director of Photography:** Jacques Marquette ASC; **Music:** Dwight Babocci, Billy Strange; **Running Time:** 97 mins; **Opened:** September 3, 1969.

Cast: Elvis, Marilyn Mason, Sheree North, Nicole Jaffe, Edward Andrews, John Carradine, Vincent Price, Joyce Van Patten, Anissa Jones, Danny Coleman, Bill Luckhart, Pitt Herbert, Med Florey, Robert Nichols, Helene Winston.

1927: The Chatauqua Tent Show – a travelling theatrical entertainment, popular from the end of last century until the Thirties – arrives in Redford Centre for a long anticipated engagement, with a new manager, in the person of Walter Hale (Elvis), who grew up in the business, starting as a singer. He is having problems with Charlene (Marilyn Mason) who doubles as a pianist, singer, dancer and general factotum, and who happens to be the union representative of a show which has no union. She is dedicated to changing all that, but Walter, with whom she has had her moments, is not so keen. She erupts constantly, but he always keeps his cool. She is good at her work, which includes keeping the peace between jealous mamas who always think that their little girls are the tops and should have the lead in the parade. One of these ladies, the local sexpot, Nita Bix (Sheree North), is usually in a horizontal position with the local drugstore manager, Harrison Wilby (Danny Coleman), an odious two-timer, for whom she works. Her daughter, Carol (Anissa Jones), is one of the more talented children, chosen for the lead in the pageant. The druggist, on the pretext of doing them a favour, unloads a box of fireworks on the children. They hide the fireworks in a corner of one of the tents which happens to belong to Charlene. Walter, happens to be in the tent negotiating with Charlene over a standby

pianist his second in command, Johnny (Edgar Andrews) has hired for the show without a salary. While they talk Walter throws away the smouldering cigarette. It lands among the fireworks and while Walter is sharing a kiss with the now melting Charlene a magnificent display begins. Charlene rushes out, in fury. An even more explosive happening puts paid to the excitement over the Chautaqua and attendances fall to zero: the lady channel swimmer, Maud (Joyce Van Patten) during one of her demonstrations, runs into the floating corpse of Harrison Wilby. Clarence, one of the Chautaqua members, who had clashed with the druggist over a crooked card game was arrested for his murder. Walter, talking to Charlene, learns that she had overheard Nita having a big row with Harrison Wilby which ended with her threatening him and slapping his face; so he is on to the real murderer. He beats down Nita's resistance and all her bitterness and resentment spills out, but she denies knowing anything about the murder. Walter tells her that if it had been in self defence she could not only get acquitted but probably also a big sum of money to help her daughter, Carol, get a start in show business.

Taking an outrageous chance at both getting a full house again he advertises that on stage the real murderer of Wilby will confess, presuming on Nita's own conscience, that she would not let an innocent man hang. On the night the tent is packed to capacity and for starters local talent is given full sway during the time before Nita is likely to put in an appearance. She eventually does, but is so drunk she passes out and Walter has to rely on Johnny to bring her round, while he goes on stage to help deal with the acts, including a number from an outraged and rebellious Charlene. Even the local Glee Club boys are unable to get any sense out of her and Walter is about to admit defeat, while the forces of the law advance to arrest him for false pretences, when a

bucket of water from Johnny and a slap in the face from Walter does the trick. Nita staggers on stage, soaked and dazed and says she killed Wilby in self-defence. Clarence is let out of jail, Walter arranges for Nita to go out of town to where she can get a fair trial and only Charlene remains adamant that she is leaving Walter, as a matter of principle, though she admits he has done something heroic. It is clear she loves him, but her own stubbornness gets in the way, so he persuades the local police force to abduct her and put her on the train with him out of Radford Centre.

Ironically, there were signs in Elvis's last three films of a touch of originality in subject characterization and direction, which obviously came too late to stop his disillusionment with the whole Hollywood machine. Here, with thirty down and one to go, in the fictional movie count, Peter Tewkesbury who made a quite riotous cowboy spoof out of *Stay Away Joe*, again directs with a sense of elegance and a sure hand. Elvis, as the manager of a travelling tent show – there's a change of roles for a start! – in 1927, when these Chautaquas (original title and much better than the silly 'Girls' syndrome) were still popular in the States before the talkies, radio and television, killed them off. The songs are few and distinctly off-beat and with one exception, strictly not chart material but fun. Nonetheless the storyline, with the hero clearing up a murder mystery in an outrageously unprofessional way, engaging in a battle of wills with his strong minded shop steward girlfriend is definitely intriguing. Presley, unaccustomedly laid back, plays with conviction and poise and his manager's white suit and hat, blue tie and shirt, well become him. His two leading ladies contrast splendidly – the firebrand union leader Charlene, charlestoning in her flapper mini skirt, played by Marilyn Mason and the sad sexy blonde, seizing at romance with any man who'll give in to her, Sheree North's Nita. She pulls all stops out for her drunken confession of killing her lover and is effectively touching. Interesting cameos come from Vincent Price as the pompous preacher of moral rectitude, Mr. Morality, Joyce Van Patten as the cross channel swimmer, covering herself in axle-grease, John Carradine as a Shakespearean actor who answers the question 'Did Romeo and Juliet have premarital relations?' with 'only in the Des Moines company'. Nice film – pity about the title.

THE TROUBLE WITH GIRLS (1969) (Singles)

Singles from the movie:

SWING LOW, SWEET CHARIOT * * *

Written by (Traditional gospel) Walter Hale steps in for the lead singer with the bible group, (down with laryngitis) in the bible swinger, which is right up his alley: he leads the dark suited trio, hand-clapping with gusto, backed by guitar and drums; Elvis's enjoyment is infectious and soon the whole crowd is rocking in unison.

Single B/W: 'Milky White Way'
LPs: 'Elvis Aaron Presley'; 'Elvis – A Legendary Performer – Vol. 4'; 'His Hand in Mine'; 'Known Only To Him'

THE WHIFFENPOOF SONG * *
(Omitted): See entry

VIOLET (FLOWER OF NYU)
Traditional.
Walter again stands in, this time with the Glee Club. (Not recorded)
With Betty Smith (Nicole Jaffe) at the piano.

CLEAN UP YOUR OWN BACKYARD * * *

Written by Billy Strange, Mac Davis. Billy Strange who wrote the soundtrack score, is responsible for this delightful

country and western gospel-type rocker morality song, with Walter and guitar, while other fingers pluck at the strings with a plectrum. To add to the swinging effect Jaques Marqette's camera performs some strange angles of its own. Drums play an active part and on stage are a local boy and girl with guitar.
Single B/W: 'The Fair Is Moving On'

THIRTY – AND AFTER

The years 1964–65 really were the watershed for Presley's career as far as his international status and ratings were concerned. In February, 1964 The Beatles (qv) made their first appearance on the Ed Sullivan Show and the US reeled from the impact. A few days later Elvis's 'Kissin' Cousins' backed by 'It Hurts Me' hit the charts. It did well, though it did reach not the automatic No. 1 position in past years expected of Presley releases. Colonel Parker (qv) had reacted to a decline in the ratings (unacknowledged by him and Elvis) by hiring King of the Quickies Sam Katzman (qv) to turn out the film *Kissin' Cousins* (qv) at a fraction of the cost of the last top quality Presley, *Viva Las Vegas* (qv), which took some ten weeks to produce with full time for rehearsals, while *Cousins* was turned out in seventeen days, with little or no rehearsal. In the event, the 'quickie' was rushed out on release a few weeks before *Viva Las Vegas*, which had a major co-star in Ann-Margret (qv) and was shown in Britain as *Love In Las Vegas*. Both films, predictably, cleaned up at the box office, although no LP of *Las Vegas* was released at that time – only one single coupling of the title song with 'What'd I Say' (the Ray Charles classic), plus an EP. However, despite the moans about being sub-standard, *Kissin' Cousins*, thanks to the patience and expertise of both director Gene Nelson and Elvis himself, with an outstanding supporting cast of experienced actors, grossed over $2,500,000. The title song reached No. 10 in the UK charts, No. 12 in the US

and stayed in the Elvis Top Forty Hits for a record 121 weeks. The Colonel reaped the whirlwind, but the star continued to worry about his new opposition and the fact that, for all their financial success, his movies were not advancing him towards achieving his original ambitions as an actor. He was never less than glamorous, charming and, when opportunity offered, genuinely funny, but the artist in him could not help recognizing that he had reached stalemate, bogged down, for the most part, in a morass of mediocrity. He, or his advisor(s), even came out with a rare justification of his position. Commenting on how it felt to be back in the British Top Ten again in an interview with George Rooney of the *New Musical Express*, Elvis said:

It feels great. You know, when I was making the top of the charts regularly, a few years back, I was the happiest guy alive. My fans were always kind to me and, no matter what type of song I did, they liked it. But when that kind of thing cooled off a little for me, I began worrying. After all, I wasn't used to that kind of thing. I spoke to my manager, Colonel Tom Parker, and he admitted to being a little puzzled as well. Honest, we got to thinking about things and we couldn't come up with an answer. We called a conference with song writers and music publishers and people like that, but at the end we didn't have a reason for the dropping off period in Britain. Here, in America, my records were still selling as well as ever, but in Britain they wouldn't get too high before they started dropping. As usual in these cases, there were always plenty of people around to tell me what was wrong and what I should do to improve my overseas position. But I always place the greatest trust in Colonel Parker. He is the man who has done most for me and I am convinced that if he says for me to do something, that is the best thing in my interest.

In the meantime I had a heavy schedule of

film-making. When I started out to be an actor, there were some people who said I'd never make it. I hope now I've proved them wrong. My films do well at the box office and the albums of the soundtracks sell in large numbers. Do you remember *Jailhouse Rock (qv)* and *King Creole (qv)*? If you do, you'll visualize me as a hard-talking, fighting kind of person. At the time that was all fine. I used to wear side-burns *(qv)*, flashy sports jackets or denims and very tight trousers. When my army stint came, Colonel Parker decided it was time for a change and he began the gradual process. The old, mean Elvis gave way to a new cleaned up version that I admit I have grown fond of over the years. *G.I. Blues* first showed the public what to expect from then on in. Luckily, they took to the film and the new image.

I get puzzled when people give the opinion that my films are responsible for my records not being as successful as they were. That doesn't figure to me at all. It's still the same person singing and we all decide on the songs before we record them. If it isn't suited to my style we forget it. With my film commitments, I don't have time to go into a recording studio and do additional songs. So when we get a film to do, we study the songs and if one of them seems like a prospect for the charts we issue that as a single. The success of 'Kissin' Cousins' has finally proved that we were right. Now let's hope we can follow up with some more hit songs from movies.

Well, they did, but the films, and with them most of the songs, grew more and more repetitious and bland. There was at that time no mention of The Beatles *(qv)* as a contributing factor to the decline. Elvis's old friend, Roy Orbison, at the time still a phenomenally successful record seller, leapt to his defence. After all, hadn't Elvis dyed his hair black out of admiration for the older star? Speaking with George Rooney he said:

If people compare me with Elvis Presley,

they are comparing me with the ultimate. Likewise The Beatles, or anyone else. They pick the best they can compare with. So long as anyone says "Are The Beatles taking over from Elvis?" instead of The Beatles have taken over from Elvis, well, then, he is still very much in the race. I think Elvis is in as good a position entertainment-wise as he was a year ago. He reached a fantastic peak of popularity and, like most people say, he is a legend in the music world. He could not hold this position for ever – but not (as some people think) because those who came along after him have dented his armour. The plain fact that he has been around for a very long time would make him not as big as he was. I say he's still very popular – there have been voting contests held in America since 1956 and Elvis usually comes out top. People compare other artists with Presley and that speaks for itself. Elvis is still the example with which to compare anyone who has great fame. But it's really impossible to compare someone whose records are mainly film titles with a group like The Beatles, whose discs are made solely for commercial markets. If Elvis devoted his sole time to just recording, as The Beatles do, he could come up with as good a record as his past major successes. In his films Elvis is in character and also his songs are part of that character. Not Elvis with his message to you.

If he spent more time in the recording studio, he could do practically anything he wanted to – the fact that he has been the number 1 entertainer in the world for the past five or six years, must have taxed his efforts, being in the limelight so long. It must have been lonely at the top all this time – and at least The Beatles have each other – Elvis has only Elvis!

I think his singing has matured and he sounds a little more sedate than he did. But he still sings as well as ever. His vocal performance on the flip of his last disc 'Kissin' Cousins' (qv), not yet released here, which was 'It Hurts Me', is fantastic. So

the ability is still there. It's simply lack of time – not lack of interest, which may be the reason why he hasn't had a No. 1 recently.

But I think Elvis should spend more time on preparation and recording – otherwise he's in like Flynn. If he wanted to, he could alter his schedule, so that he made four records a year and two films. Then he could devote three or four weeks to each release, leaving him eight months for movies. If he did this, then there is no doubt in my mind that he could make as good a record as has been made. Elvis and The Beatles are so popular now, known by young and old alike, that they won't be forgotten – not in ten or one hundred years time. They have made too big an impact on the world to be easily forgotten.

It is very difficult to say who the 'king' is. Especially as The Beatles are a group and Elvis is a solo artiste. And of course there are people who like only Elvis or only The Beatles, or like neither or love both. But one thing is for sure: they're both around to stay for a long time!

Those who say Elvis is slipping must bear in mind that to slip one must first be at the top.

Generous words of wisdom from a generous artiste – words that the omniscient Colonel Parker would have done well to heed.

Elvis turned 30 on January 8, 1965. The world's press celebrated the fact with such headlines as ELVIS AT THIRTY – GENIUS OR JOKE? He had earned the dubious accolade of being called 'an ageing rocker': many years were to pass before his nearest – and indeed only real British rival Cliff Richard *(qv)*, after the fall from favour of Terry Dean, would graduate to such an honour. It was duly recorded that Elvis's thirtieth year had been a profitable one: he had made about $1,428,000, three motion pictures, umpteen records and wound up high on what inThe Hit Parade and number six on The *Motion Picture Herald's* list of top box office stars. The Beatles had rocked, but never rolled him.

Barbara Stanwyck (*qv*) gave an interview in which she said, 'I was astonished, when we did *Roustabout* together. I've had some rather bad experiences with these "instant success" people. But Elvis is that rare exception, a young star who is also a gentleman.'

His day was spent at Gracelands, in what had come to be regarded as 'seclusion', with his fleet of cars, a sprinkling of close relatives and his 'six ubiquitous male friends' who protected him around the clock from the depredations of his more zealous admirers and who had not yet come to be christened 'The Memphis Mafia'(*qv*).

In Britain, the event was celebrated on the Sunday after his birthday by the inauguration of the International Appreciation Society, an offshoot of the 15,000 strong Official Fan Club run by the late Albert Hand, then 39, of Heanor, Derbyshire, who, alone in Britain, had 'gained' permission from Elvis's company to promote photographs, magazines and souvenirs. Hand and his wife had been personally invited to stay as Elvis's guests at Graceland and eventually made three trips to Memphis at their own expense. I once had the pleasure of visiting Albert Hand at his home in Heanor. I was already the recipient of his monthly Elvis magazine, then priced one shilling, and was impressed by his total dedication to the promotion of Elvis. The inauguration of the Appreciation Society was at St. Pancras Town Hall, London, which seated 600. Thousands competed for tickets and Albert told me that it had taken him and his wife four hours to go through 1,000 letters on the day before Elvis's birthday.

(See also: Ann-Margret; Elvis and the Beatles; G.I. Blues; Jailhouse Rock; Katzman, Sam; King Creole; Kissin' Cousins; Official Elvis Presley Fan Clubs

of Great Britain; Parker, Colonel Tom; Roustabout; Sideburns; Stanwyck, Barbara; Viva Las Vegas)

THIS IS ELVIS * * * *

Released by: Warner Brothers (Technicolor); **Producer:** David L. Wolper; **Director:** Andrew Solt, Malcolm Leo; **Director of Photography:** Gil Hubbs; **Set Director:** Charles Hughes; **Consultants:** Jerry Schilling, Joe Esposito; **Technical Advisor:** Colonel Tom Parker; **Music:** Walter Scharf; **Running Time:** 98 mins; **Opened:** April 3, 1981.

Cast: David Scott, Paul Bensch III, Johnny Harra, Dana MacKay, Lawrence Koller, Rhonda Lynn, Debbie Edge, Knox Phillips, Cheryl Needham, Andrea Cyrill, Jerry Phillips, Emory Smith.

This is the 34th (although posthumous) film in which Elvis appeared, released with the blessing of Technical Advisor Colonel Parker, the Graceland Estate and two of Elvis's long-time friends and associates Memphis Mafia members, Jerry Schilling and Joe Esposito. It begins just before Elvis's death, with Johnny Harra impersonating the 42 year-old King with positively eerie verisimilitude, albeit from behind, and then, as with *Elvis: The Movie* (*qv*) flashes back to the young boy (Paul Bensch III) showing him hanging around his black neighbours listening to their gospel singing, the original inspiration for the authentic Presley 'black sound' of his teenage days.

There is some deeply interesting and illuminating footage of his first appearance on TV after leaving the army in the *Frank Sinatra Show*, with their bizarre, not-to-be-missed duet, and his return for his first Special after his years in Hollywood. In 1968, this was Elvis at his definitive best, overcoming nerves to look and sound at his peak, slim and lithe as the sleek panther as he was christened by co-star Dolores Del Rio

(*qv*) in *Flaming Star* (*qv*) twelve years previously.

With hindsight, after the exposé in the book written by Red and Sonny West and Dave Hebler, *Elvis, What Happened?* (*qv*) published just fifteen days before Elvis's death, facts about his dependence on drugs and other facets of the darker side of his nature could no longer be concealed. The three men, with a journalist collaborator, wrote in anger and bitterness after being dismissed from Elvis's employment after years of loyal service and said they had wanted to save him from self-destruction before it was too late. It was, in fact, several years too late; his health had been deteriorating during his years of constant touring and after his hospitalization for what was designated as exhaustion but what, in fact, was due to serious internal complications, it was no longer possible to gloss over the facts with pretty phrases.

To watch the deterioration in a concert filmed and recorded for a scheduled CBS-TV Special in June, 1977, is a depressing experience. Elvis was grotesquely overweight, sweated profusely and just about managed to joke his way out of forgetting the words for one of his most familiar songs 'Are You Lonesome Tonight?'. He was like a man in a nightmare, the strain is painfully apparent and after getting through what must have been as big an ordeal for his audience as it was for himself, he was practically carried off by two helpers.

This reminded me of the sad spectacle in the late Forties when France's great cabaret star, Mistinguett, making an extremely ill-timed and delayed London debut at the Casino Theatre, forgot the words of her most famous song 'Mon Homme', which she had been singing for half a century. It was left to her young partner, Billy Milton, to lead her off and entertain with anecdotes until Madame recovered herself sufficiently to return and join him in a restrained adagio dance. But she was 76

– Elvis was only 42.

This is Elvis is a must for serious Presley admirers: the fans love him anyway and had even come to terms with his physical deterioration. This honest account of his life has gone further that any other in demystifying the King; in the meantime his music still encircles the globe and his films, crass though some of them were, preserve a youthful image of an idealized and sanitized athletic and nice guy.

The fusion of authentic film, much of it discovered by chance by the movie's creators, Andrew Solt and Malcolm Leo, when they opened a cupboard at Graceland and out fell several of Elvis's movies, and recreations of scenes and dialogue by actors is masterly. Presley's own voice is narrated by singer, Ral Donner, one of the most impressive Elvis soundalikes; Joe Esposito looks after his own dialogue, as does Linda Thompson. The remainder of the Presley family are dubbed by Lisha Sweetman as Priscilla, Virginia Kiser as Gladys (*qv*) and Michael Tovackas as Vernon (*qv*) – all blending smoothly with the camera's image of the actual events.

(See also: Del Rio, Dolores; Elvis: The Movie; Flaming Star; Girls, Girls, Girls (not the movie); Graceland; Memphis Mafia; Parker, Colonel Tom; Presley, Gladys Love Smith; Presley, Priscilla Beaulieu; Presley, Vernon Elvis)

TICKLE ME *

Released by: Allied Artists (DeLuxe Colour, Panavision); **Producer:** Ben Schwalb; **Director:** Norman Taurog; **Screenplay:** Ellwood Ullman, Edward Bernds; **Art Directors:** Hal Pereira, Arthur Lonergan; **Director of Photography:** Loyal Griggs; **Music:** Walter Scharf; **Technical Advisor:** Colonel Tom Parker; **Running Time:** 90 mins; **Opened:** November 24, 1965.

Cast: Elvis, Julie Adams, Jocelyn Lane, Jack Mullaney, Merry Anders, Bill Williams, Edward Faulkner, Connie Gilchrist, Berbars Werle, John Dennis, Grady Sutton, Alison Hayes, Inez Pedroza, Lilyan Chauvin, Angela Green, Louie Elias, Robert Hoy, Dorothy Konrad, Eve Bruce, Francine York, Red West.

Lonnie Beal (Elvis), a rodeo rider waiting for the season to start, is hired on a temporary basis by Vera Radford (Julie Adams) as horse wrangler on her expensive Arizona dude ranch/health spa, where the girls are all man-mad and perpetually hungry from the health diet on which they are rigidly kept by Pam Merritt (Jocelyn Lane), the spa's physical training instructor. The girls are all attracted by Lonnie's good looks and his singing, except Pam, who sees him as just another gigolo, after rich-pickings from the clients who are all as wealthy as they are shapely. She begins to see him in a different light, though, when she discovers an intruder in her quarters and Lonnie rushes in to protect her. By the time he arrives the man has fled and, when the police get there, Deputy Sheriff Studivant (Bill Williams) tells her he has heard she has been indiscreet in talking about a letter of her grandfather's about a hidden cache of gold. The Sheriff warns her that she could find herself in serious trouble if she doesn't keep her own counsel.

Evidently the cat is already out of the bag for shortly afterwards two masked men attempt to kidnap Pam. Lonnie manages to rescue her, but the intruders escape. They wait in the desert for their employer who turns out to be the Sheriff, who has been the instigator of all the attacks upon Pam. She shows Lonnie her grandfather's letter and explains that the villains are after the map which offers clues to the hiding-place of her grandfather's treasure hoard somewhere in a nearby ghost town. Pam and Lonnie admit their mutual attraction and they are getting along idyllically until Pam discovers Lonnie in an embrace with Vera, who has made no bones about wanting him from the beginning.

Pam then refuses to have anything further to do with him and Lonnie leaves the farm in disgust to go back on the rodeo circuit. However, his mind is so full of Pam that he finds his old skill as a rodeo rider has left him; he gets thrown repeatedly, to the jeers and boos of the crowd. He is unable to do anything right and his friend Stanley Potter (Jack Mullaney) is soon able to persuade him to return to the farm. He finds Pam about to explore the ghost town of Silverado where the gold is hidden. He and Stanley follow her and all three run into a storm which suddenly blows up from the mountains. They find themselves stranded in a deserted hotel, which had been restored by a local historical society where weird and terrifying apparitions keep materializing during the night. The villains, masked and desperate, are still trying to get hold of the map. Stanley accidentally stumbles upon the hidden treasure and gold nuggets start to pour out of the wall. The newly reconciled Lonnie and Pam finally outwit and unmask the villains, the *coup-de-grâce* to the two-timing Sheriff being delivered by Pam with a deftly aimed blow to the head when Lonnie has knocked him around into the right position: hitherto, every time she tried to help in a fight it was Lonnie she hit. The Sheriff's two henchmen had been manoeuvred into a reservoir of mud by quick thinking on the part of Lonnie and Pam and are dragged out by ranch foreman, Brad Bentley (Edward Faulkner), who has always been against Lonnie because he himself fancied Vera, the boss-lady with a roving eye. The masked and muddy villains are revealed as two of the dumbest ranch hands, Henry (Robert Hoy) and Jerry (Louie Elias).

Everything is sorted out by the time Vera throws a wedding party for the happy couple, Brad firmly by her side. The ever-inept Stanley, having fixed the 'Just Married' sign behind Lonnie and Pam's wedding carriage, is swept up into a dustbin as they drive off. As he is pulled

Flashback to the ghost town of *Silverado*
– Lonnie Beale (Elvis), a rodeo cowboy
and singer, imagines himself back in the
old days as a milk-swigging desperado,
romancing the saloon's cabaret star, Pam
Merritt (Jocelyn Lane), in reality a PTI
loved by Lonnie. *Tickle Me* (1965)

along behind the newly-weds who are oblivious of their uninvited passenger, he shouts 'Hey! What am I going to do on your honeymoon?' An odd moment, one would think, for Lonnie to start singing, 'Slowly But Surely I'm Going to Wear You Down!'

The shenanigans in *Tickle Me* are as ludicrous as the title. Yet *American Variety* reported that the film grossed between $4,700,000 and $5,000,000 making it one of the highest of Presley's money-makers, with the exception of *Viva Las Vegas* and a couple of other blockbusters (unspecified). The headline reads, 'PRESLEY'S BAIL-OUT OF ALLIED ARTISTS, A SAGA OF BUSINESS-LIKE CO-OPERATION.' No wonder during the historic meeting between Elvis and the Beatles (*qv*), when John Lennon asked Elvis why he didn't do some recording sessions of the kind of music he used to play, he explained that the sessions for his film music left him no time, and that 'the fans keep buying them anyway!' That, for Colonel Parker, was the final answer to all questions.

Even *Variety*, who always found mitigating qualities in virtually every movie at that time, found the screenplay by Ellwood Ullman and Edward Bernds 'wispy thin', but recorded that it allowed Elvis to 'rock over nine numbers from past albums to good effect'. The BFI monthly magazine's assessment was, as ever, notably sharper:

Exceptionally routine Presley vehicle, which spends nearly all of its footage demonstrating that every single female in the cast swoons incontinently before Elvis's manly charms (and songs). A fantasy sequence set in the ghost town, parodying the convention of the Western with Presley as a milk-swigging gunslinger, is so flabbily directed as to be pointless: the horror-comedy finale is only slightly livelier; and there isn't much else except for a quantity of uninspired songs.

The National press in general found little to praise on either side of the Atlantic: the London *Daily Mail's* kindly Cecil Wilson said 'It's the mixture as before. There is little new to report, except bikinis seem to be growing smaller. Or else the girls are growing bigger.'

Critics were growing as bored-sounding as Elvis reputedly felt about the songs he was being asked to sing. He himself in his performance kept up a standard that justified the inevitable Trade paper reviews: *Motion Picture Daily* glowed: 'He seems to enjoy the picture as much as his audiences will.' The *Hollywood Reporter* was even more ecstatic: 'A picture with a sharp, trim, bright decoration, lively action. Should do the customary brisk Presley business.'

Interestingly enough, top-billed after Elvis, the beautiful Julie Adams, who spent her career as leading lady in numerous B movies, plays the sexy, if mature, Vera Radford – she was 39 at the time – and is the most distinctive of the girls who romp with and ogle Elvis and the only one with any noticeable style. The nominal female lead of *Tickle Me* is Jocelyn Lane as the PT instructor Pam Merritt, undeniably pretty, and perfectly competent in her role and indeed, the standard female lead in an Elvis movie. All around her are myriads of bimbos of the same ilk, with the exception of 64 year-old Connie Gilchrist, playing her usual outspoken character – this time a masseuse. Even she can be spotted in the background, gamely rocking, while the younger, more nubile chicks cavort around Elvis in the foreground.

It is tempting to identify the whole exercise, along with other *Girls! Girls! Girls!*-type vehicles, as the reverse side of the two-way mirror Elvis and 'the Guys' – the more acceptable term for Memphis Mafia (*qv*) – used to amuse themselves with during their recreational moments back home. The Hollywood sanitized version presented him as the essentially clean-living nice guy who could be tempted by the Vera Radfords of this

world, but whose normal instinct would be to keep himself pure until leading the right girl to the altar. That way the fans could have their cake and eat it, the Mills and Boon exterior allowing them to exercise their fantasies to the full with a free conscience. Elvis motoring his bride into the blue beyond is virtually always the climax of a Presley movie – in the case of *Tickle Me* we are left with the potential query of the hero's buddy tagging along on the honeymoon in a washtub. Is this a ploy for an extra laugh or a subtle in-joke between director Norman Taurog (*qv*) and his star.

The part of Stanley, nutty friend of the hero, is pointless and ill-conceived and Jack Mullaney can do little with it, apart from playing on a slight resemblance to Jerry Lewis. Another red-herring part, that of Deputy Sheriff John Sturdivant, who turns out to be the bad guy all along, was presumably given to Bill Williams because he had always specialized in nice, open-faced good guys, but he is kept out of camera range most of the time, so who can tell? This role is a notable omission from his film listings as far as I can trace.

(See also: Elvis and The Beatles; Girls! Girls! Girls! Memphis Mafia; Parker, Colonel Tom; Viva Las Vegas)

TICKLE ME

(RCA EP – Released 1965)

I FEEL THAT I'VE KNOWN YOU FOREVER * *

Written by Doc Pomus, Alan Jeffries. Elvis's sings this as the penultimate song in the movie to Jocelyn Lane as Pam Merritt, PT Instructor at the ranch for rich young ladies where he is temporarily working. He sings it through the blinds of her cabin, which she has let down in anger to keep him out after catching him kissing his boss, Vera Radford. As he moves round to find an open window she pulls the curtains at each one of the windows, until she waits for him, apparently won over by the caressing tones of the ballad at the original

window, then lets the blind down on him saying she never wants to see him again. He sticks his head through and says, 'O.K. – goodbye' storming off to join the rodeo show. At the start of the song she is seated at her dressing table, preparing for bed, as the strings accompany Elvis at his most syrupy. The ballad swells to the addition of piano and guitar and builds to a crescendo when it seems as though Pam is going to be won over, then the mood is abruptly fractured as she lets down the blind on his head. A typical story plant, of the kind featured in every Elvis musical.
LP: 'Pot Luck'

SLOWLY BUT SURELY * *
Written by Sid Wayne.
The final song as Lonnie and Pam drive away on their honeymoon; the words indicate that his wooing will be gentle but insistant. This is a jolly rocker, with plenty of drums, guitar and washboard.
LP: 'Fun in Acapulco'

NIGHT RIDER * * *
Written by Doc Pomus, Mort Shuman.
Lonnie and Stanley are engaged in a little light haymaking while the girls on the ranch enjoy a recreation break with a beach ball, under the supervision of Pam. Lonnie picks up his guitar and the girls flock round as he starts to play and sing. He lays his guitar down and the saxophone, drums, guitars and ensemble take up the melody while he and Pam dance, accompanied by her pupils: the lyrics tell of a mysterious night rider who stole his girl away and he pleads with him to return her. The cheerful rock with a fun beat belies the tale of woe and they frolic on till one of the ranch hands tells Lonnie that Mrs. Radford requires him in her office right away. The girls, lamenting, are ordered back to their 'work-out' by Pam.
LP: 'Elvis in Nashville', 'Pot Luck'

PUT THE BLAME ON ME * * *
Written by Kay Twomey, Fred Wise, Norman Blagman.
Pam is exploring the derelict hotel in Silverado when Lonnie frightens her by appearing from behind a curtain. She tells him about the days when the place was a thriving saloon where Jenny Lind used to sing. The scene fades to the olden times when gambler Highcard Harry is playing poker, dealing from the bottom of the pack, when the Panhandle Kid strolls in through the swing doors and throws his ten gallon hat with unerring accuracy onto the barman's head and orders his usual pint of milk. He rescues the beautiful singer from the unwanted attentions of Highcard Harry, seizes a guitar from a gaucho entering down a staircase and starts to sing. The saloon's glamour girl joins him in a pas de deux, which dissolves back to Lonnie and Pam in the present day. Guitar, piano and drums accompany Elvis in this western spoof which is just not funny, despite the earnest endeavours of the players. The song and routine accompanying it are effectively catchy and attractively costumed.
LP: 'Something for Everybody'

DIRTY, DIRTY FEELING * * *
Written by Jerry Lieber, Mike Stoller.
The mood of this Lieber–Stoller rocker which follows right on from the scene where Lonnie is introduced to the admiring patrons of Vera Radford's Health Centre might well be called 'Elvis in Soft Porn Land' when he happens upon Jocelyn Lane taking her callisthenics class, bending forward to touch her toes, photographed from the back and looking up at him through her legs. The vision so disorientates him that he blunders backwards over chairs and tables and disrupts Brad Bentley's swimming lessons by breaking into the lyrics of 'Dirty, Dirty Feeling' which leaves little to the imagination. All this while he's feeding the horses from bales of hay, which he soon abandons in

favour of leading the scantily clad girls in a terrific rock 'n' roll routine all around the paddock. This harks back to the songwriters' 'Jailhouse Rock' energy, only this time Elvis is rocking with girls instead of boys in the prison scene.
LP: 'Elvis is Back'

IT FEELS SO RIGHT * *
Written by Fred Wise, Ben Wiseman.
The second song in the movie: Lonnie arrives in Zuni Wells, a Western hick town, where he was expecting to meet a friend who had promised to get him a job riding in the local rodeo – but the man has quit town. The only way Lonnie can earn his keep until the rodeo season starts is to take up his guitar, which he does and launch into this number in the town saloon, packed with an appreciative audience. He's telling his girl they have to make love – everything seems right for the occasion. A blonde in the audience evidently feels the same – she embraces him in a bear hug, her boyfriend objects and the inevitable fight starts: a slow rocker, with words that are just bound to lead to trouble, the way Lonnie sings them. He's backed by drums, bass, piano and handclapping in unison. Lonnie knocks the man out and is helped to sling him through the swing doors. A jolly plot filler: Lonnie loses his job at the saloon and is hired as a ranch hand by a lady customer.
Single B/W: '(Such an) Easy Question'
LPs: 'Elvis is Back'; 'A Valentine Gift For You'

(SUCH AN) EASY QUESTION * *
Written by Otis Blackwell, Winfield Scott (1962).
Lonnie sings to the young ladies on the health farm, asking each in turn why he's unable to get a simple answer to a simple question. A simple song, with Lonnie accompanying himself on guitar, backed by an invisible orchestra while he addresses himself to each girl in turn.
Single B/W: 'It Feels So Right'
LP: 'Pot Luck'

Elvis (previous page)   *Roustabout* – the soundtrack album (above)   Beach party from *Paradise, Hawaiin Style* (below)

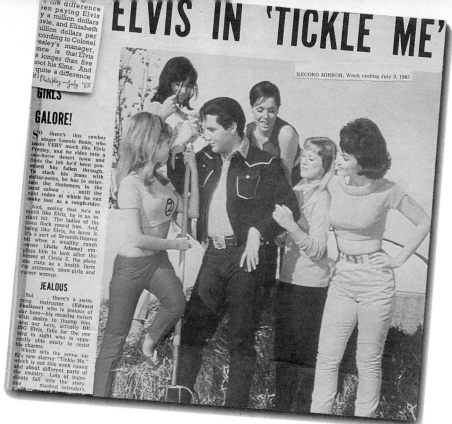

I'M YOURS * * *

Written by Don Robertson, Hal Blair.
Lonnie entertains, after some
embarrassing incidents for the rich
sponsors at Vera Radford's Health Farm.
As in most of the songs from this movie,
Lonnie declares his passion to every
individual female. The appeal, which
sent it into the million sellers, lies in the
sexy innuendo of his interpretation of
the banal lyrics and an undeniably strong
beat, with background organ underlying
the usual combo – drums, guitars, piano.
Could hardly be more repetitive – or
more financially successful!
Single B/W: 'It's a Long, Lonely
Highway'

**(IT'S A) LONG LONELY
HIGHWAY** * *

Written by Doc Pomus, Mort Shuman.
Yet another opening travelling song for
Elvis, riding for a change on a bus 'on
the road to nowhere', this time to a mid-
west hick town called Cluny Wells to
ride in a rodeo. The insistent guitar beat
drums out a persistantly jolly rhythm
that counteracts the lyrics about the girl
who left him; never is Elvis more
cheerful than when singing about lost
love. The words tell, quite wittily, a story
that his happy expression contradicts.
Single B/W: 'I'm Yours'
LP: 'Kissin' Cousins'

V

VIVA LAS VEGAS (LOVE IN LAS VEGAS in Britain) * * * *

Released by: Metro-Goldwyn-Mayer (Panavision, Metrocolor); **Producers:** Jack Cummings, George Sydney; **Director:** George Sidney; **Screenplay:** Sally Benson; **Art Directors:** George W. Davis, Edward and Edward Carfagan; **Director of Photography:** Joseph Biroc ASC; **Music:** George Stoll; **Running Time:** 86 mins; **Opened:** April 20, 1964.

Cast: Elvis, Ann-Margret, Cesare Danove, William Demarest, Nicky Blair, Jack Carter, Teri Garr.

Formula racer Lucky Johnson (Elvis) pays a visit to the gambling casinos at Las Vegas, looking to win a considerable sum of money to enable him and his mechanic, Shorty Farnsworth (Nicky Blair), to enter their car in the Grand Prix. Lucky in gambling as well as love and cars, Johnson wins a large bet, pays his entry fee in advance and heads back into town, where he encounters Italian racing champion, Count Elmo Mancini (Cesare Danova), tuning up his Ferrari for the race. Mancini makes a proposition that Lucky drive the other cars out of the race so that he, Mancini, can be sure of being the winner. Lucky says he works for no one and, in any case, he aims to win the race himself. While they are underneath a car, an exceptional pair of legs appear in their

vision: they belong to Rusty Martin (Ann-Margret), a swimming instructor, but she drives off after Mancini has fixed the whistling sound on her car, which Lucky has pretended is seriously out of order in order to keep her there. She makes off before they can find out anything about her and the two drivers, assuming the lady to be a dancer, set off on a tour of the casinos. They see lots of gorgeous girls of all nationalities and some spectacular shows – but no Rusty. They return, disconsolate, to their hotel: through the open window Lucky hears a familiar voice – and there is Rusty, giving some children a swimming lesson. He runs up, elated, onto the diving board to renew their acquaintance and is rewarded by bring pushed into the pool, fully dressed, with the wad of money he had saved to spend on his engine for the big race being sucked down the drain. The hotel management allows Lucky and Shorty to work off their hotel bill by serving as waiters. To Lucky's delighted surprise, working as staff renders them eligible to compete for the $2,500 in prizes for the winner of the annual employees' talent competition. After becoming close, then parted by her aversion to racing, Rusty and Lucky tie for first prize but a flip of the coin by MC Jack Carter makes Lucky the winner. However, in place of the much needed cash, Lucky gets a gold-plated trophy and a honeymoon for two in Vegas. Lucky's emotional mechanic,

Shorty, faints dead away at the shock of disappointment; Lucky tells Mancini he will work on his car but won't drive for him. Hours before the big race the money turns up for Lucky's engine, secretly financed by Rusty's father (William Demarest). In her excitement Rusty even agrees to work as one of Lucky's team of mechanics, as she had been frightened he would meet a fatal accident. Lucky wins the Grand Prix after all, leaving the way clear for him and his bride to take advantage of their honeymoon prize in Las Vegas.

This was virtually the last time Colonel Parker (*qv*) would splash out money for a really spectacular musical, though presumably the perks for making the plot a background for a grand tour of the Vegas night spots must have more than recompensed him. The plot is sheer tired formula – Elvis set on winning a big race and eventually doing so against all odds. What makes the movie entertaining is the punchy direction of George Sidney, co-producer, who had to his credit such classic musicals for MGM as *Annie Get Your Gun*, *Show Boat* and *Pal Joey* for Sinatra plus the teaming of a co-star for Elvis who could more than hold her own with him in the musical and dancing stakes – Ann-Margret (*qv*). They positively ignite sparks between them that help one to overlook the almost non-existent plot, and they have one delightful scene with a touch of

originality. After the inevitable lovers'
quarrel (over his racing obsession, of
course) he has delivered to her father's
house a handsome tree, having listened
to her rhapsodizing about her ideal
marriage, with roses around the door and
a real green tree in the garden. Her
animosity forgotten for the moment, she
dissolves back into the champ's arms.
The comedy expertise of William
Demarest as Rusty's hard-drinking and
understanding father greatly enhances
the story. Cesare Danova has
considerable presence as the Italian
racing champion and Nicky Blair fills the
role of Elvis's comedy henchman neatly.
David Winters' choreography is energetic
and beaty, though one suspects that
Ann-Margret practically choreographs
herself.

Although filmed first, *Viva Las
Vegas* – why the silly change of name to
Love in Las Vegas for Britain? – was
released after *Kissin' Cousins*. The George
Sidney film reached 14 on *Variety*'s
weekly list and 11 for 1964. The total
gross was £4.7 million. *Kissin' Cousins*
rated 11 on *Variety*'s weekly list, 26 for
1963, with a total gross of $2.6 million.
In actual takings it would seem that the
Colonel's money saving on the Sam
Katzman deal was a matter of swings and
roundabouts.

(See also: Ann-Margret; Katzman, Sam;
Kissin' Cousins; Parker, Colonel Tom)

VIVA LAS VEGAS (EP Released 1964)

IF YOU THINK I DON'T NEED YOU * *

Written by Red West, Joe Cooper.
Lucky Johnson, in waiter's outfit, uses
this cheeky rocker, accompanying
himself on guitar, to interrupt the
romantic dinner his rival Count Elmo
Mancini has arranged with Rusty.
Written by Elvis's friend Red West this is
an unexceptional time-filler, ending with
Rusty coyly sandwiched between the two
racing drivers.

I NEED SOMEBODY TO LEAN ON * * * *

Written by Bill Giant, Bernie Baum,
Florence Kaye.
Lucky Johnson is at his lowest ebb,
having fallen out with his girl, Rusty,
and it looks as though his dreams of
winning the Grand Prix have dissolved
into thin air. Piano and saxophone
accompany him as he wanders round the
bar, empty but for a few smooching
lovers, not actually singing, just sadly
musing – the sort of think-song that he
does so movingly: he joins in at the end.
The last number in the film, just prior to
a reversal in his fortune.
LPs: 'Double Dynamite'; 'I Got Lucky'

C'MON EVERYBODY * * * *

Written by Joe Byers.
On their first date, Lucky and Rusty
meet at the University of Nevada
Gymnasium for a dancing workout.
Rusty, in black leotard and scarlet sweater
is accompanied by gyrating male students
and the dance leads into Lucky's swinging
into Joy Byers' rousing rocker, danced
frenetically by Lucky, Rusty and the
'students', backed by drums, tympany,
guitars, double bass and lots of finger
flicking. A real fun number, in Joy Byers'
best tradition, ending with the happy
couple collapsing on the ground after he
swings her into a horizontal hold.
LP: C'mon Everybody'

TODAY, TOMORROW AND FOREVER * * * *

Written by Bill Giant, Bernie Baum,
Florence Kaye.
(Based on 'Liebestraum' by Franz Liszt)
Romance is on for Lucky and Rusty after
their first carefree day together. She
introduces him to her father. Lucky goes
into the Giant–Baum–Kaye version of
'Leibestraum' – a lovely romantic ballad
by any name and sung with depth of
feeling by Elvis, apparently
accompanying himself on the piano,
pointed by a gentle drum roll at the end.
LP: C'mon Everybody'

With some of the best numbers for years,
it is frustrating that this was not made
into a full soundtrack LP. The film opens
with:

VIVA LAS VEGAS * * * *

Written by Doc Pomus, Mort Shuman
An exciting opening and closing song for
the movie. Elvis extols the attractions of
the nightlife in Las Vegas while Joseph
Biroc's camera complements the effect.
The song also wins Lucky the award for
the hotel talent contest. (A one-take duet
recorded with Ann-Margret).
Single B/W: 'What'd I Say'
EP: 'See the USA, the Elvis Way'
LPs: 'Elvis in Hollywood'; 'Elvis
Worldwide 50 Gold Award Hits – Vol.
1'; 'This is Elvis'

WHAT'D I SAY * * *

Written by Ray Charles.
Ray Charles's hit performed at the end of
another rocker provides Elvis some fast
pelvic swinging in his old style, this time
with Ann-Margret – no mean pelvis
shaker herself – backed by drums,
guitars, saxophones and all the rock
panoply.
Single B/W: 'Viva Las Vegas'
LPs: 'Elvis's Gold Records – Vol. 4';
'Elvis in Concert'; 'Greatest Hits – Vol.
1'

SANTA LUCIA * * * *

Written by Teodora Cottrau.
Traditional Italian-type, romantic ballad,
nostalgically sung by Elvis with plenty of
strings and guitar backing in the hotel
foyer prior to the contest. Ann-Margret's
sizzling point number with the boys in a
figure-clinging swimsuit wins her top
marks in the talent contest – and no
wonder. If it could have been arranged,
this could have been one of the high
spots of the LP that never was.
LPs: 'Burning Love'; 'Hits From His
Movies – Vol. 2'; 'Elvis For Everyone'

THE YELLOW ROSE OF TEXAS

* * * *

Written by J.K. (1853) (Yellow Rose).
Written by John Sinclair (1907) (Eyes of
Texas).
Lucky takes on this rousing oldie to help
a Vegas manager get rid of Texas drunks
who are holding up his show. Martial
trumpets and brass predominate while
Elvis quotes such sacred names as 'John
Wayne' and leads the roisterers out of
the club.
LPs: 'Double Dynamite'; 'Elvis Sings
Flaming Star and Others'

THE LADY LOVES ME * * * *

Written by Sid Tepper, Roy C. Bennet.
N.B. David Stanley's comprehensive
discography records this number as
written for *Viva Las Vegas* but not used.
In fact, it's very effectively sung as a duet
with Ann-Margret on the high diving
board of the pool where she, as Rusty,
works as a swimming instructor. Witty
lyrics are pointedly interrupted by the
two stars. It has full orchestral backing,
despite the setting, and at the conclusion
Rusty pushes him into the pool.

W

WELCH, RAQUEL
(b. 1940)

Although she does not seem keen to acknowledge the fact, Raquel Welch had one of her first speaking lines in a movie in *Roustabout* (*qv*). She is one of four young people who drive up to a roadhouse called The Teahouse where Elvis as Charlie is singing. The waitress, Marge (Joan Stanley), quips that the two girls are minors and will have to drink cokes. The blonde insists they are over 18 to which Marge replies, 'Sure you are dear.' Raquel, the dark one, takes her up with, 'How can you call this a Teahouse, *dear*?' When Elvis comes on with guitar, to sing 'Poison Ivy' the male college students take the mickey because the girls find him 'cool and sexy'. Raquel has no further lines to say, but makes the most of a few sardonic facial expressions. In a blue dress with matching hair-band, she is clearly photogenic, without anything to indicate that within a couple of years she would be the undisputed sex goddess of the Sixties and one of the highest paid women in the business.

Her career did not take off until she signed up with press agent Patrick Curtis, with whom she formed Curtwell Enterprises, formed to promote her sensational looks and voluptuous figure. Curtis got her a contract with 20th Century Fox and her assets were well to the fore in the 1966 *One Million Years BC* and *Fantastic Voyage*, made in the UK. Critics remained sceptical and she

did not really receive due credit for her performance in the very tricky role of Myra Beckinridge, despite her avowed intention of being taken seriously as an actress. She and Patrick Curtis – they were married shortly after forming their famous partnership – parted company in 1971, by which time she was able to continue her career as an international star, despite her reputation for not being easy to interview or to work with.

She acquitted herself well by taking over from Lauren Bacall in the stage musical *Applause, Applause*, on Broadway, and, in 1995, in a tour of Great Britain as Bernard Shaw's *The Millionairess*, did well at the box office, despite in the main unenthusiastic critical reviews: it was thought inadvisable for her to take the play into London's West End.

En passant, it seems worth mentioning that one of Elvis's most meticulous biographers, Jerry Hopkins, in a footnote to *Roustabout*, states that Raquel Welch's film debut is in a scene where the midget, Billy Barty, tries to take a peek at two girls taking an outdoor shower; one of them, he claims, is Raquel Welch. After re-running the scene several times, along with the one at the beginning where she definitely has a line with the waitress, there is no clear close-up in the shower scene and though the girl is dark and pretty, it seems unlikely that she and her blonde friend would end up as employees at Barbara

Stanwyck's (*qv*) carni. Will the real Raquel Welch come forward?
(See also: Roustabout; Stanwyck, Barbara)

WEST, MAE
(1892-1980)

In the early Sixties there was nearly a close encounter of a potentially explosive kind when plans were announced for Elvis Presley to star with the senior sex symbol of Thirties and Forties Hollywood: Mae West, the lady who wrote her own plays and dialogue and was responsible for putting *Sex* on the map. It had, of course, been around for some time, but never had the word been employed as the title for a play, which she wrote, produced, directed and starred in in 1926. So great was the outrage that the law stepped in to stop the show. Mae was taken to court, charged with obscenity and jailed for ten days on Welfare Island, where she was treated like royalty and had a ball, gleaning material for her next play dealing with another taboo subject, homosexuality, called *The Drag*. It was a smash hit in New Jersey, but she was warned not to bring it to Broadway. In 1928 her play *Diamond Lil*, for all its outrageous sexual innuendoes, was allowed to wow them on Broadway and for the rest of her long career she played variations on the same character, which she brought to the screen in 1933 in *She Done Him Wrong*, thereby saving Paramount Studios from bankruptcy in a

Mae West sings 'You Gotta Taste All Of The Fruit' in *Myra Breckinridge* 1970. In 1964 she indignantly turned down the role of Elvis' mother in *Roustabout*. In 1978, at 85, she played a reigning sex symbol in the film version of her own play *Sextette* opposite Timothy Dalton, aged 34.

single, inexpensively produced movie. This was the same studio where Presley was to make many of his most successful films for Hal B. Wallis, who had introduced him to films in the first place.

It was Hal Wallis who announced that he had signed Mae to co-star with Elvis in his next project, inspired by an interview she gave in 1961, when touring in her latest play, *Sextette*. Asked who she considered the real show business personalities at the time, Mae, who was already being called 'the sexagenarian sexpot of show business' answered:

All we got is Presley. He's tops. A natural. A real sex personality. What we need is more like him. I mean, good in their own way, but no more exactly like him. That's just imitating him and they're a dime a dozen. Imitation is the highest form of flattery, I've had it for years. Presley is the sex personality of the times – like in the Twenties we had Valentino. Then I found Cary Grant: I said "If he can talk, I'll have him." I told him in Diamond Lil "You can be had. Why don't you come up – see me some time." He's still at it. But now we got Presley. And there's myself, of course.

Of course. But Hal Wallis made a strategical blunder by announcing that in *Roustabout* (*qv*) Mae West would play Presley's mum. 'I ain't never played mothers in my life and I'm certainly not going to start now!' She was 69 at the time. The fat was in the fire: in vain did Wallis change the character to the owner of the travelling 'carni' – a circus. There was also the little matter of billing.

When Mae made her screen comeback in *Myra Breckinridge* in 1970, she not only wrote her own dialogue but received top billing over the eponymous hero/heroine of the Gore Vidal novel played by Raquel Welch (*qv*).

The upshot was that Wallis chose another, less intractable star, Barbara Stanwyck (*qv*), who had made successful movies for him at Paramount and was also interested in making a comeback. Gallantry was the order of the day. 'It's Miss Stanwycks's film' said Colonel Parker (*qv*). Nevertheless her billing, under the title as co-starring, was noticeably smaller than Elvis Presley's.

Hall Wallis was to have an object lesson in how badly he had judged Mae West's estimation of her own sex appeal. After *Myra*, Raquel, who not only had the billing thunder snatched from her but also the film's première, when she had to fight her ways through West's cheering fans, gave an interview in which she said, 'Mae still thinks she's the hottest deal in town!' Further when the lady brought her own *Sextette* to the screen in 1978, she chose as her top leading man to play the latest of six husbands, 34 year-old Timothy Dalton, a future James Bond. She herself was 85.
(See also: Parker, Colonel Tom; Roustabout; Stanwyck' Barbara; Welch, Raquel)

THE WHIFFENPOOF SONG

Chautauqua, the original title for Elvis's 1969 *The Trouble With Girls* (*qv*) featured a short version of the 'Whiffenpoof Song', which centered round a travelling chautauqua. However in some prints of the film it has been edited out and cannot be found in most comprehensive discographies of Presley songs. Presumably the title of the film was changed because of the majority of people's lack of information about what a chautauqua is.

In fact, it was originally an American summer study course for

Sunday School teachers, founded in 1973 by John H. Vincent and Lewis Miller, Thomas Edison's father-in-law. By the turn of the century it had developed into a popular travelling cultural college. In a Presley film the word college means girls so hence the inevitable title featuring the word 'girls': *The Trouble With Girls*. This was Elvis's penultimate Hollywood movie; the chautauqua here has become a travelling tent show, of which Elvis, as Walter Hale, is the manager. The action calls for him to join a group of singers for a short rendition of the old traditional song, a favourite of college glee clubs. This version had toned down the original chorus to Gentleman Singers off on a spree/Doomed (instead of damned) from here to eternity/Lord (in place of God) have mercy on such as we/Baa, Baa, Baa, accompanied by bleating sheep.

This half-minute snatch was originally recorded in 1968 but not released for 26 years until issued on the 1995 quad soundtrack CD 'Live a Little, Love a Little'.
(See also: Jailhouse Rock; Live a Little, Love a Little; The Trouble With Girls)

WILD IN THE COUNTRY
* * * *

Released by: 20th Century Fox, a Company of Artists Inc. Production (DeLuxe Colour, Cinemascope); **Producer:** Jerry Wald; **Director:** Philip Dunne; **Screenplay:** Clifford Odets, based on the novel by J.R. Salamance; **Director of Photography:** William C. Mellor ASC; **Music:** Kenyon Hopkins; **Running Time:** 114 mins; **Opened:** June 22, 1961.

Cast: Elvis, Hope Lange, Tuesday Weld, Millie Perkins, Rafer Johnson, John Ireland, Gary Lockwood, Jason Robards Sr., Red West, Pat Buttram, William Mims, Christina Crawford, Robin Raymond.

Glenn Tyler (Elvis) is intelligent and

Elvis as Glen Tyler, consigned to the care of court psychiatrist Irene Sperry (Hope Lange) after a fight in which he almost kills his brother. *Wild In The Country* **(1961)**

talented, but has grown up always getting into trouble. During a drunken fight with his brother Hank (Red West), Glenn believes he has killed him and runs away. He is caught and brought to court where he attracts the sympathy of psychiatrist, Irene Sperry (Hope Lange). His father refuses to have anything to do with him, but Irene is pleased that Glenn is placed in the custody of his uncle, Phil Macy (John Ireland), who is

a friend of hers. Glenn goes to work in Phil's plant and moves into his other uncle, Ralph's, house where his sexy cousin Noreen (Tuesday Weld) also lives with her baby – her husband is said to be working overseas. Glenn's long-time girlfriend, Betty Lee Parsons (Millie Perkins), comes to see him but he refuses her invitation to go for a meal with her and her parents, saying he knows her father doesn't like him. He tells her to return all his letters and the stories he had written, saying he wants to burn them all. She loses patience and says sometimes she thinks he's slightly touched and warns him not to look for

trouble. In fact, trouble is sitting not too far away in the shape of Noreen, who is singing to herself on the porch steps and strumming a few chords on a guitar. She later tells him she has wanted him ever since she was 12. Noreen thinks she's pretty – 'And sad' says Glenn.

He is required to report to the court psychiatrist, who turns out to be Irene Sperry. He is sullen and unco-operative at first but when she tells him he is a free agent and can walk out if he wishes, he begins to see that she is on his side and wants to help him. He apologizes for his initial hostility and when she invites him to go ahead and say what is on his mind, he confesses that he hates his father and brother, whom he tried to kill. He is convinced he has the mark of Cain on him and talks about his mother, whom at first he would not allow her to mention. He wanted to make money to get her away from the family, who left her to work her fingers to the bone while her husband and son were lying drunk most of the time. She planned for Glenn to go to college, but there was no money and she died before his ninth birthday. Having got this off his mind he asks to leave, but makes an appointment to return.

After a hard day's work Noreen's father tells Glenn he can use her bathroom, as there is no shower. She and her father have a row and she threatens to leave after he has warned her to keep her hands off her cousin. 'He's a good clean-living boy – and stupid.' After Glenn has cleaned up, he borrows his uncle's truck and visits Betty Lee and her parents, but is too late for dinner. They end up at a roadhouse, where they run into his uncle Phil's spoilt son, Cliff (Gary Lockwood), who once framed Glenn for stealing a car, which he had, in fact, loaned him. The feud goes back to Cliff's jealousy over Betty Lee preferring Glenn, despite all his father's money. Glenn refuses Cliff's offer to join him and his friends for a drink and a fight nearly ensues over his cousin's snide remarks, but Betty Lee pulls him away.

At his next session with Irene he tells her about the incident and she convinces him to write about it because she has observed he has a way with words. Being slightly backward at school, his early ambition to write was mocked and he put the thought out of his head. When Irene goes to Phil Macy's home at his invitation he proposes marriage, but she is still hurt by her own previous disastrous marriage and will not let him divorce his wife to leave him free to marry again. He has also asked her over to discuss his son Cliff, whose wild life and heavy drinking, encouraged by his

mother despite his weak heart, could lead to his early death. Irene declines to take him on as a patient because of their own relationship, but promises to find Cliff a good consultant.

Noreen persists in her determination to win Glenn, proposing they steal her father's money and run away. He refuses, but eventually they are about to share a kiss when the situation is diffused by the arrival of Cliff in his car to buy some of Ralph's hard liquor. Glenn confesses his mixed feelings for Betty Lee and Noreen the next time he sees Irene, who has read his story and thinks it so full of promise that he ought to set out to fulfil his mother's dream for him to go to college. He angrily turns on her when she suggests showing his story to someone who could help him, but agrees reluctantly to think the matter over before their next meeting. Another set-back in Glenn's fight to come to terms with himself occurs when Betty Lee's father catches them kissing while they're out trying to fly a kite. The church-going bigot insults Glenn and his family, orders his daughter into the house and Glenn leaves angrily, straight into the arms of Noreen. They get drunk together on Ralph's liquor and call at Irene's home, shouting insults while he hoses down her porch. Irene goes to see him the next day and offers him his story back. They have an argument in front of Noreen and Irene storms off.

Ralph takes Glenn and Noreen to a local fête on her birthday and breaks the news that her husband has died, leaving the field wide open for the young couple to get married. Glenn, knowing there never was a husband, reacts cynically and a bitter fight starts, during which he knocks his uncle over in front of the vicar. Ralph sends for the police and Glenn drives in his uncle's van to Betty Lee's home to ask for help in the form of money so he can make a getaway. She persuades him to stay and face the charges; together they phone Irene, who stands as a character witness against

Ralph's charges. Phil Macy goes to see Ralph and forces him to drop the case, harking back to some shady dealings in the past of which he has proof. Noreen exults in her father's discomfiture and takes reluctant leave of her ex-lover, saying she'll always be there for him if he wants her.

Glenn asks Irene to take him back as a patient and she is only too happy to agree, taking him to see her colleague, Professor Larson, who is sufficiently impressed by his writing to agree to try and arrange a scholarship for him at his college. As they leave in her car their spirits are high enough for them to sing an impromptu duet. On the way back into town a storm blows up and they are forced to pull in at a motel, where Glenn confesses to Irene that he's in love with her. She tries to explain it away by telling him that in a relationship like theirs such a thing often occurs. 'They call it transference.' He replies 'That's book talk.' It soon becomes clear that she shares his feelings; they embrace, but she asks him to leave, despite the hotel proprietor's suggestion they 'double up', for economy reasons. We cut to the next morning when Irene is taking her red setter, Rosie for a walk. When she returns home her maid tells her Glenn has called three times and sounds very troubled. She dials a number. In the next scene she is agreeing to Phil Macy's proposal of marriage, but tells him frankly she is only marrying him to get away from another entanglement. He tells her that is irrelevant, but changes his tune when he hears that Cliff has been spreading rumours about her and Glenn spending the night together at a motel. Cliff had checked in with a girlfriend shortly after Irene and Glenn signed for adjoining rooms.

Phil finds Glenn trying to get an answer from Irene as to whether she still loves him, confronts him with his son's accusation and tells Glenn that Irene has agreed to marry him. The boy leaves telling Irene he never wants to see her again. He heads straight back to Noreen, tells her to get her father's money box, collect the baby and come with him. He stops off at the roadhouse where Cliff is drinking and knocks him out. Moments later a police car drives up and Glenn is arrested for manslaughter: Cliff has died. Outside the courtroom Phil tells Irene to get Glenn a good lawyer as he intends to hang him if he can. Giving evidence, Irene tells the court about Cliff's heart condition, but Phil denies it and says his son was perfectly healthy. Brother Hank testifies against Glenn and Irene goes home to write a letter. She then tells Rosie that there'll be no walk today, deadheads a few flowers and goes to her garage, closing the door. When the car engine starts up Rosie, aware that something is terribly wrong, tries to get in and raises the alarm. When the news of Irene's attempted suicide reaches the courtroom, Phil retracts his former statement and tells the truth about Cliff's heart condition. Glenn rushes from the court to be at Irene's side. The doctors have managed to bring her round from a coma and she rallies when he tells her he loves her. She is able to see him off at the station to take up his college scholarship; Noreen, who was in court, watches as she and Glenn shake hands: he repeats that he needs her and she says 'be sure' and promises to write. The brief kiss she gives him tells Noreen, watching from a window, that their affair is over. As the train pulls out he opens the letter Irene has posted and reads that his first story has been published. The title song is reprised as the Credits roll.

Wild in the Country deserves re-appraisal. It was already in the pipeline of scheduled Presley films in the first careless rapture of his return to movies. Colonel Parker even appeared to concur that his protégé could tackle serious roles with aplomb and might not even have to burst into song to the detriment of the dramatic impact of the storyline. However, when *Flaming Star* (qv),

though still a winner, proved less popular than *G.I. Blues* (qv), 20th Century Fox producer Jerry Wald, having commissioned several songs that were excised from the final print of the film, first opted for more serious treatment, then decided to leave the title song, which reached No. 4 in the UK, though only 29 in the US. There were two others also, which seem out of place in the context, and an unaccompanied duet with Hope Lange in a car, which fits charmingly into the situation in which they find themselves.

This presented a God-given opportunity for several clever-clever reviews in which the critics seem to be deriding the erstwhile darling of the intelligentsia, Clifford Odets, for undertaking to write a script for a rock 'n' roller, even though he was the King of the genre. In fact, the plot is well worked out, situations and characters are believable and the acting in the main excellent. What went wrong with the overall impression is the inserted songs element and the unimaginative direction of Philip Dunne, who had turned director after some twenty-five years of script writing and composing political speeches, notably for John F. Kennedy and Adlai Stevenson. His best films were those for which he also wrote the screenplay, such as the perceptive family drama *Ten, North Frederick* in 1959, with Gary Cooper. His treatment of the dramatics in *Wild in the Country* is heavy-handed, suggesting he was ill-at-ease with a screenplay not of his own composition. Reactions sounded the death-knell for dramatic roles for Presley in the future, with the exception of *Kid Galahad* (qv) in 1962 which suffered even more noticeably from the dichotomy between drama and an overload of songs.

American Variety offered the usual blandly approving review trotted out in those days, but the most surprising commendation came from Britain's *New Musical Express*: David Cardwell

headlined his critique with '*Wild in the Country* is Elvis's best so far!' He went on 'There is only one way to describe Presley's performance – superb!' He concludes 'Yes this was obviously Elvis's best film and he will be known from now on in my books as Elvis Presley, singer and film star.' This is one of the few reviews to credit Presley's beautifully modulated and at times acutely touching performance. He has been mocked for quoting from the bible in the first court scene and in the tricky situation where he and his psychiatrist Irene Sperry (Hope Lange) both realize they are falling in love, but fight temptation in rejecting the opportunity to spend the night in the same room when trapped in a motel during a thunder storm. The words put into his mouth by Clifford Odets are both apposite and movingly spoken as befits a boy from the religious background from which Presley came. The author clearly wrote Glenn's character with Elvis's past in perspective.

Hope Lange is one of the few Hollywood actresses of the time who could be convincing as a psychiatrist; the part steers her through a minefield which she negotiates with a sure and gentle touch, while Tuesday Weld as teenage sexpot Noreen – the kind of part which she always did so well – is cleverly contrasted. The only one of the female stars who fails to impress is Millie Perkins in the thankless role of Glenn's childhood sweetheart; her intrusions, full of wise advice and home-spun philosophy, seem irritating which can only be a fault in the writing or direction since she was very impressive in *The Diary of Anne Frank*. John Ireland fills one of those waiting-in-the-wings for the leading lady parts which he always did so well with a touch of quality that lends credence to the startling volte-face in the final court scene, where he suddenly changes his evidence to get his nephew out of a murder charge. The ne'er do well son of the John Ireland role, Cliff, is played by Gary Lockwood with the appropriate sneering approach: he was to change sides to become Elvis's buddy in *It Happened at the Worlds Fair* (*qv*) two years later.

Interesting supporting cast members include Red West as Elvis's brother Hank, who is obviously handy with his fists until his brother fells him with a blow from a milking stool. This was West's first speaking part and, though rather short on dialogue, he handles himself well. There is also Christina Crawford, adopted daughter of Joan, who plays Cliff's girlfriend, Monica George: she later became better known for writing the searing biography of her mother, *Mommie Dearest*. *(See also: Flaming Star; G.I. Blues; It Happened at the World's Fair; Kid Galahad; Memphis Mafia; Parker, Colonel Tom)*

WILD IN THE COUNTRY * * *

Written by Hugo Peretti, Luigi Creatore, George Weiss.

Elvis sings this over the credits, setting his character of Glenn Tyler as a simple country boy, while the camera ranges over peaceful countryside, leading up to the murky interior of a barn where Glenn is fighting with his brother Hank (Red West). It is a slow, reflective ballad, with full instrumentals, guitar and piano and repeated at the end of the movie, where the mood is again peaceful as Glenn enters the college to which he has won a scholarship.

Single B/W: 'I Feel So Bad'
LPs: 'Elvis Aaron Presley'; 'Elvis in Hollywood'; 'Elvis: The Other Sides – Worldwide Gold Standard Hits'

IN MY WAY * * *

Written by Fred Wise, Ben Weisman. Another slow ballad, sung by Elvis to the sexy Tuesday Weld who, as Noreen, is out to get him any way she can. Elvis accompanies himself on the guitar, a pot boiler to ease the plot along.
LPs: 'Elvis For Everyone'; 'Separate Ways'

I SLIPPED, I STUMBLED, I FELL * * * *

This cheerful rocker is sung by Elvis to Millie Perkins, as the good girl in his life. Ironically, the *New Musical Express* writer voices the opinion that it is unquestionably the best number in the film. He goes on to emphasize, 'in fact I would go as far as to say that this is the best ballad (?) he has sung in any film.' 'Ironically', because both this and the next song, more understandably, are not listed among any of Elvis's discs to date so they go without writers' credits.

HUSKY DUSKY DAY * * * *

This is a sweet country and western ditty which Elvis and Hope Lange duet as she drives her car away from the college where he has been favourably interviewed. The song is unaccompanied but undoubtedly perfect in the context.

WOODS, DONALD

(b. 1906)

As the General in Elvis's *Kissin' Cousins* (*qv*), Woods, then in his sixties, retained all his youthful matinée idol good looks with the exception of a slight greying of his naturally dark hair. To date, he has only made two movies since having returned to the theatre, like many of his generation, in which he had made his name in the Twenties and Thirties before making his film debut as a juvenile lead in 1934. In a string of mainly run-of-the-mill movies up to the Fifties, he played in some classics, notably the 1935 MGM version of Charles Dickens' *A Tale of Two Cities* as Charles Darnay, starring Ronald Colman, *The Story of Louis Pasteur, Anthony Adverse* with Fredric March in 1936, in which he played Vincent Nolte, and *I Was a Prisoner on Devil's Island* in 1941. His last outstanding part was as Brother Juniper, in *The Bridge of San Louis Rey* in 1944.

Donald Woods found working under the economy regime of Sam Katzman (*qv*) quite an experience. He recounts:

I had been on shoestring budget movies before – one was Mexican Spitfire, one of a series starring Lupe Velez. She was just that and frequently stormed off the set to sulk in her dressing room. They had to shoot round her until she was sweet-talked into coming back. I was reminded of her on the one occasion Elvis wouldn't leave his dressing-room, because he had not come to terms with the blond wig he hated wearing as his hillbilly cousin. When our director, Gene Nelson (qv), finally persuaded him to face the cameras he was, as always, totally co-operative and offered to stay on after his 6 p.m. deadline to make up for the few minutes delay. He never complained about the gruelling shooting schedule, which affected him more than anybody, because he had so many songs to shoot. I can't think of many major stars who would have been so amenable. He was, with that one exception, always first on set, word-perfect with his lines. He went out of his way to make things as easy as possible for everyone else.

Like another cast member in a Presley movie, Bruce Bennett, Donald Woods had a second string career as real-estate broker. 'Elvis was fascinated by this and eager to learn the ins and outs of the profession. "Just in case I may need it one day" he said. "I may be able to give the Colonel a few lessons."' It was hardly likely that either of them would ever be in need of having a part-time profession.' *(See also: Katzman, Sam; Kissin' Cousins)*

APPENDIX 1

THE MOVIES OF ELVIS PRESLEY
(American Release Dates)

CHRONOLOGY   TITLE
RELEASE DATE   DIRECTOR

1 LOVE ME TENDER
November 15, 1956 Robert W. Webb
2 LOVING YOU
November 5, 1957   Hal Kanter
3 JAILHOUSE ROCK
October 17, 1957 Richard Thorpe
4 KING CREOLE
July 2, 1958   Michael Curtiz
5 G.I. BLUES
November 15, 1960 Norman Taurog
6 FLAMING STAR
December 17, 1960 Don Siegel
7 WILD IN THE COUNTRY
June 22, 1961   Philip Dunne
8 BLUE HAWAII
November 22, 1961 Norman Taurog
9 FOLLOW THAT DREAM
May 23, 1962   Gordon Douglas
10 KID GALAHAD
August 29, 1962   Phil Karlsen
11 GIRLS! GIRLS! GIRLS!
November 21, 1962 Norman Taurog
12 IT HAPPENED AT THE
    WORLD'S FAIR
April 10, 1963   Norman Taurog
13 FUN IN ACAPULCO
November 27, 1963 Richard Thorpe
14 KISSIN' COUSINS
March 6, 1963   Gene Nelson
15 VIVA LAS VEGAS
April 20, 1964   George Sidney
(LOVE IN LAS VEGAS in Britain)
16 ROUSTABOUT
November 11, 1964 John Rich
17 GIRL HAPPY
April 14, 1965   Boris Sagal
18 TICKLE ME
May 28, 1965   Norman Taurog
19 HARUM SCARUM
November 24, 1965 Gene Nelson
    (HARUM HOLIDAY in Britain)
20 FRANKIE AND JOHNNY
March 31, 1966   Edward Small
21 PARADISE, HAWAIIAN STYLE

May 4 1966   D. Michael Moore
22 SPINOUT
November 21, 1966 Norman Taurog
(CALIFORNIA HOLIDAY in Britain)
23 EASY COME, EASY GO
March 22, 1967   John Rich
24 DOUBLE TROUBLE
April 5, 1967   Norman Taurog
25 CLAMBAKE
November 22, 1967 Arthur H. Nadel
26 STAY AWAY, JOE
March 8, 1968   Peter Tewkesbury
27 SPEEDWAY
June 12, 1968   Norman Taurog
28 LIVE A LITTLE, LOVE A LITTLE
October 23, 1968 Norman Taurog
29 CHARRO!
March 13, 1968   Charles Marquis
Warren
30 THE TROUBLE WITH GIRLS
September 3, 1969 Peter Tewkesbury
31 CHANGE OF HABIT
November 10, 1969 William A.
Graham
32 ELVIS: THAT'S THE WAY IT IS
November 11, 1960 Denis Sanders
33 ELVIS ON TOUR
November 1, 1972   Pierre Adige,
Robert Abel

MOVIES ABOUT ELVIS
ELVIS: THE MOVIE   1979
John Carpenter
    (Kurt Russell)
THIS IS ELVIS   1981
Andrew Solt
    (Documentary)
ELVIS AND THE COLONEL:
THE UNTOLD STORY   1993
William A. Graham
        (Bob Youngblood and Lloyd
Bridges) (TV Feature)

APPENDIX 2

ELVIS PRESLEY FAN CLUBS

THE OFFICIAL ELVIS PRESLEY
ORGANIZATION IN GREAT
BRITAIN

P.O. BOX 4, LEICESTER
LE3 5HY
Incorporating *Elvis Monthly*

THE OFFICIAL ELVIS PRESLEY
FAN CLUB OF GREAT BRITAIN
President: JULIE MUNDY
Promotional/Editorial Division
P.O. Box 4048
Milton Keynes, Bucks
MK6 0JH
The Official Elvis Presley Fan Club
currently has membership in excess of
20,000. For a £10 annual subscription
fans receive: The Club Magazine
quarterly; a free CD or cassette; four
intermittent newletters; a membership
card. As a bonus we also have a home
page on the Internet which features the
first Elvis radio show on the net; we
present an exclusive catalogue of Elvis
Presley merchandise direct from
Graceland; trips to the USA three times
a year; UK holidays and conventions.
*The Official Elvis Presley Fan Club
Magazine* has just been re-launched and
for the first time in its forty year history
is available on news stands throughout
the UK. Another publication produced
by the Fan Club (available on a separate
subscription) is *Elvis Monthly* which has
been in circulation since 1960.

BRANCHES OF THE OFFICIAL
ELVIS PRESLEY FAN CLUB OF
GREAT BRITAIN
Our local branches operate in order to
provide a local service to fans in each
area. They range from a few people
meeting in a house to large clubs with
extra subscription rates (above our own)
which put on larger events and produce
local publications.

AVON
Anthony Whitlock
19 King William Street
Bedminster
BRISTOL B53 1HH

BEDFORDSHIRE
Bill Hyde
38 Dordans Road
Leagrave
LUTON LU4 BS
Tel: 01582 584021

BIRMINGHAM
Michael Coyle
68 Primrose Hill
KINGS NORTON
BIRMINGHAM M38 9NT

BUCK AND NORTHANTS
Steve Tebbutt
13 Langcliffe Drive
Heelands
MILTON KEYNES MK13 7LA

DERBYSHIRE
Sheila Johnson
8 Wikeley Way
Brington
CHESTERFIELD S43 1BH

DEVON
Mark Dicken
22 Hawthorn Close
Aller Park
NEWTON ABBOTT TQ12 4TG

DUDLEY AND WEST BROMWICH
Margaret Watkins (Mrs)
341 Simmons Drive
Woodgate Valley
Quinton
BIRMINGHAM B32 2UH
Tel: 0121 427 9113

DORSET
Mrs. Linda Haycox
49 Cammel Road
West Parley
FERNDOWN BH22 8RX

ESSEX
Mike and Gyll Davis
15 Dunlin Close
SOUTH WOODHAM FERRERS
CM3 5SA
Tel: 01245 323633

ESSEX (EAST)
Miss Wendy Brown
25 Church Street
HARWICH CO12 3EA

GLOUCESTER
Diana and Ray Hill
Graceland
10 Edwy Parade
KINGSHOLM GL1 2QL
Tel: 01452 502563
Hon. Club President: Freddie Starr

HERTFORDSHIRE
Tony Dobb
28 Dormans Close
NORTHWOOD HA6 2FX

HUMBERSIDE
Mike Hawkins
1944 Hessie High Road
HULL HU4 7BG
Tel: 01482 566053

KENT
David Gabriel
53 St. Patricks Road
RAMSGATE CT11 7EJ

LANCASHIRE
Branch Leader Vacancy

LEEDS
Pat Phillips
418 Oakwood Drive
LEEDS LS8 3LG

LEICESTER
Mick Haywood
40 Hawthorne Street
LEICESTER LE5 9FG
Tel: 0116 2512001

LONDON
John Talbot
59 Beanell Road
Forest Hill SE23 1AA
Hon. Member: Sir Tim Rice

MANCHESTER (Greater)
Kath Jamieson
192 Greebham Way
Blackrod
BOLTON BL6 5TG

MERSEYSIDE
Terry Bellis
43 Brownlow Road
New Ferry
WIRRAL L62 1AV

MIDDLESEX
Tony and Pearl Cattemull
30 Addison Road
TEDDINGTON TW11 9EX
Tel: 0181 977 9610

NORFOLK
Terry Wortley
3 Collis Road
NORWICH NN7 9QE

NORFOLK (NORTH)
Ellen Knox
Sunshine Place
2 Church Bank
Terrington Street Clement
KING'S LYNN PE34 4NA

NOTTINGHAM
Glen Gee and Adele Kersey
150 Trent Road
Beeston
RYLANDS NG9 2LQ
Tel: 0115 922 0390

OXFORDSHIRE
Jenny de Fraine
49 Marlborough Road
Grandpont
SOUTH OXFORD OX1 4LW
Tel: 0865 240692

SOMERSET
Josie Gallimore
2 Hyde Lane Cottage
Bathpool
TAUNTON TA2 8BT

SUFFOLK
Glyn Mortimer
7 Tintern Close
IPSWICH IP2 9BH
Tel: 01473 6031231

SUSSEX AND HANTS
Andrew Hearn
62 Shandon Road
WORTHING BN14 9DX

TYNE AND WEAR
Les Charlton
6 Croftwell Close
Bleach Green
Winlanton
BALYDON-ON-TYNE NE21 5JE

WILTSHIRE
Valerie Morse
3 Karslake Close
Eldene
SWINDON SN3 3SX

WOLVERHAMPTON
Barbara Wilson
11 Connaught House
UPPER VAUXHALLS WV1 4SZ
Tel: 01902 772859

WORCESTER
Helen Tipton
87 Perry Fields
Sidemoor
BROMSGROVE B61 8SZ
Hon. Member: Freddie Starr

YORKSHIRE
Andrew Wolczyk
74 Burton Bank Road
Monk Bretton
BARNSLEY S71 2NQ

YORKSHIRE
Alyson Adams
West Yorkshire Branch
2 Grassleigh Avenue
Allerton
BRADFORD BD15 9AR
Honorary Member: James Burton

WALES
Martyn Collins
17 Chard Avenue
Llanrumney
CARDIFF CF3 9EL

NORTH WALES
Sylvia Rowlands
373 Caemarton Road
Bangor
GWYNED

MID GLAMORGAN
Chris Hallett
3 Canwell Place
Gawun Miskin
PONTYPRIDD CF48 2RY

SCOTLAND
Ronnie Patterson
P.O. Box 710, NWDO
EDINBURGH

Jane Boyce
114 Lochdochart Road
Easterhouse
GLASGOW
Tel: 0141 771 2221
Founder: Gerry McLafferty
Honorary Members: Scotty Moore, D.J.
Fontana.

Paul & Linda Downie
95 Gottries Road
Harbourside
IRVINE KA12 8QH
Tel: 01294 272652

IRELAND
John Kavanagh
43 Bernard Curtis House
Bluebell
DUBLIN 12
Tel: (Dublin) 4501304

'Elvis – Today, Tomorrow and Forever'.

FANCLUBS USA AND ELSEWHERE
Contact: Patsy Andersen
Fan Relations Manager
Communications Department
Graceland Division of Elvis Presley
Enterprizes Inc.
3734 Elvis Presley Boulevard
Memphis
Tennessee
38116 Tel: 901 332 3322
(Details of individual fan clubs will be
supplied as required)

BIBLIOGRAPHY

The information in this book has been drawn from many sources, predominantly from my own seven volumes of Elvis Presley news stories dating from 1956, when he began to break into the consciousness of the British press, via his US concerts, records and movies. As a show business writer and avid film and playgoer I recognized from the start a unique personality and talent; I never missed any of his movies and derived considerable enjoyed from even the poorest of them. As a contributor to such magazines as *Picturegoer* and the numerous other movie periodicals which proliferated in those days I was able to keep abreast of his considerable output of films; cuttings I amassed from such publications as *Photoplay, Picture Show, Films and Filming, Plays and Players, The Stage* and *TV and Video Guide* for which I wrote regular features and critques. Where possible I have identified the sources and apologize for those I have been unable to trace.

Baer, Richard D. *The Film Buffs' Bible of Motion Pictures (1925–72)*, Hollywood film Archive, Hollywood, California, 1972.

Cardwell, David and Hand, Albert *The Elvis Presley El-Cyclopedia* The Official Elvis Presley Fan Club of Great Britain and the Commonwealth, Heanor, Derbyshire 1963.

Gifford, Dennis *British Cinema* Tantivy Press: A. Zwemmer Ltd, London 1968.

Goldman, Albert *Elvis* Allen Lane Penguin Books Ltd, London 1981.

Halliwell, Leslie A. *The Filmgoer's Companion* MacGibbon & Kee Ltd, London 1967.
Hopkins, Jerry *Elvis* Abacus London, 1974.

Katz, Ephrain *The International Film Encyclopedia* Macmillan Press Ltd, London.

Quinlan, David *The Illustrated Guide To film Directors* B.T. Batsford Ltd, London, 1983.

Stanley, David E. (with Coffey, Frank) *The Elvis Encyclopedia* Virgin Publishing Ltd, London 1995.

Tobler, John & Wootton, Richard *Elvis The Legend And The Music* Hamlyn Publishing Ltd, London 1983. (W.H. Smith edition)

Wayne, Jane Ellen *Stanwyck: The Untold Biography* Robson Books Ltd, London 1986.